IRONIES OF ONENESS
AND DIFFERENCE

SUNY series in Chinese Philosophy and Culture
—————————
Roger T. Ames, editor

IRONIES OF ONENESS

AND DIFFERENCE

Coherence in Early Chinese Thought;
Prolegomena to the Study of Li

BROOK ZIPORYN

STATE UNIVERSITY OF NEW YORK PRESS

Published by
STATE UNIVERSITY OF NEW YORK PRESS, ALBANY

© 2012 State University of New York

Printed in the United States of America

For information, contact
State University of New York Press, Albany, NY
www.sunypress.edu

Excelsior Editions is an imprint of State University of New York Press

Production, Laurie Searl
Marketing, Anne M. Valentine

Library of Congress Cataloging-in-Publication Data

Ziporyn, Brook, 1964–
   Ironies of oneness and difference : coherence in early Chinese thought : prolegomena to the study of Li / Brook Ziporyn.
       p. cm. — (SUNY series in Chinese philosophy and culture)
   Includes bibliographical references (p.   ) and index.
   ISBN 978-1-4384-4289-1 (hardcover : alk. paper)
   ISBN 978-1-4384-4288-4 (pbk : alk. paper)
   1. Li.   2. Philosophy, Chinese.   3. Truth—Coherence theory.   I. Title.

B127.L5Z57 2012
181'.11—dc23   2011038254

10 9 8 7 6 5 4 3 2 1

CONTENTS

ACKNOWLEDGMENTS   vii

INTRODUCTION
Rethinking Same and Different   1
   Coherence and Li: Plan and Method of This Book and Its Sequel   9

CHAPTER ONE
Essences, Universals, and Omnipresence: Absolute Sameness
and Difference   19
   Essences, Universals, Categories, Ideas: Simple Location and
      the Disjunction of Same and Different in Mainstream
      Western Philosophy   23
   Same and Different in Form and Matter   37
   Two Opposite Derivations of the Omnipresent   39

CHAPTER TWO
What Is Coherence? Chinese Paradigms   49
   Coherence As Opposed to Law, Rule, Principle, Pattern:
      Harmony Versus Repeatability   63
   Is White Horse Horse?   71
   Qian Mu's Pendulum   77
   Ironic and Non-Ironic Coherence   84

CHAPTER THREE
Non-Ironic Coherence and Negotiable Continuity   89
   Coherence and Omniavailability of Value in Confucius
      and Mencius   89
   Coherence and Heaven in the *Analects*   94
   Ritual Versus Law: Cultural Grammar   103
   Rectification of Names: Negotiated Identity as a Function
      of Ritual   111
   Classes and Types in Mencius   114
   Omnipresence in Mencius   127
   Transition to Ironic Coherence: Qi-Omnipresence
      and the Empty Center in Pre-Ironic Proto-Daoism   131

CHAPTER FOUR
Ironic Coherence and the Discovery of the "Yin"   139
    The Laozi Tradition: Desiring W/holes   139
    Overview of Ironic Coherence in the *Laozi*   142
    The Five Meanings of the Unhewn: Omnipresence and
        Ironic Coherence in the *Laozi*   146
    Zhuangzi's Wild Card: Thing as Perspective   162
    Using the Wild Card   183
    The Wild Card Against Both Objective Truth and
        Subjective Solipsism   188
    Conclusion to Chapter 4: Ironic Coherence   195

CHAPTER FIVE
Non-Ironic Responses to Ironic Coherence in *Xunzi* and the
Record of Ritual   199
    Xunzi and the Regulation of Sameness and Difference   199
    Omnipresence and Coherence in Xunzi   215
    Two Texts from the *Record of Ritual* (*Liji*): "The Great
        Learning," and "The Doctrine of the Mean"   220

CHAPTER SIX
The Yin-Yang Compromise   229
    Yin-Yang Theism in Dong Zhongshu: The Metastasis of
        Harmony and Irony   250
    An Alternate Yin-Yang Divination System: Yang Xiong's
        Taixuanjing   255

CONCLUSION AND SUMMARY
Toward Li   265

NOTES   269

BIBLIOGRAPHY   307

INDEX   315

ACKNOWLEDGMENTS

This book was a long time in gestation, and the process by which it came to be was especially protracted and convoluted, which means it has been sucking the life out of an unusually large number of persons and institutions for an especially long time! The parasite now takes the opportunity to express its gratitude to its hosts.

First and foremost I want to thank my students. I mean this in the most general sense—students real and virtual—because I remain convinced that the only real point of doing academic work of this kind is for the sake of the next generation of scholars and thinkers. As for our colleagues, our friends, our peers, they are beyond hope! And we are beyond hope for them, which is, I suppose, just as it should be. We are set in our ways, we have deep investments, emotional and otherwise, in our conclusions; at a certain age our minds start to rattle along the same old tracks, it seems. So for me the only really meaningful audience for a work of this kind is the unknown future readers, the young, the curious, the undecided, the ones who are still exploring, who have not yet declared any specific allegiance, who are trying to get a general sense of where they stand, of what can be assumed, of what the possibilities are and what the cost and payoffs are for each of these options, of how things are and have been and could be.

Among my students in the flesh, I must single out Michael Beraka and Alanna Krause for their careful technical assistance with the manuscript. But I also owe an enormous debt to the discussions with and challenges posed by all my actual students over the years, which gave shape to the lectures from which this book emerged. And even more than that, it is the very existence of these students that is the real motivation behind trying to formulate and structure a global theory of this kind at all, to bother to try to express it in a consistent and intelligible form. Nietzsche, I think, got this point very right: "Whoever is fundamentally a teacher takes all things seriously only in relation to his students—including even himself." So I owe them that too. Without them I would not have had the opportunity to experience that very strange but wholesomely unnatural form of consciousness: having to take oneself seriously now and then.

Looking in the other direction, at yin's debt to yang rather than yang's debt to yin, I must also thank the teachers who many years ago first really opened my eyes to the careful and systematic study of classical Chinese philosophy, above all Professor Donald Munro and Professor Xin Yiyun 辛意雲. The model derived from both of these exemplars in how to combine detail and overview, rigor and creativity, in a single integrated process, together with the specific insights and orientations gained in the careful study of many of the classical texts discussed in this book, continues to be my guiding lodestone, which I feel has served me enormously well over the years.

I have also had the good fortune to have many accomplished and distinguished specialists read versions of this manuscript in various stages of its growth, to whom I owe enormous gratitude both for the time and encouragement they have given me and the invaluable comments they have offered. Among the very eminent minds who have done me this honor I must first mention of course my simultaneous antipode and doppelgänger Alan Cole, who has long been for me a true knower of the tone (知音) both musically and intellectually. Nothing has been more sustaining and stimulating for my thinking than the eternal riddle posed by our interactions: How can such total agreement and total disagreement of outlook coincide so exactly and in such a convivial and invigorating way? That must mean something. But great gratitude is also owed on this score to my much admired friends Steven Angle, Roger Ames, Michael Puett, Franklin Perkins, Robin Wang, Alan Dagovitz (Levinovitz), Michelle Molina, and Paul D'Ambrosio, all of whom have lent me the benefits of their great erudition, intelligence, sensitivity, and time to read and comment on drafts of this book, thereby greatly improving it.

Great thanks are also due to Nancy Ellegate at State University of New York Press for seeing this complicated project through over the course of its many metamorphoses, and for the free hand she was willing to allow me to get it done; that was by any standard an unusually complicated process that required considerable steadiness of hand and of vision on her part, as well as a degree of confidence in the author's judgment that has become lamentably rare among editors, a confidence I fervently hope that I have deserved.

Over the years during which this book was written I have suckled at the teat of many an institution as well. The Department of Religious Studies and the Department of Philosophy at Northwestern University have been my home for most of this time, and I have been treated exceptionally well there. It has also been my pleasure to be part of the faculty of the Department of Philosophy at the National University of Singapore, where some of the final work on this book was done. Financial support has been generously provided by a fellowship awarded by the Fulbright-Hays Foundation, and from an International and Area Studies Grant sponsored jointly by the American Council of Learned Societies, the Social Science Research Council, and the National Endowment for the Humanities. The official vote of confidence embodied therein, as well as the financial assistance, have been indispensable to the completion of this work.

Of course there are also many people to whom I owe gratitude on a more personal level, a lot of people whom I love a lot, maybe even including some already mentioned. I'm too shy, though, not to feel somewhat paralyzed and discomfited by the prospect of talking about this kind of emotional bond in public, making the customary front-of-the-book PDA feel almost like a slightly indecent act—shy, or perhaps self-protective, or perhaps just old-fashioned and easily embarrassed, or superstitious in a Rumpelstiltskinny way about naming names, lest this steal from their owners the power they have over me. They know who they are, don't they? Anyway: *Wovon man nicht sprechen kann, darüber muss man schweigen.*

INTRODUCTION

子曰：君子和而不同，小人同而不和

The Master said, "The noble man is harmonious [with others] but not the same [as them]. The petty man is the same [as others] but not harmonious [with them]."

—*Analects*, 13:23

自其異者視之，肝膽楚越也。自其同者視之，萬物皆一也。

Looked at from [the viewpoint of] their differences, your own liver and gall bladder are Chu [to the south] and Yue [to the north]. Looked at from [the viewpoint of] their sameness, the ten thousand things are all one.

—Zhuangzi, "Dechongfu"

當知一切由心分別諸法。何曾自謂同異。

You must understand how everything derives from the mind's differentiation of things. For when do things themselves ever declare themselves to be "the same as" or "different from" one another?

—Jingxi Zhanran, *Zhiguan yili*

Let's suppose for a moment that "questioning our assumptions" is something worth doing—because it frees us from prejudices, because it expands our powers of thought and action, because it opens up new possibilities, because to do so is almost the definition of learning and thinking per se, because it is (as a result or perhaps synonym of all of the above) fun. One way to do this, no doubt, would be to undertake the serious and sympathetic examination of alternate belief systems, of *other* types of assumptions, ones that differ in surprising ways from the ones to which we ourselves, with whatever degree of self-reflective awareness, have been committed. Classical Chinese thought is often recommended in this connection, and rightly so. But the uncovering of alternate beliefs about "what is so"—how the world might happen to be, how human beings might be constituted, and

1

so on—is perhaps less unsettling, and hence potentially less salutary, than the contemplation of alternate possibilities for *what constitutes a belief*, for what is intended in saying that *anything* is "so," or for the preconditions that are unconsciously assumed in even formulating the choice between alternative beliefs. To entertain an alternative view about what things exists or do not exist is perhaps not as disorienting in its implications as glimpsing alternative possible assumptions about what a "thing" is, what it would mean for something to exist, or the relation between existing and not-existing, or between "being one thing" and "being another thing." On these grounds, the seemingly very abstract and distant question of *what is meant by sameness and difference* may prove to be a pressing matter of profound importance. A moment's thought immediately reveals that some prereflective assumption about what counts as "the same" and what as "different" would have to serve as a defining premise in each and every possible human judgment and activity, every desire and value, every philosophical conclusion and logical principle, every cultural institution and political development.

As it happens, this consideration points us directly toward one of the most puzzling and intriguing things about many classical Chinese thinkers: the way they handle ideas of "sameness" and "difference." This is reflected in the most basic implications of apparently simple declaratory sentences— what is meant by saying "what" something "is"—and also in the most puzzling features of Chinese metaphysics, where modern interpreters seem again and again to find the material resisting analysis in terms of hard and fast notions of some set of really existing items that are factually "the same" and others that are "different." Again and again, in a variety of ways, we come across similar quandaries for interpretation: One? Many? Inner? Outer? Same? Different? And even: All? None? The persistent reoccurrence of such ambiguities, and the usually unsatisfying solutions offered for them, suggests that these either-or alternatives are perhaps not the most useful questions to ask when dealing with Chinese thought.

RETHINKING SAME AND DIFFERENT

To clarify what we're getting at here, let's put it this way: everything we can say, everything we can feel, everything we can know or want or imagine, presupposes some sense of what it means for something to be "the same as" or "different from" something else. If this list of types of experience is exhaustive, then all experience involves a strange preconscious procedure known as *identifying*: determining the identity of something. Maybe it is not an exhaustive list, if we consider some tacit or undifferentiated aspect of experience to be part of what we know or feel; possibly the above applies only to what we can *clearly and distinctly* know or feel, which emerges out of a more inchoate mass of not-yet-identified sensations that serve as a background out of which our clear and distinct ideas emerge. That would not be an unreasonable or unimportant claim. But even in that case, as long as we are experiencing *anything* as clearly and distinctly identified, we are ipso facto differentiating it from this inchoate background, which itself therefore is identified implicitly as the "inchoate-and-not-yet-identified-from-which-we-derive-identities."   One clearly differentiated item is all it takes to snap everything else instantly into the position of "everything else." We have to determine some identity for any element that is to figure into our experience, whether or not in doing so we are right or wrong about that identity, whether or not it is "really there," whether "determining" means "making so" or "figuring out what is already so." To perceive and be conscious of something requires coming to know "what it is": it is this thing (a computer, not a cardboard box), it is this sensation (smooth, not rough), it is this color (white, not black), it is this state of mind (bored, not excited). That means regarding it as "this" rather than "that," distinguishing it from "other" things, and ordering the relation between this thing and other things in some way, establishing its identity with itself at past and present moments over time, and further categorizing it as belonging to some class of things of the "same type," which is itself different from every "different type."

But how humans beings have historically gone about this, and what they thought they were doing when they did so, varies more widely than is sometimes supposed. One approach, with roots in early Greek thought, tends to do so by recourse to categories such as "universal" and "particular," requiring the multiple (different) instantiations of unchanging (same) forms or principles (many cats exemplifying the same essence of catness, or even, in another sense, many occurrences obeying the same natural law), or substances that stay "the same" in spite of their "different" relations and attributes (the cat sleeps or wakes, sits or runs, but is the same cat). Some one, selfsame something—catness—is present in some separate, different things—cats. It is different from them, but somehow also present in them, even constitutive of their identities. At the same time, this one selfsame something—catness—is different from other selfsame somethings—dogness, redness, and so on. Further, this one selfsame thing—this cat—at once instantiates many of these selfsame somethings—furriness, arrogance, fastidiousness, catness, carnivorousness. Certain very intricate problems come with such ideas, problems about the relation of the one to the many in these various senses. For one important, though I think unintended and perhaps even ironic, consequence of these ideas is that they grant an ontological ultimacy to the notions of "sameness" and "difference," which are themselves then thought to be completely "different" from one another.

There is a *fact of the matter,* on this view, about what is the same and what is different. If it is noticed that no item of experience ever seems to reduce neatly into being what it is while being purely different from every other intelligible thing, it becomes necessary to introduce questions about when and in what way it is different, pushing the pure separation of same and different up to a higher level of abstraction, or to deny reality to this contradictory thing in favor of an intelligible realm where true sameness and difference apply without intermixture. A thing cannot have two opposite predicates in the same respect and at the same time. Whatever part or aspect of something is the same is not different, and whatever aspect is different is not the same. "Same" and "different" translate quickly into "inside" and "outside": what counts as the same is everything "included" in the nature of this thing. What is different is everything "excluded." To know what a thing is is to know where its boundaries lie, and to regard these boundaries as ontologically impermeable.

We all know that Plato was Greek, and not Chinese. Presumably, we also know that Platonism formed no part of classical Chinese thinking, that no classical Chinese thinker was a Platonist. If pushed, everyone would also admit that, lacking Plato, Chinese thought cannot be strictly described as anti-Platonic either. It does not reject Platonism, having none available to reject. But what is philosophy like without Platonism to kick around? Is it really possible? If so, how does it work?

It is not as easy as one might think to answer these questions. For the roots of Platonism and its shadow anti-Platonism run deep and wide. Sometimes Chinese thought is presented as getting along just fine without wandering into the abstruse questions imposed upon Western thought by the peculiarities of Greek thinking: questions about Essences and Forms and Ideas and Universals and Particulars and Substances and Attributes, about God and Creation and Eternity and Time and Relative and Absolute and Truth and Opinion. And indeed, it gets along just fine, and more than just fine. But it is not just the cruder forms of Platonism or anti-Platonism that are lacking in it, and whose lack underwrites its most stunning and surprising developments. Why? Because even without Plato, some analogue to the problem Plato hoped to solve must be taken into account. That problem is the ambiguity of the identity of all experienced things. Here is this dog—but it is also white, and running, and hungry, and many other things besides. Here is this triangle—but it is also chalk powder. Here is this living body— but it is also, at "another" time, a corpse. Here is this good man—but while he looks good to me, he looks bad to you. Plato hoped to weed out these ambiguities and find some way to fix the definitions, the identities, of things once and for all, somewhere, in some sense. This required a step away from the empirical world to the world of Forms, where each entity was exactly what it was and nothing besides. The Platonic problem is the problem of the ambiguity, the alternate parsability and identifiability, of all experienced identities. Even without his solution, we must face this ambiguity, and if we find that it is not regarded as the same kind of problem somewhere—China, perhaps?—we have to ask why not. For in the absence of Plato, or all that we represent with the word *Plato,* or the reaction against Plato, we need to completely reconceive from the top down and from the bottom up what might be meant by the concepts of "same" and "different." And when the notions of "same" and "different" are rethought, everything else has to be rethought as well.

The pages that follow trace out some alternate ways of handling the identification of things, of sameness and difference, by some classical Chinese thinkers, and their rather enormous consequences. In place of essences, universals, particulars, substances, and attributes, we will find in the dominant Chinese traditions not simply notions of wholes and parts, but various notions of "coherence" which do not involve the handling of "sameness" and "difference" in the way sketched above. I do not mean to say that something translatable as "same" and "different," "inside" and "outside," is excluded from Chinese thought. That would be literally unthinkable. Attempts do seem to be made in the early tradition to develop unambiguous notions of sameness and difference, notably in the Mohist tradition. But these attempts run spectacularly aground, or are outcompeted in the cultural ecosystem, to be replaced by, and subsumed into, the competing model of coherence, as I hope to elucidate here. They never grow into the system of essences and universals that were hit upon in the West to solve the types of problems that attend the working out of these primitive same/different dichotomies. Once subsumed into the coherence model, the remaining ideas of sameness and difference are not regarded as mutually incompatible ultimate facts of the matter. It is that sameness and difference are *ultimately and ontologically negotiable,* and this negotiability about what they are pertains not merely to what we think they are or how we categorize them, but to their most fundamental character. The ambiguity pertaining to all experienced realities here has quite a different significance from what is found in either the Platonic problem or the Platonic solution, or for that matter in any anti-Platonic solutions. The sameness or difference predicated of them in any given context are aspects, often reversible, derivative of something else: what we will be calling "coherence."

By "coherence" I mean a way of hanging together. Already this sounds strange. Coherence, one might think, cannot be an "ultimate" category from which the others are derived, because we are accustomed to assuming that it is itself derivative of something else: whatever it is that is doing the cohering, the items that are hanging together. These items must have a prior identity, which would be ruled by the canon of "sameness versus difference": those identities would have to be just what they are, rather than something else. But is this an obvious truth, or is it merely a vestige of Platonism? In this book I hope to show the plausibility of the latter option, as exemplified in certain developments in the history of Chinese thinking.

"A way of hanging together": that could mean almost anything. But in its broadest denotation it will here point on the one hand to the mode of togetherness of any distinguish*able* (as opposed to "ontologically genuinely distinct") elements contained "within" a putative item, and on the other hand to the ways in which what is distinguished as this entire item is embedded in its environment. What would it mean if it were these factors, rather than ontological facts about what differs from what, to which we should look, in determining of "what a thing is" and "how a thing functions" and "what groups it belongs to" and "what can be reliably expected about it"? This may sound very bizarre and mysterious, or else very trivial and banal. But I hope to show that it is neither. In the epigraph from Zhuangzi at the top of this chapter, we see a prototype of the kind of outlook that is involved here: "Looked at from the perspective of their differences, your own liver and gall bladder are Chu [to the south] and Yue [to the north]. Looked at from the perspective of their sameness, the ten thousand things are all one." Does this mean that things *merely look* either the same or different when viewed in these alternate ways? Or does it mean that things *really are* the same or different when so viewed? The first would be trivial. The second would be bizarre. What I hope to show in the pages that follow is that neither of these fit the case. My claim in the following pages will be that it is something like this view, affirming neither of these alternatives, that forms the decisive consideration underlying the notions about what a thing is in classical pre-Qin thought, developing further in Han and Six Dynasties thought and continuing to be decisive themes in the theoretical forms of Chinese Buddhism, a continuity that is sometimes less than obvious, and for that reason generally ignored in attempts to confront these issues.

The "sameness" and "difference" question is also the "one-many" question, and ultimately these questions push us back to the question of "essences." It will be my contention that indigenous Chinese thought really has no doctrine of essences of the type we find typically rooted either in Plato or in Aristotle, that is, an attempt to determine, in the latter's phrase, *to ti ên einai*, what it is for a thing to be what it is. Whether as a transcendent or an immanent factor, the Platonic-Aristotelian approach to this question is to attempt to find a definitive identity for each thing, a definition that is valid in all possible contexts, after the manner of a mathematical proposition. Whether as the essence of one substance persisting through time, or as the essence named by a universal instantiated in a number of substances, we have here a notion of a kind of "sameness" that pervades either several disparate moments in time (in the case of an individual substance) or several disparate substances spread out in time and space (in the case of a universal essence). In this sense, even a singular essence is still a "universal" essence of a type, persisting unchanged through the apparent differences of the changes in the "accidents" pertaining to that substance. The claim that no equivalent of a universal essence, in either of these senses, is found in early China has been advanced before, in spite of apparent analogues to essence such as we find in, for example, the disquisitions on "human nature" in the *Mencius* and elsewhere. I will be arguing in support of this claim. But in contrast to some of the explications of Chinese thought that recognize the absence of a doctrine of essences, I will be arguing strenuously against considering what remains in the absence of a doctrine of essence a "nominalism" of the Western type (i.e., the doctrine that the universal essences attributed to things are therefore merely human impositions on what in fact has no essence of its own). Rather, in the absence of a concept of essence, *neither* nominalism nor realism can be true. Simply stated, nominalism assumes that there is a definitive constitution to the external things onto which essences are projected by humans—that is, they definitively *lack* an essence, which means that any essence attributed to them must be "merely" a name. In the absence of any concept of essence, external things cannot have the essence of lacking essence once and for all; the imposition of a name or identity onto them in a particular context can thus never be something that violates its essence of having no universal essence. This will be explained and explored in due time. What I hope to show is that in early Chinese thought we have a philosophical world without essence which is significantly different from the two other systems that deny universal essences, Western nominalism (and its extreme postmodern avatars) and Indian Buddhism. Unlike nominalism, early Chinese thought does not exclude the names or identities given to things from their essence—for there is no essence to be excluded from. Unlike Indian Buddhism, which *denies* essence rather than lacking it entirely from the beginning, this does not devolve into a Two Truths system where a *single consistent* set of provisional essences is allowed to persist as "conventional truth," bracketed by a second level of "ultimate truth" which transcends these essences. The upshot of the lack of essence in early Chinese thought is not that every putative identity must also be negated. It is that every identity is constitutively *ambiguous*. In Indian Mahayana Buddhism, every identity is both the *one* it is (conventionally) and *none* (ultimately). In the Chinese coherence doctrines, every identity is instead *several* identities at once.

Common sense—or at least the common sense that prevails in some parts of the world in some eras—seems to rebel against the rejection of any assumption of a single, objectivist "way things are," of independent facts in the world, which makes it seem that very sophisticated and perhaps decadent theories are necessary to call to these obvious assumptions of all ordinary life into doubt. The theories that challenge ontological realism veer toward the bizarre: the subjectivist turns of philosophical idealism, postmodernism, or the horror of horrors, moral relativism. But both of these extremes are symptoms of the same set of assumptions. Two simple and uncontroversial facts about early Chinese language and thought can perhaps make it more plausible that these "common sense" assumptions would not apply to them. The first is the absence of plural and singular distinctions in Chinese language. It hardly seems a stretch to assume that a culture that in its linguistic and conceptual system makes no *fundamental* distinction between plural and singular, does not place this distinction among its primitive building-block linguistic resources, will not configure the one/many problem, and therefore the same-different problem, quite the same way as a culture that does. The second factor, which follows directly on the first but is evidenced not only linguistically but socially and ethically: the absence of any theory of knowledge oriented to a *single* observer, which is to say, a mathematically singular *point of view*. This is not only a matter of the fuzzy lines between singular and plural; it also pertains to a conception of human knowledge as *always* arising within a prior familial and cultural context, where subjectivity is always first and foremost a prior intersubjectivity; where to become a full subject of knowledge always presupposes being a child of parents, learning language that comes from a specific past, seeing as referencing the viewpoint of a priorly existing subject or subjects with whom one is in an existing relationship of care, trust, and support. The lone isolated subject opening his eyes before an unnamed world is literally unthinkable here, an oxymoron. To be a subject is to already be a child of someone. It is perhaps not too counterintuitive to assert that the relationship in which a child's nascent identity stands to those of his forebears is again, strictly, neither an exclusive sameness nor an exclusive difference, but a certain kind of coherence. Now imagine a culture that regards singular and plural as inessential or secondary ontological categories, and which never posits a point of view that doesn't definitionally *come with* other points of view as part of its very constitution. Common sense in such a place will not, perhaps, think of the world as either the same or different from the ways in which it is named. The world will not be constituted of objective facts which are either so or not so, true or false, where these two categories are strictly mutually exclusive. Nor will it be the ideal creation of any single mind acting in isolation, projected without restraint or autonomously, which can thus simply make so whatever it wishes to be so at any time. It will be a world of coherence. That is the world we find in ancient China, which I will try to describe in this book.

COHERENCE AND LI: PLAN AND
METHOD OF THIS BOOK AND ITS SEQUEL

One of the most distinctive markers of the Chinese tradition's ability to get along without the notions of mutually exclusive sameness and difference, without Forms and Ideas and Universals and Particulars and Substances and Attributes, without the dichotomies between God and Creation and Eternity and Time and Relative and Absolute and Truth and Opinion, is the Chinese character 理 *Li*. It is a hidden focal point of this book, and the center-stage star of its forthcoming companion volume, although it makes its entrance as a philosophical category relatively late in the story, and thus serves as the explicit topic of the companion volume[1] rather than this one. For the swarm of meanings and shadings and alterations gathering around this character provide us with a sort of master key with which to unlock some of the most daunting enigmas in the history of Chinese thinking, illuminating a kind of prestructure paving the way for itself even before it walks in the door. Li is one of those epochal concepts whose arrival instantly reveals its own prehistory. It arrives more than once, in many forms, and never stands still. But tracing the thread of its gradual emergence and bizarre developments provides us with a way to understand all the implications of the Platoless and anti-Platoless world of Chinese thought.

The translation of this character into English has been, as we shall see in detail in the aforementioned companion volume, a very sticky problem that has aroused much controversy.[2] The main candidates have been things such as "principle," "order," "truth," "reason," "Logos," "pattern," "structure," and "coherence." We will be adopting the last-named word, "coherence," first suggested by Willard Peterson for Neo-Confucian usages, as a strong approximate marker of the character's semantic territory in many of its most puzzling and distinctive contexts. Let us note clearly at the beginning: this does not mean Li "always has the same meaning." Nor does it even mean that, purely as a translation question, the word is "best translatable as 'coherence'" in all, or even most, contexts. (Indeed, I would claim that in most situations, it is probably less awkward to translate it with such words as "guideline" "constructive pattern," "the way things fit together," "the sense made by things," "the how and why of things," "crucial information," "structure," or indeed simply "principle," or even sometimes—why not?— "truth.") It means simply that close and informed thinking about coherence will be invaluable to us in determining what it does mean, and how it is best translated, in each particular context.

The delineation of the precise senses of "coherence" that apply here, their definitions, qualifications, criteria, and ranges of application, will be perhaps the central contribution these books have to make. Once we have made clear to ourselves the many things it can mean for elements to "cohere" in this sense, and how these elements are therefore conceived, we will, I hope, find that many of the most vexing difficulties that have hitherto surrounded the understanding of this term, and indeed Chinese thought as a whole, will have been significantly reduced.

The complexity of factors involved in addressing this issue necessitates a somewhat unusual approach. The exposition given here can be read as structured somewhat like certain massive nineteenth-century European novels. We have several characters introduced independently of one another, with a detailed exposition of their lifeworlds, their background, their problems, and their aspirations, revealing the intricacies of their respective characters. These protagonists are initially unrelated. But they are destined to meet, and we feel this future bearing heavily upon them in the exposition. The aspects the author reveals to us of each of these two prospective lovers is already prefocused in accordance with those of the other; they are obscurely reflecting each other even when kept in isolation. Then we have the fateful moment of their meeting, followed by complicated misunderstandings, the painful shedding of previous entanglements, and finally their embrace and union. When I speak of Li as coherence, something similar is going on. We have, initially, two independent developments. This book will deal with what may be called the ironies of the notion of coherence as it develops in the classical philosophers who were to become most central for the mainstream developments of Chinese thought (e.g., Confucius, Mozi, Mencius, Xunzi, Laozi, Zhuangzi). In this part of the discussion, we will be focusing first on the "non-ironic" notion of coherence in *The Analects* and *Mencius,* modeled on certain features of human social interaction and evaluative behavior, and its implications for notions of how things assemble into coherent groups, what class membership is, and also the peculiar notion of "omnipresence" that emerges, to some extent as a by-product of this development. We will note how the particular approach to coherence here does not involve an ontological dichotomy between sameness and difference, and thus is neither a nominalism nor a realism in the philosophical sense, neither internalist nor externalist in the ethical sense. This has, initially, nothing to do with the word *Li* as such, which has no special importance in most of these texts.

Then we will spend some time on the contrarian cousin of this mode of thought: the "ironic" notion of coherence developed in the *Laozi* tradition and the Inner Chapters of the *Zhuangzi.* "Ironic" here means that this coherence is in a certain sense also, and necessarily, a noncoherence: the togetherness of things, pushed to its ultimate conclusion in the notion of the omnipresent, undermines the "intelligibility" of things, rather than establishing them. But it is this incoherence that really makes them cohere, and really allows them be what they are, which is what was claimed for the non-ironic coherence. The non-ironic coherence tradition claims that coherence makes value. The ironic coherence tradition claims that incoherence, and the nonattribution of value, is what makes value. Again we have no dichotomy between same and different, and no nominalism or realism. And here too Li plays no significant role.

While all this is going on we have another story gradually forming: the prehistory of the character *Li*. It starts out as a homely verb meaning to divide things up in a certain way. Intermittently it comes to be picked up as a useful marker of something that is hard to say otherwise. The companion volume will trace the development of the term from its earliest etymology and nonphilosophical uses, and then slowly taking its place as a piece of technical philosophical vocabulary. This becomes increasingly evident as the ironic and non-ironic traditions begin to encounter, absorb, and modify one another. Li is one of the fault lines of this encounter. We see it gain increasing prominence in the ironic incorporations of and response to non-ironic ideas. In these various ways it comes to denote coherence itself, as variously conceived in various compromises effected between the ironic and non-ironic traditions. The two characters of our novel meet and fall in love. They encounter all kinds of troubles and misunderstandings, and try to work it out. That is what these two books are about.

This book then, will follow the development of three types of coherence (non-ironic, ironic, and non-ironic coherence appropriating ironic coherence into itself) through the classical texts (*Analects, Mencius, Laozi, Zhuangzi, Xunzi*, the "Great Learning," "Doctrine of the Mean," from the *Liji*, and the systematic works of the Yin-Yang systems in the commentaries to the *Zhouyi* and Yang Xiong's *Taixuanjing*.

The companion volume, after looking at some modern attempts to interpret the meanings of Li, will take up the development of the usages of the character "Li" beginning with the *Shijing*, through its growing prominence in some of the later classical texts (especially in later parts of *Zhuangzi* and in the *Xunzi*), and its full-blown debut as an explicitly defined philosophical idea in the *Hanfeizi* commentary to the *Laozi*, and its great successes in the works of *xuanxue* thinkers such as Wang Bi and Guo Xiang. Its various applications in Chinese Buddhism, marking various ways of interfacing ironic and non-ironic notions of coherence and value, will then be traced as further extensions of the developments especially in Guo Xiang's deployment of the term.

An important question about method should be considered here before continuing. I must reiterate that I do not mean to imply that the term *Li* retains the same meaning in Buddhism and in Neo-Confucianism, much less in the earlier works I will look at below, nor even that there is *necessarily* any relevance of the various uses and nuances of this term, and other terms relating to similar issues, in earlier sources. A certain methodological question arises in this connection: why should anything that has been said about Neo-Confucian ideas of Li, such as I will cite and consider in detail below, have anything to do with how we are to read the Buddhist and pre-Buddhist texts? Am I assuming some kernel of unchangeable semantic essence that persists in all these very different texts, written under very different historical conditions, as parts of various agendas, over several millennia? Obviously this question itself, about "sameness and difference" of meaning, itself involves a stance concerning the very question we are considering here: universals, categories, classes, and what it means to say some "same" thing is "reappearing" at another time and place. If we were to ask this question in terms of the more typical Chinese notions to be developed in this work, we would instead ask about cohering continuations, of continuity, which strictly speaking instantiates neither pure sameness nor pure difference, and then we could say: yes, there is a coherence between these various usages of Li, though not an identity. But if the question is posed in terms of sameness and difference, my answer is simple: no, I do not think this term always means the same thing, which would be tantamount to denying any progression in the development of Chinese thought over several thousand years. I follow Nietzsche's suggestion that a word is something like a pocket into which various things are put at various times. On the other hand, I will try to show, through close, detailed analysis of very diverse usages of these terms and conceptions in different philosophical contexts, that, if we choose to abstract ruthlessly enough—pull the camera back sufficiently, as it were—we can find certain continuities of usage which may have made this particular pocket attractive as a container for these various ideas. This depends on the highly abstract nature of the continuities we will be identifying—for example, linking through their shared reference to intelligibility, value, pleasure, and so on. *What* in particular constitutes "intelligibility" or "value" in any of these cases will differ radically, and this will affect what sorts of things are identified as Li, how it is apprehended, how it is structured, and how it relates to various other terms in each philosopher's writings. I cannot claim any sort of a priori validity for this assertion, nor imply that it had to be this way. Instead, I will try to show that, for example, we will find in almost all cases that Li has a relation to value—however conceived in each case—that resonates recognizably with most of the other usages we will examine. In principle, it is always possible to give a new sense to a word that plays off its previous usages, tweaking them in a way that eventually allows its former implications to fall away. That said, some sort of continuity is presumed in doing so. Indeed, one of the central themes of my treatment of this development is the way in which an ironic usage of the term almost completely reverses its meaning—but in a way that presupposes at every step its previous usages, without which it would pack no punch. So I will indeed be making generalizations and transhistorical summary statements about "the Daoist use" or "the Confucian use" of certain terms. Whether or not it is proper to refer to, say, Laozi and Zhuangzi as "Daoists," let alone certain texts in the *Guanzi*, is to me a question of little importance. The answer to this question will depend on the answer to another question: For what purpose? Proper *for what*? I use these terms as shorthand ways to refer to a group of thinkers, for the sole purpose of making my referent known to my reader. But I have taken pains to indicate explicitly or through context the specific range of texts I am attempting to characterize with these claims, and what the range of their applicability is in each case. I hope that reading the analyses below will make these points more concretely clear.

The same consideration applies to the problem of "essentialism" when talking about "the Chinese tradition." In my view, the historicist attack on essentialism, which is almost the primary dogma of intellectual history in our day, is well-intentioned but misguided. It may seem like progress when, instead of saying, "The Chinese think like this," as the first few generations of unabashed orientalists were prone to do, we say, "Members of this school of thought in the mid-Tang period in the Zhejiang region thought like this," or better, "This guy, at this time and place, in this text, meant this." But—to make another meta-appeal to our central problem—unless we have at our disposal some way of understanding the coherence of distinct entities into a larger characteristic whole that does not depend on the category of "essence," we are just replacing a bigger "essence" with a smaller "essence." What does it mean to discern a shared feature in more than one occurrence, or a characteristic that "expresses itself" in more than one way, or in more than one moment? What does it mean to identify a continuity between two distinct moments? How can an identity of any kind have a duration of more than one moment, remaining unchanged in spite of the changes in its appearances? What does it mean to know a fact about something at all? Even if we restrict our claims to predications about a single individual, or a single text, we are still applying some kind of universal, and we may be justly criticized for creating a stereotype. Does every moment of Zhu Xi's life and every utterance he makes have to be permeated with this abstruse quality "Zhu Xi-ness"? Is every line of text X saturated with the "meaning" of text X, or X-ness? No more and no less, I would claim, than every particular instance of "Chinese thought" is permeated by "Chineseness." In both cases the answer is no, or at best yes and no. It may be a step toward an overcoming of the larger essence when we diversify and fragment it into smaller essences, but at the same time it further entrenches the habit of essentialism. My view is that we can only undermine this habit not by a self-contradictory attempt to be nonessentialist, but rather through a kind of *poly-essentialism.* That is, the hegemony of a certain essentialist reading of, say, Chinese thought can be overcome only by providing *alternate* essentialist readings of the same. The *more* of these we have, the weaker the hold any given essentialism can have on us.

This brings us to a broader point. What after all is an interpretive analysis such as this supposed to do? And, given the questions that will arise about the undergirdings of our usual thinking, how do I think it is possible to ferret out the mechanism of an alternate set of premises for thinking using only these very tools of analysis and induction that are embedded in my early-twenty-first-century academic American English prose? The oddness of traditional Chinese conceptions of "categories," and especially the idea of Li, has remained one of a handful of nodal points in almost all of the more ambitious attempts to situate the Chinese tradition of speculative thinking with relation to the European. It has even found itself a role as a postmodern staple of more general philosophical interest as well since the impressive opening trope of Foucault's *Les Mots et les choses,* describing his reaction to Borges's imagined Chinese encyclopedia. But the methodological problems we confront here would suggest that another Borges parable might be more to the point. In "Averroes' Search," Borges tells the story of the Islamic theologian struggling to find an Arabic translation of the words for "drama" and "comedy" in Aristotle's *Poetics,* at a time when Islamic culture had no theater. After poignantly describing Averroes's groping for an equivalence, Borges makes a typically self-reflective move: is my Argentinian attempt to imagine and depict the Islamic theologian's struggle to map an alien Greek concept really any less blind, groping, and doomed than that struggle itself? This is perhaps closer to the problem we confront here: How do we categorize an alternative to the category "category"? How do we replicate an alternative to "replication"? What is the universal meaning of an alternative to "universality"? What principle can we derive from something that takes the place of "principle"?

I subscribe to the broadly pragmatic view that an interpretative reading of the tradition, such as I attempt here, is no more and no less than a kind of tool, a supplementary text not at all unlike a concordance or an etymological dictionary. It is one of many different tools we have at our disposal, each of which will be appropriate for a different purpose; which tool we reach for in any given instance will depend on what we *want* at that time. We have certain texts before us that we can read in a number of ways. We confront certain difficulties, cognitive dissonances, bemusements, excitements, and questions, in the process of reading. As we turn the text this way and that, and juxtapose it with various external considerations— historical, philosophical, personal, whatever is to hand—we notice that the extent and contours of its intelligibility change accordingly. We may never get the feeling, on any of our readings, that everything there might be to say about a given text is exhausted, nor that every atom of its warp and woof become unambiguously clear. But by applying now one tool, now another— or perhaps, to slightly alter the metaphor, now one lens, now another— we find that different Gestalts emerge, different aspects, different strains of coherence. These diverse readings may or may not, when lined up side by side, add up into a single unified picture that applies for all possible lenses, for all possible purposes. I tend to think not. But it seems uncontroversial to suppose that the more lenses we have at our disposal, the more we will know about the text. To know more about the text is to know more of the ways it is capable of appearing to us, more types of ways in which it can form a certain temporarily coherent picture. This book and its companion volume are a lens through which to read the Chinese treatments of questions of coherence, value and omnipresence clustering around the word *Li*. Their purpose is to aid other readers who might have confronted some of the same perplexities as I have in working and playing with these Chinese texts for several decades. The test of their value lies in the degree to which they prove useful to other readers of these texts; when confronted with a snag, they can be referred to, just as a concordance or a dictionary might. We cannot but cherry-pick the aspects of the case that especially concern our present orientation, but we do so in the hopes that outlining what these are will allow others who are likewise saturated with these texts to come to see the same aspect there, among whatever other aspects might concern them. It is like looking at the moon and saying, "See, there's a rabbit there; that pointy thing up near the top edge is the ears," in the hopes that our companion, who has seen the moon a thousand times but never seen a rabbit there, will finally say, "Aha! Yes, I see it too." That is really all our tool amounts to: a way of saying, "That pointy part is what I'm seeing as the ears." This doesn't mean every rock and crater of the moon's surface will correspond to some part of the rabbit, nor that the alternate vision of the Man in the Moon will suddenly become inaccessible. There will be some parts left out of the picture, and there will be alternate pictures that can be constructed even of the parts that are included. But sometimes this alternate way of organizing the material will help smooth out the problem experienced by our companion—without robbing him of his ability to also see the Man in the Moon, when that suits his purposes. Sometimes he will have a problem that our alternate tool will not help solve. In that case, another tool from the toolkit should be tried.

It goes without saying that what constitutes "smoothing out" and "a snag" will depend on what the reader wants from these texts, and she may want different things at different times. This will mean different tools would be appropriate at different times. It is also obvious that such an endeavor is hopelessly "presentist": we are looking for things that will enhance the reading experience for us, such as we are here and now, and with our current purposes and interests guiding what counts as a problem and what a solution. That is where we start, from within our own present interests, conceptual schemes, language, our own biases. We start, unsurprisingly, where we are. We have to encounter a second position from our first position: we cannot invent a third position from scratch. Our initial position, of course, involves a long-developed interest in historical causality, in sequences of before and after, in vectors of influence, a sense of uncertainty and continued questing when the historical context of a text we are reading, situated by us within a particular conception of time and history, is still vague. That is the reason we will also find ourselves obliged to be historically and philologically as "rigorous" as possible when considering these texts. Indeed, such rigor is much to be treasured even if we are committed to Whitehead's much-abused but irresistible dictum, "It is more important that a proposition be interesting than that it be true" (which, if not true, is at least interesting): for a rigorous historical approach safeguards the strangeness of a text, and helps protect us from reading into it just what we have always already assumed, forcing us to stretch our conceptual and imaginative powers in the attempt to make sense of it. This recalcitrance of the text in its historical embeddedness, our commitment to faithfully facing up to an alien claim, our commitment to truth, *makes it more interesting* (again in accord with Whitehead, who follows his abuse-begging comment just quoted by adding, "The importance of truth is, that it adds to interest. . . . [O]f course a true proposition is more apt to be interesting than a false one").[3] But still, I do not think it necessary to consider this impulse to really be about finding out the once-and-for-all way it was in that distant past time. Rather, it is hoped that in the course of the encounter, rooted in a here whose nature is to grope toward a there, our initial language will gradually expand its repertoire of sayables, that its range of implications will bleed into new shadings that reveal new information about our first position, indeed allow it to morph into a synthesis that is position-one-after-its-encounter-with-position-two. This is the only way to get from position one to position three.

This is why I will try to read every thinker I discuss here as if he is absolutely right about everything. I will not point out fallacies and inconsistencies. The nature of the project requires that each position be spelled out from within, requires the expositor to serve as each contradictory position's spokesman, as it were. I take it for granted that every possible position is in some sense or other "coherent"—it is simply a question of coming up with what other premises would be required in the background to make its coherence appear to the reader's eye. Here again I believe that the only way to overcome the hegemony of truth claims is to make plausible multiple conflicting truth claims. For to critique a philosophical position really only establishes more firmly the unseen philosophical position from which the critique is made: the unquestioned premises or rules of discourse that one wields in making the critique. Critiques of hegemony only establish the hegemony of the critique. More boldly, I would claim that a critique of any philosophical position is really a failure of nerve and imagination, of subjecting oneself to the alterations in one's implicit framing notions of legitimacy that would be required to make it plausible.[4]

Twenty years ago, I boarded a bus in Taipei, and soon discovered that I did not have enough money for the fare. I was very surprised when the driver, seeing me rifling through my pockets, said something like "Never mind" and waved me on board to sit down. That was the beginning of this project. I dedicate this book to that unknown bus driver.

ONE

ESSENCES, UNIVERSALS,
AND OMNIPRESENCE

Absolute Sameness and Difference

What do Chinese thinkers mean when they make those assertions we translate in the form of "*This* is *that*"—for example, "this is a horse," or "human nature is good," or "the nameless is the beginning of Heaven and Earth"? We quickly get into trouble if, applying familiar models of particular entities that non-negotiably possess certain properties and not others, we assume that they mean "it is really and ultimately the truth about this object here that it is a horse and not a non-horse," or "it is the real and definite fact about this item in the world, human nature, that it is good and not non-good," or "that entity which is the nameless is such that it is the beginning of Heaven and Earth, rather than not being the beginning of Heaven and Earth." We get into trouble, that is, if we take these statements to be assertions about *essences,* or unchanging definitive determinations of "what it is to be this thing," putatively valid in all contexts. Equally, though, it is clear that these assertions do not mean, "I am arbitrarily projecting horseness, goodness, or beginningness onto an indeterminate blank," nor, "horseness, goodness, beginning are purely mental constructs," or "purely human social constructs." What then do they mean?

One relatively simple way to zero in on the difficulty here would have to do with the status of language, and hence of every possible proposition. Are the ultimate facts about the world adequately definable in sentences made of words? If we don't think so, we will not regard our statements that "X is Y" as meaning to assert that X is really and exclusively Y, full stop. We would have to regard the purpose of making verbal statements to be something other than saying how things really are.[1] And indeed, it has been suggested that the defining moves in Chinese speculation work on a very different model, where words are part of, say, an exemplary skill-practice, meant to guide behavior in such a way as to alter perception and evaluation, rather than to describe what is really so or what is really good.[2]

This may seem, by Occam's Razor, to be the best way to understand some of the strange things that come to occur in the history of Chinese thought. After all, it is not just that China had no Plato. It also had no Parmenides, and no Parmenidean assertion that "being" and "thought" must coincide, that the thinkable and the real would have to be one and the same. This is arguably the most basic assumption of the entire Western philosophical tradition, the implications of which the latter has grappled to think through, and the limitations of which it has fought to overcome at every stage of its subsequent development. It is this assertion that of course underwrites first and foremost the entire Platonic project most pervasively.

This point about the status and role of language in Chinese thought is important, but it doesn't really solve all of our problems. For one thing, the denial of the final definitional and descriptive adequacy of language does lead to certain inevitable problems and contradictions, the avoidance of which has been one of the main reasons for adhering to the assumption of linguistic adequacy in the West. In addition, we have to ask what language *is* doing if it's not supposed to be telling us facts about things, and whether it can really do so while excluding any claim to at least one adequate reference to something purported to be definitively so. We must assume that there are many ways to answer this question, and many uses of language. For even within the confines of the non-ultimate-reality qualification, the linguistic expressions of Chinese philosophy are not the simple reiteration of the insistence that "words do not express objective realities." They make many claims, many different claims and counterclaims, in linguistic form, and indeed many that are found nowhere else in the annals of human thinking, which are not reducible simply to this one act of bracketing. Even if construed as tentative directives for action, they arguably involve cognitive commitments that frame their efficacy, which perhaps produce as many quandaries about the relation of language to reality as they avoid. And this is certainly acknowledged by those who have done most to highlight the problems of unqualified attribution of truth claims to Chinese thinkers. Hall and Ames, for example, acknowledge that the indifference to the question of truth of verbal assertions in the strict sense does not mean that these statements are unrelated to "facticity," the difference being that this facticity is not embedded in a framework requiring a notion of the *necessity* of conclusions from premises, which in turn involves some reference to "final principles" and "atomic facts."[3] I am much in agreement. The question then becomes how we are to understand this kind of "facticity."

Another simple way to deal with this facet of Chinese thought would be to note that it tends to assume a "process orientation," rather than a "substance orientation." That is, ultimate facts are regarded as temporal processes rather than static entities. This ensures a certain mismatch with declarative sentences that affirm things to be *fixedly* one way or the other, neglecting their transformation into opposite characteristics. This could also be described as a dialectical view of reality. In this sense, for example, Zhuangzi's statement that is sometimes translated "the Perfect man has no self" (至人無己 *zhiren wu ji* 2/1/21–22) can best interpreted by simply adding an implicit "fixed" to the sentence: "The Perfect Man has no *fixed* self." The negation is of fixity, not of presence or existence of a "self" in the broader sense. This too instantly renders many of the puzzling statements found in the tradition intelligible.

But here as well many new problems arise. Are words and terms also processes, or do they somehow fall outside the general ontological claim about process? Couldn't the words themselves participate in the process that by hypothesis pertains to everything existing? In that case, there would seem to be no need for an unbridgeable mismatch between them. And whence do words then even *seem* to attribute something like stability or constancy? Is constancy really excluded by a process orientation, or just otherwise conceived? And does a term such as "process" itself perhaps involve us in problems of self-reference, exempting itself from the process nature of all other entities? Is it "always true" that things are really processes? In the Chinese tradition that most explicitly thematizes the notion of process—the *Zhouyi* and its commentaries—we find the stock trope, going back at least to Zheng Xuan (127–200), that 易 *yi* has three meanings: easy, changing, and *unchanging*. If we are tempted to interpret the last of these, as many modern Chinese interpreters do, to mean that there are unchangeable "principles" or "laws" of change, or that the fact that all things always change is itself an unchanging principle or law, we seem to be on the brink of a two-tier metaphysic of unchanging laws (or at least one "law": change) and their changing instantiations, which can easily link hands with the Western philosophical traditions with which we are already familiar. Be that as it may, it is clear that we cannot discount *some* sense of "unchanging" playing a role in this tradition. But is this exactly what "unchanging" means here, given that it is presented as an alternate *meaning* of the word meaning "changing"? The sense of "unchanging" prevents the meaning of the term *change* from being *the same* at all times: it *changes,* as it were, the meaning of change; the concept "change" itself is precisely *not unchanging.* What sort of change is it that also *means* "not change," its own opposite, its own "change"? What sort of "unchanging" also means "change"?

I do think that there is a pervasive distrust of the ultimate adequacy of language to the nature of reality in the Chinese tradition, and also that process orientations are closer to what Chinese thinkers tend to have in mind than substance ontologies and vocabularies. Indeed, I think these conclusions are by now rather uncontroversial. These points can be brought together in a more sweeping ontological comparison, made most lucidly by Li Chengyang, who notes, in his discussion of Aristotle's ontological stance, presented plausibly as underlying much of the Western philosophical tradition's approach to this matter, the assumption of a *single primary being* (or "*substance*") for any really existent entity; though any entity can perhaps be described in a number of ways, in accordance with various relations or predicates, the truth about it is an understanding of its single, unambiguous, definable essence, its primary being, which has a privileged and originary relation to all its other predicates. Li contrasts the assumptions of Chinese ontology as manifested in Zhuangzi's failure to single out any of the many alternate ways of relating to or describing something—an ox, for example—as primary, foundational, or ultimately *most* real.[4] Though I think Li makes things a bit too easy by choosing the most obvious contrast to Aristotle—Zhuangzi, no less—this approach does cut the Gordian knot and get to the heart of the matter. The contrast here is not primarily to fluidity or pragmatics (though these can be quickly derived from this point), but to the question of *ontological ambiguity*. Li's insight here is, in my view, closer to the real issue as I'd like to approach it in this work. What comes under scrutiny here is the assumption that there must be a *single truth about what something ultimately is*. From here it is a short step to asking whether *existing means being ultimately and definitively the same as or different from something else*. The question is the *definitiveness of specifiable identity* per se.

But simply asserting and accepting these provisos are on my view too summary a way out of confronting what is most fascinating and worth our while in Chinese thought. It may be possible to dig a bit farther. Rather than taking this "easy way out" right from the beginning, then, this book and its sequel will try to take the "hardest way out," focusing our attention on a term that comes to mean, among other things, precisely "intelligibility": Li 理. For Li is in most cases precisely *something to be cognized,* and something that is *capable of being discerned*. If there is any term that would correspond to what is knowable about the world, or where human cognition can accord definitively with what is really the case, it would seem to be Li. Indeed, if we were looking for a candidate in traditional Chinese vocabulary to mean something like "Truth" in the fully audacious philosophical sense, it would probably be Li.[5] For precisely this reason, an understanding of this term can help us understand why the concept of "Truth" in the traditional Western philosophical sense, involving necessity of premise-conclusion relations, ultimate foundations on principles and atomic facts, is of so little relevance in Chinese thought. An examination of how this term develops, and the vicissitudes of its usages, will help give us a more complete understanding of the relation between human knowledge and the realities of the world in Chinese thought.

We will do this first, in this book, by investigating the "prehistory" of Li, the notions of coherence that develop in Confucius and Mencius on the one hand and in the ideas collected in the *Laozi* and the Inner Chapters of the *Zhuangzi* on the other, as well as some compromises between these two views emerging in late Warring States texts. The main thrust of this story will depend on the emergence of two distinct notions of "coherence," the relation between which may be described as the dominant theme in much subsequent Chinese thought. The focus on "coherence" can be quite simply translated into the language of the just-considered provisos. Like Hansen and others, I think the criterion used to judge the validity of all statements made in ancient Chinese texts is aimed not at being "true" but at being "acceptable" (可 *ke*), and that this pragmatic criterion is meant socially and ethically, explaining why semantically opposite statements about the same topic might both be "acceptable," that is, useful in doing something in some particular intersubjective situation. Two opposite statements about what this thing is, for example, might both be "acceptable," in that the making of these two statements might be ethically important in their own situations. Perhaps it cannot be "true" that this thing is both X and non-X, but it can be "acceptable" to say that it is X or to say that it is non-X. What I want to add to this picture by bringing in the larger question of "coherence" is that "to be acceptable to say" is itself a type of cohering, between a situation and an ethical goal and an action; and that this pragmatism does then open up a particular way of talking about what things "are," but one that *folds in* this pragmatic relation of coherence to words, identities, and human actors. But why is this interesting, why should we choose to focus our attention on precisely this question, among all the questions that might arise in reading early Chinese texts? To understand this, we must take a look at the default assumptions that are arguably built into our commonsense assumptions about sameness and difference, about oneness and diversity, as derived from the distinctive inheritance of the Western philosophical traditions.

ESSENCES, UNIVERSALS, CATEGORIES, IDEAS: SIMPLE LOCATION AND THE DISJUNCTION OF SAME AND DIFFERENT IN MAINSTREAM WESTERN PHILOSOPHY

The default mode of handling the question of sameness and difference in the Greco-European philosophical tradition seems inevitably to draw upon some variant of the problem of essences or universals. In the present context, it is important to note that the distinction between "individual essences" and

"universal essences" is irrelevant. To the extent that an individual essence—
for example, "what it is to be *this cup*," as opposed to "what it is to be *A
CUP generally*"—is assumed to persist through the many moments during
which this particular cup may exist, and indeed through its various aspects
as an unchanged "this-cupness," we have a "universal" with a certain range
of application. If we take seriously the question of time, of the difference
between one moment and the next, the difference between an individual
essence and a universal is merely one of extent: individual essences are
merely universals with a relatively limited extent. Similarly, the difference
between the Platonic and the Aristotelian understanding of essences becomes
irrelevant (as does, for our purposes, the distinction between "conceptualism" and "realism"). Whether it is what Schopenhauer preferred to see as
the *unitas ante rem* of the truly metaphysical Platonic Idea (and realism in
general) or the *unitas post rem* of the intellectually derived concept (and
nominalism), we have here a way of finding a sameness within a multiplicity,
but at the same time of conceptually separating out the sameness from the
multiplicity. In one way or another, a "sameness" is discovered permeating a
number of diverse instances. It should be noted right here at the outset that
in its original Greek form this way of thinking is perhaps anything but an
attempt to make a simple and doctrinaire sameness and difference perfectly
separate; on the contrary, it is a way of highlighting precisely how complex the relation and intermixture of sameness and difference is. We might
consider briefly the role of mathematics in the earliest Greek conceptions
of knowledge as embodying an intuition about precisely this problem. For
the mathematical model, first foregrounded by the Pythagoreans, provides
the most direct template for the Platonic revolution in epistemology. The
very idea of apodictic knowledge, knowledge that is always and everywhere
true, is modeled on mathematical knowledge, whence derives the Platonic
notion of Forms, the Aristotelian investigation into essences, and finally the
wholesale separation of sameness and difference into radically distinct categories. But this very same mathematical impulse also provided a potential
undermining of a static conception of the same versus the different. As a
simple example, consider an elementary (though notorious) bit of arithme-
tic: the equation $5 + 7 = 12$. What does this "equal" sign signify here? Not
that what stands on either side of it are one and the same thing. For then
the sign would say nothing, would do no work at all. Manifestly, "$5 + 7$"
is something quite different from "12." After all, $4 + 8$ is also 12, and 4 is
not 5, nor is 8 7. But the equal sign asserts that, in spite of being different,
they are also in some sense the same. More precisely, same and different do
not apply to this relation. "Equal to" means a sublation of the categories
of same and different: it tells us that these are not ultimate, nonnegotiable
categories of ontology, that they do not tell us what things definitively are.

Equivalences between ratios illustrate the same point perhaps even more forcefully. Yet "equal to" can also be construed as asserting the ultimacy of a real sameness. There is an inherent slippage or ambiguity in the foundations of mathematics with respect to this question.[6] Obviously, I have not chosen this equation randomly: it points forward to the Kantian problem of synthetic versus analytic judgments. It should be obvious that there too the very alternative between these two types of judgment rests entirely on an assumption about the relation of sameness and differences: Does the predicate say something "different" from what is allowed in the subject, or does it merely repeat "the same" information? The particular way in which this problem of sameness and difference is addressed in the foundational moves of European ontology and epistemology produces, perhaps almost as a by-product, a set of conceptual tools that come to enforce a view of the world that takes sameness and difference as clear-cut ultimate facts. The invention of the idea of universals pervading particular instances is both an acknowledgment of the problem encountered in any attempt to divide the world neatly into samenesses and differences, and a way of containing and defusing the potential problems that come with this division. Multiple diverse characteristics or identities are noticed at one and the same location. There is an interpenetration of different characteristics found in each selfsame thing, and one and the same unchanged universal contains many diverse things. To thematize such points is to thematize a kind of interpenetration of same and different. This interpenetration, however, is subordinated to a more basic metaphysical commitment to keeping sameness and difference absolutely distinct. To give some sense of how we are conceiving this issue, let us very briefly sketch how this seems to have taken place.

It would perhaps be no exaggeration to say that the problem of the relation between the Universal and the Particular, in one of its many forms, is the central character in the drama of classical Occidental philosophy, running from the Socratic interest in definition, to the Platonic doctrine of Forms, the Aristotelian notion of essences and natural kinds, through the medieval debates between nominalists and realists, the Humean critique of induction, the Kantian response, and so on. But what is a Universal anyway, and why is it so important? And how is it that this problem seems so much less central to the classical tradition in Chinese philosophy?

Of course, human beings do not need a *theory* about how to understand sameness and difference—set theory, mereology, or a theory of universals—to apply what are later called universals, or even, more modestly, generalizations, in their practical everyday life. Indeed, a sort of Santayana-esque "animal faith" in reiterability, consistency, predictability, and so on are encoded in the simplest rudiments of sentient behavior. Pavlovian responses to stimuli involve an instinctive and unproblematic judgment about what counts as "same" and "different" with respect to the practical needs of the animal in question. In learning to identify signs of danger or promises of nutriment, an animal classifies and divides into groups. These classifications are, of course, fallible; what smells delicious—roughly similar to previous instances of nourishment—may turn out, in this instance, to be poisonous. It would not be difficult to derive the philosophical question about universals from the increasingly frequent disconfirmation experiences of this kind that perhaps come with increasing complexity and alterations of the environment in which the human animal, negotiating not only material but also social and linguistic signs, must survive. But in any case, it must be clarified that when we speak here about the importance of the problem of universals, we certainly do not mean that without having perfected some such theory, no such connections or classifications can or will be made. On the contrary, their practical application always precedes the explicit raising of this question to philosophical speculation; the latter, indeed, is dependent on just this procedure to even ask the question about this procedure. But this does not diminish the importance of the various ways in which differing cultures come to conceive of this procedure in which they had always already been engaged. For the humble fact of rough-and-ready classifying can be understood in a wide variety of ways, integrated into very different worldviews, which in turn can come to impact upon how this procedure of classifying is itself applied and handled when presented with new situations, with the inevitable experience of disconfirmation, and with the nonempirical speculative outgrowths of both confirmations and surprises that experience brings. Metaphysics both grows from attempts to make sense of this activity, and in turn comes to influence how this activity is subsequently deployed.

The problem taken up here has been on the theoretical radar at least since Lucien Lévy-Bruhl tried to distinguish "primitive mentality" from rational thought by singling out the typology of "collective representations" operative in them. Lévy-Bruhl lumps together all forms of thinking that strike him as qualitatively different from modern Western "logical" thought, including Chinese thought, and calls them "prelogical," assuming that whatever is unlike logical thought as he conceives it operates by means of a more or less similar set of procedures. The framing of *both* categories, in fact, give us insight into certain features of modern *Western* thought; the characterization of non-Western thought reveals by negation what is excluded in logical thinking as Lévy-Bruhl conceives it, what its premises make impossible. Prelogical thought does indeed make classifications, generalizations, and abstractions, according to Lévy-Bruhl, but neither the generalizations nor the abstractions so made resemble logical "concepts." Indeed, almost the first thing he says about this, the most striking puzzle of all, is that "the opposition between the one and the many, the same and another, and so forth, does not impose upon this mentality the necessity of affirming one of the terms if the other be denied, or vice versa."[7] Rather, they follow what he calls "the law of participation," which "busies itself with collective representations so interwoven as to give the impression of a community in which members would continually act and react upon each other by virtue of their mystic qualities, participating in, or excluding each other." A set of apparently disparate objects are linked and grouped together on the basis of a mystic affinity that allows them to act upon one another with special efficacy, and the name of the group names this totality of linked items. The members of this group are joined by actual though unseen interaction among real beings: they have a relationship to one another, in the most concrete sense. They *relate* to each other, actively. Unlike logical concepts, the classification is simply the name of this whole group of relating beings. It "does not . . . become compacted in a concept which is more comprehensive than that of the object[s] it embraces."[8] The objects simply fit together through their actions upon one another, and the totality of these things as fitting together and acting upon one another in this way is what is named by the generalization. Typically, the name given to the group as a whole will be the name of one of its most prominent members, namely, one that is encountered especially frequently or one that is construed to have an unusually great power of influence.

In contrast, "logical thought classifies by means of the very operations which form its concepts. These sum up the work of analysis and synthesis which establishes species and genera, and thus arranges entities according to the increasing generality of the characteristics observed in them."[9] Lévy-Bruhl is claiming that logical concepts of universality have two defining characteristics: (1) they mirror in structure the very mental operation of abstraction by which they are subjectively derived, and (2) they exceed the list of objects by which they are instantiated. The first point means that we arrive at the notion of a classification by means of a process of grouping and abstraction, making use of a criterion by which to recognize members of a given class. That *criterion itself* becomes the name of the essence being instantiated.

Suppose I have two transparent liquids. One is sulfuric acid, the other is water. I distinguish them by means of criteria: all the liquid that has the chemical composition H_2O and quenches human thirst is "water," all the liquid that has the chemical composition H_2SO_4 and burns through human flesh is "sulfuric acid." This criterion itself names the essence of the two substances: water *is* the clear liquid that quenches thirst and has the composition H_2O; sulfuric acid *is* the clear liquid that burns through flesh and has the composition H_2SO_4. What the thing *is* is synonymous with *what distinguishes it from other things*. When I name that thing, the name I give it is not one that is warranted by the entire thing, but only the aspects of it that are different from other things. Whatever is shared is necessarily left unnamed at this level. What is shared is popped up to a higher level, or a more fundamental level: it has logical priority, and brings with it an implication of causal grounding, and the apodictic sense of necessity and unilateral (transcendent) dependence: whatever is true of a member of this species is necessarily also true of all members of this genus, but not vice versa.

If I have an object composed of properties X and Y, where X is shared with others and Y is not, the *name* of the object will be Y, rather than XY. X will have a logical priority to Y. We will be inclined to think that Y depends on X, but X does not depend on Y. X-ness will be identified as X only at the higher level of X versus Z in the compound XZ, where Z is shared and X is unshared. Z will have a logical priority to X. The genus that includes these species, which identifies what is shared among instances, actually refers to a redirected difference: how this sameness differs from other samenesses, the genus represented as what is left out of the differentia of the subordinated species. These two substances belong to the same genus—clear liquids—because of the criterion I use to identify them as such: their transparency and liquidity at room temperature, and so on. These shared characteristics too are part of the essence of each substance, and their *sameness*, their *belonging to one class*, or their *being parts of one whole* are determined by the sharing of those characteristics that allow us to judge them to be parts of this class. But these characteristics themselves, these distinguishing marks, also consist only of what distinguish them from other characteristics: opacity, solidity, and so on. The same process must continue, pushing sameness up always to one order of higher inclusiveness and logical priority than the difference, where the difference alone provides actual content or putative identities.

So if Lévy-Bruhl is correct that the relations between various essences, the inclusion of species within genera, follows the same structure as that between these procedures of classification themselves, we may note a crucial *asymmetry* between sameness and difference, a systematic *level-incommensurability of difference and sameness* even in the identification of putative sameness, *because the procedure of identifying either sameness or difference depends on an act of judgment, which is the making of a distinction*. This can be seen equally as a privileging of difference (sole provider of content) or a structurally necessary subordination of difference to sameness (sameness therefore identifiable in the skewed, at-a-distance view of its higher-order category; sameness can only be seen *from below*). I literally have no way to identify the sameness without relegating it to a higher, more inclusive level (or, what amounts to the same thing, a lower, more fundamental level)—a logically prior level. The point here is that the sameness and difference are always, necessarily and structurally, consigned to different ontological levels. A mammal is an animal that bears live young and breastfeeds them. All mammals are therefore animals, and whatever characterizes animals must therefore characterize mammals. But the reverse is not the case. In a specific mammal, the characteristic of (say) live birth (the differentia) and of, say, oxygen respiration (a shared trait among all animals), are both immediately present, and equally integral to its concrete existence. But in a symbolic and conceptual system that attributes being to things in a way that is isomorphic to its procedure for categorizing them ("rational thought"), the "animality" *cannot* be ontologically commensurate, on the same level, as the "mammalarity." Respiration cannot be on the same ontological level as capacity for live birth; respiration is prior and more fundamental; all live-birthers respire, but not all respirators live-birth. This allows us to infer apodictically of a live-birther that it respirates. In this case, this unproblematically maps on to the levels of ontological dependence: only *because* something respirates can it live-birth. If respiration is removed, live birth cannot persist. And this is concretely and empirically true: the function of "giving life birth" does in fact depend on the function of respiration, but not (in an already living animal) vice versa.

However, consider the water/sulfuric acid case. By the same logic, we should put "translucent and liquid at room temperature" in the same role as "respiration," and "having the chemical composition H_2SO_4" in the role of giving live birth. All H_2SO_4 is transparent and liquid at room temperature, but not everything that is transparent and liquid at room temperature is H_2SO_4. We can conclude of any H_2SO_4 that it will be liquid at room temperature. But in fact being H_2SO_4 is not ontologically dependent on being translucent and liquid at room temperature; just the contrary is the case, the dependence relation goes the other way. The co-present and mutually pervasive "translucence, etc." and "chemical composition H_2SO_4" are now in the opposite causal relation; logical priority is still given to one rather than the other, in a unilateral relationship, but runs in the other direction. But in fact the genus is still inclusive of the species.

Logical thought, of course, has developed ways to deal with the complexities of causality and its complicated relation to strict logical priority, generating various approaches to tidying up the sometimes unwieldy relation between the empirical and the logical. Note that the exact same structure applies even if I am considering only individual substances, where the individual thing as a whole assumes the logically prior role of "same" universal ("this piece of chalk") and its various specific properties assume the role of subsumed differences ("its smoothness, its whiteness, etc."). What is shared in this smoothness and this whiteness is their belonging to this piece of chalk, which itself therefore assumes a logically prior position, even though the chalk is where the white is and where the smooth is. What matters here is the way in which the systematic asymmetry of the classificatory system necessarily generates the concept of transcendent logical priority, even for two properties that are empirically co-present and mutually pervasive in a given context. What a thing *is*, what makes it identifiable and definable, and what allows us to group it with other instances of the "same" essence, is its difference from other things. What we name when we name what something is is what is different about it. But note that the "sameness" is necessarily pushed up to a higher, more inclusive level of generality. "Clear liquid" has to become a higher-order category than "sulfuric acid" and "water," and this "sameness" of the transparent liquids gets its identity from the differentia operating at this higher level, rather than at the first level. This is odder than we normally notice. Imagine that sulfuric acid and water were the *only* two types of transparent liquid in the universe. This quart of water is both a transparent liquid and has the chemical composition H2O. Neither of these two qualities subsumes the other; each is equally pervasive in the entire volume of the liquid. But the classificatory system of sameness and differ-ence will have to regard "transparent liquid" as the more general genus that *includes* within it the species "H_2O"; any same-level identity drops out of the system entirely, while the shared sameness with another substance—sulfuric acid—is the only identity that can be assigned for what is shared among these liquids. The same-different criteria embedded in the act of classifying via differentia enforces *a one-way and univocal hierarchy of subsumption*.

The implicit ontology here is rooted in the act of making a decision about how to classify things. It is not just that the need to make such a decision is rooted in the practical orientation of active beings, who must apply a dichotomous "either/or" scheme to their actions (Do I eat this or not? Is this poison or not?), with no middle ground. It might be argued that this mode of classification leads to the objectification or ontologization of the pragmatic either/or necessary for decision making—and importantly, of one particular viewpoint for decision making, with its own *single* set of desiderata—into a nonnegotiable ontological reality. The cognitive act of distinguishing qualities is the basis of identifying, and this act of identifi-cation is translated directly into the ontological fact of identity, which is then regarded as the basis for attributing sameness among instances so dis-tinguished. We can already see a further result of a system where identities are regarded as precisely isomorphic with the act of identifying them: the unity of thought and being is built into the system, precisely because the system of differentiae preloads it into its very definition of what something "is." What exists is what I can identify, and what I can identify is what I can differentiate. That is, precisely because the pragmatic is folded into the ontological, the pragmatic is effaced; it no longer sticks out against the ontological, because they match exactly. Thought and being are one, because the very criterion of being is the criterion of thought. Ironically enough, precisely the exact isomorphism of the practical cognition and the ontological is what conceals the role of the practical cognition in the ontological. Cognition is separated out from ontology precisely by being identified with it: the identity of cognitive structure with ontological structure is precisely what effaces the relationship between practical cognition and ontology, rendering subjectivity and objectivity ontologically incommensurable.

We can now see the intrinsic connection between Lévy-Bruhl's two characteristics of logical thought. His second point means that this essence stands above the set of things that instantiate it. The essence "having the chemical structure H_2O" is not just a name for all things that have this structure, considered as a total set. The distinction between the criterion itself and that to which it is applied translates into the Socratic definition of the thing, the Platonic form of the thing, the Aristotelian distinction between "the thing which is X" and "that the thing is X," between existence and essence. The essence *transcends* its instantiations, and could be applied to an infinite number of instances. It remains *unchanged* by the size of the set of its instantiations. While privileging *difference* as the criterion for classification, it simultaneously produces a by-product of *sameness*.

Taking Lévy-Bruhl's ideas about primitive participatory collectives as more revealing of the constructing of an ideal "other" to the self-defined ideal type of logical thought than of anything to do with the mental life of non-European cultures, we can perhaps use these attempts to imagine a general foil for "Reason" as indications of the kind of impasse faced by the same-different paradox in the face of its other. The primitive participatory collections are, in Lévy-Bruhl's understanding, names for a particular whole set of items, joined by an unusually strong bond of action and reaction, which is not transcended by the abstracted title that names it, and which is structured as a whole with various parts rather than as the relation of the processes of analysis and synthesis that produced the groupings.

Let's assume that all clear liquids have a special relationship with a particular mountain, which is also mysteriously related to a particular bird, such that being on friendly terms with one of these members disposes the other members of the alliance to treat one well. The criterion for inclusion in this group is the recognition of this reciprocity between its members. This is not the noting of a single characteristic that is the same in each of member of this group, in contradistinction to a characteristic noted in another group. X is a member of the group because of the characteristic "having a close relationship of mutual recognition with Y." Y is a member of the group because of a different characteristic, namely, "having a close relationship of mutual recognition with X." Further, if the group consists only of these two members, X and Y, then there is no further essence, without changing, that could apply indiscriminately to a newly discovered member, Z. It would not have the same criterion for membership as X and Y. Rather, it would require a new one: a special relationship with X and Y, which would differ from the criterion of membership of X and Y (having a special relationship with Y and Z, or with X and Z, respectively). We see here that no transcendent selfsame essence applies to all members of this group. There is no room here for an unchanging, abstract system of same-nesses and differences. It is this that gives such groupings a decidedly "ad hoc" appearance when compared to logical taxonomies.

If I decide to name the group after one of its members—calling the whole that includes the mountain, the clear liquids, and the woodpecker by the name "woodpecker," I have chosen a part to represent the whole. This part might be chosen due to its especially great efficacy in affecting the other members, or its direct relation to all other members (its status as a central hub of their relations), or perhaps its historical connection or temporal precedence in coming to the attention of my tribe. The members of this whole may in some cases share a characteristic, either structural or functional, a similarity in appearance or activity or habitat, but this will be one among many features that indicate membership in this whole, which can easily combine with alternate markers. This similarity is not the *criterion* for membership, but rather an expression of a kind of relation-ship between these members. Much less is it the defining essence that is the *same* in all members, that makes them what they are, that constitutes their being and their participation in this universal. Lévi-Bruhl seems to glimpse a tantalizing possibility here: a kind of grouping that is not *entirely* beholden to same-different categories. But lacking any positive conception to put in their place, he finds no principle of organization here other than purely contingent ad hoc relations. What a "relation" might be outside the confines of same-different ideas is not a question that can come up here: "participation" remains a catchall category for something that is "differ-ent" from same-different logics, but it does not seem to get us very far in approaching what this participation might actually be like.

The distinction Lévy-Bruhl notices here corresponds roughly to what logicians call the difference between class-logic and mereology. The for-mer is the relation between sets and their members, applying to attributes (e.g., "redness") and their instantiations (red objects). The latter is the relation between wholes and parts. Stephan Korner notes two of the crucial differences between these two kinds of classification as follows: "First, in class-logic one distinguishes between a class and the class having the afore-mentioned class as its only member. No such distinction is made between a whole and this whole considered as a part of itself. In the former case we are presented with two classes, in the latter with only one whole. Second, the logical impossibility of instantiating internally inconsistent attributes leads to the natural assumption of empty classes, whereas the assumption of empty wholes would, to say the least, be unnatural."[10]

We can see how this mirrors Lévy-Bruhl's two characteristics of logical thinking. These apparently subtle distinctions have enormous consequences. Since a class may have only one member or no members at all, it can be the same in all cases, and can be unaffected when its instantiations change. It is an abstract form, a criterion of judgment, to be applied to whatever cases might appear, or not to be applied if no cases appear. It forms a realm of relations unto itself, relations of pure sameness and difference, profoundly unlike the way in which its actual instantiations may relate to one another. To state my position directly: it is a matrix of *sameness and difference*, rather than *coherence*. And while Lévy-Bruhl is undoubtedly naïve, Eurocentric, rightly discredited if taken at face value, and ultimately uncomprehending in the face of the ethnic other, by reading him in reverse we do get a clue to where we might look, within our own conceptual tools, for our problem in understanding the alternate modes of organization that confront us in seemingly nonlogical systems, even when they are elaborate and rigorously systematic: we may need to start our thinking from mereology rather than class-logic. This is precisely what Chad Hansen has suggested in his justly famous mass-noun hypothesis of ancient Chinese semantics, and its implicit "scope" metaphysics,[11] from which I draw obvious inspiration here, and about which more below. But of course a mereology developed in the absence of a parallel class-logic, as in classical Chinese culture, will differ profoundly from a mereology developed alongside of the growth of class-logics. It is from the latter that we get the distinctively Occidental idea of "universals." Our question will be what we get from the former, and in particular, how to conceive of the role of the mereologist who identifies these parts and wholes in the absence of a class-logic to underwrite his relationship to their relationships.

The problem of universals in Occidental thought has implications for ethics, for epistemology, and for metaphysics, and indeed none of these issues has traditionally been approached without some reference to this question, whether positively or negatively. Alfred North Whitehead, whose account of the history of Western metaphysics I follow closely here, has famously remarked that all of Western philosophy can be construed as a series of footnotes to Plato. Since Kant, it has been asserted that some sort of transcendental grounding (nonempirically-derived Ideas, categories, laws) was necessary to make real knowledge possible at all—real knowledge here defined as apodictic knowledge, knowledge that is both necessary and universal, as was then assumed to be the ideal for scientific knowledge.

The origin of this ideal for knowledge was certainly directly related to the concern with mathematical knowledge, which is nonempirical but transcendental, and thus universal and necessary.[12] Whitehead has fingered as the central dogma of post-Enlightenment thought what he calls "the doctrine of simple location," which he defines as the notion that "material can be said to be *here* in space and *here* in time, or *here* in space-time, in a perfectly definite sense which does not require for its explanation any reference to other regions of space-time."[13] But this doctrine, he points out, makes induction, and hence the possibility of any generalization or prediction about the future, impossible, as Hume had proved. Whitehead's own solution is to reduce the claims of induction—it need not imply universal validity, only validity within a particular "community" of occasions, a particular cosmic epoch—while admitting that this presupposes a metaphysical commitment, which he proceeds to elaborate in the rest of his work.[14] But the apodictic nature of even these more modest inductions seems to be sacrificed in making this move. For how indeed can we know what constitutes the limits of the relevant community of occasions for each case of induction? We find ourselves back in the infinite regress that hounds the problem of induction.

On this picture, we may view the doctrine of transcendental universals or, alternately, transcendental categories, as a necessary correlative to the doctrine of simple location of units of matter. The universals serve as a sort of halfway house to rejoin the units of matter that have been severed from one another. Simple location makes relation of any kind in space and time (the latter meaning both continuity and change over time) unintelligible and inconceivable. Universals and transcendental categories can in this sense be seen as a stopgap to refurnish—as it were, artificially and "from above"—the relatedness that was drained out by simple location.

Whitehead views simple location as a special feature of pre-twentieth-century science and philosophy, assuming sole dominance since the Enlightenment, but with roots going back to early Greek thinking. He describes the central difficulty brought about by this mode of thought as deriving from three premises:

> (i) The acceptance of the "substance-quality" concept as expressing the ultimate ontological principle. (ii) The acceptance of Aristotle's definition of a primary substance, as always a subject and never a predicate. (iii) The assumption that the experient subject is a primary substance. The first premise states that the final metaphysical fact is always to be expressed as a quality inhering in a substance. The second premise divides qualities and primary substances into two mutually exclusive classes. The two premises together are the foundation of the traditional distinction between universals and

particulars. . . . The term "universal" is unfortunate . . . for it seems to deny, and in fact was meant to deny, that the actual entities also fall within the scope of the principle of relativity (i.e., really enter into the constitution of other particular actual entities). . . . [This view] led to the collapse of Descartes' many substances into Spinoza's one substance; to Leibniz's windowless monads with their pre-established harmony; to the skeptical reduction of Hume's philosophy . . . The point is that the current view of universals and particulars inevitably leads to the epistemological position stated by Descartes . . . [in which] it is assumed that . . . the Ego . . . is a particular, characterized only by universals. Thus his impressions—to use Hume's word—are characterizations by universals. Thus there is no perception of a particular actual entity. He arrives at the belief in the actual entity by "the faculty of judgment." But on this theory he has absolutely no analogy upon which to found any such inference with the faintest shred of probability. . . . [thus leading to absolute skepticism and "the solipsism of the present moment"].[15]

The problem is that the dogma of the subject-predicate form, as expanded into the absolute dichotomy between substances and the qualities that inhere in them, severs the primary substances from one another in a way that can only reestablish a connection by means of the doctrine of real, abstract universals. The particular substances are devoid of relation and devoid of quality, and these must be imported in again by reference to the universals. Because the perceiving subject also comes to be seen as a primary substance, this makes inference, and hence all knowledge, unintelligible, and finally severs subjective experience completely from the external world, leading to skepticism and solipsism.

We might also say that the subject-predicate dogma leads us straight toward some doctrine of essences, either as real-kinds, as categories that genuinely and univocally apply to the world so as to form a single consistent system, as universals or as Forms or Ideas. As soon as we have essences of *any* of these types posited in contradistinction to that of which they are the essence, you have a reality-appearance ontology of some kind, where the former is static and the latter is changing. The dog stays the same dog whether he is standing or sitting or walking, whether he is a puppy or a decrepit fleabag. His "identity" stays the same in spite of whatever changes he might undergo. Indeed, "dogness" stays the same whether it is this dog or that dog, now or in a thousand years. Dogness is unchanging, while the particular dogs, or the particular posture and behavior of a dog, change from moment to moment. This dogness is never seen or experienced by the senses. It may be that some empirical characteristics of the dog—having four feet or a particular anatomical structure, or a relation to a particular breeding line, for example—are chosen out as its essence. Then the assertion is that as long as these particular characteristics don't change, he remains the same dog, no matter what else changes. But the split between the empirical and the nonempirical, the former being transient and the latter unchanging, remains as sharp even if these particular empirical marks are identified as the essence. For it remains the case that these characteristics are not always apparent—you may not always be able to see all four legs of the dog, and certainly not all his anatomical structure or his genealogy. These have to be assumed to persist exactly as they are even when no one is experiencing them.

Unless we have some doctrine of essences, and a nonempirical world of reality in however attenuated a form, no persistent identity is thinkable. For it appears to be a psychological rule that no part of experience can be perfectly static to the exclusion of change. All experience presents itself in the form of temporal happenings, and depends on contrasts between awareness and non-awareness; a thought even of "the eternal," as a thought, must be preceded by the lack of such a thought to be registered as such. Even the last two sentences I have written here cannot be understood literally without some appeal to a doctrine of essences—for I have just said "all" experience is such and such and that there is a "rule" of psychology. There exist "laws" or "principles" nonapparent, hidden, but reliable. But where are they hidden? As long as I assume simple location in any form (even the simple location of "identities" or essences in "conceptual space," so that each one is just where and what it is), I will need a nonempirical world of some kind to support these essences, and some doctrine of unchanging universals therein to bridge the gap between individual instances, ensuring their "sameness."

But what is especially astute in Whitehead's diagnosis above is that even the sense that there is something problematic about linking individual moments of experience or facts, since, in reality, they are absolutely isolated and need some sort of extra linkage from outside, is itself an outgrowth of the same questionable assumptions. This seems to be an assumption made by modern people as soon as they come to notice the ways in which sameness and continuity are linked to questionable doctrines about transempirical universals and essences. It is assumed that, since the universals don't exist, what does exist are simply located individual entities, absolutely isolated from one another in time, space, and identity. But simple location and transcendental essences go together. The idea of pure difference falls with the same stroke as pure sameness. The real question before us, then, is not how actually separate entities come to be connected in the absence of any intelligible realm of universals or real natural kinds, but rather whether there is an alternative to both these assumptions, that is, of genuine separation of individual entities and genuine relinking of them through universal predicates.[16]

SAME AND DIFFERENT IN FORM AND MATTER

If we had to dig out a few of the ruling metaphors behind the early Greek development of theories of universals and particulars, form and matter, potentiality and actuality, and so on, we would perhaps first think of the Pythagorean emphasis on number and ratio inherited by Plato,[17] and the images of *mimesis, imposing form on passive indeterminate matter,* and *building something,* found in both late Plato (e.g., most clearly in the *Timeaus*) and, more centrally, in Aristotle's metaphysics. Already in the Platonic theory of Ideas as presented in the *Republic,* we are offered the notion of *copying* as a way of understanding the participation of universal ideas in particular things. With Aristotle, we find ourselves again and again confronted by examples of making a statue out of bronze, imprinting a signet ring into wax, building a house, and so on. How do "same" and "different" play out in terms of these basic orientations? In all these cases, we have "the same thing" (original to be copied, shape of figure to be sculpted, signet, house-shape) imposed into formless matter. It can be imposed an unlimited number of times, and will always remain the same. Repetition, or occurrence in a different context, imprinted into a different bit of matter, does not change what it is, its essence, in the least.

But it would be erroneous to suppose that the Form/Idea/Universal side of the equation thus stands for pure sameness, while Matter stands for difference. In fact, it is Forms that differentiate things, limit them off from the continuity of formless matter. This formless matter is itself, strictly speaking, neither one nor many, neither same nor different; it is not "actually" anything at all, being pure potentiality. A Form both unifies a set of instantiations into a group defined by their identical essence and separates that set from all other such sets. All dogs are members of the species Dog because they share the same essence, the Form of Dogness. The Form of Dogness is different from the Form of Catness. All statues of Hermes have the same Hermes-shape imposed upon them, and this is what makes them part of the group "Hermes statues" rather than another group. This is a way of managing and organizing relations of sameness and difference. Catness and Dogness are "the same" in that they are both subsumed under the larger genus "Animal," and share this essence of Animality. They are "different" in that Catness is not Dogness nor Dogness Catness except in terms of this single essence of Animality they have in common. There is a single

answer to the question about what is the same and what different about
any two possible items, all of which are organized into a system that charts
in a single vision what is really the same and what is different about them.
A Form is a way of defining both sameness and difference, and of doing
so in such a way as to keep them absolutely distinct and moreover, as we
saw above, necessarily asymmetrical so as to literally "subordinate" (put in
a lower order) difference to sameness.

But this approach to the problem brings us directly into the question
of the Universal of universals, which finds an echo confined to similar
contours even in Kant's question of the relation between the conditioned
and the unconditioned. The diverse Forms, essences, Universals, and so
on are generally organized into a taxonomy of species and genus, like
an upside-down tree, branching downward, so that smaller categories are
subsumed into larger ones. Catness and Dogness are both subsumed under
Animality, and this is understood as grouping them together by means of
a second-order sameness, the essence of Animality that they both, identi-
cally, share. This subsumption works in only one direction. Pushing this
system all the way to the top, we come to the highest category, which is
to subsume all the others, indicating what all essences share as essences,
the Form of all Forms.

But if universals are what unify particular separate determinate entities, allowing them all to bear the same name and the same necessary
properties, what unifies the set "universals" so we call them all by the same
name, that is, what qualifies them to be called "universals"? We seem to
have an infinite regress here. With the separation of the world into a bunch
of distinct types or essences, we have the problem of their interaction and
mutual influence. This is the problem of the connection between the universal universal as pure unconditionality (what must apply in all conditions,
at all times and places, without exception) and the mutual conditioning of
the specific universals; are the latter still truly unconditional? Connection
between particulars is solved *within* each type by the doctrine of universals,
but this creates the same problem in spades for the relation between these
universals themselves, these essentialized "Ideas." Some such concern had
led to the Platonic notion of the Good as the universal of universals, the
Neoplatonic doctrine of Hypostases, the Kantian transcendental unity of
apperception, Whiteheadian Creativity and God, and so on. All these are
putative ways of maintaining a plurality of genuine universals that are both
determinate and unconditioned. At the same time, we have the leftover
and troublesome category of formless matter, pure potentiality, which is
strictly speaking neither the same nor different from anything else, in that
it fails to be anything actual at all. Here we confront the problem of the
Omnipresent.

TWO OPPOSITE DERIVATIONS OF THE OMNIPRESENT

The maximal exemplar of "sameness" would be something that was the same everywhere without exception, despite every apparent difference: the Omnipresent. Once we have this simple-location-plus-universals worldview in place, two opposite avenues of thought lead quite directly to the positing of some conception of the Omnipresent—some all-pervading entity or characteristic that is present in every instance of reality without exception.

The first version might be called the "idealist" derivation: Given the particular universals, which pervade some but not all concrete existences, we have in hand the idea of pervasion of the different by the same. But this pervasion only extends to some of the totality of existents. "Red" pervades, unchanged, all the different red things, but not all things. Redness is "the same"; its instantiations are "different." Similarly, all universals, to be members of a single class called "universals," and to have that which truly marks them as universals, should have a further universal pervading them; the set of all sets, or the universal of all universals. This universal universal would pervade all lesser universals in a manner analogous to the way each universal pervades its instantiations. This would be the truly Omnipresent. Plato's Idea of the Good would be the earliest and most obvious example.

The second derivation, which we might call "materialist," also emerges directly from this conception of universals. For all universals are manifestly abstractions from something more concrete: when I say this is red, and partakes of the universal Red in some way, I am singling out its redness at the expense of all the other characteristics it might have. Moreover, as noted, each universal covers part but not the whole of the totality of existents. So a universal, on this critique, is something that by definition leaves much out, excludes, is incomplete. The Omnipresent, then, would be everything universals leave out, whatever overflows the qualitative categories of thinking. It is what escapes the range of each universal, and all universals, what is abstracted from in these abstractions; on this picture it is of the nature of universals to be unable to approach the Omnipresent, for their essence is exclusion. The Omnipresent is what universals fail to reach. Anaximenes's idea of the "Limitless" would perhaps serve as an example.

It is not insignificant that these two apparently opposite ideas seem to converge inexorably into indistinguishability, both positing the Omnipresent, which in both cases veers toward necessary unknowability. Moreover, both are subject to critique for this very reason. An arch-idealist such as Hegel can say quite justifiably that "matter" or "being" is itself a universal, indeed the most universal universal, the utmost abstraction; the attempt to avoid all abstraction is itself actually the most abstract abstraction of all. A materialist or nominalist, on the other hand, can assert that all universals are merely approximate abstractions from the concreteness of reality, and indeed that it is in the nature of what a universal is, an abstraction that by definition functions only by leaving things out, to be unable to embrace the Omnipresent. Moreover, he can show quite simply that this idea of the universal universal is a particular event occurring in the brain of a particular person at a particular place and time, and not otherwise. But both of these positions rest on the assumption of the simple location of the element's empirical existence and its necessary correlate that something else, real or imagined universality, must be added to connect up these separated bits of reality: the universals. In both versions the pervaded is the different, while the pervading is the same. Here again we find that, even in asserting maximum intermingling of sameness and difference, even in asserting that their extent is perfectly equal (i.e., so that everything that is different is also the same, and vice versa), the prior metaphysical commitment to the difference between sameness and difference leads us back into the same circle of problems. Without this tradition of universals, what notion of the Omnipresent would emerge, if any? And would it perhaps be structured in a way that did not make it susceptible to these two opposite critiques?[18]

This is perhaps not the place to pursue the seemingly insoluble philosophical problems that thus follow as soon as universals are assumed to exist, nor the quandaries presented by trying to get rid of them and still maintain the same conceptions of knowledge, ethics, and being. But it is worth stating briefly some of the obvious consequences of natural kinds of theories when intended in the truly absolute sense discussed above. Not only do they exclude alternate ways of grouping and separating the elements of existence, they also assume, and, as it were, enforce, some impression of repeatability of the same, and hence a certain timelessness and changelessness, which tends to problematize or devalue the processes of transient empirical experience. This will be so as long as both the universal and the particulars are seen as determinate entities with some kind of "conceptual" simple location. Each is just what it is, just where it is in the conceptual space of the intelligible realm. Redness is not Chairness in the same way that this rock is not that tree.

Spinoza is perhaps the first to break through this conceptual knot, introducing the idea of "common notions" as opposed to "universals." The former are something that is "the same in the whole and in the part," thus no longer subject to simple location (*Ethics*, IIp40s1-s2). Spinoza, I think, has in mind things such as natural laws conceived on the model of geometrical principles, modes that are coextensive with space itself, and are whole and complete in every portion of it. The only thing like this would be the "eternal modes," which constitute the laws of nature; $F = MA$ would be one, for example, or the principle that "a straight line is the shortest distance between any two points." This is true and operative, *in its entirety*, wherever there is Euclidean space, and in fact is analytically derivable from the nature of space qua space. But Spinoza here insists on the radical difference between these exceptionless and omnipresent aspects following directly from the nature of Substance and the specific, limited "universals" that apply only in some cases, times, and places, and not others. The latter— universal essences such as "horse" or "man" or "Frenchman" or "Russia" or "capitalism"—are not truly universal (unless they can be directly and in an unbroken chain of deductions derived from the very nature of Extension or Thought, in the way the properties of a triangle can be derived from the nature of Extension [space], which Spinoza never attempts with anything but the few basic concepts of body and finitude and causality in general that make up the *Ethics*); they apply in one region of space, one set of modes, and not others; hence, Spinoza *dismisses them as fictions* derived from nothing more than the feebleness of our imaginative faculty.

Spinoza himself is aware that with the "common notions" he is inventing an entirely new kind of logical category that fits neatly into neither of the traditional categories, universal and particular, as they had hitherto been conceived, remarking, "Indeed, these mutable particular things depend so intimately and essentially (so to phrase it) on the fixed things that they can neither be nor be conceived without them. Hence, although these fixed and eternal things *are singular*, by reason of their omnipresence and wide-ranging power they will be *to us like* universals, i.e., the genera of the definitions of particular mutable things, and the proximate causes of all things."[19]

We have here the advent of a *tertium quid* which is neither universal nor particular in the usual sense, but which is the sole source of accurate reasoning. It may be argued that the radical nature of this solution was not appreciated in subsequent science and philosophy, which continues to treat laws of science as if they were universals of the older kind, and treats universals, therefore, as if they were validated by scientific findings. (And if one were sociologically inclined, one could here make an intriguing argument that this seemingly minor and subtle logical mistake, regarding conclusions about particular groups of people or eras of history as if they were scientifically determinable in the same manner as the laws and facts discovered analytically in geometry and in Cartesian physics, is what led to the inevitable growth of "scientific racism," on the one hand, and "historical determinism," on the other, of the nineteenth century, and all that came with it in the following century.)

Hegel, for example, tries another way around this problem, stressing rather the "magical" nature of universals—they are not at all like simply located things, which can be only here and not there. On the contrary, the whole point of universals is that they are simultaneously here and there, instantiated equally and wholly in very diverse particulars. Hegel notes how ridiculous it would be to ask someone to buy me "fruit" and then complain, when he brought back bananas, pears, and apples, that I had asked for "fruit," not bananas, pears, and apples, which are after all quite different determinations. The point is that we have in the universal a device by which qualitatively different determinations can coexist in the same time and place. Due to the intrinsic structure of set-theory, as noted above, the mereology that applies here is generally thought of in terms of a one-way whole-part relation—subsets within larger sets. But this, as Hegel showed, does not do justice to the magical form of determination we find in thinking through what it is to be a universal.

Hegel's point is of course well taken, and the insight behind it is very crucial to the seriousness with which I am endeavoring to consider these questions here. Nonetheless, it must be noted that even when the Hegelian sense of determination of universals is accepted, the axiological devaluing of the particulars appears to be inevitable—it is very pronounced in Hegel's own thought, for example. Indeed, we may say simply that Hegel in fact tries to make every single operative universal (horse, man, Frenchman, the Roman Empire, slavery, capitalism . . .) that Spinoza viewed as by-products of the weakness of the human imagination a Spinozean "common notion," that is, something that *can* be derived in an unbroken chain of deductions directly from the nature of the Absolute. In a certain sense this is the very heart of Hegel's entire project. The consequences of this shift from Spinoza to Hegel, of course, are enormous. Again, if one were in the mood to cast "blame" for all the disasters of the twentieth century, this might not be a bad place to look. But in any case, it is not hard to see how, for instance, my notion of "a woman" in general could interfere with my relationship with any particular woman; none would quite live up to the essence of universal womanhood as I preconceive it, all would be found lacking. No fruit is as fruity, arguably, as Fruit. Indeed, this failure of any particular to meet up to its universal, in spite of the bizarre non-simply-located form of determinateness of universals, is precisely what allows Hegel to solve the Aristotelian problem of the relation between essences: they collapse into each other in their failure to live up to their own "Notions" (*Begriffen*)—which means, ultimately, that they fail fully to correspond even with themselves, are ultimately self-contradictory.

This is ingenious, and also offers a solution to the mismatch between the abstract and the concrete: it is not that the particulars are inadequate, but that the concepts themselves are not yet "concrete" enough. But this reproduces the problem of the "unconditioned," the universal universal, which for Hegel become the Absolute Idea, which throws the inadequacy back at the empirical world with a vengeance, even as it claims that the Real is the Rational. Very little of what we normally experience, at least as we normally experience it, turns out to be "real" in Hegel's sense. This is a high price to pay, and it seems there is no other way around the way universals inevitably cast a shadow of inadequacy on all actual experience. It is possible to argue that this is a good thing, as Hegel does, but we might wish to balance it with the opposite, perhaps "Daoist-Nietzschean" consideration, which is that every universal and ideal is a curse on temporal particular reality (the only reality there is, on this view).

In this work, I will be using the term *realism* to describe any doctrine that real universals exist in the objective world, whether these are thought of as transcendent Platonic essences or natural-kinds existing only in the empirical world. The stress here is on the objective existence of unique ways in which certain objects in the world group together, privileged divisions in the world, "joints" of its own at which nature can be cut, which provide the possibility of real knowledge about how they behave, which is not merely projected by human observers. "Nominalism" will be used to describe all doctrines that deny this claim. These can range from absolute skepticism, which holds that no induction of any kind is possible from one fact to another, to strong conventionalism, which holds that universals and kinds are merely loose generalizations psychologically and socially derived, and projected by human beings, and refer to no objective realities, the latter being restricted to the realm of individual objects and events. In a nutshell: *realism regards some form of sameness among things as ultimately real, and difference as somehow secondary, derivative or illusory. nominalism regards the differences as primary and ultimately real, and sameness as secondary, derivative, or illusory.*

The tension between these two orientations goes back to Aristotle's response to Plato, of course, but in various versions it comes to define what may be considered the central issue in every new phase of Western thought. We may think here not only of the scholastic debates on this topic, but also of Kant as opposed to the post-Kantian idealists on the one hand and the empiricists on the other, and again, in the postmodern milieu, of the debates over the relation of symbolic and social systems to any brute realities putatively outside of them, namely, the question of whether apparently natural facts are or are not merely social constructions. My claim will be that the Chinese handling of these problems is properly neither a nominalism nor a realism of this kind. Instead, we will find the conception of coherence, which in later traditions comes to cluster around the concept of Li, providing an alternative mechanism for handling the corresponding questions, and an alternate vision of the relation of objectivity, subjectivity, and intersubjectivity, and with it a very different conception of temporality and the Omnipresent.

The same type of problem emerges as an intersubjective quandary: Will what I experience now be consistently matched with what that other subject experiences, at another time or even putatively at the same time? How will our names and attitudes toward it be correlated to converge into a single object, so as to allow for reliable communication and practical handling of this object? But here too full confirmation is always yet to come—for there are always possible further others, additional subjectivities, yet to be encountered, who must also share the experience for it to qualify as full intersubjective agreement. The confirmation is always, constitutively, yet-to-come, still-in-doubt. This temporal and intersubjective breaking down of the concept of reality behind appearance will be useful to remember when we consider the Chinese case, and how it manages to get along without any concept of appearance versus reality. In a nutshell, its development of notions of coherence will do this work, without having recourse to a "simply located" conception of time or subjectivity, and hence will bring with it a different set of standards for predictive accuracy.

From a logical point of view, what is perhaps most damaging to both realism and nominalism is what might be called the paradox of uncondi-tioned determination, the discovery of which is, I think, what much of postmodern criticism of traditional philosophy amounts to. It is simply this: *How can something be both determinate and unconditioned?* The problem already came onto the horizon when Spinoza flatly declared, in passing, and in a letter (Epistle 50), that "determination is negation." If determination is negation, which is a relationship to a conditioning other, determination and unconditionality are flatly contradictory and incompatible. If knowl-edge means apodictic (unconditional) knowledge, determinate knowledge herewith becomes impossible. It would seem that neither "no universals" nor "fixed and definite real universals" can solve the problem, as long as apodictic knowledge is what is required. But what other options are there? It is clear that the seriousness of this problem has begun to be felt within Occidental thinking itself from the various recent attempts to provide alter-natives to this requirement. or to these strategies for fulfilling it.

One place to look for a way out of the realism/nominalism dichotomy while still preserving meaningful knowledge is the relatively recent advent of the pragmatic tradition as developed by Peirce, James, and Dewey, and more recently by Hilary Putnam and Richard Rorty. Perhaps the classical conflict over this issue in the foundational period of pragmat(ic)ism—between Peirce (a self-described "scholastic realist") and James and Dewey (both nominalists)[20]—might suggest to us that the pragmatic method itself eludes the dichotomy, and thus is indifferent to either commitment, or perhaps can do without any reference to the problem at all. But this does not seem to be what Peirce and James themselves thought: they seemed to believe that pragmatism itself was unintelligible without a commitment to realism (Peirce) or without a commitment to nominalism (James). This would suggest that pragmatist methodology as such does not supersede the problem of a dichotomy between the two so much as postpone it; it remains unresolved.

Constructivism, in the philosophy of science, provides another possible way beyond the dichotomy. (Kurtis Hagen has profitably applied this framework to the discussion of, at least, Xunzi's thought, as we shall see below.) Constructivism holds that there *are* real distinctions and structured groupings in the world, but that there is no one unique way of naming, identifying, or describing them. The real structure of the world constrains but does not determine the ways in which it is named. It excludes some possibilities as wrong, but does not have a single determination of right; it allows a range of possible and equally valid ways of describing reality, perhaps a very large range, which are neither completely arbitrary and projected (they have external constraints) nor strictly determined by the structure of the world abstracted from human purposes (there is a wide choice of possible right answers). This approach suggests an approach to the subject/object relation, the name/reality issue, the one/many issue, that is neither strictly nominalist nor realist, and indeed is perhaps the closest to some of the Chinese assumptions that we can find among available modern theories—in particular when applied to late "non-ironic" examples of the type exemplified by Xunzi, as Hagen rightly explores. However, it is not clear, even on Jamesian pragmatist grounds of the kind that perhaps stand in the background of constructivism, how it is that we can know and register the constraints of the nonconstructed structure of nature, nor indeed if it is even meaningful to talk about them "existing"—we are back in a version of the old Kantian thing-in-itself problem here, on one reading. It is clear, at least, that we cannot think of the "real structure of the world," however non-uniquely nameable, as *determinate* in any familiar sense—and it is difficult to see how something nondeterminate can act as a constraint, without a wholesale reconsideration of what is meant by "determination" and "constraint" per se.

Simply imagining this relation on the model of a *range* of possible right answers, as, for example, we might say that we know something about the author of the *Iliad* because we know that he or she or they were *not* a diabetic Rastafarian, but we do not know whether he was one person or many, male or female, Greek or barbarian: history constrains us to exclude the work's creator(s)' allegiance to the as yet nonexistent Rastafarianism, but does not give us a conclusive answer about his ethnic identity or gender or number. If the as yet unconstructed world is "constraining" in that sense, we really haven't gotten beyond a metaphysical realism. Put another way, if the ambiguity is purely epistemological (we just don't know exactly what is so yet), we are still in the realm of realism. The ambiguity must be *ontological* (and indeed logically necessary) to really push us beyond some higher-order realism or nominalism.

But on its own terms, when faced with the problem of induction in natural science, it is by no means clear that constructivism in its present form can produce a coherent account of how this ontological ambiguity works, and accommodates the emergence of constructed determinacies with predictive power, unless it opts for a Kantian turn, which would seems to deny the "real structured world" proviso. Hegel may perhaps be read as providing an attempted answer to the Spinozan "determinate negation" problem, developing from Kantian resources a revised conception of what determination actually is such that "unconditionality" and "determination" are no longer mutually exclusive: negation as self-negation, and hence determination as self-determination, involving an active overcoming of otherness and limitation in the kind of incorporation into the self of the negation itself via a form of recognition. If successful, this would indeed point a way to the preservation of both reliable induction and determinate knowledge, as well as granting the centrally constructive role of the human knower. Whether it is in fact successful is too large a question to settle here, but we can at least note that its costs are very high, arguably requiring at once a pan-logicism that at the same time rewrites the foundations of logic, and a commitment to a nonmechanistic causality rooted in a teleological metaphysic which presupposes the "subjectivity" of substance. Hegel has forceful arguments for these moves, which rewrites precisely what "subject," "logic," and "telos" are in a way that evades some of the traditional problems that would come with making these founding metaphysical principles. But for all that we may still wonder, when all is said and done, whether the end result of his labors does not land as squarely back in a modified form of the realist camp, perhaps even a dangerously radicalized version of it, rather than actually taking us beyond the realist/nominalist dichotomy altogether.

Another—and ultimately not all that dissimilar—approach is the Whiteheadian solution itself, which, as noted above, frankly sacrifices the universality of induction, limiting it to particular communities of occasions in whose concrete relations it is rooted. Whitehead's system also dispenses artfully with the one-way subsumption relation of universals and particulars, replacing them with concrete prehensions, and with it the ontological split between subjective and objective, giving an objective and a subjective "pole" to every actual occasion. Yet Whitehead too is a "realist" in the final analysis, reinstating the Platonic Forms, which he adopts and adapts under the term "eternal objects." Even Hartshorne, who rejects Whitehead's notion of eternal objects, on the basis of a penetrating distinction between "determinate" and "determinable" (admitting only the latter), ends up declaring himself a realist, albeit a "soft" one, admitting the eternal objective reality of a few universals (notably *numbers*, and certain aspects of deity, no less), while regarding the rest as local and contingent. Process thought has obvious and real affinities with much Chinese thinking (not only in the nonseparation of subject and object, a pan-experientialism that does not reduce to idealism, and in the general process orientation, but also and in particular in the rethinking of the very notion of determination), and this perhaps accounts for an understandable temptation to interpret a term such as Li, at least in its more robust neo-Confucian versions, as something that might fill in, if not for the Forms in Plato's sense, at least for the Eternal Objects in Whitehead's. In this work I hope to show another plausible alternative.

For it is precisely with respect to impasses such as the above that I think the Chinese sources present us with interesting resources and possibilities, by considering the way this problem was handled—or was *not* handled—in the Chinese tradition. For the thesis of this book is that the "correlative thinking" dismissed by Lévy-Bruhl is misconceived when it is viewed only as a foil to the same-different paradigms of logical thought; and that the ideas of coherence that arise in the niche otherwise filled by logical paradigms does not remain simply "primitive" in the absence of a Socratic/Platonic/Aristotelian obsession with definitions and essences, which creates the notion of absolute sameness and difference embedded in the notion of universals and particulars. Rather, left uninterrupted by these developments, such "primitive" conceptions grow and develop along their own trajectory, reaching their own types of sophistication and refinement and complexity, which rival those of the Greco-European tradition but from very different premises and leading to very different conclusions. Let us now turn to these developments.

TWO

WHAT IS COHERENCE?

Chinese Paradigms

In the previous chapter we attempted to broadly characterize the typical Greco-European handlings of sameness and difference through the lens of some version of a doctrine about universals and particulars, or alternately, its correlate or by-product, particular substances with definite essences and attributes. We will now try to establish a framework for considering some classical Chinese notions of what I'll be calling "coherence," as divided into two types, the ironic and non-ironic, as a contrasting approach to the handling of certain parallel issues.

One traditional name for this kind of problem about sameness and difference is the "one-many problem." How much of the world is the same, forming a "one," and how much of it is different, diversified into a "many"? Where and what is the boundary between "this" and "something else," which warrants us in treating them as two things rather than one? How can one thing have many different aspects, or many different parts, and still be one thing? How can one quality be instantiated in many places and times? What exactly does it mean to be one or many? How does oneness relate to manyness? It has often been noted by previous scholars that there is something at least odd about the way these problem are handled, or not handled, in traditional Chinese thought. It is no surprise that a twentieth-century Chinese thinker such as Tang Junyi, taking the measure of the entire tradition, identified "mutual implication of oneness and manyness" as one of the distinctive features of Chinese thought as a whole, and his treatments of individual Chinese thinkers effectively demonstrate the way in which oneness and manyness, sameness and difference, resist the kind of analysis commonly deployed to handle similar problems in Western thought. But we may wonder if Tang's attempt at an explanation is radical enough to really resolve the perplexities here, and indeed whether it might not be too beholden to certain analytic tools derived from contemporaneous Western thought, themselves rooted in another set of assumptions about this very one-many problem, to really clarify this point.

The way to a more fundamental explanation was opened, in my view, by Chad Hansen's controversial study of ancient Chinese logical paradoxes, which suggested one reason why the question of universals might not have developed in China in a way that is at all comparable to its development in the West. Consistent with our brief discussion of mereology as opposed to class-logic in the previous chapter, Hansen claimed that classical Chinese nouns function more like mass nouns than like count nouns. Mass nouns (e.g., water) refer to one pervasive amorphous entity that is spread out in various places, and can be divided up in various ways, while count nouns (e.g., dog) come with predetermined units for counting. I can have "one dog, two dogs, three dogs," and so on, but "one cup, one quart, two pools" *of* water. This suggestion has caused some consternation in that it fits better the grammar of modern Chinese (where indeed nouns are generally preceded by a special measure word to indicate the amount of that noun which is being indicated) than classical Chinese, where individual entities can, in fact, be indicated without recourse to measure words. The lack of special forms indicating singular and plural in both ancient and modern Chinese, however, remains significant in this context. The point is that if a noun indicates primarily the entire mass of that substance, everywhere in the world, the problem of relating individual members to the general class disappears. There is no need to unify individual dogs with a universal canine essence if each dog is really just one dog-shaped scoop of the dog-substance spread out throughout the world. The implication is that rather than an additive class derived cumulatively by assembling individuals and collating their similarities, we are "dividing down" from the whole and selecting out subdivisions for closer consideration. There is no need for a two-level ontology here, where abstract essences or universals or forms, accessible to the intellect but not to the senses, "participate in" and unify concrete particulars; rather, the mass and each chunk of the mass are equally concrete and available to the senses.[1] Chinese thought does not have a one-many ontology, and thus does not have a one-many problem; in its place, Hansen says, it has a whole-part ontology, with its own concomitant set of problems.

Hansen's insights are particularly important for setting the agenda of the present work. He notes in particular the circumvention of both Platonic ideas and mentalist ideas in classical Chinese thinking. The mind is not a representational faculty that entertains ideas or perceives the intelligible realm of ideas. There are no universals, just stuff-kinds. The mind is a faculty of actively *distinguishing* among these real kinds. Stuffs are named by the act of picking them out from a background, making the distinction between *this* stuff and everything else that is not it. Correct knowledge is a *skill in making distinctions*, and applying the proper names, to masses of sensory data. It is not the matching of a set of sense data to a mental idea that represents them, or to a universal form in which they participate. The epistemology functions on the basis of only names and stuffs; no other entities, such as properties, attributes, essences, ideas, universals, or particulars, are necessary.

Some scholars have dismissed Hansen's hypothesis, due largely to the inconvenient fact that the grammar of classical Chinese in fact does employ count nouns, as already noted. Others, like myself, have accepted that he was on to something anyway, but feel a need to refine and build upon his initial hypothesis.[2] Indeed, from a purely linguistic point of view, Han Xiaoqiang's recent article, "Maybe There Are No Subject-Predicate Sentences in Chinese," is perhaps more to the point even than Hansen's original hypothesis.[3] There Han follows P. F. Strawson's analysis in linking the semantical "incompleteness" of predicates in English (and by extension, most Indo-European) sentences to the genesis of theories of universals, as contrasted to the semantical "completeness" of the subject. Predicates are "incomplete" in that they cannot stand alone, being introduced with a specific inflection in terms of tense, person, or number; they demand a connection or link to something else. It is the incompleteness that provides the possibility of linkage necessary for a proposition; without this disparity between subject and predicate, embodied in the inflection of the predicate, there can be no propositional link of universal and particular. Without the possibility of this link, however, there can be no such thing as universal and particular; without the relation of instantiation, there can be no instantiated and instantiator. If Strawson's analysis is correct, the complete lack of morphological inflection in Chinese sentences becomes more significant for the question of theory of universals and particulars, or the lack thereof, than the putative use of mass or count nouns. Han suggests that without these morphological features, Chinese sentences really cannot be construed on the model of the subject-predicate structure, and therefore do not work by attaching universals to particulars. On the contrary, Han suggests that the more useful model for understanding Chinese grammar (both ancient and modern), is the "feature-placement" sentence suggested by Strawson, rather than the "subject-predicate" sentence. "It is snowing here" is the example Han offers, which Strawson construes as merely locating the feature "snowing" within the field designated by "here." Han suggests that a Chinese sentence seeming to attribute a "property" to something—e.g., Bob is rich—really works in a similar way (e.g., "There is money in Bob"). Though Han deliberately avoids making this claim too definitively, it is clear that it consorts nicely with Hansen's stuff-mereology understanding of Chinese grammar. Instead of a subject-predicate relation, we would have an overlap of two stuffs, along the lines of the "mass-product" Hansen describes in his discussion of Mohist logic. The connection is still not between a universal and a particular, but between two concrete wholes that intersect in some part of each.

In my view Hansen is correct in finding a whole/part rather than a one/many problem in Chinese thought, and a conception of knowledge as a dividing down from a larger whole rather than a building up from individual instances to form a group, and that this has enormous consequences. However, I think we can make significant refinements on what these consequences are, and that the effacement of the subject-predicate and particular-universal structures also means that the wholes in question cannot be construed as unambiguous identities to which sameness and difference pertain in any absolute manner. I want to amend Hansen's idea in the direction of coherence, which will eliminate the attribution of the existence of "natural kinds" to early Chinese thought, that is, stuff which are either simply the same as or different from each other, and also to modify the understanding of the way in which the linguistic subject, the one making the distinctions, figures into the system of mass wholes. Folding the act of making the distinctions, the human act of naming and knowing, into the whole so divided has large consequences for how we understand the resulting metaphysical tendencies.

A. C. Graham slightly amends Hansen's suggestion:

We might say that while the English translations use count nouns for individuals or classes, the Chinese uses mass nouns which carry with them instructions as to where the primary division is to be made. There are also words, some of them important in philosophy (ch'i [氣], tao [道], li [理]) which carry no such instructions, so that there is no contradiction in dividing out Yin and Yang as "the 2 ch'i" yet also picking out as "the 5 ch'i" the Five Phases, or the 5 atmospheric influences, whatever one chooses to select from the mass. On this approach a lei [i類] "kind," such a jen [人] "man" or ma [馬] "horse," is a mass like cattle exhaustively divisible into similar parts (like Greek genos "genus" in its original sense of a race which could die out, not a class which may become empty of members): the shih [實] "object" which . . . we described as "concrete and particular" is a chunk out of a mass which is no less concrete than itself. This does not of course alter the fact that, irrespective of language, discontinuous and constant objects enforce on us a priority over divisions we can make as we please. Even if a shih

"object" is a chunk out of a mass, the most convenient examples of
it will be individuals . . . in the Mohist account of naming . . . not
a pool or drop of water but a horse. But that the objects are indeed
conceived as divisions is confirmed, as Hansen notices, but the fact
that where we would speak of class and member or whole and part
the Mohist logic uses only a single pair, *chien* [兼] and *ti* [體], and
defines *ti* as a "a division in a *chien* [體分於兼也]." (Canon AC *ti,
fen yu chien ye*).[4]

Graham accepts the implication that the Chinese tendency is to divide
down from the whole, adding however that these wholes often come with
built-in instructions about where the main "cuts" or divisions were to be
made, and that *in several important cases there are more than one possible ways
legitimately to make these divisions*. The idea of "built-in instructions about
how to cut something up" will be quite a useful hint for us in considering
the ways in which coherence comes to be understood, and all the more
so the idea that several alternate, even incompatible, sets of instructions
might be not only applicable but indeed built in, with the full authority of
objectivity, as it were.
    Graham makes a further claim of great importance in this connection.
In his general discussions of the distinctive Chinese solutions to the "is/
ought" question—what Donald Munro has called the "fact/value fusion" in
Chinese thought—Graham notes the "subjectivising, Chinese" assumption
that "the knowing of a *li* [i.e., an organic pattern of nature, in Graham's
interpretation; this is the word we will be translating as "coherence" in
the companion volume to this work] [is] inseparable from the reactions
it patterns."[5] Graham sees coherence as an organic pattern, a network of
connections among things; *but these "things" include human responses*. The
organic pattern is not merely an objective network to be observed and
studied from without; our own reactions are also parts of this network of
connections. The mind is not set aside as a separate ontological category,
but is part of the whole.
    A further refinement of these ideas, from another angle, can be derived
from the speculations of David Hall and Roger Ames on the distinctive characteristics of the dominant modes of "Han thinking" as a whole, which they
characterize as privileging what Graham had identified as the "correlative,
analogical, metaphorical" mode of classification over the "analytic, causal,
metonymic" mode. Correlative groupings are loose, metaphorical and ad hoc
in character, producing concepts that are "image clusters in which complex
semantic associations are allowed to reflect into one another in such a way
as to provide rich, indefinitely 'vague' meanings. Univocity is, therefore,
impossible. Aesthetic associations dominate."[6] It is, they further stipulate,

the language of process, "the only language that gets us close to the immediate sense that 'all things flow'. . . . The language of correlativity is the
result, the sign, and the reward of feeling the flux of passing circumstance."[7]
One makes one connection in one situation, another in another situation.
These connections need not be mutually consistent; they are temporary,
beholden to a situation obtaining in a particular moment of experience:
the correlations themselves "flow." The correlations made in this mode are
"non-foundational since they are only a matter of empirical experience and
conventional interpretation."[8] They are nominalist, pragmatic, historicist,
thus always necessarily ambiguous and negotiable.

Hall and Ames see one of the most important examples of this in the
"seemingly ubiquitous distinction between yin and yang," which is "no more
than a convenient way or organizing 'thises' and 'thats.' This is clearly a
consequence of the nominalistic character of Chinese intellectual culture."[9]
In contrast to this is the causal, analytic mode of making connections,
which may perhaps be linked to the metonymic rather than metaphorical
function of language (although Hall and Ames are quick to stress that this
hard-and-fast distinction itself is a function of a causal, analytic approach
stressing metonymy over metaphor). This is, the authors suggest, possibly
relatable to the distinction between classification and abstract definition
in early Greek thought, as noted by Paul Feyerabend. The Platonic tradition sought the definitions of things, "measuring rather than classifying," as
Whitehead put it, the quest for definitions arising again in association with
the concern with mathematical exactitude and universally applicable truth.
(Indeed, Whitehead sees this tendency to count and measure rather than
merely categorize, as even Aristotle tends toward, as the basis for the development of all precise knowledge of the world.) This can be seen as again
promoting the positing of a supermundane realm where these nontransient,
nonempirical, nonhistorical truths resided, whereas correlative thinking is
primarily horizontal in the sense that is involves the association of concrete
experienceable items of immediate feeling, perception, and imagination
related in aesthetic or mythopoetic terms, usually without recourse to any
supramundane realm.[10] Correlative thinking allows a free-form association
of items that might "cohere" with a given class, again very much including the subjective or cultural axiological reactions to things experienced
together with them.

Hall and Ames sum up their interpretation by offering a new paradigm
for understanding *order* in Chinese thinking: the "Focus and Field" model.
Field means "sphere of influence," and is to be conceived of as a necessarily vaguely and incompletely bordered "area within which the influences of
and upon an agent may be discernibly experienced and perceived."[11] Focus
means a "place of convergence or divergence."

They continue:

[A]t any given moment, items in a correlative scheme are characterizable in terms of the focal point from and to which lines of divergence and convergence attributable to them move, and the field from which and to which those lines proceed. . . . It is important to recall that fields and foci are never finally fixed or determinant. Fields are unbounded, pulsating in some vague manner from and to their various transient foci. This model of field readily contrasts with the one-many and part-whole models. The relations of human beings to their communities, for example, are not established by the presumption of "essences" or "natural kinds" defining membership in a set of such kinds, nor by the presumption of the contextually defined mereological sets wherein the parts constitute the wholes in an additive or summative manner. There is neither "one" (in the sense of an essential unity) nor "many" (in the sense of many instances of one essential kind). Nor are there "parts" which add up to "wholes" which are no greater than their sum. Instead there is a vague, unbounded field, both constituting and constituted by its discernible foci. Alternatively, there are a variety of shifting foci, the influences upon which and from which are resourced in a vague unbounded field. Thus, our model is neither one-many, nor is it a nominalized version of the part-whole model. The focus/field perspective employs a "this-that" model. . . . Our focus/field model must be understood in terms of the general vision of *ars contextualis*. It is the "art of contextualization" that is most characteristic of Chinese intellectual endeavors. . . . *Ars contextualis*, as a practical endeavor, names that peculiar art of contextualization which allows focal individuals to seek out the viable contexts which they help to constitute and which in turn will partially constitute them.[12]

We will be making much of these particular suggestions in what follows. Most importantly, we find here a model of classification that avoids not only (1) the one-many problem, as did Hansen's suggestions, but even (2) the definitive whole-part model of dividing down, and indeed (3) the very assumption of once-and-for-all essences attributed to either the part or the whole, or for that matter to either the focus or the field. I will disagree somewhat with both Hansen, Graham, and Hall and Ames about what the consequences of these insights are, largely by expanding upon their premises. One of the issues that requires some reconsideration concerns the categories of "nominalism" and "realism" invoked by both Hansen and Hall and Ames. These are philosophical terms derived from the European intellectual tradition to denote two opposed and mutually exclusive approaches to the question of sameness and difference. Nominalists typically claim that what really exist are concrete particular beings—this cat, this feeling of love for that person—and that general terms and universals—"Cat," "Love"—are mere names used by human beings to group them conveniently, corresponding to nothing with ontological ultimacy. Realists, of whom Plato is the greatest example, hold that the general term denotes something actually real, often more real than the particulars that imperfectly instantiate it. Both Hansen and Hall and Ames claim that the Chinese tradition is profoundly and overwhelmingly nominalist in orientation. In Hansen's case, however, this does not exclude an affirmation of stuffs as real kinds, whose *difference* from one another is an ultimate fact of nature. He notes that the idea of "a class" is employed by nominalists as a way of avoiding these abstract entities beloved of realist epistemology. But, Hansen adds, classes, with the exception of Russell and Lesniewski's mereological notion of class, are themselves abstract entities. A class is not necessary to the whole-part stuff ontology, he thinks.[13] But the stuff-kinds are at least viewed by Hansen as real kinds existing in nature, independently of the distinguishing function of the active human mind, which can thus divide either correctly or incorrectly. Hansen, of course, is well aware of the later Daoist critique of this view, which could perhaps be viewed as genuinely nominalist (although we shall have reason to question this below). But the assertion of the view that the stuffs simply are separate entities in reality tips this view toward at least a certain weak kind of realism that, in my view, clashes with Hansen's nominalist claim.

Hall and Ames, on the other hand, do give a thoroughgoing nominalist account of Chinese approaches to sameness and difference, in that they are always context dependent, the samenesses and differences, the groupings, are not only not ultimate ontological substances, they are also *not fixed*. They change with context, with situation. The *identities* of things, how they are identified, differ in different contexts. This is a crucial insight. But at the same time, there is a sense in which Hall and Ames slightly overstate the nominalism of the tradition, in that, as I will try to show, the actual approach taken by Chinese thinkers to the question of kinds and categories is neither strictly nominalist nor strictly realist in the Western sense. The simplest way to make this point is simply to say, with A. C. Graham, that the act of judging things to be same or different, the human act of naming itself, must be included in the Chinese understanding of what is real. Nominalists claim that general names, and the identities they confer, are not a part of reality, but are instead *merely* human conveniences. In the Chinese case, this is a meaningless distinction: the human conveniences, and all the deeds by which they are effected (assigning ad hoc names, for example), are part of reality, and indeed in some sense the most crucial and revealing part of reality. The names given to things, therefore, *do* in a sense reveal an ultimate truth about things. For a realist, there is truth in the names given by the wisest humans to things: the names derived from the use of reason to discern the essences of things as they exist in the intelligible realm. Most of the Chinese thinkers could also say there is truth in the names given by the wisest humans. But for the realist this truth is independent of the action of these wisest humans in actively *assigning* this name. The Chinese thinkers tend to see the truth in that very act of human giving of names—a truth about humans, and *therefore* a profound and ultimate truth about the universe. The changeability of the names likewise reveals a truth about things, about the universe: it reveals, for example, that the wisest humans change the way they name things according to circumstance.

This changes the picture decisively, and allow us to reconsider some of the issues raised in the previous chapter from a new perspective. There we noted the distinction made by Lévy-Bruhl between the procedures of "rational" thought and the "logic of participation" he saw in primitive thinking, including that of the Chinese correlative systems, which he seems to have seen as clearly inferior. Lévy-Bruhl's ethnocentric prejudices have rightly aroused much resistance, both in terms of its general characterization of primitive thinking and in terms of its applicability to the Chinese case. Sinologists such as Granet, and, later, Hall and Ames, for example, while not necessarily rejecting the general idea of a logic of participation, see the Chinese development of this basic premise as reaching a degree of sophistication and complexity that achieves a form of validity at least equal to that of mainstream Occidental rational thought. Others, like Graham, see both correlative thinking and analytic thought as universal human functions that exist in both "primitives" and "moderns," with varying degrees of emphasis.

But within the confines of anthropological theory itself, Claude Lévi-Strauss later came to reject the entire framework of (the early) Lévy-Bruhl as hopelessly ethnocentric, insisting instead that the nonanalytic classificatory schemes found both in "savage" thought and in Chinese correlative systems represent a "science of the concrete," which is not, as Lévy-Bruhl thought, devoid of thinking, but rather employs an alternate, purely "horizontal" form of thinking that is, in its own way, as empirically grounded and as valid as scientific thought, limited by its methods of observations—its limited access to empirical data—rather than by the poverty of its mode of thinking.

Hall and Ames, like Granet before them, argue that correlative thought is characteristic of the Chinese tradition as a whole, although they are careful to add that this does not mean the total exclusion of analytical thinking, but merely its subsumption into the dominant correlative forms of thought. Lévi-Strauss had attempted to clarify Granet's generalization about correlative thought by means of an appeal to Roman Jakobson's concepts of metonymy and metaphor. Lévi-Strauss's use of these terms was far from simplistic, never reducing any system to simple metonymic or metaphoric thinking alone, but tracing concretely the ways in which they interact and compensate for and transform into one another. But I think Hall and Ames are nonetheless right to see this attempt at clarification as a step backward, inasmuch as the very distinction between metonymy and metaphor is itself alien to Chinese thinking; the significant fact is that Chinese thinkers skip freely between what we would call metonymy and metaphor in their classifications and connections; *both* evidently qualify for the kind of coherence that is aimed at here, in various contexts.

Nonetheless, Michael Puett's return to Lévi-Strauss in trying to unravel this issue reveals an important shortcoming of this "cultural essentialist" reading of the Chinese tradition. Puett's close reading of Lévi-Strauss identifies the real issue here as a conflict between *continuity* and *discontinuity*. Systems of *totemism*, such as we see in primitive classificatory systems, recognize a real discontinuity among species in nature, and make various metaphorical or analogical connections among them. This system is what Puett calls "polygenetic," assuming genuinely distinct and discontinuous groups, with genuinely distinct ultimate origins in the natural world—a view that Lévi-Strauss considers empirically warranted. In contrast, systems of *sacrifice* deny radical discontinuity, introducing an unwarranted "vertical" factor not found in nature—the realm of ancestors, gods, the dead—and presupposing a basic continuity between these realms. This is what Puett calls a "monogenetic" system. These are two alternate systems, and one does not grow out of the other. Puett asserts that Lévi-Strauss would not consider Chinese correlative thinking a type of expanded polygenetic totemistic science of the concrete, but would rather see it as "lacking in good sense" in the same way that monogenetic sacrificial systems are.

Puett himself, however, rejects the notion that we can characterize an entire culture monolithically as belonging to either the polygenetic or the monogenetic system. Instead, he offers a persuasive historical account of the development of the monogenetic theory in China as a polemical stance attempting to establish a monogenetic worldview characterized by complete continuity, in contrast to a prior assumption of polygenetic discontinuity. The underlying goal behind this move toward continuity is to establish the possibility of "self-divination" for certain elites, who could thereby bypass the authority of the traditional sacrificial system and appropriate its authority to their own persons. Within Chinese culture, then, we find not a single system, but several competing claims. Granet sees totemism in the ancient history of China, overcome later by the sage-kings who establish the "continuity" of a sacrificial system. But as Puett points out, by Granet's own account, "the origins of Chinese correlative thought do not lie in an attempt to make the social world correspond to the natural order." They do not, that is, assume the existence of objectively given continuity between nature and man. Rather, the sage-kings *establish* emblems of natural things, arranging them in their proper place. "Rendering the names correct" is, Granet says, the ruler's first responsibility.[14]

This stress on human agency and participation in *creating* continuities brings us back to our main point. Puett is correct, I think, in asserting that neither continuity nor discontinuity is a universally accepted assumption for all Chinese thinkers. But this stress on the ultimate status of the human agent in the process of forming correlative connections points us toward the distinctiveness of *the particular type of continuity* that is established, by hypothesis, by the polemics of a particular set of elites in late Warring States and Han China, which, as Puett himself stresses in another connection, presupposes a set of assumptions that make this polemic possible and persuasive. The real question, adopting Puett's own approach, is the success of the self-divination theme as a dominant and enduring mainstream trope in Chinese culture. Assuming something similar may have been attempted in other cultures, why is it that it became so attractive and feasible in the Chinese context, to the extent that, indeed, one might see some form of this trope in Chinese thought of all later schools, in the Confucian notions of sage, the Daoist notions of the True Man, the Chinese Buddhist notions of instant enlightenment and Buddha-nature, all of which assume that a human person can become a godlike being with the ability and authority to realize, represent, and in some sense even determine the ultimate nature of the universe?

What I will be arguing here is that the possibility of *establishing* real continuities by means of human actions and cognitions presupposes that neither *pure* continuity nor *pure* discontinuity were operative in the Chinese framework. Things are neither the same nor different; they can be made as much really one and the same as it is possible to be, or as really different as it is possible to be, by connection with another real thing that connects up with them in a particular situation: that other real thing is human action, designed for human purposes. This is neither the continuity that is assumed in sacrifice, which preexists rather than being created by human participation in that continuity, nor the discontinuity of totemism or modern science, which assumes an objectively existing gap that cannot be bridged by any human action. Humans are not connected up with things in a continuous framework with a character of continuity that is independent of their own actions. Things are neither the same nor different. The qualities we find in things are neither definitely present in them nor definitively absent from them, neither merely nominal nor merely real. We may say that there is a presupposed continuity here in that human needs, human desires, human actions, human language are "included" in the system, as Graham asserts. But this kind of continuity is not a once-and-for-all fact with a certain determinate character; rather, it is susceptible to radical qualitative alteration, and is so by virtue of this very continuity, by virtue of the need for its own active enactment of particular forms of continuity. The various ways in which this Ur-continuity-discontinuity can be made continuous are themselves discontinuous, or, more simply, every two items with continuity between them can also (subsequently or elsewhere, in its continuity with some other time or place or deed) be discontinuous, and vice versa. This allows us to see both the diversity of continuities and discontinuities in the various positions advanced by Chinese thinkers, and to understand the presuppositions that make them possible. Indeed, in this work we will be stressing the sharply contrasted notion of continuity-discontinuity operative among the "non-ironic" and the "ironic" thinkers in the early tradition. This will, we think, help add further nuance to the claims of Hall and Ames in a way that is more compatible with Puett's discovery of the sharp "discontinuities" within the tradition.

Along the same lines, we will find that Hall and Ames's rejection of "transcendence" is itself premised on a transcendent exception by its own definition: it assumes an absolute separability between transcendence in the strong sense (they define it as any claim for absolute independence of any item) and interdependence. But what we will find here instead is a kind of second-order interdependence between interdependence and independence. There is a necessary independence of sorts posited as a by-product of interdependence itself. The perpetual "negotiability" of the ways in which things are patterned and grouped is indeed a striking feature of the tradition, and their characterization of the search for both knowledge and right conduct is indeed fruitfully understood as an "art of contextualization." But this art brings with it a demand to overcome every attempt to restrict the range of legitimate contexts applicable in any case, as Hall and Ames themselves note, as when they remark on the way this allows "individuals to seek out the viable contexts *which they help to constitute* and which in turn will partially constitute them" (emphasis added). One does not merely depend on one's contexts; one also determines what contexts serve as contexts for one's identity, and in what way. We must not imagine a fixed contrast even between a whole set of fixed relationships, which is itself independent, contrasted to the members of these relationships, who are dependent on the matrix. Hall and Ames want to stress that the matrix of relationships does not transcend its members, that it is constituted by them. But this means, as we shall see, not only that it cannot *exist* without its members, nor merely that it has no existence above and beyond their interactions, but also that its *character* is not fixed in advance as a frame that determines the character of these relationships. To be "independent," in other words, does not mean merely to be separable; it can also mean to incorporate apparently "other" items into oneself, of which one is the determiner rather than the determined. The whole is dependent on nothing outside itself, by definition, though it is dependent on its parts in a different sense. In just the same way, any member of a whole wherein there are no selves standing outside the relationships is independent in the same sense as the whole is independent: *there is nothing outside him.* The full interdependence of members in such a relationship entails not only the effacement of an independent identity within the context of a *fixed set of contexts and relationships,* but also an ability to play the role of determining the character of that whole and its relevant relationships. I will argue that this drift toward a consideration of the paradoxical character of the whole, and its reflection on the paradoxical identity of each part, is a persistent and seemingly unavoidable consequence of exactly the kind of web of relationships Hall and Ames describe as excluding any kind of independence, which reaches its full development only when every possible context is endorsed as bringing with it its own "tradition" of interrelated uses. Interdependence of all coherences does not exclude the independence, the transcendence, of these coherences. Instead, the character of absoluteness, of transcendence, becomes omnipresent, applicable to every possible coherence. In other words, each coherence, precisely because it is so thoroughly relative, is also in another sense absolute. It is not only determined by its contexts, but determines its contexts.

This is important, for otherwise, if we try to establish a picture of only relativism, interdependence, and nominalism, truly thoroughgoing interdependence fails: we are unwittingly positing an exception, another absolute, an independent entity beyond the reach of this interdependence: the frame or field within which these interdependent coherences are so conceived. This is the global vision that embraces this play of interdependences, and apprehends them as such, which becomes exempt from interdependence. These seem to be the only options. One is an attempted universal interdependence, which inadvertently posits an exceptional absolute frame of vision, leaving us again with a two-tiered metaphysic of two incommensurable and distinct ontological orders, the field and the contents. The other is a more thoroughly digested interdependence which reestablishes the transcendence, not as an additional outside frame of reference, but as an inescapable category applying to every relative instance itself, so that all entities are in the same boat, all coherences necessarily have this double status. The category of transcendence, the independent, is thus not so easily dismissed. This is not because there really is a certain particular transcendent reality, nor because existence is unintelligible without reference to it, or because it is built into our cognitive apparatus. Rather, it is precisely because of its own unintelligibility, its incoherence, that it forms a necessary limit case to all tests of coherence. This will allow us to comprehend the claims advanced most explicitly by Guo Xiang and the Chinese Buddhists, but already unmistakably adumbrated in other places, that transcendent absoluteness ends up being a synonym, paradoxically but precisely, for interdependent coherence itself; when we say one, we say the other.

In particular, then, the problem of the All, the Omnipresent, will have a new significance in this context, which will lead to an undermining of both realist and nominalist understandings of the relation of human knowledge to the real world, and provide some insight into the importance and persistence of the high value placed upon *negatives* of various kinds in the tradition—of "nothingness," "non-doing," "namelessness," "desirelessness," "identitylessness," and so on. Above all, it will reconfigure the relation between sameness and difference, and with it, the relation between something being identifiable as something and failing to be so identifiable, between coherence and incoherence. Indeed, it is "coherence," rather than the notions of "whole" and "part" that derive from it, which will prove to be our central concept here.

In preparation for the detailed exploration of these matters, it is necessary to make some preliminary remarks about exactly what "coherence" means in this context. Indeed, the English word has another connotation besides "the way things stick together," which is brought out nicely by Hall and Ames's addition of the term *intelligibility* to their gloss of this word in their emendation to Willard Peterson's suggestion of this term as a translation for certain Neo-Confucian uses of Li, as will be discussed at length in the companion volume to this book. When we say something is "coherent," we also mean that it is intelligible, that it can be read by us as having some unified and consistent qualitative quiddity. It can be used as a value word as well, as when someone critiques a philosophical position or work of art, perhaps even a political platform or a human personality, for being incoherent. This critique suggests that it is in conflict or contradiction with itself, that it fails to "read out" as a single sustainable entity, perhaps that it is in the process of self-destructing. In these usages there is an implied reference to a relation to human subjectivity, valuation, and response, which may be considered a second-order coherence, namely, the degree to which this whole quiddity coheres with (i.e., satisfies) human desires. Similarly, intelligibility itself already suggests a correspondence to our cognitive apparati, and our ability to read a unity into an assemblage of parts, seeing them as a "single thing" or "single quality."

But what is a single quality? What is unity? What is readability? The latter term is particularly thought-provoking, in that it makes present for us both the nominalist and realist aspects bound up in this notions. Coherences are there to be read, but are not coherent with our selves until so read. In this chapter I will try to make clear at least what intelligibility, readability as a unity, means in the early Chinese tradition—in particular, as we have seen, readability as a unity between our own values and the multiplicity of elements found in the world. And here we will find a thread leading between nominalism and realism, a "third way," which characterizes the Chinese tradition as a whole, situating objectivity and subjectivity in a different kind of relation to one another and to intersubjectivity, and bringing with it both an alternative approach to the problems of universality raised above, and also an alternative conception of the Omnipresent.

COHERENCE AS OPPOSED TO LAW, RULE, PRINCIPLE, PATTERN: HARMONY VERSUS REPEATABILITY

What makes a particular grouping of items coherent? While it is conceivable that a set of items can be made coherent because they follow a rule or law that directs them to be arranged in this particular way, it is not this law-following itself that is meant by coherence. That is, the type of orderliness that pertains to coherence is not identical to orderliness in the sense of "being arranged in accordance with a law," or "the quality of instantiating the same law or rule in every instance."[15] It is not even the application of the same relation again and again between each of the parts. Coherence is not "lawfulness," inasmuch as the latter implies the imposition of a command from outside—whether from a transcendent lawgiver who threatens punishment, on the model of social legal codes, or in an "autonomous" moral law where one *part* of the person (his true nature, for example), or one moment in time, legislates from outside for other parts or moments.

Neither does coherence mean accordance with a "principle" or "pattern." For these terms imply repeatability, reiterability, the recurrence of "the same" in different instances; the same ratio, the same form, the same relations. This repeated same something is supposed to be fully specific, determinate, and repeatable. Normally, when we say, "I have grasped the principle or pattern," it means, "I can extend the same procedure I have applied in a previous case to hitherto unencountered, new cases." The same is present in the different. This obviously is premised on the possibility of reiterability, repetition of the same, which is already premised on the presence of some kind of universal. For without a universal, essence, or Form of some kind, it is impossible for any selfsame "simply located" thing to be in two places at once. If someone gives me a pattern, say, 2, 4, 8, 16, ———, I can fill in the blank by "grasping the principle." I apply the same to the different. I perform the same operation in each case: "double the previous number" is the principle. It is the same procedure, and it is perfectly determinate—a universal, essence or form. The fact that this model for such perfect sameness derives from a mathematical example is perhaps no accident.

But if we are thinking instead about coherence, the case is slightly but crucially different. What is called for in order to find a coherence among diverse items is not determinately the same in each step, but *whatever* can cohere—bring diverse parts together so as to become readable as something single and determinate—with the existing situation or the preceding steps. *It is something that harmonizes with what came before, not something that repeats what came before.* The standard in this case need not be preestablished and independent, unconditioned and definitively determinate, standing above their instantiations. It is to highlight this point that I placed the words of Confucius at the beginning of this book: "The exemplary man is in harmony with others, but not the same as others; the petty man is the same as others, but not in harmony with others" (*junzi he er bu tong; xiaoren tong er bu he* 君子和而不同，小人同而不和 *Analects*, 13:23), for this may stand as our motto when trying to understand coherence and how it differs from "principle" or "pattern." It is a question of harmony, not sameness. Mention of "harmony," however, brings us into potentially murky territory, not least because it is so favored a trope among popular writers about the "Chinese View of Life" (to use the title of a not atypical example of this genre), favored above all for its nebulous and innocuous palatability. But what, after all, is "harmony"?

In a recent series of articles,[16] Chenyang Li has undertaken a more rigorous analysis of this concept, beginning with an etymological analysis of the various terms for harmony used in ancient texts, most centrally the character *he* 和 and its variants. He concludes that the terms derive from depictions of instruments that were used to mix either sounds (i.e., musical instruments) or flavors (i.e., a vessel in which to combine wine with water); and the founding metaphor of the combination of either sounds or flavors continue to be the baseline of early expositions of the concept. Alan Chan has suggested that these two alternate sources have radically different implications, making "harmony" a deeply contested metaphor throughout the tradition.[17] Chan interprets the musical metaphor as tending toward a sense of hierarchy and compliance, on the model of a ruling melodic tone or a prior note which is subsequently harmonized with, with the food metaphor offering a more pluralist implication of diverse elements contributing equally to a collective flavor, each preserving its own individual character and without any of them necessarily leading or dominating the others. Chan makes many important and insightful points in explicating the way this inner tension plays out in various thinkers from later in the Confucian tradition. We find in the pre-Confucian sources cited by Li, however, that the two metaphors are explicitly used to illustrate one another. Yan Ying (晏嬰, ?–500 BCE) is quoted in the Shaogong 昭公 Year 20 chapter of the *Zuozhuan* 左傳 comparing *he* to the blending of ingredients—water, fire, vinegar, sauce, salt, and plum added to fish and meat—in the making of soup, "compensating for deficiencies and reducing excesses." He then goes on to extend this model to the combination of sounds in a piece of music, saying, "Sounds are like flavors." (*Sheng yi ru wei* 聲亦如味). The key here is that these various ingredients or tones must "complete one another" and "complement one another" (*xiangcheng* 相成, *xiangji* 相濟). Yan Ying goes on to explicitly relate this to the relationship between rulers and ministers: to "harmonize" means not to always agree, not to be "the same as" (*tong*) the ruler, not to simply say yes when he says yes and no when he says no. In other words, harmony is contrasted to sameness with the latter explicitly conceived as mimesis and obedience, as the exact replication and agreement between a model or rule and its implementation. All *following* in the sense of compliance would here seem to be relegated to the side of "sameness" rather than "harmony," and for that reason rejected. It is perhaps to accentuate this that Li has made the insightful point that *he* is perhaps better translated not simply as "harmony" but as "harmonization": a constant process of finding ways to harmonize, rather than the accord with a preexisting pattern, since any kind of compliance would, as compliance, ipso facto be relegated to the side of "sameness." In this connection, Li quotes the very telling early attempt at a kind of *definitional statement* about *he*, from the "Zhou Yu B" chapter of the *Guo Yu* 國語周語下: "when sounds correspond and mutually promote (*bao* 保) one another it is called *he*" (*shen ying xiang bao yue he* 聲應相保曰和). What is striking here is this mutual "promotion" or perhaps *preservation* of the related item—and indeed, Li suggests several implications of the strange use of the crucial term *bao* here: "protect, nurture, rely, and assure." To unravel the meaning of this, we must turn to another key passage invariably cited in this context, the discussion of *he* in contrast to *tong* (sameness, agreement, unison) offered by Shi Bo 史伯, a pre-Confucian scholar-official, in the "Zhengyu" chapter of the same text, the *Guo Yu*:

> Now the King [You of Zhou] avoids those who loftily and brilliantly make themselves known while preferring deceitful flatterers who remain concealed in darkness. He dislikes anyone who is well developed and armed with accomplishments, associating instead with those who insist on remaining stunted and depleted. Thus he excises harmony and adopts sameness instead (去和而取同 *qu he er qu tong*). Harmony is what brings fruition and life to things, while sameness leads to no progeny or continuance. To balance the different with the different is called harmony; this is why it can

flourish and grow, and why things all return and converge around what has this harmony. But if you take the same and just add it on to the same, this leads to extinction. Thus the former kings used soil to mix together minerals, plants, water, and fire so as to produce various types of things. Hence they blended the five flavors to provide fitness for the mouth, strengthened each of the four limbs to protect the body, harmonized the six tones to sharpen the ear's hearing, ordered the arrangement of the seven orifices to serve the heartmind, balanced the eight body parts to complete the human person, invigorated all the nine internal organs to set them to their purest virtues, brought together the ten diverse social ranks to train the hundred disparate parts [of the society]. . . . For this reason the former kings selected wives from other clans, sought wealth in the [various different] possessions offered from the various directions. In selecting ministers they chose officials who remonstrated, and tested them with many affairs, endeavoring [to discover their allegiance to either] harmony or sameness. Sound that is monolithic is unlistenable; objects that are monolithic make no pattern; flavors that are monolithic bring no satisfaction; things that are monolithic bear no discussion. Since the king abandons this type of thing (i.e., harmony) and involves himself only in sameness, it is obvious that Heaven will take away [its mandate]. Could he avoid defeat?[18]

The contrast between harmony and sameness is here spelled out in the broadest terms: harmony is defined as a balance between two terms which are "other" (他 *ta*) with respect to one another, but which nonetheless form some kind of unity—a *balance* of qualitatively different entities that cohere into something that is *experienced with pleasure* as a new coherence. This type of unity is compared to another type of unity, that of sameness, the oneness of monotonous sounds and flavors, which (recalling again the *Zuozhuan* passage cited above) also implies a relation between ruler and minister where the latter merely agrees and flatters and never disagrees. The value is placed on harmony, and we are offered very specific reasons for this, which we will encounter most explicitly in our discussion of the "Great Commentary" to the *Book of Changes*, below: harmony is not only an intrinsic aesthetic pleasure in its own right, but also leads to continuance, to *progeny*. Continued existence and fertility are seen as relying on a balanced grouping which is itself harmonious in the same sense, an equilibrium that will lead to further creation of equilibrium-centered groups, and so on into the future. Sameness, on the other hand, is both unpleasant (at odds with, hence not cohering with, our true desires) and self-destructive. "Harmonizing" means these differences coming together in some way that will facilitate further harmonizings, so that this intelligibility can be sustained and continued. Coherence would then refer to those readable groupings found in the past (or in the given present) that can be selected out to be so harmonized with. We also see here the importance of setting up exemplary officials, who have manifested their normative standard, in high positions, as will become clearer when we consider the *Mencius*: this is what allows for a harmonious social totality to form. For harmony itself, as the giver of continuing life, attracts the people: they converge around it and cohere.[19] To be "one," to be "a unit," means to be a social harmony, to be constituted by this cohesion of othernesses, to be a social group, with an exalted center toward which a periphery is attracted and around which forms a coherent whole.[20]

Anyone who has ever tried to sing harmony vocals in a rock band will appreciate the delicate intertwining of normativity and freedom involved in this notion. Coming up with a harmony line to a preexisting melody is as different from the freedom of composing a melody from scratch as it is from the compulsion of singing in unison or conforming to a preexisting score. One's options are effectively limitless, constrained only by the range of one's voice and of audible tones. One can always go another octave up or down, within that range, and this will decisively change the nature of the resulting harmony. Moreover, as anyone who has ever considered the McCartney harmonies to early Beatles Lennon melodies will know, the harmony can actually change the significance of the melody itself, making it in effect a different melody, although all the notes remain the same. One is not free to sing any note at all, but the options of what note to sing are limited only by the range of possible notes. You can get a note wrong, but not because you have failed to sing the sole correct note, for there is no sole correct note to sing, nor even, really, a predetermined *finite* set of right notes, except in the sense that there is a finite set of audible notes *simpliciter*. The range of right notes expands wherever the range of possible notes expands. We don't have to delve into the mysteries of Cantorian mathematics to appreciate that there are two different types of infinity operative here. The number of whole integers is infinite, but the number of odd integers is also infinite, even though there are only half as many of them. Similarly, the right ways of harmonizing are infinite, even though this infinite set is always smaller than the infinite set of possible notes, so that there are always also a lot of potentially wrong ways to harmonize.

We tend to think of harmonizing as implicitly appealing to a second-order requirement for conformity: you can sing any note as long as it exemplifies, isomorphically as it were, the *rules of harmony*. This would be a sameness governing the realm of harmonizing. My suggestion here is that the second order of sameness-oriented laws and rules is precisely what we do not seem to find in most Chinese conceptions of harmony. Rather, the relations are reversed: instead of harmony being a subset, a special case, of sameness (precise instantiation of a rule), apparent samenesses are a subset of the broader demand for harmony, a special case of harmony. This idea will help us grasp the apparent exceptions to the sweeping generalizations we are making here, for example, the isomorphic sameness orientation of neo-Mohist epistemology, the Legalist notions of law, and Dong Zhongshu's theistic and realist theory of names.[19] Considered purely in isolation from their broader cultural and historical context, these exceptional cases were perhaps groping toward a "sameness" concept of the more familiar Occidental type. In the crucial opening sallies of *Mencius* 6A, in fact, Mencius contrasts his notion of "human nature" to other types of categories, using the stock example of "whiteness," as something that is *truly* the same in all its various instantiations, unlike the morally relevant sense of "the nature," which he will explicate instead as a coherence in the sense I am describing here. It is clear, therefore, that I cannot be claiming that some notion of sameness, or an unchanging universal, was literally *unavailable* to these thinkers, or outside the possibilities of their linguistic or conceptual system. But I do want to argue that these conceptions of sameness emerge within the broader understanding of coherence, as a special case of the same, rather than the other way around—and indeed that this might perhaps help account for their relative unimportance in the subsequent development of the tradition. In the case of the Mohists, at least, I would argue that they were; the notion of "sameness" plays a crucial part in Mozi's political thinking as well, as we can see clearly in the "Shangtong" (alternately, "Esteeming Sameness," (尚同) or "Conforming to the Superior" (上同) depending on the version) chapter of the *Mozi*. The *Mohist Canons*, indeed, distinguish between four types of sameness, which are strictly defined: the predicate "same" (*tong*) is applied (1) when there are two names for the same actuality; (2) when two parts belong to a single whole; (3) when two entities are contained within the same space; and (4) when two things "possess something by which they are the same" (有以同 *youyitong*). This last is named "The sameness of type" (類同也 *leitongye*).[22] Sameness of type is defined here by means of a tautological reference to sameness. We may take this as meaning one of the three previous types of sameness. In that case, sameness of type would seem to be the precise inverse of the second type of sameness, which pertains to two parts of the same whole. Sameness of type is a sameness that pertains to two wholes that share a part (that "possess" some part that is the same), or which have a part that is the "same" in one of the three previous senses. So if two coherent wholes possess a part that is either an intersection of the two, or contain elements which are themselves parts of some other whole, contiguous in some space, these two wholes can be said to be of the "same" type. We will see other conceptions of type, rooted in notions of feeling and response, coming out of the Confucian tradition, and rooted more obviously in a notion of harmony. But even here, we must note the whole/part ontology that undergirds this definition of sameness; it is a far cry from the notion of the genuine repetition of a form or universal.[23] Even if we were to interpret the last Mohist definition of sameness more Platonically (for example, as something other than a tautological definition referring back to the previous three types of sameness; "possessing that by which to be the same," taken out of that context, could conceivably be read as "possessing the universal form"), it would seem that there simply were not cultural resources to make sense of such an idea in the commonsensical notions of the literate culture of the time or after. They were either ignored or were absorbed into the broader "harmony" paradigm. Here we must again follow Chenyang Li in viewing the harmony-sameness relation not as a dichotomous either-or, but as constant copresence with variable degrees of emphasis, and further, with various relations of one side subsuming the other in the various traditions and thinkers. When Confucian thinkers emphasize harmony, they do not mean to exclude any possible form of sameness, which would make now sense, but just the "over-presence" of sameness. In this way we can agree with Alan Chan's observation of the coexistence of several conflicting implications in the usage of these terms, but understood as resulting from the various alloys or combinations of the alternate paradigms, which will have different implications depending on which is the subsuming and which the subsumed.

For it goes without saying that, if we wanted to, we *could* express harmony as a kind of sameness, as a way of naming a shared characteristic of all the harmonizing elements, or the instantiation of some "same" universal feature in all of them. Most simply, we could always say, "All the elements harmonizing here share the characteristic of being members of the set of harmonizing elements." I may ask, "Which of the following items does not have something in common with the others: a cigarette standing upright on its filter, a round ashtray, a wedding ring, and a book of matches?" The obvious "sameness" answer would group the three items instantiating the universal "roundness": cigarette, ashtray, and ring. The "harmony" answer would group around the human function of smoking: cigarette, ashtray, and matches. The latter would be an example of a harmonizing, the joining of disparate elements around a common goal. Now, I could always say that these elements share the feature of "being used to smoke," but the point is that we do not *need* to use this way of describing the matter. We can think of this shared characteristic, instead, as a roundabout way of describing the manner in which these items happen to cohere in this particular action, predicated on the particular human desire in question. (Whether this would, in turn, count as the type of coherence later called a Li would depend on whether the activity of smoking per se cohered with other human values, such as health, continuance, balance, and so on.) If we wanted to, we could perhaps specify that harmony here means the kind of sameness that always involves a reference to this kind of relationship: a shared trait of "joining together in a particular human function." They must cohere around the unstated figure of the human being smoking, enjoying his smoke, wanting to smoke. But this assimilation of harmony to an elaborately qualified type of sameness seems like an unnecessarily roundabout way of handling such cases.

Nor does the Wittgensteinian idea of a set of family resemblances, which do not necessarily have any single particular trait in common, exactly describe the kind of grouping we have when we speak of harmony rather than sameness. For Wittgenstein's account tends toward a strong nominalism, and excludes the act of naming itself from the set of things made to intertwine in the resultant class name. The family resemblances are described, as it were, from outside, by a dispassionate peruser of old photographs. The family resemblances pertaining to the harmony we are describing here are instead those observed within the family, at the family reunion, as it were: they are affective bonds of responsiveness and recognition between the members of the formative group itself, converging into a coherence. Indeed, as we shall see, perhaps the model of "harmonious coherence as family grouping" here is closer to the structure of the Corleone family in *The Godfather*, with its internal bonds of loyalty, hierarchy, honorary non-blood members, and so on, as formed under the pressure of a shared project and convergence toward the same goal and value: the continuation and flourishing of the family itself. The key point to note here is that it may therefore include an adoptive member, such as the *consigliere* Tom Hagen, who bears no physical or genetic resemblance to any of the prior members. This is very different from a set of particulars each of which instantiates "the same" universal, or a group of particulars passively arranged and objectively observed, which are found to have a shifting chain of ad hoc resemblances.

Hence, we will avoid watering harmony down by describing it as a subset of a kind of sameness, the instantiation of a sameness. We could, on the contrary, describe sameness as a subset of harmony, as, for example, a shorthand way of describing the interactions of a clustering social group. *The question is which is to be seen as a subset of the other.* I will claim that the Chinese traditions tend to see the samenesses as special cases of a broader harmony, and even rule following, obedience, and repetition as items whose sole value lies in their coherent harmonizing with a "something else."[24] So I will not prohibit myself from saying words like "same" and "different" or their avatars in making particular interpretative suggestions—indeed, it would be impossible to do so. But when doing so, I intend sameness as a derivative of harmonic coherence, rather than the other way around.

Thus, coherence requires at least two terms, for there can be no harmony without otherness, and otherness requires at least duality, a balance that reminds us of the structure of polarity and parallelism which we will find again in the Yin-Yang dyad. This harmonious coherence is conceived of as an equilibrium that is life-continuing, productive, and can be viewed as modeled especially on the dyads that form the cardinal social relationships in much Chinese thinking. As Mencius puts it, "When those below respect those above, it is called esteeming the noble. When those above respect those below, it is called honoring the worthy. Esteeming the noble and honoring the worthy are one single Rightness (義 yi)" (5B:4). In other words, there is a coherence not only of the two different roles (a "harmony") but also, it is asserted, some kind of coherence to the opposite normative principles operating from the two opposite directions. The superior's proper treatment of his inferior is both opposite to and identical with the inferior's proper treatment of his superior. This hierarchy between the two poles involves a reciprocal regard moving in both directions, and it is asserted that the significance of the two contrary halves of this relation, each of which includes the other in its regard, is "one." The coherence here implies the simultaneity of two opposite structures, two reciprocal relations. It involves apprehension of the one by the other, and action in accordance with spontaneous reactions to the behavior of the other. What is "one" is not just the coherence-around-a-center as a whole, but also the relations of each peripheral element to the center. It is not just the parts that are different but harmoniously coherent, but the very relations of these parts to the center, their very way of cohering. These relations are not the *same* relation, as in the radii of a circle, but more like a dyadic pair of opposite relations, standing in harmony to another. Hence, we must speak of a second-order coherence of coherences modeled on this social paradigm. We will find many alternate explorations of this notion of coherence in the early philosophical works.

IS WHITE HORSE HORSE?

As a further clarifier of the nature of the issue at stake here, it might be worthwhile to briefly consider the ever-fascinating and perplexing paradox of the White Horse, attributed to Gongsun Long, which was the key testing ground of Hansen's theory in its earliest incarnation. For it will serve as a useful touchstone for us here as well. The problem is to discover what sort of commonsensical ontological or assumed linguistic theory could make the claim "A white horse is not a horse" at once (1) interesting, confusable with an admissible statement, not immediately refutable, and yet also (2) surprising and unconvincing to early Chinese philosophers. We may regard the paradox as one of the fault lines where something distinctive in the ontological and/or linguistic assumptions of the tradition bursts forth, a kind of localized pimple indicative of global systemic difficulties not evident elsewhere. It provides us with a marker of the problems that set the agenda for the direction the tradition ultimately takes, why it veers at this crossroads away from a sameness/difference model and toward a coherence model (although, to say it again, this very fact proves that the sameness/difference model was an underdetermined possibility here as everywhere). Early in the twentieth century Fung Yulan offered an interpretation of Gongsun's paradoxes as deriving precisely from his unprecedented discovery of Platonic Forms as pure essences, which he named *zhi* (指), the focus of another dialogue attributed to Gongsun Long, the "Wuzhilun" (物指論).[25] The claim is then simply that the concept "White Horse" and the concept "Horse" are not identical concepts, which is trivial but true, but would seem astonishing and incomprehensible in the absence of clear specifiers of abstraction. The "Platonic" reading sees the absence of a Platonic tradition as the reason no one understood or cared about what Gongsun was saying. Janusz Chmielewski suggested reading the dialogue in terms of set theory (the set of white horses is not the set of white objects, nor the set of horses, though it is a subset of both; the intersection of these two sets is not the same as either set); but as Hansen pointed out, it was a highly irregular kind of set theory that admitted neither the intersection of sets nor the inclusion of the empty set. Hansen's mass-noun hypothesis was shaped largely in response to the White Horse problem, and his explanation of the dialogue is, in my opinion, far more plausible than the Platonic reading (although he admits that, on textual rather than contextual grounds, it is impossible to rule out the Platonic reading). Hansen reads the discussion of White Horse here as pertaining to a mass sum (i.e., the total of the two named stuffs, the white and the horse, modeled on the Mohist ox-horse, which includes all ox-stuff and all horse-stuff), rather than a mass product (like the Mohist hard-white, which is only the intersection of hard-stuff and white-stuff, which pervade one another where they intersect), which it is *permissible* (but not true) to say is not horse (in Hansen's language, it is "assertable"), because *part* of the compound is white-but-not-horse. Crucially, it is also assertable that white horse *is* horse. The more limited aims of the paradox (to demonstrate that white horse is not horse is *also* assertable rather than that it is *alone* assertable) accords closely with the pragmatic view of language: it is sometimes acceptable to call the total mass of whiteness-and-horseness "horse" and sometimes "not-horse." This part of Hansen's solution I heartily endorse. Hansen's reading also has the advantage of explaining Gongsun's reputation as "one who separates the hard and the white," as well as plausibly accounting for both the motivation and the unconvincingness of the dialogue.

Graham adopts a modified version of Hansen's mass-noun reading of the dialogue, translated onto an analogue of "blade" and "hilt" and "sword" to follow the argument, making its focus the relation of whole and part, which Graham holds, very plausibly, is the focus of other works attributable to Gongsun, most notably the "Wuzhilun" 物指論, which Graham translates as "Pointing Things Out," and the "Tongbianlun" (通變論), which Graham renames "The Left and Right dialogue." But he rejects precisely the pragmatic reading of the paradox's aim; Graham seems to think the argument is still meant to assert the *exclusive* propriety of white horse *not being* horse.[26] Bo Mou's recent "double reference" account of the White Horse argument, on the other hand, has taken precisely the assertability of both "is horse" and "not horse" as the real point of the dialogue. Bo Mou identifies the differences between the "semantic referent" and the "pragmatic referent" as generating the apparent paradoxes, which are meant precisely to encourage us to take *both* into account, since "the semantic referent without the pragmatic referent is blind, while the pragmatic referent without the semantic referent is empty"[27]—which is a stricture rooted in a concern for both a pragmatic (ethical) and a linguistic (epistemological) probity.

More recently, Manyul Im has argued that the argument is really intended as a *reductio ad absurdum* of existing linguistic theories, in effect a protest against theories that did not prohibit or immediately and clearly refute precisely this kind of sophistry.[28] I do not here want to attempt a comprehensive interpretation of the White Horse dialogue, and an attempt to disentangle its many textual problems, which I will save for a later work. But in the current context, I will note that, while I heartily support Hansen's "assertability" modification, and see his "mass-sum" approach as a great improvement over the out-of-the-sky Platonic interpretation, it seems to me that neither the Platonists nor the post-Hansenists give a convincing account of what to me is the key argument, which actually rules out the Platonic reading. The argument that "white horse" is semantically different from "horse" is iterated in various ways, and can be read as meaning simply that the compound, whether of stuffs or of Ideas, is not identical to the elements in the compound considered separately. But there is one argument that asserts rather that the compounded elements themselves are *not the same elements when compounded.* It is the line: 以「白者不定所白」, 忘之而可也。白馬者, 言白定所白也, 定所白者非白也。

I translate this as follows: "'White' does not specify what is whited, so [in considering what white is,] it [i.e., the latter, what is 'whited'] can be disregarded. But 'white' in 'white horse' *does* specify what is whited. Something that specifies what is whited is thus not the same as 'white.'"[29]

This line is cited by Fung Yu-lan as indicating the distinction between "White" as Universal and "White" as instantiated in a particular, noting that they are not identical. But I believe, with Yiu-ming Fung, that this line is what specifically *rules out* the idea of "white" as "the universal white" in Plato's sense. For the claim here is that when white modifies something in particular, it is no longer the same thing as white *simpliciter*. But that the "white" that modifies a white horse and "white" as a universal considered in isolation *are* one and the same thing is precisely what the theory of universals demands. Note that this precise line is what also rules out a simple nominalist interpretation: it *is* possible to abstract "white per se" which modifies no particular white thing. The point here is that when white enters into a relation with horse, it is not the same white as it was before this relation, or whiteness *simpliciter*. The relation matters. "White not specifying" is not exactly "white specifying"; but "white not specifying," I would claim, is white conceived in the matrix of *another* coherence, not of no coherence. White is not self-standing, whether when modifying or not modifying a concrete object: it is a *different* white when viewed in one way and in another way, when considered in relation to, say, other non-concrete-object-modifying colors, or when considered in relation to a horse. So even in trying to revive the Fung Yu-lan approach to the paradox, Yiu-ming Fung must make a crucial adjustment, suggesting "a new realist interpretation" of the Dialogue. To do so, he makes an enormous distinction between the abstract universal terms used by Gongsun Long and those of the Platonic tradition:

> Gongsun Long's idea of "*zhi*" [指] is similar to but not exactly the same as Platonic "Idea." Generally speaking, *zhi* (or one specific example, horse) for Gongsun Long is like Plato's universal (or one specific example, horseness) in the sense that they both exist not in the phenomenal world and both do not have the sense of concreteness defined by physical characteristics of phenomena, but they are different from each other in the sense that Gongsun Long's zhi can emerge into phenomenal thing through its jian [兼] (combining or joining) with other zhi or through its ting [*sic*, meaning *ding* 定] (specifying or fixing) into a concrete thing while Plato's universal can be exemplified into each of its instances without any meaning of emergence. In Plato's words, his Idea is absolutely transcendent and unchanged as an ontological ground which can be exemplified but cannot participate into the phenomenal world in a cosmological sense; on the other hand, Gongsun Long's zhi can emerge into phenomena though before emergence it is transcendent and unchanged as a separate simple. Just like the metaphysical Dao in Daoism, Gongsun Long's zhi plays a double role of ontological ground and cosmological origin; it is quite different from Plato's and

other Western philosophers' metaphysics in terms of the separate role assigned to their key terms of ontological and cosmological entities, respectively.[30]

But a universal that is not the same in all its instantiations is simply *not a universal*. Fung sees here a whiteness as a kind of dual-status unseen force, at once ontological and cosmological, which he compares to the Dao of the *Laozi*, which he interprets similarly as both cosmological and ontological, which both pervades and is actually active in bringing about the ontic existence of the particulars. In this book I will suggest an alternate way of accounting for both the pervading of one of these "nonidentical universals" across apparent separated particulars which however does not yield a single unchanged entity doing the pervading, and its creative role in actualizing individual events without having to posit a preexisting Dao or preexisting nonidentical universals (which is an oxymoron). The key throughout this dialogue is coherence, and indeed, all the arguments can be read in the same way. It is not just that "white horse" is not the same as "horse." Even "white" and "horse" in "white horse" are not "the same" as they are outside of this combination. White horse is a whole, a total Gestalt. It is not produced by adding two preexisting qualities. The assumption behind the plausibility and irrefutability of the paradox, on its own grounds, is the shared *holism* of the tradition, which is ontologically *prior to* fixed sameness or difference: the only identity of any item is the way it functions in whatever unions of elements it may enter into, or may be seen as entering into. It literally is not "the same thing" in one whole and in another—or, more strictly, it is "in one sense" the same element and "in another sense" not the same element. Here, we as it were combine the interpretative perspectives of Graham and of Bo Mou: the dialogue is about the relation of parts and wholes, with the intent of showing that the whiteness in white horse both is and is not the whiteness in something else. It is the necessity of the *double meaning*, the presence of both sameness and difference, that is the thrust of the argument. It is, we must say, a coherence of white and horse, which creates with it, when it comes into existence, a new "whiteness" and a new "horseness." What are assumed here is neither selfsame universals nor selfsame mass-stuffs, which are in turn ultimately different from other selfsame universals or stuffs. Rather, we are assuming multiply determinable continuities, which it will be permissible to read out one way when viewed in one context, and another way in another context. In this we are perhaps approaching the position of Cheng Chung-ying, who in a recent overview has somewhat modified his earlier realist reading of the dialogue, which had taken a view similar to Fung Yu-lan's of *zhi* as abstract qualities "apart from concrete experience of the world." Like Yiu-ming Fung, Cheng modifies his earlier realist reading, but in a direction more in line with our current discussion: "Now I wish to stress the importance of seeing determinations (as *zhi*) as both naturally arising and epistemological[ly] recognized with our conceptions which fit with our experiences *in totality* and *as a totality* [my emphases]. In this sense I wish now to take the concrete realist position which means: *There are natural qualities in things which require our experiences and cognition. . . .*" Cheng further notes that this approach brings out a new approach to the interpretation of qualities that is compatible with nominalism, conceptualism, and realism, each to be stressed in different contexts.[31] The stress on the integration of qualities as emerging from their coherence with the totality of experience, in a way that evades a dichotomization of nominalism and realism, consorts well with the approach we will be taking in this book.

Zhuangzi will later describe the method behind this paradox, disapprovingly, as "using horse to show the not-horseness of horse" (以馬喻馬之非馬). We now see what this means: he is using a (white) horse to show that the horseness [in coherence with white so as to form white horse] is not the same as the horseness [outside of the coherent compound white horse]. Zhuangzi will agree with the conclusion, but not the method: it is indeed—*sometimes, and in a sense*—permissible to say a white horse is not a horse, but Zhuangzi prefers to do so by "using not-horse to show the not-horseness of horse" (以非馬喻馬之非馬也). This is an appeal to another kind of coherence, an ironic coherence between any coherence and its negation—as we shall see in the discussion of Zhuangzi, below. Xunzi, on the other hand, will design a linguistic theory precisely to exclude the "permissibility" of this kind of assertion—by clarifying the proper definition of permissibility, though not of truth, *also in terms of coherence*—in this case the coherence with human desires, satisfactions, and communal strength. Xunzi does not, cannot, refute the claim on the grounds of any ultimate samenesses or differences that are mistakenly identified, but rather objects to the probity of this method of naming as he would object to the ambiguous use of names for weights and measures in a marketplace. My claim, on the linguistic front, is that "horse" neither instantiates a universal, nor names single selfsame preexisting entire mass-stuff of horse-stuff. Rather, the meaning and range of reference of "horse" is made coherent anew around and in relation to anything that is called horse. This "horsiness" of this "horse" is not the same as that in other "horses." Nor are this horse and other horses all "parts" of one preexisting Horse-stuff. Rather, this horse is called horse because calling it horse makes it coherently horse in coherence with other "horses," and makes other horses coherently "horse" in coherence with it. The horsiness of all horsiness is not the same horsiness, nor is it ontologically different, in the sense of excluding some other more extreme form of sameness. When a named is used on two different occasions, what is so named is seen, not as same, not as different, but as *cohering*, as *coherent*.

Note the contrast to the ontological level-asymmetry we found in Lévy-Bruhl's model of "rational thought." There, horseness would have to subsume white-horseness unidirectionally, as animality subsumes mammality, as clear liquid subsumes water and sulfuric acid. "Respirating thing" and "lactating thing" reside on distinct ontological levels, although in the concrete animal this ontological distinction is far from apparent. Here, in contrast, "white," "horse," and "white horse" all reside on the same ontological level; white horse is *not* unambiguously or unidirectionally subsumed into horse. To be a horse is no more fundamental or inclusive than to be a white horse. They are simply alternate coherent ways of reading this thing here: some white, some horse, white horse. In continuity with harmonizing whitenesses and their concomitants, it is coherently white; in continuity with harmonizing horses and their concomitants, it is coherently horse; and in continuity with white and horse, and with other white horses and their concomitants, it is white horse. "Bob is rich" means "There is money to be found where Bob is found"; "the horse is white" means "there is whiteness to be found where the horse is found." But there is also horse to be found there where the white is, and there is also white-horseness to be found there where the white and the horse are. Each is found there when a finder finds himself in coherent continuity with the relevant context, the one that links this thing coherently to whatever group of other things highlights in the finder's experience the coherent white there, the coherent horse there, the coherent white-horse there." The whiteness, the horseness, and the white-horseness are all there equally in the horse. And this is precisely why "not-horseness" is there too: for whiteness and horseness are both there, both assertable there, both experiencable there, and they are both not white-horseness.

QIAN MU'S PENDULUM

If we are looking for a model with which to grasp the peculiarities of this particular conception of harmony and coherence, there is much to be gained by considering closely the opinion of the great Qian Mu, who offers the following typically homely but arresting characterizations of the distinctive thinking of the mainstream Chinese philosophical tradition:

> Wherever there is a circle or a pendulum range, there will be what can be called a center. This center is not on the two sides, nor anywhere outside, but rather lies within [the range of the swing of the pendulum]. A pendulum swing or a cyclic process never actually comes to rest at that center, but the center is always there, and is

always still and solid as a center. It is as if the center were controlling the motion. The ceaseless and infinite motion seems eternally to be under the command of the center, completely controlled by the center, and thus we can say that it is perfectly moving and perfectly still, perfectly changing and perfectly constant. . . . Confucians want to point out a fixed center in this infinite cyclical back and forth, and they call this center "human nature." This is also what the Neo-Confucians of the Song and Ming dynasties liked to call "the Center which has not yet become manifest," "knowing the resting place," "stillness," "the master," "the constant." The Song Neo-Confucians said that this human Nature is precisely Li [coherence], but were unwilling to say that the Nature is qi [vital energy], because qi is just the motion, whereas Li is the Center of that motion. If there were truly pure qi with no Li, it would be like an unbridled horse—no one knows where it will run to. Heaven and earth would not be able to become heaven and earth, humans and things would not be able to become humans and things. There would be absolutely no way of handling or explaining the myriad different types and forms of things. The reason we now have this "Heaven and Earth," and these "humans" and these "things," is because within the qi there is this Li. Because there is Li in qi, there is constancy and predictability, which is called "the Nature" when viewed as active and emerging from within, but is called "the Decree" when viewed as passive and coming from without. But in reality this one motion is at once active and passive, internal and external, indivisibly, which is why the Nature and the Decree are seen to have a common source. Both are ways of describing this motion itself, but emphasizing different aspects of it.

"The Good" is what we call the constancy in this eternal change, the center in this unceasing motion, this relatively easily grasped and known nature. Good is just the constant tendency of this motion. . . . Whatever is separated from it by a great distance is called bad. Good is just the center of this motion, evil is nothing but going beyond it or not coming up to it. . . . Although human affairs also go through endless transformations and never stay the same, there is a constancy or a center to them. If you try to separate yourself from this constancy or center and just move straight forward, you will find that it is impossible. For example, peace and struggle are phenomena that arise alternately in human life; they usually form a cycle, a back and forth, moving from peace to struggle and then from struggle back to peace. Within this process too there is a center or a constancy. Struggle must search for peace, and peace must resist struggle (that is, must not be afraid of struggle). So peace which is close to struggle and struggle that is close to peace are both capable of continuing, and both can be called good. But struggle that is far removed from peace and peace that is far removed from struggle are both far removed from the center, so that neither can form a constancy or attain any continuity. Going too far and not coming up to it are equally bad, and both of these can be called evil. Evil is just whatever cannot be constant [i.e., is not sustainable]. The same is true of sickness and health. Usually people think a healthy person is free of sickness, but in reality if there were no sickness, how could there be the work of metabolism, assimilating and excreting? The function of excretion is a type of sickness that is not far removed from health (and hence is good). The same is true of work and rest; to rest so much you can no longer work is evil and not good, and to work so much you can no longer rest is equally evil and not good. But people usually think of life as positive, death as negative, peace as positive and struggle as negative, health and work as positive and sickness and rest as negative, and then they start thinking that the positive side is good and the negative side is evil. But according to the theory we are developing here, as long as evil stays close to good, it is no longer evil, and indeed, if good is too far removed from evil it is no longer good.[32]

I quote this passage at length because we will have many occasions to refer back to it in the pages that follow. I do not claim that this model applies perfectly for all Chinese thinkers.[33] Rather, I would like to suggest that in considering each Chinese thinker we are better off searching for something like this model and the ways in which he diverges from it than assuming something along the lines of the universal/particular model, and the particular handling of sameness into difference that it implies. For this brilliant metaphor gives us a key by which to unlock many of the problems that we will find confronting us there, to be contrasted with the basic metaphors of mimesis, or imposing a shape onto a material, that inform the Greek speculations. It is crucial to note, first of all, that the sort of "coherence" indicated here necessarily includes both sustainability and value, which are here seen as one and the same, and inseparably connected to the idea of intelligibility (the graspability of the still, virtual center as opposed to the motion of the pendulum itself) and to "centrality," a neutral point connecting to two extremes conceived as a dyadic opposition. It also provides us with a strong sense of why it is preferable to speak of "coherence" for such ideas, rather than simply some form of "harmony." For what is at stake here is literally the holding together of the parts, their grouping with one another as a condition of their being as what they are. If any part flies off to too great a distance from the center, and the opposite extreme, it ceases to be sustainable as itself (e.g., health too far from sickness ceases to be health). It is the coherence between the parts that not only sustains the whole, but sustains each of the parts as such. And this coherence with the whole, and with the center, is really just a shorthand way of designating the relation to the other parts, or better, the opposite part. The "center" is picked out and privileged because it alone provides the whole "coherence" in the other sense: intelligibility. The whole can be identified, grasped, predicted, only through the center. The center is what "shows up" to observing awareness of the circulation between the extremes.

We might note also the rather *approximate* nature of this center as a summing up of the motion involved: it is determinative, in that "too great" a distance from it will lead to a part's demise. But this does not necessarily specify the exact range of each motion, which might be more or less distant in any case, swinging a little erratically from time to time, as long as it doesn't exceed a certain range. In other words, the "control" of the center, on this model, allows for a certain randomness. It is not conceived here as control in the sense of the issuing of a command that must be exactly obeyed, or laying down a track guiding every detail of the activity. Note also the manner in which this centrality is both immanent and transcendent: it is a function of the two poles, does not really preexist them, and has only a virtual existence, but at the same time it is their "controller" in the sense that their behavior and determinate identities are derivable from their relation to this virtual center. It does not belong to a separate ontological realm, being itself merely a certain fact about the two poles, that is, a way of describing their relation to one another.

We spoke in the previous chapter of some of the founding metaphors underlying the classical Greek methods of conceiving the unities of things in terms of a repeatable Form being imprinted into a formless matter. Such a notion of Form embodied both sameness and difference, while at the same time keeping them perfectly separate, with group membership defined by the sharing of a single selfsame essence, distinct from every other essence except those that subsume it higher up in a single unchanging hierarchical taxonomy, imagined as a downward-branching tree. Hence "Dog" and "Horse" are "the same" in that they share the selfsame essence of "Animality, Vertebrate, Mammal," etc., but differ in that each has a specific essence modified by its distinguishing feature. The "realist" interpretation of this arrangement will emphasize the reality of the sameness of the shared essence, while the "nominalist" will emphasize the difference between individual species or individual members of a species as what is ultimately real. But in either case, what is the same and what is different really pertain to these existing things in an unchanging way in all contexts.

It is useful to consider, in contrast, how same and different are to be conceived on the pendulum model. Again, although of course it would be possible to describe this situation in terms of a sameness (what the two extremes have in common is the characteristic of "not being too far from the center"), this description is clearly less useful than one that stresses the interfusion of same and different here. We have an alternate way of organizing sameness and difference here. For built into this idea of the extremes and the center is the sense that what constitutes the difference between these two extremes is precisely continuity with its opposite, and what constitutes their own identities with themselves as well as their continuity with one another is precisely their nonexclusion of difference. What joins them as members of this coherence is not so much sharing a certain characteristic, but rather precisely the harmonic coherence of their differences from one another. What makes health health? Its nonexclusion of sickness. What makes sickness sickness (rather than death, which would be the end of sickness)? Its nonexclusion of health. What makes health and sickness belong to the same coherence? Not their sharing of a single essence, but rather their complementarity. On this model, are health and sickness different from one another? They cannot be, because a health from which all sickness is expunged here ceases to exist as health, and vice versa. The same? But if the two sides are the same, there is no swing, and thus no center, and thus no two sides. Are they different from the center? But the intelligibility of each is merely an aspect of the intelligibility of this center: what we see is only this one thing, identified by the character of the intelligible center; the rest is an unknowable blank. The same? But the center is a merely virtual, approximate point defined by the swing between the extremes, such that a pendulum resting at the center point would cease to function as the center. If it were "all center," it would be "no center." In this single concrete image we can see how profoundly inappropriate these questions are to the case at hand. To get a concrete example of how this alternate notion of sameness and difference would play out in the case just described, the relation between a dog and a horse, the reader is asked to consult the discussion of the "Shuo gua" commentary to the *Zhouyi,* in chapter 5 of this book.

Perhaps more to the point, if we consider closely the point about intelligibility, we can see how this notion inevitably tends toward an idea of nested identities which connects to what we will be calling the ironic model of coherence. For what is identifiable, on Qian's view, is always a center. Activity that does not yet turn around, that does not revert into a finite range, that is continually moving forward and hence is constitutively unfinished, cannot be identified and known. All that we know are cycles, which are intelligible only as their approximate centers. But this means that when we speak of "health" and "sickness," say, as the two extremes within one cycle, identified perhaps as the center intelligible as "physical life," each of these two extremes must be a kind of center in its own right (for they have been identified, and identification is only of centers). Hence, within the larger vortex of "physical life," we have two smaller vortices of "health" and "sickness." This sort of nesting would have to go on indefinitely, as long as there are identifiable elements. As an aid to visualizing this, we might expand the pendulum model into three dimensions, somewhat along the line of the Rutherford model of atomic structure (it should go without saying that this is merely a heuristic device; I do not mean to suggest that the early Chinese had in any way anticipated the knowledge of atomic structure; quite the contrary). The cloud of vibrating electrons is knowable only as a unit, which is located at and as the nucleus. But if we focus on trying to identify any further component, say, an electron, on this model we will find another swarm of vibrations grouped around a virtual center, as which this swarm is identified. Expanding outward, we will find that the entire "atom" is an electron—in this case, one of two extremes of a pendulum swing—in a larger "atom." Each element is a vortex. Its center is the vertex by which it is grasped and known. This sense of mutual inclusion might play out, as in the non-ironic conception of coherence later found in, for example, the schematic charts of the sixty-four hexagrams of the _Zhouyi_ broken down into their Yin-Yang line components, as a one-way subsumption model, superficially similar to the taxonomy of species and genus we find on the universal/particular model. But the composition of each level by means of the vortex of mutually entailing opposites, each of which is also composed of some pair of opposites, skews this comparison decisively, particularly with respect to the highest level, but also in terms of the interconnections between the lower levels. In the full-blown ironic version, this will be pushed to the point of undermining any fixed knowability concerning the ultimate identity of any of the components. But even in the non-ironic version, there will be many interesting complications to the conception of sameness and difference among the component parts, which we will be examining in detail on a case by case basis in the pages that follow.

Centrality in this sense is itself value, is itself the connection of diverse and opposed particulars, is itself intelligibility: the three meanings of coherence with which we have been grappling. A center unifies, is discernible, and is value (sustainability), as Qian's analysis suggests.[34]

Coherence in the sense used here is then not merely consistency among elements of a whole, in the sense that they can coexist without interfering in one another's continued existence, are mutually compatible and not contradictory. It is also not merely the relation of coherence in the logical sense of mutual support or mutual entailment of a number of elements. Among available conceptual constructs, our notion of coherence perhaps comes closest to the notion of a Gestalt, which is a combination of elements that form a relation that emerges a single readable figure, an intelligible whole, which also has some sense of value attached to it ("a strong Gestalt"). There is also an important element of ambiguity to a Gestalt, as illustrated by the well-known images of the vase-faces, or Wittgenstein's duck-rabbit, which can point us toward the development of the ironic sense of coherence. It is possible but not so inevitable to include a sense of continuance to the value implication of the strong Gestalt. But the Chinese notions of coherence imply a quantitative balance between dyadic opposites (the opposite poles of the pendulum swing), and with it the sense of temporal periodicity, which does not seem to be as clearly a part of the basic notion of a Gestalt. The pendulum paradigm helps us grasp the way in which the coupling and balance of the dyadic elements is always also unquestionably a quantitative relation, a kind of proper proportion. When the pendulum goes "too far" quantitatively in either direction, it disrupts the balance, loses its connection to the center and to the other extreme. Maintaining this proportion, and the ability to revert to the opposite, is precisely what allows both sides to continue forward in time, and it is this that constitutes value. It is intriguing that, although 數 shu, number, and 度 du, degree, are often linked with Li in early texts, indeed used at times as a parallel synonym for it, we find there none of the interest in exact mathematical measurement that is so prominent in Greek thought. Balance is undeniably quantitative (implies neither "too much" nor "too little" of the two components: 過, 不及 guo, buji, See Analects, 11:15), but we never find an attempt in early Chinese thought to quantify it. Rather, we find an aesthetic sense of altering quantitative proportions "by feel" in order to produce a qualitative change, as in the cutting of jade to make it a marketable product, or the adjustment of mixtures of ingredients in a recipe, or the adjustment of tones into an experienced harmony. It is especially noteworthy that this balance is generally conceived, as here, in terms of the proportioning of two opposite qualities, a dyad of terms. Another important disparity between the notion of Gestalt and the Chinese ideas of coherence is the fact that the former does not lend itself so easily to the notion of inclusion of the observer, and thus the multiplication of further inclusive Gestalts growing around the original one. A Gestalt is more usually conceived as something viewed from outside, as an objective presence. The Chinese ideas of coherence would be more like a Gestalt that includes not only, say, the lines on the page that can form the emergent figure of a triangle, but also the eyes, nervous system, and present desires of the living being experiencing that triangle. A coherence would be a Gestalt, but with the dyadic periodicity, the ability to create further Gestalts which form a larger Gestalt with the original one, the inclusion of the observer, and the value element stressed and developed to a much greater degree. With these adjustments, we can perhaps view coherence as a modified version of the notion of Gestalt: it is a kind of quantitative but not quantified dyadically structured Gestalt that includes also the observer in its configuration.

IRONIC AND NON-IRONIC COHERENCE

We can note in the above reflections an implicit tension in the idea of coherence, which will serve as an engine of many further developments. For what after all is the criterion for coherence? It is not just any set of items that stick together. In early Chinese thinking, it must always be a set of things that form a coherent grouping also with some human desire. This is clear from the description of flavors and tones that are pleasing to the palate, to harmony, above, and will be relentlessly present in the early philosophers from Mencius to Xunzi to Laozi and Zhuangzi. We can now offer an initial set of criteria for coherence: A grouping counts as a coherence when it creates pleasure, such as the harmonious enjoyment of a flavor or a musical harmony. This pleasure may be described as a further coherence, a metacoherence, that is, the cohering of this harmonized set of elements with some human desire. Usually it is associated also with (a) stability, balance, or equilibrium (a joining with what threatens the health and stability of the organism would be experienced as displeasure), generally conceived as a balance of two opposite qualities in a *roughly quantitative but not strictly quantified* sense, and (b) progeny, growth, continuance. Indeed, this sense of coherence as implying life, continuation, and growth runs through the Mencian reflections on *xing* or Human Nature, on the one hand, into the Neo-Confucian glosses of Li as ceaseless production and reproduction (生生 *sheng sheng*), as derived from the "Great Commentary" to the *Book of Changes*. It is a balancing of contraries that must keep within a certain distance of one another in order to maintain and extend their existence, which is to say, which must be able to change into one another, moving freely from the one to the other. This makes it intelligible as having some particular identity, and this is also the source of its value, which is its ability to sustain itself and create beyond itself.

But this model also brings to our attention an intrinsic countercurrent to coherence, within coherence itself when so conceived, that will have enormous consequences. For there is, as it were, a flip side to the notion of continuance and ceaseless progression—for it can also be viewed as implying a kind of infinite regress. This has consequences for coherence as intelligibility, for intelligibility requires both a particular disjunction between the whole and part, a qualitative contrast between them, and yet at the same time an indissoluble conjunction between them. When total coherence is accomplished—the togetherness of the whole with nothing left out—coherence in the other sense—knowability—is necessarily lost: the whole is unintelligible, can have no name, has nothing outside itself with which to be contrasted, can have no determinate, knowable characteristics. In terms of coherence as readability: when a readable characteristic becomes fully intelligible, one passes smoothly over it, it is no longer noticed. Perfect intelligibility erases intelligibility. In terms of coherence as grouping: when parts cohere perfectly, they become a whole forming a part in a larger whole, demanding a larger context, until the largest, and necessarily incoherent, unintelligible whole is reached. Perfect togetherness and harmony of parts presses forward to a greater whole, which must itself be indeterminate. In terms of coherence as pleasure: when a desire is consummated, it dies. Perfect harmonic coherence between a human desire and some object eliminates the relationship between them altogether. As is noted in the *Zhuangzi*, "To forget the feet indicates the fitness (or comfort, 適 *shi*) of the shoes; to forget the waist indicates the fitness of the belt; when consciousness forgets right and wrong it indicates the fitness of the mind. . . . He who begins in fitness/comfort and is never unfit/uncomfortable has the comfort of forgetting even comfort."[35] Once all the parts cohere into a single something, readable as a one, this means that it has been absorbed as a single unit into something else. The search for ever more coherence is, in other words, inherent, and thus ceaseless. Each coherence cries out for further context. The parts can only cohere if the whole coheres with a greater context, and then this context, including the previous whole, becomes a new internally consistent coherence in search of a yet larger context. We judge something to be coherent only when it coheres with an outside (in the first example, with some of our desires)—but this proposition alone ensures an infinite regress, for once the new coherence is found it becomes the inside seeking a new outside. There is just no limit to how far down or how far up coherence goes; we can keep dividing and keep assembling indefinitely. This flip side implies that the ultimate intelligibility of any definitive identity must be questioned, for the identities of the individual parts was originally conceived as dependent on their relation to the whole; if the whole is unintelligible, there is a sense in which the intelligibility of the parts is also threatened. I call this "ironic" because it means that any attribution of identity can only be meant provisionally, not quite fully literally, inconstantly, temporarily: a name that can be named cannot be a constant name. Whatever coherent name is named, thus, must have something other than a literal meaning—what I call an *ironic* meaning, with an ironic coherence. Indeed, coherence per se can only be attributed to anything ironically, for because what is "truly" coherent is incoherence: each identity, fully thought through, reveals itself to be an effacement of its original putative identity. Put another way, this point concerns the role of "the negative" in this way of thinking, which the pendulum model of coherence also helps us understand. The claim that "coherence" means both "intelligibility" and "value" might suggest that whatever is intelligible is therefore valuable, and therefore that it is impossible even to denote or be aware of the unintelligible or the negatively valued, even as something to be denied or resisted. But the pendulum always suggests a small g good opposed to a small b bad, but also a big G Good which denotes the sustainable relationship between good and bad. Unintelligibility appears within the system of any intelligible coherence in two ways: as the negatively valued half of the constitutive pair, and as the threat to the dissolution of the pair that this embodies. The loss of the health/sickness balance is also the loss of health and the succumbing to sickness. One half of the pair "stands for" the death of the pair, when taken alone, although this is only so because simultaneously it is the presence of both halves of the pair that sustain the desired half. One can "know" the undesirable only in this form of incoherence signaled within any system of coherence, which is always constituted by its relation to a set of desires. This odd asymmetry is the actual conduit leading to a certain inevitable drift from the non-ironic to the ironic conceptions of coherence. Only what is coherent with our desires is intelligible, but the contravening of our desires is intelligible as well, because it is necessarily coherent with them: it is a necessary part of the balance that sustains them. But the very presence of the possible contravening of our desires is a necessary component of the coherence of our desired outcome, and this coherence between what is coherent and what is incoherent with our desires is what allows for the coherent threat of incoherence, allows one to refer to, resist, refute, reject incoherence, which would be strictly impossible if incoherence did not have its coherent avatar within the system of coherence and intelligibility. That coherent avatar of incoherence, the coherent appearance of incoherence itself, is a marker of what we mean by ironic coherence: the coherence (togetherness) which is coherent (readable) only as incoherent (unreadable), the presence of absence, the being of non-being, the dao which is not a dao, the self which is not a self. It is this "ironic" treatment of coherence that we will find in the Daoist works, and it will continue to be the central theme of interest in Neo-Daoism and Chinese Buddhism works as well. But the Confucian texts such as the "Great Learning" and "Doctrine of the Mean," and indeed the entire Yin-Yang system of the *Zhouyi* commentaries, sketch out some non-ironic solutions to the same difficulty, as we shall see below.

I will thus be speaking of "ironic" and the "non-ironic" notions of coherence. These terms need to be carefully defined here at the outset to make the rest of this project comprehensible.

1. The "Non-ironic" notion of Coherence is found in *The Analects,* the *Mencius,* and the early pre-ironic proto-Daoist texts of the *Guanzi.* "Coherence" in this sense means the hanging together of items into groupings, but also coherence in the sense of intelligibility (visibility and readability) and as value. This coherence has a premise and a consequence, each of which are further instances of "coherence." The premise is that these particular coherent groupings "cohere" with human desire and cognitive faculties. In other words, human responses to the world are included among the items that must cohere intelligibly. As we have seen, this involves pleasure and continuity, as premised on balance and proportion. The consequence is that, once these coherences are attained, they lead to the formation of an actual group or species. A coherence coheres with human experience and thereby causes further coherence, either of the human body or personality, the human group, or both.

2. The "Ironic" notion of Coherence is found in the traditional version of the *Laozi* and the Inner Chapters of the *Zhuangzi.* All students of Chinese thought will no doubt have noticed the sudden prevalence of "negative" terms in these texts: terms prefaced with a negation, with "not," with "nothing" (*wu*). We are suddenly confronted with a valorization of *not*-doing, *not*-knowing, *not*-being. These are, of course, not to be taken literally. The are explicitly described as "doing without doing," "knowing without knowing," "being without being." A doing that is nonetheless a not-doing: an ironic form of doing. The word *doing* is now used in an ironic sense only, parasitic on its earlier uses but systematically subverting them. The true doing is, ironically, the doing that does not "do." The true knowing is the knowing that does not "know." The true being is the being that does not "be." This means "what actually accomplishes what X (doing, knowing, being) originally claimed to accomplish is actually not what we call X, but precisely the omission of X. The true X is a non-X. At the back of this, in terms of our current analysis, we can discern this thought: the true coherence is the coherence which is not "coherent." The idea of coherence is here considered "ironic" in the specific sense that it retains a sense of grouping, of "togetherness," and indeed extends it, but also sees that true togetherness of all things further entails an effacement of coherence in the sense of "intelligibility." Therefore, "ironically," the true coherence (togetherness) is incoherent (unintelligible, indiscernible, not definitively identifiable as such).

3. We will also be examining attempts to combine the ironic and the non-ironic usages, which come in two opposite types. The first is the "non-ironic" incorporations of the "ironic" sense of coherence, found in the *Xunzi*, *Liji* texts such as the "Great Learning" and "Doctrine of the Mean," and more elaborately developed in the Yin-Yang concept of *The Book of Changes* (*Zhouyi*) and its Appended Commentaries, along with two further elaborations thereof: the works of Dong Zhongshu and the *Taixuan jing* of Yang Xiong. These developments take place for the most part independently of the development of Li as a central philosophical category, and so will be dealt with in Part One. The second type of compromise proceeds in the opposite direction. It consists of the "ironic" incorporations of the "non-ironic" usage, such as we find in several passage from the Outer and Miscellaneous Chapters of the *Zhuangzi*. This development is inseparable from the growing prominence of the term *Li*, and thus will be addressed in the sequel to this work. The remainder of that forthcoming work will take up the complex intertwinings of the ironic and non-ironic notions of coherence, as embedded in various developments in the concept of Li, as they appear in the Wang Bi/Han Kangbo commentaries on the *Changes*, Guo Xiang's commentary on the *Zhuangzi*, and the Huayan and Tiantai schools of Chinese Buddhism.

THREE

NON-IRONIC COHERENCE AND
NEGOTIABLE CONTINUITY

Let us begin by looking at the non-ironic notions of coherence as they take shape in the texts of the early Chinese philosophical tradition. As noted in the previous chapter, what we are calling the "non-ironic" notion of coherence focuses on three related themes, namely, (1) a *grouping* that is a source of both (2) *value* (as sustainability, pleasure and continuance, usually premised on a quantitative balance between and inclusion of opposite poles) and (3) *intelligibility* (knowability as having a particular qualitative identity). *Intelligible and value-engendering groupings* is the sort of "coherence" we will find to be the central conception explaining much that is mysterious in these texts, in particular the ways in which they avoid the claim that sameness and difference are nonnegotiable final realities in either its realist version (samenesses as fixed nonnegotiable ultimate realities) or its nominalist version (differences alone as ultimately real), and yet also do not adopt the skeptical position that both sameness and difference are arbitrary subjective projections. Similarly, it is what allows them to circumvent claims that the intelligible characteristics of things and the values they embody are either purely internal or purely external to the human observer who identifies and values them. It will also be the matrix of a distinctive notion of omnipresence unlike both the "idealist" and "materialist" versions of the European tradition, as described in chapter 1.

COHERENCE AND OMNIAVAILABILITY OF VALUE
IN CONFUCIUS AND MENCIUS

My intention here is not to give a comprehensive account of the ethics and worldview of the *Analects* and *Mencius*, but rather to call attention to some aspects of these texts that are especially relevant to our problems of mereology, of structures and procedures pertaining to classifying sameness and difference, of conceiving wholes and parts, and their implications for notions of intelligibility, value, and omnipresence. Obviously, however, I cannot do the latter without to some extent adumbrating an interpretation of the assumptions and goals of the texts as a whole. It will be noted that I depict early Confucian ethics here as motivated and justified purely in terms of its relation to human pleasure and desire. I take Mencius very literally at his word when he defines the good as "the desirable" (7B25)—that is, anything at all that anyone at all is capable of desiring.[1] "Good" here is inseparable from desire, a function of desire, parasitic on desire; and desire is parasitic on pleasure, and may be directed to anything anyone takes pleasure in. It should be obvious that I use both these terms in their broadest possible sense: including not only physical and sensual desires and pleasures, but also desires for and pleasures in peace of mind, self-respect, interpersonal harmony, good social order, the approval of spiritual forces, and so on. My view is that *all* of these are types of what I'm calling *coherence*, and it is this alone that will serve as the criterion for which desires and which pleasures become preferred over others, how they are related to each other, and what it means for them to do so. In my view the use of these global terms, far from blurring the distinctions between different desires and pleasures and putting them all on the same level, will on the contrary give us a way to understand the way in which they come to be related to (and distinguished from) one another in early Confucianism, the way they come to be organized and grouped on the basis of, and in terms of, their preexisting continuity of sameness and difference. In addition, I am hoping in this way to do justice to what I consider one of the most distinctive features of the early Confucian approach to ethics: its simultaneous relentless commitment to normative ethical endeavor and human social roles, and its startling and constantly iterated deep continuity with the natural and spontaneous, the biological and even gustatory aspects of human experience. I am hoping the focus on coherence in its many modes can help make sense of early Confucianism in a way that accurately reflects its prima facie ambiguous and confusing continuity between consequence and motive, transcendence and immanence, internalism and externalism, autonomy and heteronomy.

In an obvious and perhaps even trivial sense, I therefore regard Confucianism as understanding ethics as grounded purely in terms of human desires and consequences. But I am not sure whether this means it is a "Consequentialism" in the sense delineated by Bryan Van Norden, in his spirited and illuminating discussion of Confucianism ("Ruism") as a type of virtue ethics, conceived "thinly" along vaguely Aristotelian lines.[2]

For clearly the distinction between "consequentialism," "deontology," and "virtue ethics" does not rest on the presence or absence of a concern for consequences in the broad sense in which I use the term here (meaning *causal effects* of any kind); they are distinguished by *what* consequences they consider decisive, and the way in which they construe the means-ends relation pertaining to these consequences.

This is most obvious in the case of virtue ethics: the achievement of "human flourishing" or "*eudaimonia,*" or "beatitude," or "*arête*" are (again, trivially) *desired consequences*. The desire may be of a particularly refined or unusual kind, or may be a meta-desire having to do with the relation of other desires, but in my view it is simply incoherent to speak of any evaluation of actions, of any kind entirely abstracted from consequences, broadly conceived. The evaluation itself is already a consequence. More specifically, to have succeeded in doing God's will is a result, a potential consequence of an action, the production of one state of affairs over another, whether this involves concrete rewards or simply the condition of being in obedience to God. To endeavor to accord with universal norms involves a desire, and to succeed in doing so is a satisfaction of that desire.

In Kantian deontological ethics, it may seem that a moral deed is not evaluated in terms of a consequence, since there is no second fact in addition to the deed in question that needs to be consulted to make this evaluation. It is evaluated purely in terms of its motivation, which must be a disinterested will to fulfill duty for duty's sake. But the fact that there *is* a motivation at all already puts it sufficiently in the realm of desire and pleasure as I understand them here. Kant's notion of autonomy already *folds in* the desired consequence; in fact, the power and perhaps inevitability of deontological ethics lies precisely in the fact that autonomy in Kant's sense is *tautologically* a case of "getting what one wants": autonomy *means* to do what one wills oneself, in accordance with the intrinsic structure of the will itself, rather than what is imposed upon one from an alien source. To desire something is intrinsically to desire the satisfaction of that desire, which means to have things go in accordance with one's own will rather than in some other way, for a state of affairs to be made so by one's will rather than by some alien force. "My disinterested fulfillment of duty without reference to my personal happiness" is a state of affairs. To want that to be what is the case due to my action is to want to get what I want, which is what it means to want at all. The fact that this tautology converges with its apparent opposite, a complete disregard for any consequence, is perhaps the strongest attraction of deontological ethics, their genius.

I confess that I am unable to understand what motivated action or agency could be if not rooted in some form of desire, which is intrinsically aimed at some sort of consequence, making one state of affairs the case rather than another. Nor is it clear to me what is gained by making the differences between physical or selfish desires and spiritual or altruistic desires ontologically absolute. It is tempting to see this sort of distinction as motivated purely by some sense that this continuity is, as Nivison puts it "unlovely,"[3] a worry that maybe morality itself is in that case not "moral" in the deontological sense,[4] rather than by a desire for theoretical clarity, which indeed seems to be sacrificed when we exclude the continuity between nonmoral and moral desire, *creating* what Nivison himself calls the "paradox of virtue."

Sharing Van Norden's preference for "methodological pluralism,"[5] I see the move away from both consequentialism and deontology and toward virtue ethics, construed as minimizing this apparent dichotomy, as a positive step away from this kind of needless worry, and find much that is clarifying in this approach. Like Van Norden, I see the difference between Confucianism and Mohism largely in terms of the interest of the former and disinterest of the latter in impalpable human states of satisfaction derived from human character and relationships themselves, rather than from material consequences. I also applaud Van Norden's great emphasis on the ethical particularism in early Confucianism, verging close to relativism for deeds but not for agents, and his virtue ethics approach helps to make sense of this in a way that perhaps makes it less alarming to readers accustomed to thinking of ethics as requiring categorical and absolute demands, and those worried about Nivison's worries. I don't share his views about the final role of Heavenly warrant for ethics in Confucianism, nor the teleology that goes with it (both of which, again, would for me in any case simply be other kinds of desired consequence; to in fact succeed in doing what it is our *telos* to do, for example), but the virtues and flourishing he describes are much the kind of consequence I think Confucians most care about. Virtues and flourishing, however, are further analyzable into forms of coherence—bringing out their continuity with other forms of pleasure, social order, and the relation to Heaven, as I'll try to show below.

Confucius as depicted in the *Analects* offers very few general speculative pronouncements, as opposed to ethical comments or responses to specific situations. It is intriguing, however, that this very fact is itself commented on in terms that single out for us a few key phrases. *Analects* 5:13 has Zigong remarking, "We have been able to learn about the expressive forms of the master's cultural accomplishments (*wenzhang* 文章), but not about his words on human nature and the Dao of Heaven" (性與天道 *xing yu tiandao*).[6] These two things Confucius does not speak of at length point us directly to the problems of omnipresence (the Dao of Heaven, assuming for the moment that it would be the most global term available in the discourse of the time, something relevant to every instance of reality) and sameness and difference in the setting of something like a defining class characteristic for human beings (Human Nature). That he is at least reluctant to speak of these things is of course significant in itself. It points us back to the question of the adequacy of language and the process orientation discussed briefly at the beginning of chapter 1, and tradition has often regarded Zigong's remark as indicating not that the master considered these matters unimportant but, quite the contrary, that he considered them too important to be distorted with something so misleading as fixed verbal speculative teachings. This would prove a crucial point of contact with what we will call the "ironic" tradition, which lays immense stress on the unintelligibility of fixed and definable coherence, either in a narrow "particular universal" (such as Human Nature) or the omnipresent "universal universal" (such as the Way of Heaven)—and of course this passage in the *Analects* has been jumped upon by Daoist and Buddhist commentators who wish to stress the continuity with Confucianism. Perhaps even more telling and intriguing is the gloss offered by Zhang Zai 張載 (1020–1077), which would become official Cheng-Zhu Neo-Confucian doctrine. For Zhang reads this passage as meaning that we do not "get to hear" (得而聞 *de er wen*) Confucius's views on these two things because precisely these two things are always innate within us. What we learn about them is not "got" from outside, is never a new acquisition, since we have always had them. Human nature is omnipresent among human beings without exception and inalienable to our being as humans, and the Way of Heaven is strictly omnipresent in all places and events, so it is innate to all things, never lacking, and hence can never be "obtained."

Confucius does, however, have a few things to say about both of these topics. These will be crucial to us for sketching the beginning of the conceptions of coherence operating in the *Analects,* and further into the non-ironic tradition. I will begin with those remarks that are relevant to the question of omnipresence, which are both more numerous and more readily interpretable than those relating to types and classes, for which they additionally form an illuminating premise. For already in this text, we can find some very significant and peculiar ways of hinting toward a certain notion of the pervasion of some observable quality throughout a range of items, and by extension of a kind of Omnipresence. Significantly, these are not always directly concerned with the Way of Heaven, as 5:13 has already suggested. They are focused more squarely on the normatively universal Course of Kings Wen and Wu, the "expressive forms of cultural accomplishment" that Confucius sets himself up as an advocate for, and the ritual program entailed therein.

When asked from whom Confucius had learned what he knew, Zigong replies:

> The Way of Kings Wen and Wu has not yet completely fallen to the ground; it is to be found present in living people. The more worthy know its major aspects, but even the less worthy know

its lesser aspects; hence *there are none who do not have the Way of Kings Wen and Wu in them*. So from whom did our master *not* learn? And yet how could he have had any one constant teacher? (19:22; emphasis added)

This is my "key passage" for interpreting the *Analects*. Here we are presented with a sense in which a certain *specific cultural tradition*, to which special *value* is attached, is omnipresent within the members of a particular community. We are told that it can be found everywhere in that community, but the decisive thing here, the turning of the tables, is that what really actualizes this omnipresence is Confucius himself, that is, his ability to recognize the coherence of these various cultural forms, to ask the right questions, to "thread them together," to borrow a trope he uses elsewhere. The presence of the particular concerns, values, and projects of Confucius is what makes this omnipresence effectively present around him. What actualizes this presence as something readable, the Way of Wen and Wu, is the way it is connected to, interacts with, *coheres* with, the dispositions, cognitive and ethical, of a certain human being, Confucius. This is neither a nominalism nor a realism, and this Way is neither purely internal to Confucius nor existing independently outside him. He does not invent it ex nihilo, but nor does it simply impose itself upon him. If he were not there to see it that way, the fragments of the Way of Wen and Wu, though present everywhere, would not *cohere* into anything intelligible. It is the focus provided by his own activity and presence, his own orientation and disposition of character, that make it come together sustainably and discernibly around him, to be seen as, and indeed to genuinely function as, a resource for his own particular inquiry. The things out there in the world are neither the same as what Confucius sees, nor different from it. He sees an aspect of what is there, and by so seeing makes this aspect, as present in many places, cohere into a particular presence. It is not the only thing there is to see there, nor does it have any independent privilege over other ways of seeing, at least not the privilege of being "the one objectively correct way to see things." The privileging of this way of seeing comes with Confucius's very act of so seeing it, which is what demonstrates and indeed *accomplishes* its coherence and its *value*. The way this eludes both nominalism and realism with respect to real coherences in the world should be noted. It is closely resonant with the Mencian approach to similar problems, discussed below.

COHERENCE AND HEAVEN IN THE *ANALECTS*

To proceed farther in coming to grips with the problem of omnipresence in these texts, we must take up a perennial problem in the interpretation of

Confucius and Mencius: their conception of "Heaven" (天 *tian*). As Philip Ivanhoe and others have noted, the usage of *tian* by both of these figures seems to stand in an odd intermediate position between the full personal theism of Mozi and the full naturalistic atheism of Xunzi. These two extreme positions map easily onto familiar conceptions, and thus appear relatively unproblematic. But the intermediate position on *tian* in the *Analects* and *Mencius* appears to be shot through with an uncomfortable inner tension, making it seem contradictory when the categories of either theism or atheism are applied. Confucius speaks of Heaven as possessing knowledge (9:12), as having intentions or direction that it favors and even "mandates," as even having a special mission for himself (7:3, 9:5). But he also distances himself from any direct intervention of Heaven in the rewarding of virtue, in micromanaging events, responding to explicit prayer, or even articulating its will. We find similar ambivalences in Mencius. Is Heaven personal or impersonal for these thinkers? Does it have an intention, or no intention? What is Heaven for Confucius and Mencius?

Ivanhoe suggests a possible solution that melds profitably with our reflections on coherence here. As is often the case, it rests on the ambiguity of singular and plural in early Chinese grammar, where our unthinking assumption of one or the other obstructs an understanding of the texts and leads to unnecessary confusions and apparently irreconcilable paradoxes. Ivanhoe suggests that the Zhou concept of *Tian*, like the earlier Shang concept of *Shangdi* that it gradually largely replaces, "lacks a distinct personality." And yet, "it was thought to be conscious, purposeful and capable of action."[7] How can we conceive of this power which has no personality, is not a person, and yet is conscious, purposeful, an agent, and moreover endowed with a specific moral agenda? Ivanhoe briefly suggests a possibility: we might conceive of Heaven as a *collective body*, something like a jury or a committee.[8] A collective body may have discernible intentions, standards, powers to act and underwrite missions, as well as its own ethical agenda, and yet be devoid of what we would normally call a particular "personality." In particular, it would be conceived along the lines of the collective body of ancestors, as in the earlier Shang notion of the spiritual realm consisting of the spirits of the deceased, who, as Ivanhoe also notes, were thought to maintain their personalities, their concern with specific purposes in the world, and their consciousness of their earthly life in inverse proportion to the length of time they had been dead. In other words, their personality *fades out* as time goes by after their deaths, and with it their specific earthly interests; they fade more and more into the impersonal qi, or into the faceless collective body of the universal nonhuman forces as a whole. Already here we have a notion of personality and nonpersonality which is not dichotomous; whether or not something is "personal" is a matter of degree, and often will not admit of a straightforward yes or no answer. (Indeed, in accordance with the coherence model, we must regard even a human individual as a coherence that is at once both personal and impersonal, a cohering of parts which have both personal and impersonal aspects, which can be viewed as a unified person, and also as a diffuse set of parts with valences falling outside that coherence, i.e., existing as part of many alternate coherences at once.)

If we accept Ivanhoe's suggestion about the authoritative power of Heaven as a collective entity, we can now easily conceive the ways in which it operates, in line with the notions of selective coherence we have seen at work in Confucius and Mencius, in a way that preserves both its normative and intentional active structure and also its negotiable, open-ended nonactive structure. In fact, we might go a step farther and question whether *tian* is in fact a proper noun naming a deity; we might take it, instead, as a kind of synecdoche, like "Capitol Hill" for the United States legislature.[9] Heaven is the *sky*, the place to which, it is speculated in the *Zuozhuan*, the ethereal gusts of conscious *qi* comprising the *hun*-soul of deceased human beings return. These still semi-personal *hun*-souls would temporarily abide as quasi-persons, maintaining for a while their conscious interests in the state of the world and their connections with living beings and existing human clans and polities, before melding into the mass noun–like bulk of the sky's *qi*, Heaven. This would determine the general overall moral tenor of Heaven at any time. Heaven is the bowl of light pure *qi* into which all the deceased ancestors are mixed, like lumps of batter, lending it for a time their consistencies and flavors. Persons of exceptional moral charisma would naturally have a greater influence on the overall flavor of the batter. A sage would be like concentrated vanilla extract, staining the entire mix with its vanilla flavor with just a few drops.

Naming "Heaven" as the sponsoring power of the Zhou dynasty is, then, not a naming of a single specific deity linked to a single specific ancestor, but to the consensus flavor of the collective institution of Heaven. Even 上帝 *Shangdi* could possibly be construed as an agnostic name of a rank rather than the personal name of a god: meaning, "the highest spiritual power, whoever it may be." But certainly the Zhou dynasty's *tian* looks even more deliberately vague: the spiritual powers-that-be up in the sky. This notion would consort well with the decoupling of the deity-descendent relationship, where sponsorship of the new dynasty is not dependent on an existing blood relation linked to a specific lineage. Heaven, like Capitol Hill, acts, has intentions and preferences, sets limits, can be struggled with or called on for support; but it cannot be a character in a story, the protagonist of a narrative or legend, or walk in the cool of the evening.

Implied here also would be a margin of diversity within the ranks of Heaven, varying factions or undertones to which one might chose to ally oneself. That subset of the heavenly forces with which my own aims and orientation and desires cohere would be my Heaven: the spiritual forces of the world that would underwrite and aid my endeavors in that direction. But this other way of grouping and underlining elements in this same collective group, seen differently, could be coherent with other aims as well: your Heaven, aiding you in your aims, could be an overlapping but not identical Heaven. All would have a role to play in the general functions of Heaven, like the weather, the rain, the wind; but some parts of what is blended into that general cosmic force might be in coherence with your aims, while others might be in coherence with my aims.

What I am suggesting, in a word, is this: Heaven means, for these thinkers, those forces, personal and impersonal and everywhere in between, that are in coherence with the particular mission of the Zhou dynasty and its successors, Confucius and Mencius. Their own actions and orientations choose out and actualize the relevant specific character of Heaven, among all the spiritual forces in the world. Heaven is not the creator of the world; Heaven is a subset of deceased humans and other forces and tendencies, which *cohere* into an identifiable collective entity, with its own character, unified intention, and unified direction of influence, by means of the selective action of "joining oneself" to it and seeing and acting in such a way as to realize and *continue* this coherence. It is not a purely external force to Confucius, just as a collective body in which one is a probationary member is not exclusively external; he will himself join it (and indeed, this helps explain what is meant when Confucius is himself compared to "Heaven" in 19:25, and also why a later Confucian writer of the "Zhongyong" [33] would go so far as to describe the "perfectly sincere" [至誠 *zhicheng*, perfectly internally coherent] person as "So Vast, he is himself Heaven!"), and is already a contributing member.

Moreover, in precisely the way in which we saw that Confucius both "inherits" and in a certain sense "constitutes" the coherence of the "culture" which he represents, he inherits and constitutes the character of Heaven. As is always the case when one is acting within and on behalf of a group of which one is a member, one neither arbitrarily or ad libitum creates or projects its "will" ex nihilo nor receives purely heteronomous commands which one must rigidly execute. As in the case of the participation in the cultural grammar of ritual (discussed below), or the lineage of a particular familial clan, Confucius is nonnegotiably a member of a group, prior to any choice, and yet at the same time decisively constitutes the nature of the group of which he is a part, from which he can only depart in terms of his prior commitment to that group, but which nonetheless requires his own present deed to be actualized in a particular way. He cannot choose not to be a member of this group, but he can choose what sort of group it is that he is a member of. Just which forces of world, nature, culture, and deceased semi-personal spiritual powers are considered to be contributing members to the collective body of which he considers himself a part depend on his own "take" on the trajectory of the tradition he connects to. He is educated in this tradition, and selectively emphasizes those aspects to which he, in both the literal and figurative senses, "connects."

Those elements and powers that cohere with his own ethical intentions are named "Heaven." They are real, as a collective body is real, and have a discernible nonnegotiable range of intentions and agendas. But since a collective body is intrinsically multifarious, there is always room for changes of emphasis, inclusion and exclusion of one or another particular wing or faction within the group, limited by the demands of coherence. Confucius's Heaven will be neither the same nor different from the Heaven of the Duke of Zhou or of Mencius. It is not the same, because more elements have been added as time goes by, and the particular personal presences that have faded to lesser influence have been subtracted. It is not different, because at each stage a coherent general will, in accordance with the circumstances and particular orientation of the present agent—Duke of Zhou, Confucius, Mencius—*and also coherent with the past traditions of collective actions of this collective entity Heaven*—produce different reads, angles, emphases, characteristics for its present force.

Heaven is neither personal nor impersonal, just as an entity such as "The Communist Party" is neither personal nor impersonal. It is a tradition of personalities with various temperaments, intentions, and agendas, which however can be viewed as cohering to at least some minimal degree when some collective action or decision or stand is required. Here the contrast of ritual and law, to be elaborated in detail below, is decisive. These collective decisions may not be decided by direct vote or strict rules of procedure, but more likely, in the Confucian "ritual"-based notion of order, in accordance with various degrees of influence, seniority, hierarchy, moral charisma, fading and emerging as time proceeds. Heaven does not speak. This Politburo gives no explicit directives. Heaven is a tradition, which can cohere in many different ways with its present self-appointed representative. Confucius aligns himself with certain elements in the traditions of the Zhou Heaven, with the deceased and gradually fading personalities of particular exemplars in the past and with the fuzzy-edged realm of natural, cultural, and spiritual impersonal power into which they are merged. Once again we are clear of both sameness and difference, of both nominalism and realism. Heaven is a real power that provides a normative direction and a special mission to Confucius, but simultaneously it is his own mission that defines the exact character of the Heaven whose member and proxy and identifier he is.

The translation of *tian* as simply "Forces" has been suggested by James Behuniak Jr., which he glosses as "'the broadest set of interlocking patterns' within which events proceed."[10] Elsewhere, he further glosses *tian* in a particular context as "the history, experience, culture, institutions, and general processes that have shaped human emergences since Xie was minister to Yao and Shun."[11] The latter gloss suggests that "broadest set of interlocking patterns" should be taken to mean "broadest presently relevant pattern that coheres out of available forces so that they interlock into a congenial and consistent force coherent with the present endeavor," rather than, "the overarching set of interlocking patterns of which all sub-patterns are always component parts."

If so, this is close to my meaning here. Note that although *tian* acts as the limiting facticity, which may either facilitate or frustrate my present endeavor, it is still constitutively relative to the desire for the good defined by that endeavor. If Heaven is not supporting my current plan, it means even the broadest and most powerful coalition of available forces that are in support of my plan is still insufficient to push it through, that the total balance of power at the moment includes overwhelming elements that are at odds with that plan. Here we must apply our pendulum model: Heaven is *constituted* at any time, definitionally, by its relation to our desired good: whatever forces cohere with our desires are the relevant forces constituting a coherent, intelligible Heaven. It is thus in these pre-ironic times definitionally "good," that is to say, always on the side of our dominant aspirations, moral or otherwise. And yet it can thwart these very desires. It is precisely the limiting force that frustrates our best intentions.

This is the "bad" side of the pendulum swing, necessarily complementary to the "good" side we desire: the balance of the two, the overall coherence in terms of which they are alone even intelligible, is what sustains the good, and is itself not good but Good. We can experience the thwarting limitation of Heaven as intelligible, but only within the context of, and in the contrast against, the greater coherence of its relation to our desired good. This does not at all mean that Heaven is really going to satisfy our desires ultimately. It only means that we have no choice but to recognize the superior power of Heaven, not because it is a bare fact, but because *even in terms of our own desires* there is no other choice.

It is the structure of our own desires that defines a certain set of forces coherently as Heaven, but this structure itself requires coherence with those forces for its continuance. The idea is not so esoteric. It is not so dissimilar from what we find in the Book of Job: God is not good in the sense of giving me what I want or enforcing moral justice, but since the only possible way I can get what I want or experience any justice at all is to exist, I must be on God's side as the sole source of that existence. More directly relevant, our conclusion here is close to that of Franklin Perkins, who offers a brilliant and closely reasoned analysis of the problem of Heaven in *Mencius*, concluding that for Mencius the purposes of *tian* are not necessarily moral or benevolent, and yet *tian's* nonbenevolent plan involves the creation of individual natures of things (*xing*), and the individual nature of humans is to be benevolent. By being benevolent, by pursuing our own inborn moral desires, we are following Heaven's plan *for us*, but this in no way guarantees that Heaven shares our desires for benevolence—Heaven desires *us* to strive for benevolence, as part of a plan and nature of its own which may or may not be benevolent in the same way, and which may or may not reward our benevolence in any way other than the very fact that it is a satisfaction of our inborn, *tian*-created nature; and so in being benevolent we are in accord with Heaven, even though Heaven itself is not benevolent and offers no further reward for our benevolence.[12]

Although Perkins's account is consistent with an "objectivist" notion of Heaven, it is also consistent with our "coherence" account. Our existence is our coherence with Heaven—with the broadest coherent set of efficacious forces of all kinds. The exact character of the set of forces coherent with our own existence is correlative with that existence, with its desires, its tendencies, its nature. We do not create Heaven ex nihilo: we are constrained to find a coherent Heaven among prior existing continuities, one that is consistent with what we find ourselves being and wanting. In the language of Hall and Ames, Heaven is the coherent field that organizes itself around the focus that is ourselves. But this field necessarily includes the other swing of the pendulum, the thwarting of ourselves, our perishing as much as our birth, our frustrations as well as our satisfactions—without which it could not provide the intelligible field that makes this focus intelligible, desirable, coherent. For that reason the intelligibility of the field is also the desirability, the Goodness, of that field. Health is health-and-sickness; Goodness is goodness-and-badness; Benevolence is benevolence-and-amorality; Justice is justice-and-injustice. It is a matter of mere nomenclature whether we call Heaven benevolent or not-benevolent. We will see this compelling corroboration of this interpretation, I believe, when we turn to Mencius's discussion of Heaven and Human Nature.

But for now let us stick to the *Analects*. From here we can proceed to the other significant passage in that text with implications for the idea of omnipresence, to be viewed in tandem with the passage about the Way of Kings Wen and Wu. It is found in one of the few places where Confucius *does* speak about Heaven, which also includes one of his only references to natural phenomena. Confucius says he wishes he did not have to speak, just like Heaven doesn't speak. So in one of the rare places where Confucius *does* speak about Heaven, he speaks precisely about the fact that *it* does *not* speak. Zigong says, "But if the Master did not speak, what would we, your disciples, have to transmit (述 *shu*) about you?" That is, what teaching, what example, what accomplishments, what norms? But Confucius replies that this not-speaking of Heaven does not make it devoid of accomplishments; it gives no explicit instructions, and yet "the four seasons proceed through/ from/in it, the hundred [various, all] things are born through/from/in it" (17:19). The ambiguity created by the condensed preposition here leaves much room for speculation concerning the exact relation between Heaven and natural processes, but it is clear that this passage suggests some sort of pervasion of the presence or influence of Heaven throughout the set of all natural entities. We find here again the tension between the normative and the naturalistic notions of Heaven: it produces natural things, which could simply be a reference to the processes of nature; but inasmuch as its production of things is here adduced as an achievement worthy of being transmitted as an instructional model, like the deeds or teachings of a master, we can conclude that the fact that it produces these things is viewed as having something praiseworthy or instructive about it. This could be the example of the ceaseless creative process of nature, as some in the later tradition have read it, or more simply the congeniality and use of Heaven's products as bounty to man: the seasons of the agricultural calendar and the crops, which gives us food. It is not impossible that this refers quite straightforwardly to Heaven as the sky in its meteorological function: when the sky proceeds through the weather patterns of the four seasons, this has the effect of making agricultural products grow. Indeed, this sense of the term is neatly connected with the other meanings of Heaven (normative, intentional, semi-personal) throughout the tradition. This strikes many of those outside the tradition as quite odd: the naturalistic and normative senses seem hard to reconcile.

It is of course possible to simply view Heaven as a purposive moral agent who straightforwardly and intentionally creates both man and things for man's use, and who also makes nonnegotiable moral demands upon man as part of the package. But generally when an ethics is grounded in a notion of a ruling or creating deity, which serves as ultimate warrant for its ethical program, it puts this idea front and center, explicitly invoking it whenever challenged, needing no other justification, as we find in both Mohism and in more familiar Western theisms; it is not glanced off coyly in occasional corners, relegated to vague stylized allusions, going unmentioned in crucial discussions of the system's main tenets, which are instead justified on entirely independent grounds. The very fact that the topic of Heaven's will is so studiously avoided in the *Analects,* and the Mohist response to this omission, are strong evidence that a straightforwardly normative and purposive Heaven is not what the Confucians have in mind. I would suggest that here again we have the perspective of a certain set of desires as the defining criterion: from among all natural phenomena, those which serve man's desires (creating food, the continuation of life) are picked out, and thereby the coherence of value is identifiable in every locus, just as in the case of Confucius finding the Way of Wen and Wu somewhere in all his interlocutors. This does not require the exclusion of the indifferent process of nature—which after all does not "speak," an indication of its disanalogy from human partners—nor of the reality of its value-bearing work. Heaven really does produce things people want and need. But it does so by not being reducible to these human purposes, nor by "ordering them" to be so: it does not speak, it gives no explicit instructions or commands, it makes no laws. It does so, instead, by being coherent with them, by forming a discernible entity with its own discernible tendency *when viewed from the perspective of these human purposes.* Those powers of nature that are susceptible to becoming elements in a total Gestalt which is consistent with and supportive of Confucius's own aspirations, in coherence with the tradition of Kings Wen and Wu, which he also finds around him, are Heaven. Whatever other powers there may be are simply defined out it, are not elements comprising the coherence Heaven. A universal continuity is not assumed, but created from a welter of forces that in themselves are susceptible to both continuity and discontinuity. The connection between value and continuity which we may perhaps draw, looking at these two passages in tandem, plays directly into our theses about coherence in the present work, and will come back frequently in our discussions of Confucian treatments of these problems. Value, as a particular way things are stuck together, a certain continuity between things, past and present, can be found and continued further as a certain type of coherence between the present observing and desiring being and the given environment of variously groupable facts.

The "birthing" and "proceeding" of the various things and seasons are all loci in which the activity of Heaven can be equally found, and in this limited sense Heaven is omnipresently in evidence in every time and place. Heaven would seem to be not the things themselves, but the creative power behind them, and not the seasons themselves, but the medium or force that accounts for their progress. It would then be in evidence everywhere, but not literally omnipresent; it would be *findable* at the roots of any particular thing or event. This is perhaps again in keeping with the performative role of the human subject in the previous passage; the cultural value is findable everywhere, but that doesn't mean that all things are equally valuable. Rather, in each person, some degree or aspect of the Way of Wen and Wu is in evidence, and can be found by the discerning eye. The value comes in a casing or frame of the not-necessarily-valuable, which has to be selected out. This is less omnipresence than a kind of "omniavailability," as it were.

This available quality of Heaven becomes actually present when someone sees it as such, when someone ties all the fragments together with her own activity and vision, thereby making it cohere into an intelligible something that is present wherever such a one may then turn her gaze.

We should note here another important feature of this passage. Confucius, we were told, does not often speak of Heaven. But here it turns out that by not speaking about Heaven, Confucius is *being like* Heaven. Heaven too does not speak, least of all about Heaven. By not-disclosing it, he is revealing it in his own behavior, exemplifying it. Heaven accomplishes its aims without commanding them, or giving explicit directives. Confucius does the same. This will be one of the crucial links to the ironic tradition, where the idea of "doing by not-doing" becomes quite central. But in the *Analects*, we can best understand the efficacy of wordless teaching, and nonexplicit efficacy, through the Confucian notion of *ritual*.

RITUAL VERSUS LAW: CULTURAL GRAMMAR

To understand this we must consider the contrast between law (刑 *xing*) and ritual (禮 *li*) in the *Analects*.[13] This conception of ritual is of course highly idealized, but structurally it is of supreme importance for later philosophical reflection about universality and omnipresence, about coherence in general. Judging purely on the basis of the *Analects*, it would seem that the following differences between law and ritual are stressed:

Law is coercive, sanctioned by force; if broken, one is susceptible to physical punishment. Ritual is noncoercive, sanctioned by social pressure, example, and persuasion; if broken, one is subjected to shame and possible exclusion from the community, but not physical violence. "If you guide the people with government and regulate them with penal law (*xing*) they will just do what they need to do to avoid it, and thus devoid of a sense of shame. If you guide them with the example of your own virtuosity (德 *de*), and regulate them with ritual, they will come to have a sense of shame, and thus become rectified" (2:3). Indeed, we find the Confucius of the *Analects* apparently opposing the death penalty (12:19), which seems to have been accepted as ethically unproblematic by all Chinese governments from ancient times to the present, in favor of the noncoercive persuasive example of virtuosity.[14]

Law—at least statute law, law as commandment—is explicit, clearly stated, and made public, possibly in writing. It is not a law until someone says it is—someone with the power to enforce it. The word comes before the fact. Ritual is initially implicit, unstated and unformalized, a set of unwritten precedents and usages, which may later be formalized, codified, charted, filtered down, tweaked, revised. It is sanctified originally only by tradition, usage, precedent, to which further authority may be added through endorsement by succeeding generations and authorities. The fact comes before the words—the words of many, not of one—which then may streamline, interpret, and modify the facts.

Law is created by and enforced by a centralized authority. Ritual is based on preexisting custom, which is then edited, revised, and systematized by successive sages; it can be modified, albeit slowly and circumspectly, according to current usage, but never created ex nihilo.

Law is blind to position, special circumstances, and rank; it admits of no exceptions, but is applied evenly and mechanically; it is egalitarian and absolute, and effective with equal force at all points in the social fabric. Ritual is rooted in the specific ranks, positions, circumstances, and admits of exceptions for unusual circumstances; it views some persons, times, and places as more intensely weighted than others. What is right for one is not right for another. As long as ranks are hereditary and unchangeable, this means a principled opposition to any form of egalitarianism. When ranks become temporary and changeable, this produces a highly constrained and rotating egalitarianism, namely, one where what is right for one circumstance is not right for another circumstance, or time, where the actors switch roles or play multiple roles while the hierarchy of the roles themselves are rigidly fixed, and where there is necessarily always a hierarchy, that is, where one part of any whole always has greater weight and centrality than others. This would apply, of course, only to the heirs to the positions of authority, the sons in the lineage, for example. A son's subordination is a promissory note for his future domination of his own family. The wives and daughters are not so lucky, although they may have similar roles of dominance to play to their own inferiors in the hierarchy at any given time—daughters-in-law, maidservants, children, and so on. Ritual is a rotating "oligocentrism": some but not all roles within the group play determining, dominant roles, and the occupants of these roles change over time.

Following Chenyang Li's inspired metaphor, building on and diverging from the work of Kwong-loi Shun, we might view ritual as something like a cultural grammar—a *grammar of behavior*.[15] Like a grammar, it is conventional, not natural, existing as a function of a particular community and its history. It is learned as a skill, in native speakers of a language, primarily through emulation, typically in a relationship with a parent or caretaker with whom a child has affective bonds, who teaches through example a structure of communication with built-in evaluative attitudes. Communication and immersion in the grammar of the native tongue and an attitude to the world all take place simultaneously with, perhaps even synonymously with, an emerging sense of oneself. The rules of the grammar are typically learned as rules after the fact, if at all, and can be difficult to formulate definitively; but an inability to state what the rules of grammar are is not an impediment to utilizing the grammar masterfully. It has a normative force, telling us what is right and wrong in the use of language. A sentence that is grammatically incorrect fails to signify, strictly speaking, within the linguistic context, or, if the intended meaning can nonetheless be gleaned, limits the range of communicability of the idea.

Poor grammar can be used to shame people: one's degree of mastery of one's language's grammar can be a mark of social class, marking what "kind" of person one is. Grammar is necessary for the expression of any ideas in the language, but does not itself prescribe what ideas will be expressed, except by implicitly making some ideas more easily expressible, and some less so, and perhaps excluding some possible ideas due to its particular structural limitations. Greater mastery of the grammar allows a greater range of different things to be expressed by means of it. In spite of its normative and conservative structure, without which it could not function at all, it admits of exceptions, particularly in the hands of masterful stylists, but these literary effects will only work if they are seen to be deliberate breakages deployed for emphasis or stylistic effect; the breaker of the grammatical rule must show that he also has complete mastery of what the broken rules are. These exceptions to grammatical rules presuppose the general application of the rule for their effect, and gain their force because they are only occasional and bring with them an implicit contrast to the normal rules. It can change over time, but only very slowly, at the peripheries, and in terms of stable existing practices.

Grammar is inherently conservative, but also always in a process of change, with fuzzy edges, as long as the language remains a living language. It is not created by any one person or at any one time, and it is not enforced by any centralized agency. The penalty for failing to observe is a loss of status, shame, and exclusion from communion with other members of the language group, or loss of recognized membership in a prestigious subset of that group. Ritual functions in a similar way. *Ren* 仁 (Humanity) is related to *li* 禮 (Ritual), as Li masterfully develops his idea, as literary virtuosity is related to the basic rules of grammar. When Confucius calls someone *ren*, it is as if he calling him a literary virtuoso. Literary virtuosity is the ability to use the grammar of a language in ways that are at once new and surprising and also comprehensible to other speakers of that language. The broader the range of ideas one can express, over the greatest scope of subtlety and nuance, the greater a virtuoso one is in the use of that language. It presupposes a thorough mastery of the basic grammar of the language, a penetration into its subtleties, which allow for extraordinary literary effects; but it is not identical to or constituted by merely this mastery of grammar. It can even break the rules of grammar for occasional effect, and in some cases thereby, through the spread of these usages, even influence the future evolution of the grammar. On this model, perhaps we can say that the sage is something like a literary genius. The genius extends virtuosity to the point where his new use of language becomes exemplary, introduces new tropes, and can change the language, as Shakespeare or Emerson or Goethe or Nietzsche did in their use of their inherited languages.

The relevance of all this for our current discussion can be discerned by looking at *Analects* 17:21, one of the most extensive and detailed discussion of the grounds and nature of ritual in the work:

> Zai Wo said, "The three year mourning period is too long. If the exemplary person ceases his ritual practice for three years, the ritual will deteriorate; if he ceases his music for three years, the music will fall apart. The period that it takes for the old grain to wither and the new grain to arise, and for the fires to be rekindled—a year—should be enough."

> Confucius said, "If you ate fine delicacies and wore brocaded clothing [a year after a parent's death], would you feel at ease? (安 *an*)"

> Zai Wo said, "Yes, I would feel at ease."

> Confucius said, "If you would feel at ease, then you should go ahead and do it. But the exemplary person, when he is in mourning, finds that even the finest food doesn't taste sweet, hearing music brings him no pleasure, he is not at ease in his dwelling. This is why he doesn't do these things. But now if you are at ease, then go ahead and do it."

> Zai Wo left, and Confucius said, "Zai Wo is not benevolent (仁 *ren*)! It is only after three years that an infant can even live outside the embrace of his parents. The three year mourning period is the universal mourning of all under heaven (天下之通 喪也 *tianxia zhi tong sang ye*). Did Zai Wo get three years of love from his parents?"

Zai Wo here offers two arguments for a proposed change of ritual practice. The first is pragmatic: the three-year mourning period has negative pragmatic consequences, even in terms of Confucius's own value system: it is detrimental to the flourishing of ritual and music. The second is naturalistic: a model in natural phenomena is given, and suggested as a binding pattern for humans: one year is the natural period for one round of growth and decay in nature. Confucius ignores both these arguments: neither a pragmatic argument alone nor a natural (or divine) argument alone, nor indeed the two in tandem, is decisive for making an ethical evaluation. In themselves, apart from a reference to the particular agent, a disinterested consideration of either practical benefits or Heaven's procedures gives us no determinate ethical guidance. Instead, Confucius asks instead if Zai Wo would "feel at ease" if he did these things after a year. The appeal now seems to be directly to human subjective experience, to the feeling of "ease." This suggests an ultimate source of value that is both pragmatic and naturalistic, but in a different sense: it concerns the (naturalistic) patterning of, and (pragmatic) consequences for, *human feeling.*

This feeling of course does not stand alone: it is part of a larger set of patterns and consequences, in terms of which it has its coherence. But these patternings of feeling and these consequences for feeling are not only one factor that is calculated in, they are the *decisive* factor, given supreme veto power. But what is most significant about this is again how it falls between prescriptive and descriptive, and between nominalism and realism. We can see here how ritual is supposed to be noncoercive, but nonetheless normative. Zai Wo is directed to consider his own feelings. He is not instructed on what to feel, and twice he is told that if he *really* feels this way he should go ahead and act accordingly, whatever the precedent or rule might be. This is the noncoercive side. The normative side comes when Confucius posits the behavior and feelings of the exemplary person in contrast. This is meant to shame Zai Wo, to perhaps spur him to further introspection, and to inspire him to emulation. But more importantly, *the very fact that Confucius does not give an order, that, like Heaven, he does not "speak" (i.e., give a specific directive), is itself meant to be exemplary and normative.* The saying of "go ahead and do it" is itself an *exemplification* of ritual, of noncoercive "yielding," which is itself normative and meant to inspire emulation and shame. The relation of Confucius to Heaven is a ritual-emulative relationship, not a law-following relationship.

When Zai Wo leaves, Confucius critiques him behind his back. Waiting to do it behind his back is another exemplification of ritual, for the benefit of both Zai Wo and the other disciples. The critique is exceptionally mild. Confucius simply notes that Zai Wo is not benevolent (*ren*), but then again Confucius does not admit that any living person is benevolent. It is a term of praise Confucius applies only to dead exemplars. Zai Wo has made a fool of himself, like a bumbling writer of prose attempting a new jazzy phrase or usage that violates traditional grammar, such as, "It ain't no even whatever," trying to make it an accepted usage, and even adding elaborate explanations of why it's so good—a sure sign of protesting too much; any time what's so good about a trope has to be explained, and reasons given for why it ought to catch on, you can be sure the trope is a non-starter. The phrase doesn't quite *work*—and so Confucius notes that Zai Wo is, to continue the metaphor, certainly no virtuoso of prose, that is, he is not *ren*. His suggested revision of grammar is confused and confusing, does not speak from any genuine emotion, it evokes no resonance, it expresses nothing: it fails to communicate.

The grounds of the judgment can be seen when Confucius then gives his own reason for the feeling of unease if the three-year mourning is ignored; a sense of automatic resonance with the previous kindnesses and care of the parents for three years of earliest childhood. During that time the child is entirely dependent on the parents for his sustenance and place in the relatively coherent pattern of the world; now that the parents are dead, they are entirely dependent on the child for their sustenance and place in the relatively coherent pattern of the world. Confucius's final remark is ambiguous; it asks literally if Zai Wo "has" three years of love "with respect to" his parents, which could either mean, "Doesn't he have three years worth of love *for* his parents?" or, alternately, "Didn't he get three years of love *from* his parents?" I have adopted the latter interpretation here. If this reading is correct, Confucius seems to mourn for Zai Wo himself, attributing his failure not to some defect of his own, but to a possible dearth of love from his parents. To continue our metaphor, this would be like saying, "Alas, he's no virtuoso at prose, he just doesn't get the resonances of syntax and allusion of our native tongue; didn't his parents model correct speech for him when he was acquiring basic linguistic competency? He has no sense of the most basic cohesion of deep structure in our language!" Of course, we are talking here not about actual linguistic structure but about a grammar of behavior and affect; the parents model the appropriate behaviors and affects, as competent users of this grammar, in their care for their child, who is thereby also to learn this very grammar.

What makes these behaviors and affects "appropriate"? Not merely their accord with an arbitrary convention (which would line up with externalism in ethics and nominalism in ontology), nor unmodified natural facts (internalism, realism), but communicability. A good sentence needs to say something but also to say it in a way that others can understand. To say something is to add something new, something that genuinely pertains to one's own experience here and now; otherwise, nothing has been said. But to be understood by others is to bring this present experience into a form of accessibility for other experiences. One must make this personal new idea comprehensible to others in terms of existing grammar and language. Without the internal and unique, there is nothing to communicate; without the external and shared, there is no way to communicate. Making-communicable is precisely what the grammar does. Making-communicable is precisely what ritual does. It brings the experience of the parents toward their helpless infant children into a form that is accessible, available, many years later, to the child toward his helpless dead parents. It makes these two opposite experiences coherent with one another.

This brings us to what is crucial here, the declaration that this is the "universal" (*tong*) mourning of all under heaven. This term might at first glance suggest a universality of the no-exceptions kind. But it is asserted here in spite of the fact that Confucius has just admitted, and even apparently condoned, exceptions to it. It is "universal," but that doesn't mean everyone does it, or even necessarily that everyone *should* do it. Rather than fake his feelings, Zai Wo is advised to not do it. This would of course disqualify him from participating in the community of "exemplary men"—but this dropping out would in that case be a good thing. This is still a harsh punishment, and a forceful sanction, with considerable normative power. The penalty for nonobservance of ritual is shame, loss of status, and exclusion. But in spite of this acknowledgment and arguable warranting of its nonobservance, Confucius describes this as the "universal" mourning of *all under heaven*. This suggests that we should not be too quick to understand *tong* to mean anything close to "universal" in the logical sense of admitting of no exceptions; it would be preferable to take the term *tong* in its more literal sense: unrestricted, unobstructed, pervasive, or communicable. It does not mean something applying in each and every case without exception, but only something that can be transferred, can appear in more than one place, can get from one place to another: it is what is *communicable*. It is somewhat like the omniavailability of value cited above: the Way of Wen and Wu is *tong* in the community, which means that it is *findable* everywhere, but in different degrees, and in different aspects. It is findable by the discerning eye of Confucius, but this does not mean everyone is or should be practicing it. This is as close to "universality" as we can get on the ritual model. It admits of, even requires, exceptions. But it links up the elements through which it flows into a coherence, makes them coherent. Ritual, the cultural grammar, is the medium of the communicability of behaviors, allowing them to come together as an intelligible, value-bearing coherence.

Apodictic knowledge must have, in Kant's words, two characteristics: it must be universal (admitting of no exceptions) and it must be necessary. To continue the Kantian theme, we might consider what "necessity" means in the *Analects*. The term that springs to mind is of course 必 *bi*, and although Confucius claims to have eschewed this—the attribution of necessity, or a necessary, exception-free application of any rule (9:4; compare 18:8)—he does also use the term positively in many places. This in itself is quite illuminating: even the rule "I never enunciate rules that admit of no exceptions" admits of exceptions. But one well-known usage of this term is very revealing for our present purposes: "In the proceedings of any three people, there is necessarily my teacher. I choose the good among them as something to follow, and the non-good as something to change" (7:22). Here we have another explicit enunciation of the principle of selection, the central importance of the discerning eye: in one sense there are teachers, but in another sense Confucius *makes* them his teacher by means of his selective gaze. Even more crucially, it can be seen how the nonexemplification of the chosen good also serves as its exemplification: by means of negative example. When someone fails to teach me anything that is worthwhile, he is thereby teaching me something worthwhile. We see the same structure of negation as instantiation in Mencius (6B16): "My refusal to teach someone is itself just a way of teaching him." Structurally, this perhaps gives us a hint on how to understand the "universality" of a mourning practice that is not everywhere observed: it is exemplified even in its nonobservance, which provides an occasion for experiencing and consolidating it further, or goading introspection about it, as in the example of Zai Wo. *Given the gaze of Confucius committed to a particular value orientation*, rooted in a certain selected set of human sentiments, the Way of Wen and Wu, the three-year mourning, and the teacher are available to be found everywhere, even in their nonappearance. It is for this reason that they need not be literally universal and necessary, and yet they are inescapable as long as the underlined condition at the beginning of the previous sentence is in place. They are normative and predictive only in this special sense.

This is the kind of "universality" and "necessity" that apply in a conceptual framework structured by ritual rather than law. Heaven does not speak: Heaven gets its work done through ritual, not through law. The cosmos is a ritual cosmos, not a lawful cosmos. And ritual, as we have seen, works on a coherence model, rather than the nonnegotiable application of universals to particulars, or the absolute separation of particulars. Ritual is not the application of "the same" rule or law to "different" instances: it is a way of effecting harmonious coherence. It is to be noted that the very first mention of the term ritual (禮 *li*) in the *Analects* (1:12) explicitly links ritual and harmony, and harmony specifically as a value: "Of the functions of ritual, harmony is the most valuable. It is this that is most beautiful in the Way of the Former Kings. It is to be followed in small and great matters alike, and yet there are thus some things in it [i.e., those that do not promote harmony] not to be practiced.[16] But to see harmony and try to practice it directly as harmony without regulating it with ritual is also not to be practiced." What matters in ritual is harmony. What matters in harmony is ritual. What is to be practiced is the overlap of these two. Neither harmony alone without ritual, nor ritual alone without harmony, are to be practiced. May we not call this the harmony of harmony and ritual? The direct pleasure of a coherence of parts, like that of diverse flavors or tones, is harmony. The inherited grammar of cultural forms of behavior is ritual. Ritual is a second-order coherence, whereby the coherence of a harmonious, pleasurable existence can be made pleasurably coherent, communicable, with other people in one's culture, and, just as importantly, can continue the coherences of the past into the future. Pleasure, continuance, balance: such is the norm of the ritual cosmos. But as things harmonize coherently in any given case, some of the elements of ritual may be left out; or, conversely, some of the elements of first-order harmony and pleasure may be sacrificed. Such is Heaven's work, which thus gives no universal pronouncements or directives, and does not name or value things once and for all according to a fixed canon of sameness and difference.

RECTIFICATION OF NAMES: NEGOTIATED IDENTITY AS A FUNCTION OF RITUAL

Against this interpretation, Confucius is sometimes alleged to have had at least some kind of realist concept of language on the basis of the famous doctrine of "Rectification of Names." The sole passage where this is explicitly mentioned in the *Analects* is 13:3:

> If names are not rectified, speech will not go smoothly. If speech does not go smoothly, endeavors will not succeed. If endeavors do not succeed, ritual and music will not be established. If ritual and music are not established, punishments will not be accurately applied. If punishments are not accurately applied, the people will have no place to set their hands and feet. Hence the exemplary person's names are necessarily speakable, and his speech is necessarily practicable. In his relation to words the exemplary man cuts no corners.

This authenticity of this passage has sometimes been questioned for several reasons.[17] It shows an anachronistic interest in the theory of language, which is nowhere else clearly in evidence in the text and does not become a focus of technical discussion in Chinese thought until a later period. It uses an extended chain of "if . . . then" arguments in a form that is also lacking elsewhere in the text, but becomes a staple of later Warring States argumentation. Also, its apparently approving reference to punishment is seen to be out of line with the rest of the text, for example, 2:3, cited above. However, let us provisionally accept its authenticity; in any case, it is clear that this doctrine became a commonplace of Confucian thinking sometime in the Warring States period. The reference to punishment is not

necessarily incompatible with 2:3, which after all does not *prohibit* punishment, but merely expresses a preference. Indeed, to prohibit punishments
would be in a certain sense tantamount to prohibiting prohibitions, just as
the actual exclusion of sameness would itself be a sameness, a rigid adher-
ence to an everywhere selfsame law. It is more consistent to see Confucius
as advocating not the exclusion of punitive law by ritual, but rather the
subordination of law to ritual, as this passage clearly states. Similarly, the
stress on harmony does not mean the exclusion of all concepts of sameness,
but rather their subordination to harmony. Law is to be a subset or function of ritual, as sameness is to be a merely instrumental and negotiable
function of harmony.

A number of other passages in the *Analects* are commonly used as
glosses of the doctrine, although they do not mention it by name, most
notably 12:11: "Duke Jing of Qi asked Confucius about governing. He said,
'Let the ruler be a ruler, the minister a minister, the father a father, the
son a son.' The duke said, 'Excellent! Truly, if the ruler is not a ruler, the
minister not a minister, the father not a father and the son not a son, then,
although there may be rice, would I ever get to eat it?" Here the reference
is explicitly to names as social roles, job descriptions for constituent members of the social fabric. The effect of this matching of performance to job
description is indicated rather bluntly by the duke: to get the food into
his mouth. Indeed, in either of these two passages where something like
rectification of names is the most explicitly propounding, this effect is the
sole justification offered. I see no reason to think this is merely a crudely
mercenary interpretation on the part of a craven duke putting an exalted
doctrine into terms he can understand, especially since it accords quite
closely with Confucius's own justification for rectification in the longer (dis-
puted) passage just cited. The justification is thoroughgoingly *consequentialist*.
No other justification is offered anywhere for the rectification of names.

What is crucial here, however, is the way this consequentialism grounds
a procedure that *looks* so realist, so concerned with matching things to their
proper definitions once and for all, and objecting to multiple, ambiguous, or
relativistic applications of names. This can provide us with some insight into
the convergence of normativity and negotiability in these early Confucian
works. The names and identities of things *must* be fixed, *should* be fixed, in
accordance with the norms of grammar facilitating cultural communicability of all desired goods, from material objects to feelings of satisfaction in
communicability itself. They must be fixed, because they are not yet fixed,
except in the omniavailability of the coherence made possible by the discerning eye of the sage.

This discerning is itself a coherence between the entire range of his
desires, themselves hierarchized and made coherent by ritual, and the forces

of tradition and nature which he selectively stresses and organizes in his gaze, as in the case of the Way of Wen and Wu. This involves both the rectification of the names assigned to persons according to their place in the grammatical coherence of the social hierarchy, so that each behaves and receives as befits his own declared station, including the distribution of goods according to the privileges of rank, a crucial aspect of ritual, but also the secondary rectification of the names of *things* that comes when human social roles are thus rectified. Rice becomes truly rice when it is eaten; the good rice becomes the truly good rice when it fulfills its function of getting into the mouth of the duke. Left out in the fields to rot, it is not rice but garbage. In the mouths of commoners, this same rice intended for the duke is not rice but contraband. In 13:3, the reference is perhaps broader, but the pragmatic focus is at least as strong. The reason to rectify the names of things as well as roles is to get things done—especially to get ritual working right, and, subordinated to it, law and punishment. This is also a criterion for what counts as a "rectified" name. This does not mean that there is a real name for each thing in the world, a unique indicator of its essence. It means, as Xunzi's discussion of this doctrine will later make explicit, that the same names are to be used for the same things, with "sameness" defined in accordance with the requirements of a certain set of human desires, and of ritual, the system of harmonizing the desires themselves (within and among members of the human group) and maximizing their satisfaction—the harmony between the desires and the available objects.

A process of adjustment, of picking and choosing, is present even in what is defined as what. Sameness and apparently essential definitions are a function of harmony, not vice versa. The names, the identities, the categories of things are determined in accordance with their place and function of the system of ritual, which is itself the cultural grammar enabling the virtuosity of *ren*, which like literary virtuosity, is a deployment of existing cultural forms to enable *maximal communication*. "Grammar" in this metaphor, as Li Chengyang himself puts it, means syntax, "the rules whereby words or other elements of sentence structure are combined to form acceptable sentences and phrases."[18] Grammar is a kind of structural format of combination or coherence of elements that allows them to form meaningful units. It is how combinations create intelligibilities: coherence. It is, moreover, a cohering of these present forms of coherence with past forms of coherence: the tradition of the language or cultural forms of meaning in which one speaks or acts. Earliest Confucianism is a kind of moral *communication*. This communication means a joining of the inner and the outer, an expression of the most personal and intimate, the novel particularity of the virtuoso's experience, in a form that can move other members of the speech/cultural community to an analogously new experience of their own, one that is simultaneously recognized as communicably public and as ownmost. It is to cohere with the other users of this stable but slowly changing grammar—past, present, and future—making them cohere with each other, in a way that is coherent to them.

CLASSES AND TYPES IN MENCIUS

We mentioned already that, in addition to the Dao of Heaven, there was something else Confucius was reluctant to talk about: Human Nature. He does, however, offer one comment on this subject: "In nature (性 *xing*) they are similar, in practice [due to their differing educations], they are far apart" (17:2). Another term is introduced in relation to the coherence of all members of the human type: "Where there is education, there are no natural types [類 *lei*, here implying further differentiated classes or castes of humans]" (*Analects* 15:38). These two terms, *xing* and *lei*, come to play a central role in non-ironic discourse, especially in the *Mencius* and *Xunzi*, where they are closely connected to the question of categorization, classification, and universals. Even in this unassuming early usage of these terms from the *Analects*, we can already discern an emphasis on the "universal universal" for the human group (disregarding any inborn distinctions among members of this group), but bringing with it an emphasis on the "particular universal" of humanity (or the cultured Chinese) as contrasted to animals (or uncultured barbarians) (5:13).

Mencius picks up both of these implications. The human "type" is genuinely distinct from all other types. But this is not a simple "natural kind" in the sense of an objective species in the world with its own fixed essence, of the Aristotelian type, much less the instantiation of a Platonic Idea. Nor is it simply a nominalist claim, asserting that the ultimate fact about humans is their individual differences, so that those designated as "human" have nothing real conjoining them into an identifiable set other than this designation itself. As Kwong-loi Shun has shown, in analyzing early uses of the term *xing* in texts such as the *Guoyu* and *Zuozhuan*, this term does not refer to a static, objective fact about a particular set of entities, an "essence." Rather, it already folds in precisely the subjective element. As Shun puts it, "in the *Tso-chuan* [*Zuozhuan*] and the *Kuo-yu* [*Guoyu*], the use of 'hsing' [*xing*] has evolved to refer not just to the direction of growth of a thing over a lifetime, but also to needs and desires that a thing has in being alive or to certain tendencies characteristic of a thing, where such tendencies may or may not be ethically desirable."[19] In other words, the term includes a reference to direction and to desires: to the act of valuing. Indeed, the term *xing* is used interchangeably with *sheng* 生 in many early texts—the same character without the "heart" radical—which has led many commentators to speculate that they were in fact one and the same word in early times. But *sheng* implies both "birth" and "life." It can mean what is inborn, what one is born with, and thus, by a very slight extension, what one always has, what is constant and characteristic about this particular creature as such: something like an unchangeable identifying characteristic, an essence. But it can also mean "being and staying alive," growing, living, which brings with it the ideas of direction, need, and desire. Both constancy and change are directly implied in this term, combining "what makes this identifiably present as this thing (its constant character)" and "what values it embodies" and "its continuance into the future"—i.e., intelligibility, value, and continuance, crucial components of what we are calling "coherence." These considerations alter the contours of the picture decisively, and helps explain some of the difficulties we find in Mencius's treatment of human nature.

"Sameness" and "difference" translate quite directly into "internal" and "external": what is "internal" to me is in some sense "the same" as me, what is "different" is "external" to me. If internal and external can be defined definitively and nonnegotiably, sameness and difference can also be so determined. The question of "internal" and "external" is of course the focus of one of the central dialogues in the *Mencius,* the debate with Gaozi over whether Rightness is "internal" or "external," which comes in the context of a discussion about what constitutes human nature.[20] The question about Rightness concerns whether it is to be construed as part of, internal to, that nature, or not. Interpreters have been much confused by the fact that Mencius can sometimes superficially sound like a nominalist and sometimes like a realist with respect to natural kinds when he defends the goodness of human nature against Gaozi. When Gaozi suggests that the relation of human nature to Rightness is like that between trees and the wooden vessels that can be made from them, a trope reminiscent of the "vessel/unhewn" trope found in Daoist works, although deployed with a different intent, Mencius sees the inevitable Daoist conclusions to which this leads, and gives a straightforward pragmatist argument against it: this implies that you must damage the nature to make Rightness, and this will make people dislike Rightness (6A1). Here, Mencius seems like a pragmatic nominalist: we had better *call* this the Nature, as it more useful for us this way.

But then Gaozi says human nature is like whirling water, which can flow out toward either good or evil with the indifference of water that may flow east or west depending on where a channel is opened up for it. It has its own intrinsic impetus to move in either direction. Mencius answers by changing the metaphor: although water is indifferent to east or west, it is not indifferent to up and down, and although it can be forced to fly up, its nature is definitely to flow downward (6A2). Here Mencius sounds like a realist: human nature has a definite, real, unchangeable nature. In particular, the "Goodness" he speaks of has a role that does not function like other possible predicates, and appears to trump the nominalism of his preceding response. This, as we shall see, is only apparent: Goodness in Mencius's sense will fold the previous pragmatic nominalist move into itself.

We have had the two opposite extremes adumbrated in 6A1 and 6A2. It is in 6A3 that the argument turns directly toward our key issues of the types and shared qualities, in the context of his ethical theory. In this dialogue and the one that follows (6A4) we have the nascent and unsteady "sameness/difference" model explicitly distinguished from the developing "coherence" model most clearly, showing us both the availability of the former in the tradition and also why it will come to be entirely subsumed within the latter. Gaozi contends in 6A3 that "the nature" is a generic term that simply means whatever one is born with, the innate.[21] Mencius asks if he means that "the nature" of all born things is the same, that is, just the quality of inbornness as such, just as "the whiteness" of all white things are "alike" (猶 you). Gaozi says that is what he means, to which Mencius replies, "Does this mean a dog's nature is the same as a cow's nature, and a cow's nature is the same as a human's nature?" (6A3). This rhetorical question obviously implies a negative response. Xing is seen here as a very special "universal," one that is at once the most general and the most specific, both differentiating and unifying.

Thus far it might be possible to read Mencius as granted this sense of real alikeness, if not sameness, to all the whites, but not to all the "natures," simply as a clarification of Gaozi's own meaning, without accepting it. But in 6A4 he explicitly differentiates[22] the type of class membership pertaining to terms of ethical concern, such as Rightness and Human Nature, and that applicable to ordinary general terms such as "white" as analyzed in Mohist logic. Unlike the later Gongsun Long dialogue discussed in the previous chapter, Mencius does not yet try to argue that this same/different model of whiteness itself is insupportable; in these pre-ironic days it is still sufficient to dismiss the broader question of general types for things in general as an irrelevancy. As the White Horse controversy and the subsequent ironic and post-ironic developments show, the later tradition will have to find a way of bringing even these ordinary terms into the coherence model, which almost sets the agenda for later Chinese metaphysics considered as a whole. Basically, what Mencius does here for "nature" and "human nature" will later be done for *any* apparently unchanged or seemingly universal term, even of the most ordinary object or quality. But this still leaves unclear exactly what Mencius himself means by xing, human nature.

The attempt to resolve this tension by reducing Mencius's apparent pragmatic nominalism to an ultimate commitment to realism, or, conversely, his apparent realism to an ultimate nominalism, specifically in relation to

the term *xing*, have produced continuing perplexity among Mencius's interpreters. It is here that we hope our alternate model of coherence can help.
For in the terms we've been developing here, Mencius is saying that Gaozi's
position is "incoherent" and in a very specific sense: it does not cohere
with the most important of human desires, the desire to make the human
personality coherent, and to make the human community coherent with
this personality, and finally, most importantly, to make the human community itself coherent as having this intelligible, sustainable, and valued
character, its "human nature." Calling certain features "the nature" is better
(the nominalist component) because it picks out and groups, thereby making genuinely intelligible, the coherence "humanity." It is "omniavailable"
within all members of the community; but it does not actually cohere (come
together sustainably and intelligibly) until it is so named.

The key passage for understanding this, I think, and a more useful
starting point for any discussion of Mencius than his pronouncements on
the goodness of human nature, on the floodlike *qi*, on the heartmind, on
Heaven, on the relation of benefit and rightness—giving us the lever by
which to understand all of them—is the following, which brings us straight
to the heart of the matter:

> The way the mouth is disposed toward flavors, the eye toward forms,
> the ear toward sounds, the nose toward scents, the four limbs toward
> comfort is a matter of [Human] Nature (性也 *xing ye*). But there
> is also decree (命 *ming*) in them, so the exemplary man does not
> call them [Human] Nature. The way Humanity is involved in the
> relation between father and son, Rightness in the relation between
> lord and minister, Ritual in the relation between guest and host,
> and Wisdom in the worthy, the sage in the Way of Heaven are all
> matters of the Decree. But there is [Human] Nature in them, so
> the exemplary man does not call them Decree. (7B24)[23]

Mencius here posits the real existence of a group of genuine human inclinations, *all* of which can be described in two alternate ways. All of them
are "the Decree"—i.e., simple given facts of the matter, which we can do
nothing to alter—and all of them are Human Nature, which here means
what is inborn and what is distinctive to human beings, what they attain
without making an effort, and how they will grow if both unobstructed and
properly nourished—i.e., we may say, if given the appropriate context, a
context with which they are coherent. This largely boils down to a question
of how to *name* those natural impulses. Mencius states explicitly that there
is no qualitative or elemental distinction between bodily desires and the
seeds of morality, a point he makes repeatedly, most noticeably (in the very

next entry in the *Mencius*) in his flat definition of the Good: "The Good is the desirable (可欲 *keyu*)" (7B25). I would argue, as mentioned above, that this bold statement must be taken in its most direct and elemental sense: whatever *can* be desired is the good (not, for example, in the tautological sense of "what is *truly* worth desiring is the good").

This is clear also in Mencius's frequent comparison of moral desires to gustatory pleasures. In one place (6A8) he compares the desire for life and the desire for morality to the appetite for fish and bear claw (a delicacy), respectively, simply a matter of greater and lesser desire. In another (6A7), the desire for Rightness and Coherence (Li) is said to please the heart in just the way fine foods please the palate. We will say more about these two examples, and the general question of larger and smaller desires in the Mencius, below. But what is crucial in the passage just quoted is that the exemplary person (*junzi*) *calls* one set of desires "the Decree" and the other "the Nature" for pragmatic and pedagogical reasons. A different holistic alloy of simple facticity and distinctively human potentials is made from these elements in the two cases. In other words, "the relation of benevolence to the interaction of father and son" is a natural fact just like the mouth's desire for good flavor (6A8), but since the former and not the latter can be expanded into a full virtue, it is preferable that the former be retrospectively described as "the Nature" rather than "the Decree," a term that should be reserved for facts of the latter type. This passage implies that "the Decree" (natural facticity, which is unchange-able by human agency) and "the Nature" (which for Mencius possesses the potential for "good") can both be applied to *all* the functions listed: the mor-ally relevant as well as the morally irrelevant or potentially harmful. Either of these two terms (equivalent to "value"—the nature—and "non-value"—the decree) can be applied to the *total* field of value and non-value. "Value" would then be a name we give to the totality "value plus non-value" (in this case, the total set of spontaneous responses and attractions) when it comes to be contextualized within a larger whole (i.e., that which includes the fully devel-oped virtues deriving therefrom), while "non-value" would be what we are to call *this same whole* when it is not so contextualized. When the "value" side of the dyad is the focus, the whole is called "value"; when the "non-value" side is the focus, the whole is called "non-value." Focus in this case would be a function of the greater whole to which the dyad was able to penetrate in its developmental relations. When integrated coherently into the larger whole, the parts that form the bridge to this larger whole—for this reason called "good"—become the focal aspect which serves to determine the overall quality of the whole set of spontaneous human inclinations, and thus can be legitimately used as a name for that whole. When this total dyad is isolated, or incoherently self-conflicted, the non-value side is illuminated, and it is then in its entirety to be called "the Decree."

Mencius wants to restrict the usage of the term *Human Nature*, giving it a narrower range than its "literal" meaning—delineated clearly in this passage—in a way that is coherent with his own value perspective. Henceforth, the term *Nature* as used by the Exemplary Man will signify not just what is inborn, effortless, and coherent in human beings, nor whatever can form a coherent whole if unobstructed and nourished, but rather what differentiates this group, human beings, from all other groups of living creatures. Mencius argues that the human type is differentiated from the other types by a very small difference. Quantitatively speaking, they are almost the same (Mencius 4B19, 4B28). Mencius offers us several criteria for which inclinations among all those existing in the human being are to count as the Nature. The distinguishing marks of this group are *to be* singled out as significant, privileged with the name "Human Nature" and cultivated as such, for the following reasons:

1. Because certain of these spontaneous inclinations in humans are not shared by other animals. However, this "defining quality of the group" is not viewed as a universal or natural kind that defines or unifies the group, as it were, from without. Rather, these are the qualities which, when fully realized and embodied by a particular member of the group, namely, a sage, actually serve as the "efficient cause" of the actual, literal "unity" of the group. That is, as Mencius says, people actually gather around a sage, a person who fully exemplifies "Human Nature," and form a coherent social group by spontaneously cohering with him, feeling the coherence between their own desires and his behavior. They are drawn to him, and cluster together with him, due to his exemplification of these qualities; their liking for these qualities, and the behavior that follows from it, are in turn coherent with these qualities, and group them with him (6A6, 6A7, 5A7).

2. Because the objects of certain of our spontaneous desires—namely those for Benevolence, Rightness, Ritual, and Wisdom—are not reduced by being shared, but rather are increased in intensity when others also partake of them. This is not true of the natural desires for material things (wealth, food, etc.); when I possess these things, that means you do not, and vice versa. To share them with others means to decrease my own store of them. The natural desires for Benevolence and the others, on the other hand, are like the enjoyment of music; the pleasure is increased the more they are shared. By letting others partake of them, I have more myself. Thus the pursuit of this set of desires

circumvents the problem of the scarcity of goods. The expansion of these desires therefore satisfies the most desires, brings the greatest joy, and leads to a further coherence between different selves, rather than a confrontation or competition between them, which would result if we privileged desires for material goods or honors that are in limited supply (1A2, 1A7, 1B3, 1B5, 6A8, 7A23, 7A27).

3. Because these desires can be attained without depending on external conditions; as Confucius said, "When I want to be Benevolent, Benevolence is there." Mencius echoes this sentiment (6A6, 7A3). Again, they therefore allow for greater satisfaction of desires.

4. Because the development of this set of desires (development again meaning the spontaneous growth allowed by placing them in the right context, i.e., a context that nourishes them and does not obstruct this growth) also allows the flourishing of the *other* set of desires, the desires for material goods, pleasures and honors, which spontaneously rally around them, exactly as the people rally around the sage (4A9, 6A6, 6A14, 6A15). This nature is a harmonious coherence which, when humans harmoniously cohere with it, leads to further harmonious coherence.

Tang Junyi, one of the few scholars who seems to agree with me that 7B24 is the decisive passage for understanding Mencius's doctrine concerning "the Nature," chronicles his progressive interpretations of the criterion being adduced here to distinguish between the Nature and the Decree. His early view, he says, was that the Nature concerned desires that are internal in the sense that their satisfaction can be obtained without external support (my reason 3). He cites Fung Yu-lan as contributing also my reason 1, to wit, that these are the features that distinguish humans from other animals—a point that perhaps bears on Feng's interest in equivalents to Platonic forms and formal definitional essences in Chinese thought. This point of view obscures, in my view, the peculiar Mencian twist on this point, namely, that this is not just a distinguishing feature in the passive sense, but is actually what makes the species "humans" literally and actively cohere as a group. Finally, Tang abandons his earlier view and finally arrives at a view that corresponds to my reason 4, which also includes considerations I classify under reason 2: the Decree-desires are limited by, and encompassable in, the Nature-desires.

Tang's analysis emphasizes the hierarchy between the two: the Nature is a "higher" level that controls and subsumes the Decree-desires, which are "lower." Referring to 6A15, his emphasis is on how the large (the Nature) can include and control the small, but not vice versa. Tang identifies the Nature with the mind, in particular its own tendency for growth and generation, and the Decree with the natural desires for visceral pleasures, and goes on to distinguish four senses in which the Nature controls and subsumes the Decree: (1) the mind includes the natural desires, seeking to satisfy the desires of both the self and others; (2) the mind inherits and continues the desires, as in the filial project of continuing the family line; (3) the mind brings the desires to their full realization in practice, as in Mencius's notions of how virtue transforms the physical body and brings it to perfection; and (4) the mind transcends the desires, as in the prioritizing of the moral desires evident in martyrdom and sacrifice for the sake of the Nature-desires.[24]

This is a useful refinement of the point, with which I am in general agreement. However, rather than represent this as an abandonment of the criteria listed as 1 and 3 above, I would prefer to see these four criteria as operating simultaneously. Kwong-loi Shun makes a similar suggestion after enumerating three explanations of the reason to privilege the ethical dispositions. The first two are among the reasons I have just offered: their uniqueness to humans as opposed to other animals, and their lying within human control. The third, representing Tang Junyi's mature position, is purely normative: "their development has priority over other pursuits," which is to say, "they are pursuits to which other pursuits should be subordinated."[25] As is no doubt abundantly evident by now, I am unable to understand what this "should" means if it is regarded as a self-standing datum of some kind, unrelated to the other criteria and to the naturalistic problem of the satisfaction of human desires, including the desires for self-respect or ritual probity or harmonious relationship, in continuity and *coherence* with the physical desires.

Shun notes, correctly, that the three reasons are not necessarily mutually implicative either logically or empirically, but goes on to suggest that for Mencius at least, on the basis of his utilization of all three reasons, they "are not unrelated." My proposal here is that, for Mencius, what we call "normative" and "descriptive" are equally parts of the coherence of the entire set of desires and conditions pertaining to human beings, and both of these aspects can therefore be picked out in the very act of identifying a coherent "nature" or "decree." What we call the "normative" dimension is the "sage's" act of finding this set of dispositions coherent, intelligible, *as* the Nature or the Decree, and furthering that coherence with the social system of which he is a coherent part by going on to *call it that*. For anything to be considered the Nature, it is necessary for it to fulfill all four. Each is a necessary but not sufficient condition for this classification; only all four together are decisive.

Hence, I must disagree with Tang on a more fundamental level. Tang reads Mencius as making a realist claim here, adducing the actual criteria for what really is the Nature and what really is the Decree. This ignores the explicit claim of the text (noted by Dai Zhen and Jiao Xun, whose reading Tang cites but rejects), its most distinctive feature, that is, the statement that "all this is Decree, and all this is the Nature, but the exemplary man *calls* some parts Decree and some parts Nature." It is the nominalist—one might even say performative—side of Mencius's doctrine concerning the Nature that Tang is unwilling to acknowledge here.

Indeed, we can see here already the contours of a distinctive position concerning coherence, or types and classes, which is neither nominalist nor realist. On the one hand, the names that identify what is what, which items can be classed under what category, are created by the intervention of the exemplary person; he calls some aspects of the human person Human Nature, and others merely the Decree, not because these are different natural kinds existing objectively external to his judgment, but because doing so coheres with his own value inclinations, as described above.

However, this is not pure nominalism, for two reasons. First, as we have seen, there are in fact real distinctions between these different items on the basis of which different classifications can be made—there are certain criteria which the exemplary person uses to decide which things go in which group, and these criteria directly relate to real observed facts about these elements. The more crucial point, however, is that although these sets of similarities and differences really exist, and this way of grouping things does in fact point out genuine coherences in the found world, they are *not the only way* in which things could be grouped; there are potentially other sorts of coherences, which would cohere with other value orientations (those of nonexemplary persons, for example), which would be *equally findable* in the world.

Mencius does make a crucial "realist" claim, right in the passage where he refers to Li/coherence (6A7): there he tells us that "there is" (有 *you*) a sameness to what human mouths enjoy in flavors, what eyes enjoy in sights, and so on, up to and including what hearts delight in among the available coherences and ways of fitting together (義理 *yi* and Li). The sages and exemplary persons are the ones who, like gourmet chefs, discover those coherences and rightnesses that are most pleasing to my, human, heart, even before I know what they are. It is especially noteworthy that Mencius in this passage describes these preferences shared by all palates and all hearts belonging to members of the same "species" (*lei*) as 同 *tong*, "the same," precisely the word that was contrasted negatively to *he*, harmony, in the passages from the *Analects* and the *Gouyu* quoted previously. This "sameness" is certainly being adduced as a criterion for membership in such a species.

Mencius gives the example of planting grains; if the conditions of the planting are the same (the soil, the time, and so on), the same seeds will mature
in the same way. If they differ, it will be because of environmental factors.
But Mencius concludes, significantly, by saying, "Thus whenever things are
judged to be of the same species-type, it is a matter of adducing wherein
they are similar" (故凡同類者舉相似 gu fan tongleizhe ju xiangsi). Xiangsi
means a resemblance, and the ju (raise, adduce, as an example) here can be
read as a remaining hint of the pragmatic allegiance—a *decision* to adduce
the side of similarity, in spite of equally real differences.

Mencius uses the term xiangsi (similar) as a definition of "sameness"
(tong) throughout the rest of the passage.[26] He quotes a certain Longzi as
saying, in this connection, "When someone makes a shoe without knowing
the foot it is for, at least I am sure he will not make a basket." Mencius
remarks, "The similarity (xiangsi) between all shoes is due to the sameness
(tong) of all feet in the world." The pragmatic implication of this example
is, I think, quite significant here. Feet are similar *enough*, for the purposes
of the desire for footwear, to give us some parameters of what makes a
decent shoe as opposed to a basket. The reference to a particular purpose
and desire—in this case, to be effectively shoed—is what determines which
aspects shall be adduced (ju) as sufficiently similar (xiangsi) to allow us to
classify all feet as member of the same (tong) class in this case. This is what
I mean by a conception of sameness that is subordinated to a notion of
harmony; it is the harmonious relation to an other—the human desire—that
makes these items "the same." Their alleged sameness is a function of this
harmony, and not vice versa. They will remain the same as long as this
harmony persists—and no longer.

This sense of sameness remains, if we examine the overall context
of Mencius's thought, subordinated to the stress on harmony, or the coherence of qualitatively different elements in a social totality to maximize the
satisfaction of desires. Indeed, the one other important usage of the term Li
in the *Mencius* explicitly relates it to *harmony* of differences, playing on a
musical metaphor. Mencius tells of various ancient sages, each of which is
a "sage" of some one particular virtue, with "sagehood" defined as in 7B25:
sageliness means to have something desirable—a good, a virtue—within
oneself genuinely and to the point of fullness and fruition, creating an
illuminating greatness which has the effect of transforming other people,
serving as an exemplar that inspires them to change. Bo Yi was the sage
of strict purity; his example inspired the lax and cowardly to become more
principled and firm-willed. Yi Yin was the sage of responsibility; Liuxia Hui
was the sage of easy-goingness—literally, harmony (he), i.e., harmonizing
with other people and with his situation. Confucius, however, was the sage
of timeliness. Mencius describes this Confucius as the "great symphony,"

literally, the great collecting together, presumably of all the other virtues just listed, to the point of completion. He explains this musical trope as follows: "The great symphony means that the metal chimes and the jade responds. The metal chime is the stripelike-orderly coherence (條理 *tiaoli*) of the beginning of the piece. The response of the jade is the stripelike-orderly coherence of the end of the piece. The orderly coherence of the beginning is a matter of wisdom, while the orderly coherence of the end is a matter of sagehood" (5B1). Here, "timeliness" is presented as a kind of second order harmony, beyond the monolithic harmony of Liuxia Hui: one that creates a harmonious coherence between being harmonious (easy-going) and being strict, participating and withdrawing, combining all these contrary virtues as the sounds of various musicians combine to form a harmony. This means coherence both of the beginning and the end; coherence of the beginning is wisdom, that is, one's own practice, making one's own character a harmonious blend of the various contrasted virtues. Coherence of the end is a matter of sagehood, that is, the power to inspire and to serve as an exemplar, which means the broader coherence between the self and others. It is coherence in a further sense of "reaching" other people, as the archery metaphor that follows makes clear.

This conception of harmony as a combination of differences, rather than strict sameness in the sense of absolute conformity or reiteration of a genuinely selfsame thing, is evident whenever Mencius speaks concretely about his understanding of either personal or social coherence. The sages discover what coherences in the world cohere with a heart that is, for these purposes, sufficiently similar to mine—that is to say, a human heart, or that part of it which is "the greater part" of the organism (6A14, 15), the one that allows the other parts *also* to be satisfied, so that the organism coheres and is not at crosspurposes with itself. Mencius gives the example here of nourishing the shoulder as opposed to the finger; a healthy shoulder allows the finger also to flourish, whereas nourishing the finger while starving the shoulder will result ultimately in destroying the finger as well.

The privileging and development of this greater part further allows the human social group to harmoniously cohere in the same way around this exemplary member. He whose organism coheres around that subset of inborn desires to which it is suggested we give the name Human Nature serves to inspire a further, broader coherence in the community. This distinctively human heart is the "nature" of the human-heart, the privileged set of desires, which Mencius above singles out as the Nature as opposed to merely the Decree. This claim about a common set of desires that will be found shared by all human hearts is the crucial weak point, the realist assertion, that will later fall subject to Zhuangzi's skeptical relativism. But the point still stands that, for Mencius, there exist an overabundance of real coherences in the world, and also in our own desires, which do not necessarily cohere into a single synordinate cosmos until the intervention of the exemplary man realizes the potential to make them cohere harmoniously.

The second reason Mencius is not a pure nominalist is that this way of grouping is performative not merely on an epistemological level, but on a literal physical level: by making these decisions about which ways to group things linguistically, actual changes occur in the real world that produce the genuine coherent social group so named. Coherence is an actual social effect of naming. We may perhaps go so far as to say that it is because the sage picks out just these coherences from all the coherences in the world, these coherences that cohere with his own value preferences, that a genuinely coherent species called "human beings" *comes to exist*, at least manifestly. The sage has the virtue of "making manifest the virtue of manifestation (明明德 *ming ming de*)," as the "Great Learning" puts it. In telling how Heaven selected Shun as Yao's successor, rather than Yao's son, Mencius states that spontaneously the minstrels sang of Shun and people went to Shun to resolve their problems, not to Yao's son (5A5). Elsewhere, he quotes an Ode that makes explicit the relation of this "attraction" to the Nature: "Heaven produces the teeming masses/Where there is a thing there is a norm/ The people hold to their sacred constancy/And are attracted to superior virtue" (6A6). The word here translated as "sacred constancy" is *yi*, originally denoting a type of ritual implement which was constant in the sense of being used not for any one special ceremony, but present and integral for all rituals. "Holding to the *yi*" is a metaphorical figure for remaining oriented toward the element that is common in all instances of ritual, something present in all enactments of sacred sacrifice to the valued ancestor. The Ode, as used by Mencius, gives us a sense of what is meant by the "virtue of manifestation": by being manifested in one person, it draws others to rally and group around him. It is their "nature" ("sacred constancy"—what is always so) to be so attracted to the manifestation of their own "nature," *which is in fact what makes it their nature,* what makes them a genuine coherent group. By manifesting (being expressed in a greater and greater range), being made apparent, being made coherent (readable, and harmoniously grouped), it brings further manifestation, further coherence: manifesting the virtue of manifestation, cohering with the coherence. A new coherence is created which was not there to be picked out before, and a truly coherent social group is formed. Human nature is in this sense "created" by the sage not only epistemologically; it becomes a real fact in the world once he has created it, a datum among the coherences, which any further valuation will have to either adopt or ignore. The crucial premise is that human response is included among the data that must cohere for there to be true coherence: value, "the desirable," is included among the elements that must be included to make a true coherence, which introduces a definitional relation to human desires. This makes sameness and difference, as functions of this coherence, fundamentally negotiable. What counts as "the same thing" in one context will not necessarily count as "the same thing" in another context.

We can now see how the nominalist/realist problem impacts on our understanding of Mencius's moral theory. Given the holistic premises discussed above, Mencius is in the strict sense neither an internalist nor an externalist, in the sense in which Edward Slingerland has usefully introduced these terms. He does not hold that our inborn nature is good in the sense of objectively being, or necessarily growing into, perfect accordance with the highest ethical norms if left to itself, or prior to interference from external sources. Nor does he hold that goodness is grafted onto a nature that has no internal resources to receive it. He holds that the inborn nature has a great number of potentials, among which are some that, if allowed and encouraged to grow and flourish, have the power to integrate the others into a "good" whole. These others have the power to *be* so integrated. For this to happen, a performative act of deeming precisely these selected potentials as what "truly" belongs to one's nature—not in the objective sense, but in an almost voluntaristic sense, ultimately motivated by a form of enlightened self-interest on the part of the far-seeing sages. They see that their own desires are best satisfied through the satisfaction of the desires of others, and that this is to be achieved by deeming things in this way, grouping this set of impulses as the nature and those others as merely the decree. We "have always been good" only retrospectively, in the wake of the deed of choosing to see it that way, which is done by seeing oneself in continuity with— coherent with—the tradition of past sages who so saw it. By using the term *Human Nature* in a particular way, Mencius creates a harmonious grouping between past usages of the term by sagacious exemplars of the tradition, the totality of human inclinations, and the group of existing humans. By seeing the Nature in this way, and acting accordingly, he serves as a "Center" to the swinging pendulum, holding together the material desires of the Decree and the cultural and ethical desires of the Nature, the tradition itself, and the human community. These different things are made coherent through this deed, like the extremes of the pendulum swing, which is to say: (1) they are *held together*, grouped, so that none moves "too far" from the others; (2) they are *intelligible*, can be known and identified as a recognizable characteristic; (3) they create maximal pleasure and satisfaction, actualize value ("the desirable"); (4) they are sustainable and can thus continue into the future. This is what we mean by non-ironic coherence.

OMNIPRESENCE IN MENCIUS

Mencius does not present any unambiguously explicit notion of the Omnipresent, but he does make some pregnant statements where he hints at something that later tradition could pick up to construct the Confucian conception of Omnipresent value. Among them we find the following passage, which combines some of this sense of "picking and choosing" applied to an omniavailability, in a way that is deeply resonant with the key passage on "decree" and "the nature" quoted above. The topic again is "the Decree":

> Mencius said, "There is nothing which is not the Decree. But we only willingly accept what is correct in it (順受其正 *shun shou qi zheng*). For this reason, he who understands the Decree does not stand beneath a tottering wall. It is one's Correct Decree to die only after one has completed fully the practice of one's Course. To die in fetters, on the other hand, is not anyone's Correct Decree." (7A2)

We start here with a bald statement of omnipresence: everything is the Decree, everything is given, everything is fated reality that is beyond our direct control. But right away, Mencius oddly retracts this with a qualification: while everything is, in the literal sense, an unchangeable given fact, on the other hand human agency makes a choice within this reality, which changes its nature. The term *correct Decree* could also be translated as "the Decree proper," that is, the real Decree, the Decree properly so called, one's Destiny as opposed to one's Fate, as it were. What makes the choice here is what we accept willingly, again what accords with (*shun*) our real commitments and desires—our Dao, our course for attaining what we value. Only to die after fulfilling this is the real Decree; to die without attaining it, frustrated and imprisoned, although technically it too is the Decree, is not the "real, correct, proper" Decree as such. In this passage, we have both a literal omnipresence and a pragmatic, revised dichotomy, with the latter mattering more. The Decree in the meaningful sense is not everywhere. And yet the fact that the Decree is literally omnipresent is more than just a grudging concession to the opposite position. It allows the value-dichotomous contrast between Decree proper and its absence to become much more fluid, situating it at the interface between value and valuelessness, hence, in accordance with our pendulum model, at the genuine locus of value. This comes down to the omniavailability of value in a way that is quite parallel to what we have just seen in Confucius. For example, we find Mencius saying:

> The exemplary person deeply apprehends it (深造之 *shen zhao zhi*) with the Dao, for he wants to attain it within himself. When

he attains it within himself, he dwells in it peacefully and stably. Dwelling in it peacefully and stably, he partakes of it deeply. Partaking of it deeply, in choosing it he meets its source both right and left. This is why the exemplary person wants to find it within himself. (4B14)

The "it" which the exemplary man deeply apprehends with the Dao is perhaps his own experience, the object of his study, whatever he turns his attention to. In his commitment to his Course, the exemplary man finds its reality within himself, and *as a correlate to this*, finds "its source" everywhere he looks, both right and left. It is omniavailable; that is, its source, from which it *can* be derived, is available everywhere. This omniavailability is strictly correlative to the depth with which he has apprehended it and "dwells within it peacefully and stably" within himself. This "peacefully and stably" (*an*) again points to the human affect, the satisfaction of a human desire and the pleasure that comes with it.

This is the same term Confucius shockingly advanced as the ultimate criterion of the legitimacy of ritual obligation to Zaiwo in *Analects* 17:21, cited above. Here, by actualizing the values of the Dao within himself to the point where his commitment to it yields pleasure and peace, the depth of internalization transforms into an omnipresent external reality. Here again we see a kind of overlap of what appear to be nominalist and realist premises, in this case yielding a weak sense of omnipresence, which is neither the "idealist" universal of universals nor the "materialist" concrete overflow that universals cannot appropriate.

Perhaps this is also what is going on in Mencius's famously obscure and seemingly mystical dictum: "All things are provided in me. There is no greater joy than to examine myself and find realness/sincerity/internal coherence (誠 *cheng*) within me" (7A4). Again, we have a depth of internalization of values (sincerity or unseen coherence within the self)[27] making available a completeness of external presence.

The other notoriously mystical Mencian dictum about omnipresence, the famous "floodlike *qi*" passage (2A2), follows the same pattern.[28] First, Mencius sketches a picture of the human psychophysical organism which is roughly parallel to his picture of the structure of the social totality, a microcosm/macrocosm picture. Just as the true ruler should guide and direct his state, in fact make himself an exemplar around which they spontaneously gather and thereby become a truly coherent social group, but cannot force them to follow him, and Mencius presents a relationship between the "will" (志 *zhi* the deliberate commitments and long-term value-orientations of the mind) and the *qi* (the spontaneous life force of the body) modeled on that between his ideal of a ruler and his people: the ruler should guide and direct his people, in fact making himself an exemplar around whom they spontaneously gather, thereby becoming a truly coherent social group, but without being able to *force* them to follow him, and also allowing for a certain degree of reciprocity of leadership in that the people may overthrow a ruler and thereby sometimes "take the lead. Mencius sketches a connection between the courage of this *qi*, the emotions and spontaneous reactions of the body, and the value commitment of the will and mind. An unmoving mind and will inspires a firm, settled, courageous *qi*, which gathers around it spontaneously just as the people gather around the sage king who exemplifies the best of their own essence. But just as the people can also move the ruler, the *qi* can also move the mind. Hence, even though "where the will goes, the *qi* follows," it is still necessary to "maintain the will but without doing violence to the *qi*." One must neither let the *qi*, the spontaneity of the organism, grow wildly and without cultivation, or force it to grow, like the man of Song who pulled on his sprouts and thus killed them. If properly nourished, this *qi* becomes the floodlike *qi*. This *qi* is "supremely vast, supremely firm; if unceasingly nourished and undamaged, it fills the space between heaven and earth." But again, this omnipresence is for Mencius dependent on the organizing, nourishing power of the value commitment of the will, the conscious commitment. Hence he says, "This *qi* must be matched with rightness and the Dao; without these, it is depleted. For it is generated from the accumulation of rightness; it is not that rightness comes along later and appropriates it." That is, just as the people too have the moral nature that allows them to recognize and be attracted to the exemplary ruler, the *qi* itself is nourished, moved, and cultivated by the moral virtues and value commitments of the will, not merely borrowed by this will as a neutral source of power. The *qi* itself has a something real in it that allows it to be drawn to the moral aspirations of the will: the *qi* has its own "nature" which becomes manifest within it when it is attracted to this moral aspiration lying outside of it, in the will. This attraction to the good *is* the good moral nature of the *qi*. But it is only to be *called* the nature: Mencius does not say the *qi* could not be drawn in other, immoral, ways by other attractions that are equally intrinsic to it, just as in the famous example of the baby at the well in 2??, he does not say that in addition to the spontaneous feeling of commiseration one would *not* also feel, equally spontaneously and from an equally inborn source, indifference, *Schadenfreude*, malice—nor indeed that one's flash of commiseration would necessarily last more than an instant or lead to any actual attempt to save the child. All he needs, and all he asserts, is that everyone feels at least a flash of commiseration that is not motivated by any ulterior aim. The *qi* may have many conflicting spontaneous impulses at any time, and be attracted in many divergent directions. These may all be equally intrinsic, but only those that can be grown in a direction that coheres with the moral aspiration (and that facilitates the mutual coherence among desires, fosters their satisfaction in independence of external factors, distinguishes humans from other creatures and allows human beings them-selves actually to form a coherent social group) *should* be called the nature, because of the positive consequences such an act of naming would have on this very process of bringing out the natural attraction toward the good. For Mencius, human nature is *good*, really and genuinely good, but strictly speaking it is good *among other things*. The passage goes on: "If one's actions cause dissatisfaction in one's mind, [this *qi*] is depleted." Again, the question is one of direct satisfaction, the sincerity found within, trueness to oneself; this is what nourishes the *qi*, and makes it omnipresent, "filling the space between heaven and earth." Then one "finds its source" everywhere. We can consider this another instance of the omniavailability of value, which also crosses the line into the realness of the *qi* and of external reality. It is an internal value commitment that organizes the world around itself, creating value by discovering it and discovering value by creating it. This is neither realism nor nominalism.

Can this omniavailability, as we have seen it advanced by both Con-fucius and Mencius, be called a kind of omnipresence? Yes, but obviously only if we understand "presence" to mean "availability." A case can indeed be made for such an understanding. In a certain sense, just to say something is present is to say that it is to-hand, that it is available; we may not be seeing it, or touching it, or noticing it, but it is present if we can see or touch or notice it or use it *whenever we choose to do so*. The table is present in the room even when I'm not noticing it, which means it is available to my notice at any time.

But it must be noted that this concept of presence stresses the aspect of *choice*, of selecting-out from among alternatives, and as it were underlines the participation of the human subject in the process of presencing. There are always many different things available, but the ones that are actualized depend on the action of the human being. In one sense all these things are "present" and available, but in another, only those are relevantly available which a human being might desire, and which can only be brought to bear through this desire and action. All things are the Decree, but only those we accept willingly are our Proper Decree. So when Mencius says that his floodlike *qi* fills the space between heaven and earth, or that all things are present in himself, we have as it were two contrary ways of making the same point: his own power and spontaneity are findable everywhere to just the extent that all things are available to his value-commitment, to the extent that he can "find its source" everywhere. There is a continuity between the *qi* of his own body, which is altered into an optimally functional and coher-ent whole by the spontaneous influence of his will, and the rest of the *qi* in his environment, which forms the social and natural worlds. Just as the body is affected by the will, the world is affected by the will-cohered body. We have a coherence within a context, which makes this context coherent with it; then this coherence of coherence-and-context on the first level becomes a new coherence, which in turn makes its own context, the rest of the world, also coherent with it. This concentric picture of the extension of value becomes, in texts such as the "Great Learning" and in much of Confucianism, a key aspect of the Confucian "oligocentric" conception of omnipresence as omniavailability.

TRANSITION TO IRONIC COHERENCE: QI-OMNIPRESENCE AND THE EMPTY CENTER IN PRE-IRONIC PROTO-DAOISM

Our taxonomy of ironic and non-ironic coherence forces us to cross traditional delineations of classical Chinese schools. For our next example of the development of non-ironic thought is to be found in a series of texts that are usually classified as Daoist in character, rather than in Confucian thinkers of later periods, such as Xunzi: the "Four Chapters" of the *Guanzi* which, according to some modern scholars, are representative of the "Daoism"—sometimes described as Huang-Lao Daoism—of the Jixia Academy in Qi, around the middle of the fourth century BCE.[29] These four chapters are, in the order of their putative composition, the "Neiye" ("Inner Training"), the "Xinshu shang" and "Xinshu xia" ("Techniques of the Heart/mind, parts one and two"), and the "Baixin" ("Purifying the Heart"). Others, notably Harold Roth, suggest that some of the texts, particularly the "Neiye," precede even the *Laozi*. Based on internal evidence, I would place the "Neiye" and part but not all of the "Xinshu shang" to roughly the time the *Laozi* was taking shape, and possibly slightly before. As Guo Moruo has noted, the "Xinshu shang" appears to be divided into a primary text and its commentary; the primary text may be quite early, but the commentary portion shows signs of being somewhat later, particularly in its detailed string of definitions of specific terms and careful glossing of their connections, and its uses of the term *Li*, for which an attempted definition is also attempted, the first in the tradition.[30] For the remaining portions of these chapters—the commentarial portion of "Xinshu shang," the "Xinshu xia," and the "Baixin"—I would agree with Zhang Dainian's broad assessment, namely, that they date to sometime "after the *Laozi* but before the *Xunzi*."[31] Based on their lack of clear references to the existing *Laozi* or *Zhuangzi*, and its rhymed parallelisms, I am willing to entertain the hypothesis that the "Neiye" and the primary portion of the "Xinshu shang" can be discussed together with the Guodian *Laozi* fragments to give a picture of something I would like to call *pre-ironic proto-Daoism*.

Any speculation about the relation of this pre-ironic Daoism, or "Jixia Daoism," and the *Laozi* text is of course highly risky at this point, as new archeological discoveries could overturn any conclusions we might tentatively draw.[32] I would also not like to jump too quickly to the conclusion drawn by Chen Guying and others that these texts represent "Huang-Lao" Daoism—a category that is itself highly questionable. Indeed, I am not so convinced of the early dating of these texts that I would like to hang much of the current argument on it; and in fact, what I am calling pre-ironic Daoism here would fit neatly into the category of what I will call ironic appropriations of the non-ironic, to be discussed in a later chapter, which is where I place the remaining, clearly later, portions of the "Four Chapters." But given the present evidence, we might construct a story that looks like the following, picking up on a connection between the "Neiye" and Confucian-friendly form of proto-Daoism proposed by Graham prior to the Guodian discoveries.[33]

The Guodian fragments of the *Laozi* text, found in a tomb sealed around 300 BCE, contain about one-third of the present *Laozi*. It has been noted that these fragments lack the virulent anti-Confucian polemics of the received *Laozi* text. Although we do find parts of, say, chapter 5, chapter 17, chapter 18, and chapter 19, which in the received version are among the most outspokenly critical of Confucian virtues such as Benevolence and Rightness, the Guodian versions lack precisely the critical remarks.[34] The "Inner Training" of the *Guanzi* combines "Daoist"-sounding rhetoric with an even more Confucian-friendly stance, explicitly positing a role for the Odes, Music, and Ritual as aids in dissipating emotional disturbances that prevent the stillness of the mind, regarded as crucial to cultivation of the Dao. These traditional aspects of Confucian cultivation are thus not only not regarded as obstacles to the Dao, or as derivative secondary substitutes when the Dao disappears, but as positive aids to its cultivation.

This type of claim allows us to postulate a proto-Daoism, which has not as yet come to criticize the Confucian values of Benevolence, Rightness, Ritual, and the like, viewing its own method as rather the best means to attain these virtues, rather than a rejection of them. This would be the pre-ironic Daoism as represented by the Guodian fragments of the *Laozi* and the earlier portions of the *Guanzi* chapters. It is pre-ironic in that, while it has begun to have reservations about the efficacy of both moral virtues and discursive knowledge, it does not undertake a radical critique of them or assign these key terms new, "ironic" meanings. Rather, it embraces a more moderate position that reverses the priorities of cultivation that make virtue and wisdom possible. The *Guanzi* chapters in particular develop a theory of qi cultivation as a basis for the spontaneous manifestation of the virtues and of wisdom, reinforced in places with the use of these virtues as a means of that very cultivation. Moreover, while "the Dao" is already spoken of as omnipresent, formless, and indescribable, this unknowability is not yet pushed to the full radical consistency found in, say, the first chapter of the received *Laozi* text, or the Inner Chapters of the *Zhuangzi*. That is, we do not find claims of systematic elusiveness of an a priori nature, to the effect than any statement about the Dao, because it is a statement, is ipso facto misleading, or that only an unproclaimed or strictly unnameable Course can be the real Course. Rather, the Dao is knowable through other methods— i.e., qi-cultivation—and straightforward statements about its nature continue to be made without the immediate erasure that we find in fully developed "ironic" Daoism.

The "Inner Training," for example, states:

> The Dao is not far away; it is by attaining it that the people are born. The Dao is not separate [from us]; it is by attaining it that the people have knowledge. . . . The reality of the Dao hates tone and voice, but if one cultivates the heart/mind and stills the intention,[35] the Dao can be attained. The Dao is what cannot be spoken by the mouth, seen by the eye or heard by the ear, *which is why we instead cultivate the heart/mind and rectify the body [to attain it]*. It is what people lose when they die, and what they obtain to live; it is what things lose when they fail, and what they attain in order to succeed.[36]

Note here that the indescribability of the Dao leads to no extreme skeptical or ironic results, and does not lead to self-reflective criticisms or erasures of statements just made, or about this statement itself. Rather, it points unproblematically to another way in which the Dao *can* be "attained": through psychophysical cultivation and stillness of the mind. Note also that the Dao serves as a purely positive "life force"–like item here associated with positive things such as life and success, but which is not operative in failure and death—indeed, failure and death mean the loss of the Dao. In the ironic Daoist tradition, as we shall see, failure "succeeds in failing" by virtue of the Dao, as it were, and death too is accomplished by Course (Zhuangzi); in the *Hanfeizi* commentaries to the Laozi as well, we are told that the Dao, in its "yielding," participates in and makes possible both success and failure, both life and death. The latter position is, however, really just a further thinking through and radicalization of the premises established in pre-ironic Daoism.

The "Inner Training" suggests that the body can be made healthy and well-ordered, the virtues generated, and the world brought to order through one technique: stilling the mind. It is stillness of the mind, the emptying of any specific content, that serves as the unifying center of the psychophysical organism and even its environment, bestowing on them their coherence in just the sense we have spoken of in the Confucian context: holding together elements in a balanced, intelligible way that generates some specific values, notably sustainability and pleasure. Indeed, *huan* 歡, happiness, is identified here with that which creates life, and hence with *Qi* and Dao; all particular emotions are swervings away from the preexisting centrality of this happiness: "Human life necessarily arises by means of its happiness. To worry is to lose the guiding thread (紀 *ji*), to be angered is to lose the proper starting point (端 *duan*). The Dao can find no place in worry, sorrow, joy and anger. Still your attachments to desire, rectify any encountered disorders, neither pushing nor pulling it, and good fortune will revert to you of its own accord." We see here the close connection between pleasure, measure, centrality, and valued order, now directly related to "neither pushing nor pulling," the ultimate stillness of the intentional mind. The results of this process follow the same pattern: "If the body is not rectified, Virtue will not come; if one is not still within, the heart-mind will not be well-governed. When the body is rectified so as to bring Virtue into it, heaven's benevolence and earth's righteousness arrive of their own accord, overflowingly."[37] What holds the parts together, keeps them in their proper order (i.e., the order that allows them to produce whatever is considered valuable), balances them, and makes them intelligible as what they are, is here precisely the *non-interference of the center.*

The trope of "non-doing" (*wuwei*) appears perfunctorily already in the *Analects* (15:5) in reference to the perfect governance of the sage-emperor Shun; there, we can assume that it refers to the perfection of ritual propriety, which is able to effect order noncoercively through the charisma and influence of the exemplar. In Mencius 2A2 we noted the picture of the psychophysical human organism as a microcosm of the state, with the mind playing the role of ruler and the qi of the people. Here we have these two models brought together more explicitly (particularly in the "Techniques of the Mind, Part One," which explicitly describes the mind as occupying "the rank of the ruler," 君之位 *jun zhi wei,* within the body), but the nonactivity of ritual propriety has begun to take on some more radical overtones: here, the mind is genuinely still, unmoved by emotional involvements, and even by worrisome attempts to be ritually proper; this, however, has the same kind of influence seen in Shun's ritual nonaction, the magical effecting of coherence throughout the realm (the body). The action of the center is now literally nil. But it is precisely the absence of the imposition of any activities of the center on the two extremes—the fact that it doesn't move off into them to do something to them, but remains unmoved—that makes it central, and thus what makes the parts cohere. It is by remaining radically unlike them, remaining separate from them, in this sense, that it connects them. But its presence is felt precisely in its absence: that is, not-being-there in the other parts is its mode of being-there in them. Because intelligibility is thought of on the coherence-around-a-center model already taking shape in Confucianism, this paradox is easily comprehensible. But in this conception we are beginning to see the dawning of the ironic form of coherence.

This development is in its own way still consistent with the idea of Dao as "omniavailability of value," realized through cultivation, which we have seen in the non-ironic tradition of Confucius and Mencius. Here it seems that the traditional value-implications of Dao in the older sense (the traditional virtues) are made manifest throughout heaven and earth to one who has successfully attained Virtue, which in these texts is done through stilling the body and mind. But this text goes a step farther. It asserts not only that the traditional values can be attained through stillness, but that this stillness itself can be accomplished through dispelling excessive emotional states, which can be attained through the traditional practices and virtues of Confucianism: "In stilling anger, nothing is more effective than the *Odes*. In dispelling worry, nothing is more effective than music. In regulating joy, nothing is more effective than ritual. In holding firm to ritual, nothing is more effective than reverence. In holding firm to reverence, nothing is more effective than stillness. When one is still within and reverent without, he can return to his nature, which will then become profoundly settled."[38]

The Confucian virtues and the state of stillness are mutually reinforcing. Stillness is induced by the virtues, and then further becomes source for their maintenance. Mencius, as we have seen, adopts a similar theory, perhaps learned from Gaozi, whose outlook seems close to that of these pre-ironic proto-Daoist texts; but Mencius stresses that the moral virtues are indispensable elements of qi-cultivation from the beginning, rather than its by-product, or, as in this passage, mere supplementary aids to stilling the mind. It is not too much of a stretch to arrive at this omnipresence of "Dao" if omnipresent qi is already endowed with the potential for value-laden effects, as a "dao" in the older sense—a guiding discourse—was supposed to have had, namely, a directed set of practices that lead to the attainment of some valued goal.

Thus we find that a certain form of omnipresence of Dao, *the* Dao, is already a fait accompli here, and that this is closely connected with what small degree of irony does get connected to the term. It is by no means obvious why the term *Dao*, which in Confucius and Mozi means any kind of guiding discourse, comes to be the term used for the omnipresent source and substance of all things. In these *Guanzi* texts, however, the Dao's omnipotence seems to be closely related to the theory of qi as the stuff and origin of all things. Indeed, in some places the terms *Dao* and qi seem to be used interchangeably, as in the formulation that "Dao is that by which the body is filled" ("Inner Training"), and equally (in a phrase also used by Mencius) that "*qi* is what fills the body" ("Techniques, Part Two"). Such a direct equivalence between Dao and *qi* is not seen in the *Laozi,* and is ambiguous at best in the Inner Chapters of the *Zhuangzi.* We may speculate that the Dao retains some of its original sense in the connection to the art of *qi*-cultivation: Dao is the guiding set of techniques directing this art, and De (德) is the attainment of virtuosic mastery in these techniques. The omnipresence of the Dao is thus correlative to the omnipresence of *qi,* dispersed in the form of air and condensed in the form of all palpable bodies.

The Dao is omnipresent because *qi* is omnipresent, just as we might say that the Way of swimming is present wherever there is water. *Present* here obviously means, as in the Confucian texts, *available.* The omnipresence of the Dao is here really the omniavailability of the Dao, as in Confucius and Mencius. In the present case, this would mean both that this technique, swimming, can be applied wherever there is water, and also that, inasmuch as *qi* is both the "water" in this analogy and, in its condensed form, the creatures in this water, the Way of swimming is what the water does to itself. Water is swimming. *Qi* is Dao. *Qi* means breath, the movement of condensation and dispersion of the air, the source of life. It is what is lost in death. All things are made of it, but it is also, like the steam rising from rice from which the graph is said to derive, the source of energy and life. *Qi* is also associated with weather patterns, the turning of the seasons, and thereby the process of agricultural growth, the emergence of food and life. To study the Dao of *qi* is thus to "work the weather" which produces all things, to study *qi* itself, and to master this Dao is to master the Dao of all things. The "Way" of *qi* would be the process of condensation and dispersion itself—that is how *qi* behaves—and that is the source of all things.

But importantly, in contrast to the condensed versions—called "things"—the *qi* is formless, is uncategorizable. It is no particular identifiable thing. Inasmuch as it is the whole process of condensation and dispersal, it cannot even be said to be any one identifiable *state*; the pendulum swing between the poles of condensation and dispersal can be identified with neither one state or the other to the exclusion of the opposite state. Here we see the beginnings of a notion of the coherence-generating center that serves as an alternative to the Confucian center, which, as we have seen, resides in the exemplary central personage of a social grouping. The center, here as there, is identified with the whole, since the center is what gives the whole its character, what makes it coherent in the sense of intelligible, identifiable, as well as holding it together. But in this case, the character of the whole—now not merely a social group, but the totality of all things—is precisely nothing-in-particular, the *qi* in the state of vacuity, tenuousness, emptiness: 虛 *xu.* It is here that we find the one of the seeds of the paradoxes of the ironic tradition. The term for the omnipresent, what is found in all things, is "Non-thing,"[39] the unintelligible—"incoherent"—as such.

In sum, we see in these pre-ironic texts a type of omnipresence derived from the formlessness of *qi* and a conception of coherence as both limitation and unification derived from the notion of noninterference, basically building upon the Confucian model. As in the Confucian model, ordered unity, coherence, is attained by the ruling member restricting himself to his proper role. In the Confucian model, this role is that of exemplifying the Confucian virtues, thereby creating a ripple effect that organizes the whole as this pattern is emulated by the parts. The ruler's characteristics are to spread out beyond its sphere. In this pre-ironic Daoist model, the proper role of the ruler is noninterference, stillness, which orders the whole. The seeds of the ironic tradition lie here. For it is by not spreading out and infecting the whole, by truly limiting itself, that the ruling member actually does spread its organizing power through the whole. Here we see an early form of the convergence between two opposed forms of coherence: coherence as the making-coherent in the sense of intelligible and definite of the subordinated parts of the whole (the two extremes in the case of the pendulum swing) by limiting oneself to one's own sphere, thereby limiting each part to its own sphere, and the making-coherent in the sense of being unified with all those parts and the center as one whole. The center effects real joining by separating them, and really effects them by separating itself from them. This is one source of the conception of the ironic form of ruling, of guiding, of affecting: affecting by being still, by not interfering, but not affecting. And equally, it is one beginning of the ironic form of cohering: by keeping each locked up in its own proper place, they are genuinely connected.

FOUR

IRONIC COHERENCE AND THE
DISCOVERY OF THE "YIN"

THE LAOZI TRADITION: DESIRING W/HOLES

Let us now take a look at what I will call the "ironic tradition," and the transformations of the idea of coherence that take place there. I call coherence "ironic" when it disassociates the three aspects involved in non-ironic coherence: "harmony (hanging-together in some mutually enhancing way)," "value (coherence with past and future, and coherence with some human desires, i.e., "sustainability" and "goodness")," and "intelligibility." Non-ironic thinking regards these three aspects as at least linked and sometimes as interchangeable. Ironic thinking divides them so that what is "coherent" in one sense is not "coherent" in the other sense: it is *ironically* coherent, with "coherent" used to mean also "incoherent." In a nutshell, the ironic notion of coherence puts "harmony" and "value" together, but regards this alloy as precisely the negation of "intelligibility." Real value emerges from a coming-together, which undermines all attempts to define, perceive, deliberately target or grasp coherently either this value or this togetherness. The characteristic marks of ironic texts are the sudden abundance of negations (non-doing, non-being,[1] etc.), the virulent critique of positive values (e.g., the Confucian virtues of Benevolence and Rightness, or of any positive "dao," i.e., any purposively value-directed course of self-cultivation and study), and the new, ironic double meaning given to the key terms of the previous tradition: a Dao that is a non-dao, true benevolence that is non-benevolent, and so on. The prime exemplars of this turn of thought are to be found in the received *Laozi* text and the Inner Chapters of the *Zhuangzi*.

The *Laozi* as we have it in the "received" (Wang Bi) version is, we may surmise from current evidence, probably not the work of a single person, and indeed seems to have been composed over a long period of time from gradually assembled sayings, possibly in several different versions. I mentioned above, in discussing the "proto-Daoism" found in the *Guanzi*, that we can perhaps see in the early parts of Guodian fragments of the *Laozi* text an early version which is still consistent with this "pre-ironic" Daoism. I want to argue, however, that the received version of the text represents the amalgamation of these pre-ironic fragments into a whole which takes a definite editorial stance, and can be read as a coherent whole, representing full-fledged "ironic" Daoism.[2] I hope to show that, in spite of its presumably slow and accretional composition, the received *Laozi* text can be read as a whole that has a more or less coherent philosophical position.

In this chapter I will thus be crediting the tradition of thinking evidenced in this text with the discovery of some ironies built into the notions of coherence, intelligibility, desire, and value that are regarded as having an inescapable character, a type of necessity we might call *the dyadic a priori*. It would be equally useful, perhaps, to identify it as *the ironic a priori*. I call it *a priori* because, as I will try to demonstrate, it here comes to be regarded as a necessary, always preexistent, nonempirical, inescapable condition of experience and assertibility. What is at issue here is the contextualization of any intelligible coherence within a greater whole which is itself unintelligible and incoherent. For if intelligibility per se depends on a prior context, this context itself cannot be intelligible without leading to an infinite regress. This leads to an ironic self-undermining of intelligibility, an irony of contextualization that is strictly unavoidable, being a condition of the possibility of coherence per se. This development can also be described simply as the discovery of what will later come to be called the Yin half of the Yin-Yang dyad, the receptive, responsive, feminine, still, unformed, dark half of the dyad—the "that" that comes with any "this," the background context that comes with any foregrounded content.[3] This can also be described as the "unintelligible" (i.e., "dark," hard to see, difficult to make out) and devalued side of any dyad. Yin will later be the general term used to denote the context that coheres with any coherence, a necessary complement to every valued intelligible coherence (Yang). In a simple formula, ironic Daoism uses this incoherence that necessarily accompanies and makes possible any coherence to drive a wedge between coherence as "intelligibility" on the one hand, and coherence as "real value," "harmonious balance," "sustainable continuity," and "sticking together," on the other.

Hall and Ames have already invoked the term *irony*, with some reservations, as characterizing the overall Daoist attitude toward existence.[4] But what I have in mind here is rather a particular literary trope. The Daoist use of terms that traditionally signify coherence is always, I claim, ironic, in the specific sense of indicating the impossibility of coherence in the literal sense, and yet, ironically, indicating that *this impossibility is a higher form of coherence*, in the sense that it fulfils the original promise of coherence more successfully than the original, non-ironic coherence did. The Daoist use of the term *dao* is an *ironic* use of the older term. It is closely equivalent to looking out the window at a rainstorm on the day of the picnic and saying, "Oh, great weather for a picnic." This means that the weather is precisely *not* great, is the opposite of great, in the expected sense: we wanted a sunny day for our picnic. However, the real irony, and the key Daoist insight, is this: this rainstorm really *is* great, much greater than the sunny day we were hoping for: it is only the rain that makes it possible for the crops to grow, providing the food we wanted to eat on our picnic. Without the kind of weather that sometimes provides rain, there is no picnic. Strictly speaking, we have two levels of irony here: "great" is used in the ironic sense, meaning the opposite of great. But, ironically enough, this non-greatness referred to ironically as "great" is what is *really* great. "The Dao" is the ironic opposite of any given dao—and thereby the real dao. The promises fulfilled by ironic coherence are the promises of value implied in non-ironic coherence: coherence as sustainability, balance, and value—i.e., second-order coherence with past and future, and with some set of human desires—and value-bearing togetherness. In the *Laozi* these values are still the older values of continuance, life, sustainability through time. The impossibility is still limited, in the *Laozi*, to the aspect of *intelligibility*. What is intelligible is here regarded as never truly valuable, never actually fulfilling of our truly coherent desires (what we will be calling "stomach" desires, following the trope in *Laozi* 12), and limits rather than facilitates value-bearing togethernesses. It is here that we find an immanent explanation to the insistent "doubleness" of key terms in the *Laozi*, which has in one form or another been a continual catalyst of puzzlement and ingenuity for its commentators, giving us a way to understand the insistently *dual status* of Dao, of Name, of Sage, of "the One," of Non-Being, and so on. In the case of Being and Non-Being, it has been noted that there seems to be some conflict between the symmetrical "horizontal" pairing of *you* and *wu* (e.g., in ch. 1 and 2), and the asymmetrical "vertical" pairing of the same terms (e.g., in ch. 40). A good recent example is the work of Bai Tongdong, who has recently addressed this issue in depth, painstakingly teasing out a powerful and consistent reading of the text based on a distinction between two separate and hierarchically arranged senses of the two terms, marking them as *you*1 and *you*2 and *wu*1 and *wu*2.[5] While in general agreement with Bai's approach, I hope here to elucidate to a greater degree the way in which these are not in fact completely separate senses of each of these terms, but rather a way of indicating and exploiting an ambiguity that is inescapable in both senses, pointing in each case to the other sense of the term. For me this necessary "both-horizontal-and-vertical," where each necessarily leads into the other, is the key to the text. Ironic coherence is a consequence of the simultaneous symmetry and asymmetry of two paired terms that is built into the failure of the attempted non-ironic notion of coherence. The same applies to the other crucial double-sensed terms in the work.[6]

Indeed, more expansively, this riddle of the overlapping multiplicity of meanings of the term *Dao* has been recognized as a key feature of this text by many astute commentators. Tang Junyi is perhaps a representative example of this sort of sensitivity to the text. Tang offered an analysis of six separate senses in which the term *Dao* is used in the *Laozi*, as follows: (1) Dao as the unifying totality of the various principles in all things (有 貫通異理之用之道 *youguantongyilizhiyongzhidao*), expressed in their concrete characteristics and behavior, existing immanently within them rather than beyond them; (2) Dao as the nameless objective transcendent metaphysical substance (形上道體 *xingshang daoti*) from which all reality emerges, which is beyond all apperception and predication; (3) Dao as named and manifested (道相 *daoxiang*), that is, through such terms as weakness, return, mother, mystery, and the like; (4) Dao as identical to De, Virtue or Virtuosity, which Tang sees as a sometimes used in distinction to Dao but at other times as an alternate denotation of the ontological identity and cosmological function of Dao; (5) Dao as the guiding principle for the cultivation of Virtue and other practical applications, in ethical and political life; (6) Dao as ideal or original state of persons and things.[7] What I hope to add to Tang's discussion with the following exploration of the implications of "irony" as it pertains to the problem of coherence generally is the inner connection between these various senses, and indeed, the disclosure that they are not different meanings at all, but rather various applications of one and the same meaning, alternate paradoxical connotations of one and the same denotation: they all mean "the unhewn." More specifically, they are all ways of indicating the ironies activated in the notion of coherence per se when faced with the notion of Dao as "the unhewn."

OVERVIEW OF IRONIC COHERENCE IN THE *LAOZI*

I will be speaking here of the received Wang Bi version of the Laozi text as the joint product of a tradition of writers. There are no proper nouns in the work, which makes it highly unusual among independently circulated pre-Qin texts (the four Guanzi chapters, if they were circulated independently, would be another example) and points to the deliberate omission of perhaps the most pervasive form of coherence grounding the Confucian works, namely, *coherence with a tradition* as the decisive standard of true coherence with the most salient human desires. The standards established by the sages or exemplary persons are, as we have seen in Mencius and will find again in Xunzi and the *Zhouyi* tradition, crucial for determining which among the multitude of competing coherences were to be chosen out as conducive to the greatest coherence. This aspect of coherence is pointedly omitted from the notion of coherence as presented in the Laozi tradition.

We have, instead, two other terms traditionally used to denote a kind of coherence, intelligibility, and value: Dao 道 and *ming* 名, or name. These are the first topics presented in the first chapter of the received text. The following is an attempt to translate this chapter in terms of its relevance to the preoccupations of the present work:

1. A guiding course can be discoursed;[8] but then it will not be a sustainable [i.e., reliable] guide.

2. An intelligible value [i.e., a name][9] can be explicitly valued; but then its value will not be sustainable.[10]

3. Without any intelligible value [i.e., indiscernible, incoherent, unintelligible, unvalued] is the beginning of heaven and earth.

4. Made intelligible in accordance with its value [to us, it can be called] the mother of all things.[11]

5. Because [there is an aspect of us that thus] consistently desires nothing [from it, inasmuch as it is incoherent and thus value-less to us], we are enabled to watch for its hard-to-see subtleties [namely, those aspects of it that do not accord with our values, and thus tend to escape our notice].

6. Because [we also] consistently desire something [from it],[12] we are enabled to watch for its easy-to-see manifest outcomes.[13]

7. These two emerge together; they are two names for one and the same meaning.[14]

8. This sameness is what we refer to in calling it "obscure."

9. The further obscurity [i.e., sameness of the two, doubleness] of this obscurity itself is the gate to all subtleties.

Let me start with a brief paraphrase of the meaning of this chapter, which will be elaborated in detail below: (1) It is possible to posit a way to make the things we want and value available to us: a course by which what we value can be brought about, or (2) to posit a concept of value that serves as the ideal toward which our actions aim. A way can be taken as a way, named as our guiding way, made into an ideal. But in making this way explicit, and embracing it as an ideal, we actually undermine its efficacy to reliably and sustainably produce what is valued. (3) Before anything is intelligible, discernible, and available to be valued, it is first something indiscernible and thus unvalued. So anything at all that we can notice or name or value comes from a prior state of not yet being valued or intelligible: a state of lacking that name and that value. By the same token, considering all knowable and valued things en masse, the entire known world of knowables and desirables, we must conclude that it emerges from a prior state of not-yet-intelligibility, namelessness, which is also, to us, valuelessness. What is not yet named or even noticed ipso facto cannot be valued. In this sense, it is the absence of anything intelligible or valuable, anything coherent, that is the true *source* of all valued coherences. (4) But then again, since as such it is the true source that provides what we want and value, of all that we see and know and name, we could give it a name pertaining to its function as "invisible source," make it intelligible to ourselves as valuable, in a paradoxical way: the Mother of all things. For a "Mother" is an emptiness, a uterine void, which has no socially recognized (sur)name or value, who does not herself have the social status, eminence, or "value" of her sons, and yet is this void is their actual source. "Mother" is a special kind of word, a name that names only a void, a name for namelessness. It is a positive presence of an absence, a substantialization of a void, a description of indescribability, a valued valuelessness. It is this ironic kind of presence, an absence-as-presence, that is the true creative "source" and "course" (both terms now also to be understood in the same ironic way). (5) Since it is unintelligible and without value, in one sense we are always and sustainably without any desire for it; we are unable to desire it, being unable to conceive it or assign any definite intelligible identity to it. But since (as the text later makes clear) our awareness is conditioned by our desires, this lack of desire creates a useful epistemological by-product: unconstrained by any particular goal, we are able to see what we normally neglect in our purposive deployments of looking and seeing and knowing. We see the unexpected and otherwise unnoticed formlessness and valuelessness at the root of all the forms we value. We see the unsuspected roots of our values in the valueless. (6) But then again, since it does provide what we value and desire, we also consistently have desires with respect to it. Being primed by these specific desires for what we value, we are able to notice "the Mother's" productiveness of value, its power to produce what we want, the emergence of the formed from the formless, and to see more clearly the real nature of the array of intelligible, valued things before us, to wit, precisely their rootedness in this namelessness and valuelessness (i.e., in the precise exclusion of their name, identity, value). We grasp the intelligible and valued better by knowing their secret alliance with, rootedness in, and emergence from the unintelligible, the valueless.

(7) The valued and disvalued, the intelligible and its own undermining, emerge simultaneously, come forth together (同出 *tongchu*): when we name something, we implicitly also name with the name "namelessness" that to which it is contrasted, from which it emerges, against which it is nameable. The positing of any valued coherence is also the positing of its own prior and surrounding incoherence (its indiscernibility prior to its emergence, and its undiscoverability in the contrasted background around it), which is what grounds it and makes its presence possible. The emergence of the coherence and the incoherence, these opposites, are aspects of a single event. Every coherence (name, value) has a double meaning: it names both the coherence and the ultimate incoherence with which it is coherent, and it is this coherence (togetherness) of the coherence and the incoherence that alone makes any coherence coherent (intelligible). At the same time, the namelessness has now been named: we have to call it "namelessness," or "the dark," "the obscure," "the subtle," "the low," "the female," "the mother," and so on. These are names for namelessness, strange ciphers that exist within the system of names and yet simultaneously gum up the smooth functioning of that system, pointing beyond the system. They are simultaneously both within and without the system of names, simultaneously named and unnamed. They are surds, which, in attempting to mean what is no part of the whole system of names, actually end up meaning both (a) "the unvalued part" of the whole, the background that is left over after named part has been picked out, and also (b) "the entire whole, which is subsequently divided into named and unnamed." Though in a different way, we find here as much as in the non-ironic tradition that "same" (*tong*) is not really absolute "mathematical" identity such as we would find in the repeatability of an abstractable essence: it is, rather, a necessarily *paradoxical* simultaneity of opposites in every coherence. We have two contrasting names (or ways of discerning and valuing) for "the same" meaning (異名 同謂 *yiming tongwei*), two ways of describing the same cognitive event, but the point here is that this event cannot be reduced to either one of the two without remainder. Nor can it be a "third," what stands beyond them, a further namelessness behind the contrast between name and namelessness, for this is preemptively folded into the previous dynamic; namelessness, as indiscernible, cannot be identified as one or many. This "sameness" is comprised simply of this co-presence of two apparently mutually exclusive meanings. Every coherence, every value, is always shadowed by its concomitant incoherence, its concomitant disvalue. The "value-bearing togetherness" of the source and the emergent, of the unintelligible context and the intelligible content, lies in this inescapable doubleness and simultaneity. (8) Here we have the advent of the second-order, "ironic" coherence that obtains

between first-order coherence and first-order incoherence: this doubleness is itself double, for it is at once coherence (coherence and incoherence are necessarily always "together") and incoherent (always ultimately grounded in, emerging from, returning to, the unintelligible). (9) Doubleness is at once double (coheres into *no single meaning* exclusively) and single (inescapably bringing about both sides *simultaneously*). The word *obscurity* is one of those names for namelessness that has a built-in double meaning, denoting both (a) the unintelligible as opposed to the intelligible, and (b) the whole prior to the division between intelligible and unintelligible—all in the course of attempting to say (c) neither the "intelligible" nor the "unintelligible." In short, this word for the irony underlying every name is itself constitutively ironic. Even irony is ironic, means itself and also its opposite. The "good" in "good weather" is ironic (it means the opposite of good), but its irony is also itself ironic (it really is good). This is the gate, the road of access, to all the subtleties that follow in the rest of the text.

THE FIVE MEANINGS OF THE UNHEWN: OMNIPRESENCE AND IRONIC COHERENCE IN THE *LAOZI*

Let us examine this line of thinking in more detail. The term *dao* originally means course, way, road, speech, tradition of guidance. There can be a dao of the ancient sage kings, or of good government, or of Heaven and earth, or of particular arts, in all cases meaning a model for a proposed course of action and attention, meant to lead to the acquisition of the mastery of a skill. As a verb, the word means simply "to guide." By following the guidance and example provided by a dao, one learns to embody and attain the value it prescribes; it is a means to an end, a Way to attain a prescribed value. "Guiding discourse," the translation suggested by Chad Hansen,[15] is an English compound term that captures many of these implications. It connotes both a way of connecting with a tradition and of adopting and attaining the goals held to be valuable by that tradition.

The term *ming* literally means "name." It is arguable that, in spite of the more philosophical sense given to the term after a certain late date (as paired with "actuality" 實 *shi* or "form" 型 *xing*), the primary meaning of "name" in pre-Qin texts, especially in ordinary discourse, is social. It signifies one's reputation in a community. Name is *fame*, and unmodified it is already a value term: a *good* reputation. This meaning, that is, the effect one has on one's community, or one's contribution to it, is, I claim, the most immediate reference here, and the structural model of the usage of the term in this text. We can see that this is mainly how the term is taken in early commentaries to the *Laozi*, including those embedded in apocryphal texts such as the *Wenzi* (a kind of Daoist gleaning from scattered texts, especially the *Huainanzi*, recast into the mouth of Laozi), where we find the following explication of the dyad "Named" and "Nameless":

> What has form is the completed things; the formless is their begin-ning. The completion of things is the making of useful objects (器 *qi*), while the beginning is the unhewn (樸 *pu*). Form has sound but the formless is soundless. Form is produced in the formless, and thus the formless is the beginning of what has form. What is broad and thick has a name; so the named (有名 *you ming*) is noble and complete. The stingy and mean have no name [fame]; so the nameless is lowly and unesteemed. The wealthy have a name [are famous], so the name is honored and favored; the poor have no name/fame, so the nameless is base and insulted. The male has name/fame [is renowned], so the named is evident and bright. The female has no name/fame, so the nameless is hidden and reticent. Those with an abundance are famed, so the named is lofty and esteemed. Those without enough have no name/fame, so the nameless is burdened and below. To have merit is to have a name. To have no merit is to be nameless. The named is produced from the nameless, so the nameless is the mother of the named. The Way of Heaven is "the mutual production of being and non-being, the mutual completion of difficult and easy [*Laozi* 2]. Thus the sage holds to the Way, is empty, silent, subtle and minute. . . ."[16]

Named and nameless mean here simply what has been credited for some achievement, for the obtaining of some preconceived value, and what has not. Indeed, a quick look at the Inner Chapters of the *Zhuangzi* makes it clear that in earliest (ironic) Daoist works the term *ming* never applies to "nomenclature" in the sense of a system of names. It is not a topic of lin-guistic theory as it is in the Mohist canons; rather, it seems consistently to mean "fame." Hence, the first chapter of the *Zhuangzi* asserts, climactically, that "the Consummate Person has no [fixed] identity, the Spirit Man has no [particular] *merit*, the Sage has no [one] *name*."[17] Name is here again closely related to merit (功 *gong*), or credit for an achievement, and when contrasted to "actuality" (實 *shi*), as occurs later in the same chapter, it means reputa-tion as opposed to actual merit. *Ming* is a word for the blossoming of an influence within the community, the coming to prominence or visibility of someone who will, in the terms discussed in the previous chapter, come to act as a beacon or inspiration for others: the rich, the exalted, the famous, the powerful, the exemplary, the virtuous. When they come into the position that will allow them to exert this magical influence, attracting and inspiring others to cluster around (cohere with) them and emulate them, they are said to have a "name."[18] We may say, indeed, that "name" means "coherent and valuable-coherence-creating intelligibility" as such.[19]

Name, then, also suggests a form of coherence; the coherence between (1) some person or deed and (2) the needs and values of a certain community. This is what makes something or someone stand out as identifiable to the community. This gives something an intelligible identity. Name is what can be seen and known, and is recognized as such by the community as having value, that is to say, cohering with the recognized needs, ideals, and values of the community. This means also that it is "readable," intelligible, due to its "coherence" with preexistent standards for interpretation; one knows how to read it "as" such and such, because it coheres adequately with a preexistent interpretative frame. Intelligibility, again, is a form of coherence, between an object and a context and a human observer. This context includes both the total semiotic environment and, again, particular human habits, desires, and cognitive dispositions.[20]

The first lines of the received text make a point about both these forms of coherence, after the acceptance of which coherence can only be understood ironically. It tells us that whenever coherence succeeds, it fails, and that the true coherence (value, togetherness) is incoherent (unintelligible), and necessarily so.

The idea behind this, as we can piece it together from the text as a whole, can be formulated in very simplified terms as follows:

1. For something to be regarded as an object of valuation is for it to be coherent not only in the sense of (1) "sticking together" as an intelligible object, but also (2) in the sense of cohering with our desires. But we find encoded in the text a presentation of two different types of desire:

   a) the desires of the "eye," which are attached to a particular coherent intelligible socially determined way of "cutting out" valued objects, and have no intrinsic point of satiation;

   b) The desires of the "stomach," which arise spontaneously, are not sparked by a particular intelligible object, and follow an autonomous course of arising and decay, with a built-in limit of satiation.

Laozi 12 tells us: "The five colors blind the eye, the five tones deafen the ear, the five flavors dull the palate, chasing and hunting make the mind insane, hard to attain goods impede man's progress. Thus the sage in ruling is for the stomach and not for the eye; he eliminates that (彼 bi) and adopts this (此 ci)." The five colors and so on are socially determined values; the particular colors, tones, and flavors that are selected out of the total spectrum and assigned special value and "names." Orientation toward them creates what I am here calling "eye" desires. What I am calling the stomach desires are those described as typical of the infant described in chapter 55: "His bones are weak, his sinews are soft, but his grip is firm; he doesn't yet know of the joining of male and female, but his penis is erect: the ultimate potency! He screams all day but does not grow hoarse: the ultimate harmony! Knowing harmony is called the Sustainable; knowing Sustainability is called Clarity [明 ming—we will have more to say about this term as used in the Zhuangzi]. Helping life along is called inauspicious. Controlling your energy [stomach desire] with the directives of your mind [eye desire] is called forcing it." The stomach desires are not sparked by a particular evaluative purpose, the pursuit of a particular preconceived object intelligible to the "eye" of knowledge. The example here is sexual desire: the infant has no arousing images or concepts of sex to incite his desire and spur him toward the attainment of an imagined satisfaction. But he has an erection, a spontaneous arousal of sexual energy triggered by no particular object. This objectless desire is a "stomach" desire. When we desire food, we have on the one hand an inchoate stomach sensation and on the other hand some images of "desirable" foods to which this state of the stomach is attached. We might wish to obtain caviar to satisfy our hunger; that would be an "eye" desire. But the acquisitiveness for an object lends itself to cease-less seeking, to greed: we can want more and more, we gluttonously desire to stockpile the caviar, all the good foods, for our enjoyment. The stomach desire, on the other hand, spontaneously ceases as soon as the stomach is full. It has a built-in point of satiation, and therefore a built-in periodicity, cycling naturally from hunger to satiety and back. Stomach desires move in a circle, a rhythm, a rise and fall. Eye desires suggest a straight line, an infinite trajectory of getting more and more, getting better and better.

An alternate form of "knowledge" is here suggested, one that cor-responds to the stomach desires: "clarity" (ming). This is defined as "know-ing sustainability" (知常 zhichang) (16, 55) or as "seeing the small" (52; cf. 34). Sustainability, in turn, is defined as "stillness, which is returning to the root" (歸根 guigen), which is again "returning the [destined source of] life" (復命 fuming) (16), or "knowing harmony" (知和 zhihe) (55). "Harmony" here refers, I think, to the *true* (ironic, unintelligible) coherence. This true harmony is the coherence between the hewn-out object (the named, the valued, the intelligible) and the unhewn context (the unnamed, unvalued, unintelligible) in which it is embedded, from which it emerged and to which it reverts. "Knowing" this harmony is precisely "seeing the small," to wit, being aware of the "hard-to-see subtleties" (眇／妙 miao) of chapter 1, that is, becoming aware of the unseen and unvalued at the root of the unseen and unvalued. Note here especially the direct connection, once again, between harmony and "sustainability," the coherence with the past and future—con-tinuance, lastingness, life. But here this "true harmony" is, in fact, the constant undermining of the original coherence of the intelligibly hewn object. Consistently in the *Laozi* text "knowledge" (知 zhi), unmodified, is depicted as negative, while "clarity" (明 ming) is depicted as positive. These are the "eye" and "stomach" modes of apprehending the world, respectively.

2. For something to be regarded as an object of *zhi* or eye-knowledge is for it to be coherent in the sense of intelligible, which means (1) its parts stick together in a pleasure-inducing way, sticking together therefore also (2) with a particular context of other surrounding items in a particular way, and also (3) with particularly disposed human faculties. Whatever is known in this manner, as "eye-knowledge," must serve as the object of an "eye" desire. It is noticed here that this always implies the co-presence of a context, an outside, with which the coherent object of knowledge and desire is also cohering or sticking together. It can appear as this object only when given together with this context. Coherence of the elements making up an intelligible unit implies coherence with what is outside that unit.

3. Both of these senses of coherence are indicated by the term *ming,* name, which we have seen to have the sense also of formed, intelligible, effective, existent. Whenever there is a name, an intelligible object of desire or knowledge, it can be regarded as having been "cut out" from a larger whole. The career of any known object can be traced back to its beginning and forward to its end, describing a typical course from unnamed to named and back to unnamed in a kind of bell-shaped pattern. They are like "straw dogs" (5)—starting out as worthless grass, made temporarily into a valued discernible object, and then "returning" to their original indiscernible value-lessness. "Returning" in this sense is the characteristic motion of the Dao, as the reversal toward namelessness (unintelligibility, incoherence) necessarily haunting every particular coherence (16, 25, 40). Perceiving this "other side" to every coherence is called "clarity," that is, "knowing the sustainable," the only sustainability that can be found, as opposed to the pretended coherence of particular intelligible values and coherences. This is the (ironic) "clarity" (*ming*) of the "stomach desires," contrasted to the "knowledge" of the eye desires. It is associated with "stillness," "emptiness" and all the other indiscernible, proto-Yin, devalued qualities (see "column B" below) (16, 55).

It is crucial to note here, then, that both *dao* and *ming* are terms with built-in value implications. A guiding discourse can be used to guide beings; but this use, this explicit status as a guide, will undermine its success in guiding them. A ruling principle may be named and praised, but then this renown will not last, for it will undermine itself. But the overall message of the *Laozi* remains optimistic; there *is* a way to attain sustainability: to create without being master, to rule without being seen, to do without doing, to achieve without taking credit, to know the masculine by holding to the feminine:

Know the masculine by keeping to the feminine,[21] and you will be the ravine of the world. Being a ravine to the world, the power of sustainability (常德 *chang de*) will not be separated from you, and you will return to the state of an infant. Know the bright by keeping to the dark, and you will be a model for the world.[22] Being a model for the world, the power of sustainability will not go awry, and you will return to the ultimate point of not yet being manifestly present and apprehensible. Know the honored by keeping to the disgraced, and you will be the valley of the world. Being the valley of the world, the power of sustainability will be whole, and you will return to the unhewn state. (28)

Sustainability *can* then be attained, ironically, but via a very special method. It involves an instrumental use of anti-value: the positive side is attained as sustainable only by "holding to" the negative side (cf. 22, 36, and *passim*). This will prevent the exclusive positing of the positive as the sole value, as what alone is positive, and hence will prevent its demise, its inconstancy.[23] This is not to be conceived as a merely formal and symmetrical presence of the two opposites, in equal parts, simply thrown together. Rather, there is a very definite asymmetrical structure here: *know* the male (et al.), but *hold to* the female (et al.). The two components in this stable (sustainable) alloy are differently bonded. One of the two has a privileged place: the negatively valued half of every pair, which is "held to" rather than merely "known." That is, it functions in the manner of "stomach," rather than objectified "eye," desires. This devalued background is the beginning of any coherence, from which it emerges, and into which it fades into unintelligibility; in this dimension too, the counsel is to attend to the beginning, the transitional border between not-yet-intelligible and intelligible, and privilege the former (63, 64). The exact nature of this privileging is more evident elsewhere: "The heavy is the root of the light, the still is the master of the active. . . . To be light [without being rooted in the heavy] is to lose the root, to be active [without stillness] is to lose the master." (26) Here too the "root" and "master" is found in the conventionally undesired half of each pair. If you wish to be "light" (i.e., take things lightly, be carefree), you must be "rooted" in the "heavy" to pull it off, to make it a "sustainably" applicable strategy. The achievement of the desired end (lightness, activity, male, brightness, etc.) as a constant course is made possible only by privileging the opposite quality, which controls and makes possible the positive quality, serves as its grounding and root, what makes it persist without being overturned. Similarly, to "hold to" the negatively valued half of any pair is precisely what allows one to "know" (implying also, "know how to, be able to achieve") the positively valued half. Only in this way can the achievement of the desired end be made sustainable. A stable masculinity, eminence, carefreeness, activity, and so forth, one that will not fall into its opposite, must already possess that opposite, be vaccinated with it as it were, and, what is more, give it the preeminent and ruling position in its own activity.

Whenever a coherence is made explicit, there is *necessarily* ("consistently, sustainably") an inherent vector toward a context; once this coherence with context is seen as coherent, it forms another coherence, which requires a further context, and so on ad infinitum. This is seen in a new emphasis on the question of "beginnings," hitherto rather downplayed in Chinese thinking, which looked rather to the coherence of tradition, or to a limited line of precedents, without worrying about an absolute beginning. The beginning is the point of transition from non-X to X, from a prior context to a particular coherence. This beginning is seen to be necessarily unintelligible.

4. This larger whole is thus the "not-yet-cut," the unhewn (樸 *pu*) raw material as opposed to the "vessel, useful object" (器 *qi*), which is socially valued and intelligible as a particular thing (28).

5. This unhewn has a double status:

a. In contrast to the valued vessel, it is the leftover detritus. This means it is valueless, in contrast to the value of the vessel, and that it is formless, nameless, unintelligible, in contrast to the intelligibility of the vessel.

b. As what is prior to the cut, and thus prior to the contrast itself, it encompasses both what is later called the vessel and what is later called the raw material, the value and the valueless, the intelligible and the unintelligible.

The *Laozi* text, as A. C. Graham has pointed out,[24] uses a great many parallel dyads to illustrate this relationship between the valued coherence and the disvalued context. These can be arranged in two columns as follows:

Column A (the Valued/Coherent):	Column B (the Disvalued/Incoherent):
Name	Nameless
High	Low
Male	Female
Vessel	Unhewn Material
Moving	Still
Full	Empty
Adult	Infant
Bright	Dark

In all cases, the items in the second column have the double status in relation to the first column item: they are both the *opposite* of the first column item, and *what exists prior to* the contrast, and hence *encompasses* both the first column and the second column items. The items in column B are thus stand-ins for the unintelligible that is the encompassing "coherence" of *both* A and B, in the sense of their togetherness.

6. Thus, this unhewn (B) is:

a. B as opposed to A, i.e., the *source* from which every vessel (intelligible object of knowledge, valued object of desire) comes, and the *end* toward which every vessel tends to return.

b. Both A and B, i.e., the *stuff* of which the vessel is made, the substance of which it is composed whether it is vessel or detritus, what is "constant" in either case.

c. Neither A nor B, i.e., what is neither "named" nor "nameless," neither "formed" nor "formless," since both of these pertain to what is in the system of cut-out names, whereas B is what is prior to any cutting whatsoever.

d. True B as opposed to so-called "B," i.e., not what is named "nameless" but what is devoid even of the name "nameless."

e. The true A as opposed to so-called "A," i.e., the *pattern or principle* of arising and returning, the inherent tendency back toward its unintelligibility and valuelessness which is always immanent in it, which determines how A acts, permeates A, makes A A, sustains A as A, and hence is the real locus of its identity as A. A is A as opposed to B only because A is value, and the unhewn (B) is the real value of A. The unhewn is thus the real A.

This same complex relationship pertains to all the members of columns A and B above. This fivefold relationship rests on the double meaning of the B terms. That is, B in all cases is (1) the opposite of A; (2) the totality of both A and B; (3) neither A nor B; (4) the true B; and (5) the true A. The unhewn is the opposite of the vessel. The (pre-cut) unhewn is the totality of both vessel and (post-cut) unhewn. The (pre-cut) unhewn is neither the vessel nor the (post-cut) unhewn. The (pre-cut) unhewn is the truth about the (post-cut) unhewn. The unhewn is the truth about the vessel (i.e., the vessel is taken as the locus of value, but the true locus of value lies in the anti-vessel, viz., the unhewn, which is what truly satisfies the original definition given to "vessel"—its valuableness). It is this last consequence—that "B" is the true "A"—that constitutes the "irony" of the Daoist tradition. "Non-Dao" is the true "Dao."

This inescapable doubleness of meaning is played out in the pointed paradoxes presented by the text about coherence, developed not only in terms of value and disvalue and visibility (intelligibility) and invisibility (unintelligibility) but also in terms of the derivative ideas of "greatness" and "smallness": the greatest is the smallest, that is, the most coherent (valuably unifying) is the least coherent (intelligible). From this unhewn whole, names (values) are "cut"—that is, divisions are made in the originally homogenous and useless (valueless) raw material, so that everything must fall on either one side or the other, the valued vessel or the refuse carved away from it. The unhewn itself is in this sense technically pre-value, the whole from which both value and anti-value emerge. These names, coming in value-opposite pairs, lead to eye desires, which identify an object and assign an intrinsic value to it as object. Thus, a return to the unhewn whole leads one back to having no (eye) desires (37). Invisibility, that is, the lack of a posited value, which the text designates as the "smallness" or "namelessness" of the unhewn (32), is a condition for desirelessness, since it implies that there is no object to be seen and grasped by deeming valuation and eye desire. Here we see the string of connections between the small, minute "ungraspable," the unhewn, and desirelessness (i.e., no "eye" desires, not no "stomach" desires). The unhewn whole, which one would assume to be bigger than any part, is thus called "small" in a very special sense: namely, in the sense that smallness means in this text what is subtle, difficult to perceive, what is nameless, not yet evident, not yet given a value-name, not yet emerged as a particular (hence one-sided) object of desire. The whole is not yet divided into names, it is not eminent as one name or the other, and hence cannot be an object of deeming "eye" desire. On the basis of the five meanings of the unhewn, we can now more fully understand the double status of the text's attitude also toward these desires: we are in one sense to "eliminate" eye desires (if they are conceived as only A versus B), but also we are told to preserve eye desires and even protect and enhance them (if you remember that they are actually unsevered from the cycle of stomach desires, are themselves manifestations thereof, B as the totality of A and B, and as the true A). Hence, we are told in chapter 12 that the five colors harm the eye: it does not say that obsession with the five colors distracts us from something more worthy, such as colorlessness, or spirit, or Dao: it tells us that it harms our ability to *see colors*. Eye desire harms *the eye*. The text is both pro-eye and anti-eye at once, which is only intelligible if we discern the multiple senses built into the meaning of the B category, the central *irony* of the term *Dao*. The text takes the same double attitude to Dao, to names, and to desire, and the structural reasons for all of these are to be found in the five meanings of "B," of the unhewn, outlined above.

Smallness also implies the incipient, the hard-to-discern state of something that is just beginning, which is not yet recognizable as what it will become[25] (64). This suggests that the meaning of the term *unseen subtlety* (*miao*) also indicates the unseen presence of the opposite of whatever is apparent in any given situation, and its potential reversal into its opposite. This is what accounts for the impossibility to attain any consistent way of naming it, of fixing any constant course for it. In order there is a seed of disorder, which is as yet "nothing," "nameless," "an unseen subtlety."[26] (58) Thus, the simple negation embedded in every affirmative, the incompleteness of any description, the failure to yield any constant course, actually means that the opposites will tend to reverse into one another. The unhewn whole haunts all partial, specified actuals; they contain more than they seem to, they also contain the seed of their opposite, for they have been cut and posited out of the totality of themselves and their particular discarded anti-value background.

The unhewn is then both the "largest" whole and the "smallest." The text is quite explicit about this paradox, calling the course both the "Great" and the "Small." This correlates again to what we may call the two prongs of Laozi's fork: the constant co-presence of doing and non-doing, desiring and not-desiring, the hidden and the manifest, the Small and the Great. Indeed, it is only now that we are in the position to understand the connection between the two sides. The unity of the unseen mysteries and the manifest outcomes was merely noted in chapter 1, but is spelled out more clearly in chapter 25 and chapter 34. Chapter 1 simply told us that these two apparent opposites are really two words for the same meaning. Chapter 14 told us one way in which the named comes from the ungraspable, in that it is called "The faint, the subtle, the minute." There, it is the very failure to find a specific form that is itself given a "name" (*ming*). This name is "the great image" (35), that is, the "shape of shapelessness," "the image of thinglessness," (14), thus, the name "namelessness," the form "formlessness," which is embodied in all the B-category items. The images of creative void (the voidness of value that creates value in ch. 5, the empty hub in ch. 11, the still root from which things grow and to which they return in ch. 16) further underscored this connection between none and all. It is Chapter 34 that tells why the ungraspable void may be regarded equally as either small (the unseen, the beginning, the subtleties, without desire) *or* as large (the names for all, the all-encompassing mother, which can be an ironic object of desire):

The Great Course overflows everywhere, able to go either left or right. All things depend on it for their birth and it refuses none, and although it accomplishes this task it does not get the name [credit] for it. Though it clothes and nourishes all things, it *does not act as their master*. Thus it sustains freedom from desire [concerning it and all that derives from it], due to which it can be called the small [which plays no observed, valued or desired role in things]. [But by the same token,] *all things return to it*, though it does not act as their master, due to which it can be called the great. So it is precisely because it never deems itself great that it accomplishes this greatness.

Here, the two contrary aspects are again spelled out as two ways of describing the same situation. It is "small" because it (1) does not make itself master (is not posited as valued, B as opposed to A), although it (2) nourishes and produces all things and is their beginning and end (is the actual source of value, the real A). It is "great" because it (2) nourishes and produces all things, and is their beginning and end (the real A), although (1) it does not make itself master (B as opposed to A). These are two ways of saying the same thing, with reversed emphasis. This smallness means inapprehensibility, its never taking the discernible role of master, the lack of a constant guiding course or of an already manifest object to be deemed as desirable. To perceive that all things derive from it and yet to perceive its absence of lordship over them, to perceive its "smallness," is to be free of desire concerning it, and concerning all particular objects seen as so deriving from it; rather than seeing them as eye-objects, as posited values, which excludes anti-value, they are seen as expressions of the unhewn Dao; but since they are all this unhewn Dao, and this unhewn Dao is not itself any particular thing and thus cannot be the object of an eye desire, they too are not seen and desired as half of a pair of names divided out from the unhewn whole. One strives after no values, because all values are seen to derive their value from the valueless. Because it is unknown to them, it does not create eye desires in things (nor, of course, does it have any desire to play the lord over them). It can be called great, on the other hand, because "all things return to it."[27] "Return" here means turn to it to provide their coherence, as the social group coheres around the sage king in the *Mencius*, as the spokes of the wheel all return to and converge around the empty hub in *Laozi* 11. As Ivanhoe puts it, "The Confucian draws people toward him through the power of his ethical excellence, which inspires similar behavior and attitudes in others. He is like the Pole Star or the wind—forces *above* the people to which they submit or defer. . . . Laozi's sage also draws people to him, moves them to submit or defer, and influences them to behave in certain ways. But he draws people toward him and wins their allegiance by placing himself *below* them, welcoming all and putting them at ease."[28]

Things cohere not around the bright, the high, the eminent, the full, but around the dark, the low, the neglected, the empty, and this "cohering" is simultaneously a "returning to" in the sense of emerging from and dissolving back into that lowly empty center that unifies them. All things return to their roots, which are equally unintelligible and lowly, and as indiscernible, are "one" in the sense of the lowest, or the most lacking, as none (14).[29] This "one" is the emptiness toward which all things return as "converging," which is conflated with the process of return of the bell curve of rise and fall from formlessness to form to formlessness (5, 16) and with the built-in cyclical returning motion of the stomach desires from hunger to satiety, from wanting to not wanting, from valuing to not-valuing. It is around this noneness to which they return that they genuinely cohere. This is the "One"[30]—not merely a unity but also the *lowest* number, a noneness, a valuelessness in which all things are rooted—i.e., the real source of their coherence, value, and harmony (39, and *passim*). "One" is unity only as a function of its lowness: it is both A and B because it is B as opposed to A.

As source of value, then, it is, in its own ironic way, doing what a "Dao" is supposed to do. As principle of operation, it also does what a "Dao," a guiding discourse, was supposed to do. As unintelligibility, it provides the real togetherness of any coherence with its context, with every context, with whatever lies outside it, whatever lies before its beginning and after its end as an intelligible coherence. As incoherence, therefore, it provides real coherence. This is the central irony of the ironic tradition.

By contrast, the intelligible object of desire and knowledge (eye-knowledge), which is supposed to cohere with the minds and hearts of the social group so as to cause it to cohere as a genuine community, if taken in complete isolation from the stomach, A in complete separation from B, creates "sameness" rather than harmony, and thus competition, strife, disunity and incoherence. "Not esteeming the worthy will cause the people to be free of strife; not placing value on hard-to-attain goods will cause the people not to become thieves. Not displaying the desirable will keep the people's hearts from disorder. Hence the sage's rule empties their minds (eye desires) and fills their stomachs (stomach desires); weakens their ambitions (eye) and strengthens their bones (stomach). . . ." (3) "Sameness" would pertain to an eye-object, the object of an eye desire. When any object, coherent value, is made explicitly desirable, all the desirers rush toward it, trying to get the "same" thing. This creates strife, conflict, disharmony: the very "coherence" (intelligibility) of the object undermines the "coherence" of the group that serves as the context which endowed it with coherence.

The recommendation of the text is not necessarily the complete elimination of everything that we experience as eye desires. It is more centrally concerned with the reintegration of eye desires back into stomach desires, a maintenance of the eye desires' connection to, rootedness in, stomach desires, of which they are, ultimately, expressions. The problem with eye desires is that they become removed from the stomach, become autonomous and "constant." Eye desires are in fact "cut out" of stomach desires, remaining embedded in them and then, if not artificially enhanced by the application of ideals and values and virtues, fading back into them: in the ideal natural state, they retain this connection, to be cut out against their background of unhewn raw material like an embossed relief rather than a free-standing statue. But even when going awry there is "Dao"—the unhewn—in them, they too are made of this raw material that we see as their background. My lust for pornography still involves my physical sexual hormonal flow and the entire economy of my non-aim-specific biological life; my lust for caviar still is made from my stomach's cycle of hunger and satiety, from which it is formed. An eye desire is a shaping, a channeling, a carving out, a directing of the amorphous formless energy of a stomach desire into a particular focused form—in short, a "guiding," a "dao"ing. Chapter 28 gives us this relationship most explicitly, as we have seen: "Know the white, but hold to the black"—know the eye desires, but hold them to the stomach desires, so that, as the final line of the same chapter says, "The greatest cutting does not sever" (大制不割 *dazhibuge*). This means that the eye desires both are and are not a "part" of the stomach desires, just as the named both is and is not a "part" of the nameless. We see a further application of the "both/and" relationship propounded in 28 developed in terms of "mother" and "sons" in 52: the eye desires are the sons, the stomach desires are the mother, and both are to be preserved, and their relationship maintained, to ensure the flourishing of *both*. The ironic double meaning of terms is once again the key to the text.

A simpleminded model might be helpful to clarify this. To do or experience anything I want to do or experience, I have to be awake. I desire wakefulness, consciousness, clarity, vigor, activity. These seem to be unambiguous goods. But being awake is actually part of a cycle that includes both wakefulness and sleep. Being asleep is a state of complete inactivity and unconsciousness, in which I can neither do nor experience (discounting for the moment dreams!) any of the things I avowedly, and perhaps legitimately, want. Sleep is the total negation of everything I want. The *Laozi* sees human problems as analogous to a case of chronic insomnia. Because I want what I want so exclusively and obsessively, I cannot get to sleep: I'm obsessing on my plans and projects, and besides, why waste valuable time sleeping and missing out on everything? Staying awake for days on end, I start to lose my ability to work, to concentrate, to get any of the things I want, or even to enjoy them if I happen to get them. Dr. Laozi may say, You need sleep. But if I *try* to sleep, directing my will to this new project "sleep" in the same way as I do my other projects, it will of course only make it more difficult for me to sleep. So I must devise other strategies to disrupt my customary mode of desiring. I must raise some questions about their inherent desirability, teach myself to notice their rootedness in disappearing now and then, their cycle of appearing and disappearing as the essence of their desirability, cultivate some insight into the elusiveness of "sleep" as an object of desire and the paradox of "wanting" to sleep, and so on. "Sleep" is itself a term like "mother" or any other B term: it resists direct targeting as an object of the will, and at the same time, seen as the substratum of all the non-sleep goods, undermines my usual mode of desiring those non-sleep goods. So to cure my insomnia I need the double meaning of sleep—real sleep as the negation even of "sleep" as definite conscious aim—and of non-sleep, of both the undesired and of the desired. (We may note here in passing that Dao is in this sense the precise opposite of certain understandings of the traditional monotheistic God, a monster of constant consciousness, wakefulness and willing of the good!) The further implication is that, once we do get a normal night's sleep, we'll be able to do all those things we were straining to do in our waking life all the better, and without having to strain; all these things come naturally to one who gets a good night's sleep. So straining for either the goods of wakefulness or for sleep impedes sleep, and when sleep is impeded, so is the attainment of the goods of wakefulness. This leads to a vicious circle: thus impeded, one strains all the harder for the goods of wakefulness, making sleep that much more elusive, and therefore making the goods of wakefulness that much more elusive. This perhaps also clarifies in what sense the eye desires are not to be eliminated, but rather reintegrated: what makes the porn or the caviar good at all is the fact that it's a temporary, perhaps occasional, manifestation of non-porn and non-caviar, as conscious excitement is fine as long as it doesn't end up interfering with the sleep that makes it possible. Whether or not every single possible eye desire can be rehabilitated as a form of stomach desire is, it seems to me, left inconclusive in the text as we have it.

An even more simpleminded example might tease out some further implications: A flower grows out of dirt and manure. "Dirtiness" is excluded from the coherence "floweriness," if this coherence is made explicit, defined, seen as intelligible as such. But the coherence of flower requires coherence with non-flower—dirtiness—to be coherent. Seeking floweriness in its purity, as a pure form, exluding all non-floweriness, means either picking the flower, hence killing it, or creating a plastic flower, also dead and not truly flowery. The unintelligible incoherence of flower-plus-dirtiness is the true coherence of floweriness, the flow of emergence and return into dirt which, ironically, is the true "constancy" of floweriness, as opposed to the sham constantly coherent floweriness of the plastic flower. The true coherence is the incoherence that sees the flower as an aspect emerging from the dirt, always permeated by the dirtiness of it and ruled by the trajectory of emerging from it and the tendency to return to it. This does not mean eliminating the flowery, nor the articulated distinction between the flower and the dirt, but rather calls for maintaining the sense of the connection between the coherent and the incoherent. To see the life, continuance, coherence (including coherence with our really coherent, "stomach," desires) of the flower is to see its constant hounding by, rootedness in, tendency to revert to, incoherence, disvalue and death. Again our key line is the end of chapter 28: "The greatest cutting does not sever." (大制不割 dazhibuge) Plato felt that triangles that were infected with lots of other non-triangly stuff were not triangles: they had all sorts of other characteristics. If I draw a triangle in ink on a piece of paper here, there is, in addition to triangularity, lots to do with "ink" and "paper" and "here and now" involved. Also, the triangle appears triangular from head-on, but from some angles and in some lighting it looks like a line or a blur or a part of a square. Plato wants a triangle that is triangly all the way down, and from all sides, and to all observers. The pure triangle, divested of all this non-trianglish stuff, is the real triangle, the intelligible triangle, the Form of the triangle. For Laozi, on the other hand, the pure triangle is the destruction of the triangle. The more purely triangly it gets, the less triangle is there. The pure flower is the dead flower. The more purely flowery it gets, the less flower we have. The pure good is worthless. Make things too "good," by any standard of good at all, and the good is destroyed. Any pure dao fails to dao. The real daoing is done by not being daoed.

Here we arrive at the model of omnipresence as it emerges in the ironic tradition. Though it is one of the first things anyone learns about Chinese philosophy, we should be surprised that "the Dao" has come to be used as a term for "the omnipresent." We can see now, however, that the kind of omnipresence it is should not be conflated with the notions of omnipresence we briefly outlined in chapter 1, as derived from Greek notions of form and matter, predicated on absolutized notions of sameness and difference. Rather, it derives from an ironic subversion of the Chinese model of coherence as discussed in the last chapter, and for that reason bears some unusual contours. Like some of the concepts of omnipresence in Greek (and for that matter, Indian) thought, we can indeed say that the Dao is everything and nothing. But it is not, like them, everything and nothing because it is all matter (and hence everything) deprived of all form (and hence nothing), or because it is all form (and hence everything) deprived of all matter (and hence nothing). Form is what is the same between two chunks of same-formed matter. Matter is what is the same between two chunks of differently formed matter. Form is what is different between two chunks of differently formed matter. Matter is what is different between two chunks of same-formed matter. But none of this goes into derivation of the omnipresence of the Dao. The Dao is everything because the unhewn is the raw material of all hewn vessels, the stuff of all things, which bears some superficial resemblance to the idea of "matter." It is the "formless" which is the stuff of all form. But formlessness is also the *source* of all form. The unhewn is the beginning from which the hewn emerges. It is also the end into which the hewn resolves. It is thus also the *course* of all form, the determining principle of rise and fall from formlessness to form to formlessness. Formlessness denotes the opposite of any particular form, the exclusion of it, and at the same time it is the word for the ultimate and entire reality of any particular form, its beginning, its course and its end. Formlessness means both "column B as opposed to column A" and "what precedes the division between columns A and B." It is, again, all five of the following: (1) B to the exclusion of A, (2) the totality of B plus A, (3) neither B nor A, (4) true B, and (5) true A. This is a characteristic paradoxicalness that is not found in Greek or Indian conceptions of omnipresence. Form is the hewn is coherence: the contextualization of a composite item embedded in a background from which it is distinguished by its value, its relation to human desire. To restate the matter in these terms, formlessness, the unhewn, incoherence is thus at once (1) the opposite of coherence; (2) the totality of both coherence and incoherence; (3) neither coherence nor incoherence; (4) the true incoherence; and (5) the true coherence. It is the opposite of value: the worthless. It is the totality of value and disvalue: the omnipresent field in which both appear, and which indeed appears *as* both. It is neither value nor disvalue: the field deprived of both. It is true disvalue: not the so-called disvalued which is really operating usefully in the system of knowing and discourse. It is the true value: what alone is truly of worth and true gives things continuance, life, coherence with past and future, sustainability, identity, coherence with the world. It is in this sense that the Dao is everywhere and nowhere, is everything and nothing. Simply stated, it is *both* the "materialist" omnipresence *and* the "idealist" omnipresence, joined in an ironic turn of the ethical omnipresence of value as disvalue, disvalue as value. This is an omnipresence that is the very process of transformation from the disvalued and unknown, to the valued and known, to the disvalued and unknown. Hence, it is not a static omnipresent something that is just inertly present. Nor is it simply an omnipresent fact waiting to be known; its relation to knowing and not-knowing is embedded in the very mechanism and structure of its omnipresence. Its omnipresence is none other than its absence; there is no question of whether it "exists" or "does not exist." Hence, I call it "ironic" coherence.

Looking back to Tang Junyi's five meanings of the term *Dao*, we are now perhaps in a position to understand their inner connection. Tang's meaning 1, Dao as the immanent totality of all things, is our "Both A and B." Tang's meaning 2, Dao as the nameless and fully transcendent reality, is our "Neither A nor B" and "True B." Tang's meaning 3, the named and manifested Dao as weakness and lowness and femininity and the like, is our "B as opposed to A." Tang's meaning 4 (Dao as Virtuosity), meaning 5 (Dao as the ideal state of a thing), and meaning 6 (Dao as the prescriptive rule to be followed) are various dimensions of our "True A." We can perhaps now see that rather than being five unrelated meanings, which just happen to be attached to the same word, these seemingly opposed or even para-doxical connotations of the term are all simply alternate ways of denoting the same thing, the unhewn, the B category with its built-in ambiguity and the systemic paradox of naming and value embedded in it. The discovery of these ironies and double meanings of coherence and omnipresence are the central contribution of the ironic tradition.

The technical term *a priori* I have been using here is sure to raise some hackles. From what has been said above, I hope both the intended meaning and the justification for this term have become clear. The question rests mainly on an appreciation of both the all-inclusive comprehensiveness of the term *ming*, name, in this text, and its self-referentiality. It would otherwise be possible to regard the *Laozi*'s claims as resting on empirical induction, without concern for their "necessary" applicability, derived from the observation of certain particular facts and coherences—cycles in nature, or the customary connection of certain social facts to one another. But I claim the element of necessity, and a full a priori quality in the sense of inescabability of the dyadic undermining of context to any coherence *no matter what coherence* happens to appear in experience, just by virtue of being a coherence, and as a condition of any and all possible coherences, including the one involved in this claim. This entails the claim also that some coherence or other must be posited, that coherence is inescapable, for even the thought of no-coherence is another coherence. This ensures the fully inescapable, a priori nature of the situation. I make this claim, in spite of the fact that nothing like a rigorous argument is presented in the text, because of the self-referentiality of the term *ming*, again, and its all-inclusiveness; but what serves as the true guarantor for this a priori implication comes from the confirmation of what comes closest to a rigorous argument for the dyadic a priori, which comes in the second chapter of the *Zhuangzi*, the Qiwulun or "Equalizing Assessments of Things." It is to this discussion that I now turn.

ZHUANGZI'S WILD CARD: THING AS PERSPECTIVE

The *Zhuangzi* was traditionally regarded as the work of Zhuang Zhou (fourth century BCE), but is now generally regarded as the work of many hands, reflecting many distinguishable strains of Daoist thinking.[31] The part of the text thought to come from Zhuang Zhou himself (the "Inner Chapters," or the first seven of the thirty-three chapters of the traditional Guo Xiang version of the text) takes a further step in extending the earlier Daoist preoccupation with the spontaneous bodily life over purposive cultural aims, moving to a critique of the fixed valuation of even the concept of "life" itself, as part of the general critique of valuation and conceptualization in general. This is achieved by means of an intricate epistemological and linguistic agnosticism and perspectivism, rooted in insights into the indexically dependent nature of evaluative knowledge and of language on perspective, and the unceasing transformation of these perspectives. Let us examine the development of this line of thinking in detail.

Zhuangzi's work begins with the striking story of an inconceivably vast fish named Kun, who transforms into an equally enormous bird named Peng. Peng, we are told, must fly high in the air to get enough wind underneath him to support his enormous wings. This makes him seem both uselessly grandiose and incomprehensibly bizarre to the smaller birds watching him from the earth, and we are treated to their ridicule of his outlandish extravagance.

This story may be regarded as Zhuangzi's dramatic entrance, his self-introduction to the reader. For Peng is the first of Zhuangzi's many masks, serving as a cutting but good-natured rejoinder to his friend Huizi's taunts about the uselessness of Zhuangzi's big talk, presented in the final two dialogues of the first chapter.[32] The story introduces us to three intertwined themes that are at the heart of Zhuangzi's project:

1. *transformation*;

2. *dependence*; and

3. the limitations of *perspectival knowledge*.

Peng's position is incomprehensible to the little birds, as Zhuangzi's is to Huizi. These birds can only thrive in their constricted particular environment, which alone gives them a function, an identity, a value. Their identity is *dependent on its coherence* with this particular environment. However, merely flying high in the vastness of the air is no escape from this problem. The text goes on to remark that even if one breaks free of such a narrow realm, like the mythical philosopher Liezi, who could walk on the wind, one is still dependent on coherence with *something* for one's usefulness and identity, for one's happiness—in this case, the wind. The dependence of Liezi on the wind is still rooted in commitment to a *fixed perspective and identity*, predicated on a particular coherence with a particular environment, like a scholar who depends on the esteem of a particular ruler or community as the guarantor of his value and status.[33] If Peng were merely Peng and noth-ing more, if he had a fixed identity and thus a fixed definition of what suits him, he would be no better off. But this bird is actually a *transformation* of the enormous fish, Kun, representing the very oppositemost perspective. And this, for Zhuangzi, is the heart of the matter: *the way perspectives transform into other perspectives.*

Zhuangzi then introduces the notion of genuine independence and freedom, which he describes as a way of "charioting upon what is true both to Heaven and to earth, riding atop the back-and-forth of the six atmospheric breaths, so that your wandering can nowhere be brought to a halt" (乘天地之正, 而御六氣之辯, 以遊無窮者 *chengtiandizhizheng eryu-liuqizhibian yiyouwuqiongzhe*). This passage suggests that one can become completely independent of things not by separating oneself from things, renouncing one's involvement with and responsiveness to them, but rather, ironically, through *complete* involvement with them, in a sense through com-plete dependence on (all of) them. Rather than being dependent on this or that, and far from being dependent on no thing at all, one is dependent on *any* thing at all, because one's identity, and with it one's conditions of depen-dence, is able to transform unobstructedly. This means an ability to cohere with whatever environment may confront one, and to do what we have seen "cohering" is supposed to do: continue into the future unobstructedly, producing value and pleasure. Whatever happens to come one's way, one is able to "ride upon it," to make it the chariot upon which one goes wandering through new vistas. The identity of Peng, the highest and largest and most visible in the sky, is free and unfettered only because he is able to transform from the smallest and lowest and most hidden: Kun, a fish egg that is also a vast fish, in the depths of the sea. It is this transformation of perspective and identity that Zhuangzi indicates when he asserts that "the Consum-mate Person has no fixed identity." This ability to cohere, value-creatively, with any environmental context, obviously requires a very special sort of "identity"—an ironic identity. Hence, the passage in question actually does not directly say that "if one did this, one would then be independent," but rather says, "If one did this, one would then be dependent on—what?" This dependence on "what?"—not as an answer but as a perpetual question—is the ironic independence of the ironic Daoist identity, the perpetual "who?" It is this "who?" rather than a definitive lack of a self, that is denoted in the following line, asserting the lack of a fixed identity, along with the lack of any one particular merit or name, that is, recognized value. Lack of any certain merit, lack of any particular value, lack of any fixed identity—these all denote the same thing. The Zhuangzian person does not possess any particular value or merit or identity, but is able to produce endless values and merits and identities. But how is this possible?

This will be the theme with which chapter 2, "Equalizing Assessments of Things," begins. The arguments made in this chapter on these issues—transformation of identity, dependence, and perspective—represent the core of the *Zhuangzi's* philosophy. The remainder of the Inner Chapters may be viewed as containing applications of the considerations sketched out in chapter 2 to different situations and contexts.

This chapter begins with Nanguoziqi saying, "I have lost me," after looking as if he had "lost his opposite."[34] "Losing me (*sangwo* 喪我)" is paired with, indeed seems to be identical with, "losing his opposite/counterpart (*sang qi ou* 喪其耦)." "Me" and "the opposite/counterpart" appear to be opposites, but the losing of one is synonymous with the losing of the other, for in losing one, both are lost. Here, the great question of the mutual definition of dyadic pairs, the two extreme swings of the pendulum, makes its unmistakable appearance. For here we begin to see concretely what a "whole" with which one must cohere is for Zhuangzi, and indeed for the tradition in general. It is not an undifferentiated mass of indifferent matter or *qi*, as we might think from an unreflecting reading of some of the passages in the text. Instead, the primary idea of a whole is of a correlative pair, which Zhuangzi pares down to its purest and most abstract form: This and That, or Self and Not-self.

The question is then asked: "What do you mean, you lost you?" The answer that is given seems at first unrelated; we are told about the piping of earth and heaven, which are the sounds that emerge from the hollows of trees and rocks as the wind passes through. This is not only a clever continuation of the wind imagery from the chapter before, but a striking metaphor of the voices of philosophers arguing their rights and wrongs with each other from their various perspectives, as Guo Xiang, Wang Fuzhi, and many others have noted. They can all be perceived, in all their cacophony and conflict, as a harmonious piping of the one blower, the wind. In the same way, perhaps, the philosophers' arguments can be heard as the pipings of Dao. Perhaps this can be construed to mean, "I no longer see my viewpoint as my own, but instead as that of the blower, the Dao, and the same goes for the viewpoints of others." This would mean that we all share one ultimate identity, that of the Dao, as all the pipings are the sound of the one wind.

This "monistic" interpretation gives us part of the answer, but does not go far enough; it must be supplemented by carefully considering the exact nature of this monistic identity: for it is, in fact, an *ironic* identity, an ironic coherence. Nanguoziqi concludes by saying, "It goes through all the ten thousand differences, allowing each to go its own way. But since each one selects out its own, what identity can there be for their rouser?" This *what identity?*, this *who?*[35] This "who," in my view, is a gloss on "I lost me." This question word is Zhuangzi's typical yes/no, the same yes/no we saw implied in the structure of "'I' lost 'me,'" the simultaneous presence and absence of the self, and Zhuangzi's insistence on ending all his discussions with a wavering pair of questions, rather than a conclusion. The blower, then, is the self, always both present and absent in the sounds. The true self, in short, is "Who?." Or, to put it otherwise, the true self is, "Is there really a true self or not?" The Dao has no fixed identity, and when I identify myself with the Dao, I have lost me—not thereby gaining another definite identity (i.e., that of "the Dao"), but rather adopting the identitylessness of the Dao, which is present only as identities other than its own, as non-Dao identities, just as the wind's sound is present only as specific hollow sounds Indeed, it is thus perhaps this question itself—the "who?"—that most adequately evokes the wonder of the unfixable multifariousness of the wind's sonic identity. The true self is, in a word, unintelligible, or, more to the point, *unintelligibility itself*. It is this incoherence that is now put forward as the true coherence, what brings all things to be, what creates all value, what continues the process of transformation and holds together every dyadic pair as its center. The sounds of the pipings, and the views of the philosophers, do have a kind of "harmony" or coherence among them—but the exact nature of this harmony is very much the issue that confronts us in this chapter, for it is a harmony that depends on their equal dependence on the unintelligible, the incoherent "what?" that lies at the source of each of them. This harmony is an *ironic* harmony.[36]

What are the sounds, then, supposed to represent? A few lines later the answer is given explicitly: "Joy and anger, sorrow and happiness, plans and regrets, transformations and stagnation, unguarded abandonment and deliberate posturing—music flowing out of hollows, mushrooms of billowing steam!"[37] As a first approach, then, these varied tones are images of the shifting and transformation of different human *moods*, which are arranged here, significantly, in contrasting dyads: joy versus anger, plans versus regrets, and so forth. These conditions of our consciousness, these moods, these colorings of our experience, come and go, swinging from one side to the other. These are our *perspectives* on the world. When we are joyful, we see a world of joy; when angry, a world of anger. Where do these perspectives come from? What is their basis? What controls them? Which is our "real" mood, our real identity? Who is the blower? Above all, *what does the ceaseless transformation of perspectives depend on?* In this question we have a compressed reprise of the three themes introduced in chapter 1: transformation, dependence, and perspective. That is why Nanguoziqi lost "himself" in contemplating these pipings: he sees only the transformations, and no "true ruler"—source, controller—among them other than the posing of the question about the true ruler.

This point is made more forcefully a few lines farther on, when the question of true controller is raised explicitly. First we are told that "the self" as such is correlative with these, its objects (note that initially the "objects" are not things in the outside world, but the self's own emotional perspectives): "Without *that* there would be no me, but then again without me there would be nothing selected out from it all."[38] It seems as if there's some controller—but no sign of him can be found. It is like the body itself—do the parts rule each other in turn, or is there a real enduring ruler to them all? And again, we end up with the same deliberately ambiguous conclusion: it has no sign or form, is identified with no one part or stage in the transformations, and yet it has its unmistakable functions, again presented as a pair of opposites and their coherence. "Its ability to flow and to stop makes its presence plausible, but even then it shows no definite form. That would make it a reality with no definite form." These words are echoed and expanded upon in chapter 6 to describe Dao itself: "Dao has realness and reliability but no form or deliberate activity" (有情有信, 無形無為 *you qing you xin, wu xing wu wei*).[39] We may perhaps infer from this that the Dao is to the world as the non-contrastive, non-definite, incoherent self is to the passing emotional perspectives. It is both present and absent—in other words, "I" have lost "me."[40] We have the ironic wedge between the different senses of coherence. It is coherent in the senses of continuing the process of transformation, holding opposites together, and bestowing value, but incoherent in the sense of being unintelligible.

The wind, on this reading, would represent Dao. But what is that? Zhuangzi is suggesting that it cannot be expressed in any one particular manner, as any specifiable identity. The way is no specific way. It is unknowable, unspecifiable, just as the tone of the wind is no particular tone, is any and every tone. Zhuangzi tells us that "knowing consciousness cannot find the source" of these moods and perspectives, the sole true determinant of their identity. We cannot know the sound of the wind *as such*, the sound that is the source of all the other sounds, that makes them so. Nor can we know Dao as such, the entity that is the source of all entities, that determines their becoming. But we are then told that there always *seems* to be a "genuine ruler"—Dao, Wind—serving as the controlling source of all these shifting phenomena. It's just that we can never find any one specific characteristic to identify it with. It is neither there nor not there, like "the sound of the wind" in each particular tone. It always seems to be present, but cannot be grasped as definitively here or there.[41]

But why is it that the source of the varying perspectives, a fixed single real identity, can *never* be discovered? This brings us to the crux of Zhuangzi's argument. Zhuangzi claims that the way we see things, the way we consciously know, is itself determined by our perspective, our mood.

But the question about the origin of this way of seeing things is posed as part of that way of seeing things. The question about where moods and perspectives come from is posed from *within* some particular perspective; a perspective is attempting to see and verify *its own* becoming. However, Mood X cannot witness its own transition from not being there to being there, for by definition it cannot be there to view what preceded its own emergence. Whatever it sees and knows is ipso facto a part of the world that exists *after* its emergence—the world of anger, the world of joy—not the preexisting cause or source of that emergence. Knowledge of the source of X would require an ability to stand outside of X. It might try to get around this problem by drawing conclusions about its preexistent source based on inferences rather than direct witnessing. But this conclusion and the premises of the inferential procedures that produce it do not really stand outside of X; they are themselves manifestations or aspects of X's own experience, internal to it. Since all assertions about the origin of a perspective are internal to that perspective, there is no perspective-independent way of verifying their reliability, of inferring a nonempirical source for them, or of adjudicating between conflicting accounts.

That is, Zhuangzi does not advise us to recognize any single definite, unchanging cause of these transformations, whether it be the Dao or the whole, and to comprehend it and surrender to it. This would still be "taking a mind with some particular completed perspective (in this case, *the perspective of the whole*) as your master (隨其成心而師之 *sui qi chengxin er shizhi*)." But Zhuangzi does not recommend this. What then does he recommend?

It is at this point in the text that the connection to the disputes of philosophers is explicitly made: "Sayings are not just blowings; sayings have something they say. It's just that what they say is not fixed."[42] Zhuangzi's argument proceeds from this consideration of an individual's moods succeeding one another in time to the more technical problem of conflicting truth claims. He has an imaginary objector—perhaps we should hear Huizi again here—saying, in effect, "Okay, that may be true for things like shifting moods, but when we make philosophical arguments, there *is* a fixed standard: words are not wind, words refer to something, and this gives them a consistent reliability, a standard by which to be judged."[43] Zhuangzi, in response, brings us back to the question of dependence. What words *depend on* for their meaning, what they putatively refer to, is actually no more fixed than the shifting moods, the sounds of holes in a windstorm, or indeed, "the chirping of baby birds." For the fixing of a scheme of reference, by which alone words are given meanings, is also wholly dependent on a perspective. So are words arguing philosophical positions really any different from blowing breaths or chirping birds (perhaps the derisive little birds of "Xiaoyaoyou"), from the changing modes and emotions an individual goes through, or not? Again we end in a question—Zhuangzi is subtle enough to see that to conclude definitively even that words can conclude nothing is unnecessary. All he needs to make his point—i.e., to evoke the perspective that he wants to evoke—is to make it questionable whether words—including his present words evoking the question about the conclusiveness of words—conclude anything definitive. Words can raise questions, including questions about words and their conclusiveness and power to refer unambiguously, without any of the usual epistemological quandaries that come with, for example, using words to *demonstrate* that words can demonstrate nothing. Zhuangzi is not using words to say that words say nothing, which would be an obvious contradiction. He is, rather, using words to raise a question about whether words do anything but raise questions—which far from being a contradiction, is perhaps the very form of the unquestionable! For "do words raise questions?" itself, if taken as a question and answered *either positively or negatively,* already demonstrates that words *do* raise questions. Even to answer, "No, words do not raise questions about words" demonstrates that words *do* raise questions about words. This "instantiation by means of negation" is the real structure of the absolutely reliable state of mind, intriguingly parallel in the structure of Descartes's *cogito* and Spinoza's "conceivable only as existing," but in Zhuangzi's case it is precisely and specifically *doubt*, not thinking in general—the "radiance of drift and doubt (滑疑之耀 *guyizhiyao*)"—that accomplishes this completely incontrovertible position. The statement "there are sometimes disagreements" is confirmed whether one agrees with it or disagrees with it. It is the obvious fact that precedes and conditions any discussion, and yet it is also the one absolutely true proposition, which is confirmed even by being denied. It is thus the only true omnipresence, instantiated even in its negation, as present in its presence as in its absence.

More technically, Zhuangzi develops this point by means of a consideration of two central terms, which figured prominently in the specialized vocabulary of the logicians and debaters of his day: *shi* and *fei*. *Shi* 是 means both "this" and "correct." Graham has ingeniously covered both senses of the term by rendering it into the somewhat cumbersome English phrase, "That's it!" which implies both correctly identifying something as what someone intended to refer to, and the affirmation of correctness. The term has two different antonyms. One is *bi* 彼, meaning "other, that." This is contrasted to the term in the sense of "this." The other antonym is *fei* 非, meaning "wrong," both in the sense of untrue (of an assertion) and in the sense of morally objectionable (of an action). Graham renders it as "that's not [it]!" These terms are, as A. C. Graham and Chad Hansen have persuasively argued, what linguists call "indexicals." Indexicals are words whose referent depends on what one is pointing to when one utters them. When I am pointing to a chair, the word *this* refers to the chair. When I am pointing to the table, however, *this* refers to the table. Zhuangzi argues that our notion of "right" is in exactly the same boat: it is "this," my own perspective, that is defined as the standard of "right," and what that is will depend on who I am, and what my perspectival mood is at any moment. But these are always changing and transforming. What words refer to is dependent on the assigning of a meaning to the primal division between "this" and "that." If we cannot agree on what "this" means, we cannot agree on what "right" means. But we can never agree on what "this" means, since it is dependent on perspective. Since all other designations are dependent on the consistent meaning of "this," Zhuangzi holds that all the meanings we assign to words are equally relative to perspective. Not meaning the same thing by "this," we also cannot really mean the same thing by "finger" or "horse," much less by words such as "right" and "wrong." Zhuangzi can thus agree with the conclusion of Gongsun Long, as we discussed in chapter 2: a word such as "horse" means something different for each context, each perspective, with which it is made coherent, and it is thus sometimes permissible to say that "a white horse is not a horse." But unlike Gongsun, he does not need to arrive at this conclusion by contrasting one meaning of horse with another, derived from alternate compounds that just happen to exist side by side (white-horse-coherent-with-white-things and white-horse-coherent-with-other-horses), but might not have existed, since no intrinsic relation of opposition pertains to these alternate perspectives. Rather, Zhuangzi can "use not-horse to show the not-horseness of horse"—the second perspective doesn't just *happen* to be there, it is posited simultaneously, as a necessary concomitant, to the first. "Non-horseness" *always* goes with "horse," it is "the non-horseness *of* horse." Any perspective necessarily posits an alternate perspective; when you have horse, you also have non-horse, and this non-horseness belongs to the positing of horseness, providing a new perspective, outside the perspective of the horse or the perspective that decided to call it horse, which sees horse otherwise. What is viewed from the perspective of horse will not be seen the same way from the perspective of non-horse. This means that the multiple meanings of horse, horse's simultaneous non-horseness, is strictly unavoidable.

Now, just as "the wind" is something that is known and heard nowhere but in all the sounds, the "true self" is nowhere but in all the changing emotions, and the "truth" (Dao) nowhere but in all the different words, positions, and arguments of the philosophers. In this sense, they're all correct. For all are indeed "this, self, right"—from their own perspective. This is where things start to get interesting. They are not said to be correct *because* each is an expression of universal Dao; that is, they are not just correct *sub species aeternitas* or in the view of the Whole, to perceive which each must relinquish its own perspective. Rather, each one is "right" *precisely from his own petty limited partial perspective*, and this is affirmed as the truth, as what brings the "*shi*"-ness, or rightness, or *value*, into things at all. Their *shi* comes from being a part, and seeing things from a partial angle, *not* from seeing things as from the perspective whole. "Dao" is derived from this consideration, not vice versa.

Thus, the Confucians and Mohists are equally partial, each *shi*-ing what the other *feis* and vice versa. But if one really wanted to make sure that everything each affirms is negated and vice versa, as each side of the debate seems to do, the easiest way would be to use the *obvious* (明 *ming*) state of affairs, namely this fact itself, the fact that they negate each other.[44] The obvious fact itself solves the problem, and ironically achieves what they themselves wanted to do, namely, negate each other! They are negated by negating, they are affirmed by affirming, all from their own individual limited perspectives. The fact that everyone has a different perspective and view is obvious—that's why there's an argument in the first place. But that obvious fact is what solves the problem, settles the argument: You wanted to negate them? They are thereby negated! You wanted to negate both of the disputants of that other argument, or affirm both, or affirm one and negate the other? They are both negated, and both affirmed! Take your pick! Hence, "The sage steers by the radiance of drift and doubt."[45] As Zhuangzi says a little later, "Things are affirmed by affirming them, negated by negating them. Ways are formed by walking, things are so because they are called so. Why right? Because someone holds it to be right. Why wrong? Because someone holds it to be wrong. Everything has some perspectives which hold it to be right and some which hold it to be wrong, so there is nothing that is not right, nothing that is not acceptable."[46] It is not a question of digging down to the inner essence of things, or seeing the truth behind appearances, for instance, seeing that in their ultimate essence all things are expressions of the whole or Dao, the wind blowing through all the holes, which is Good, and therefore, despite appearances, all are really good. Instead, Zhuangzi redirects us to the appearances themselves: the obvious appearances are of everyone having his own view, the chaotic welter of everyone affirming himself—and in this way all things are affirmed, the wind's "great harmony." The affirmation of everything comes then not from a unicentric penetration to the one true transcendental perspective, which can never be explicitly posited as anything more than a Who?, but rather from a going along with the surface phenomenon where each thing affirms itself. Indeed, it is just this welter of contrasting and conflicting individual perspectives that itself produces this Who?, this quality of Whoness, which is nothing but the impossibility of settling into any definite identity or perspective as definitive. Who? is in effect a shorthand way of indicating the drift and doubt of the shimmering unsettled surface, not a way of grounding, transcending, or going beneath it to a true knowledge of its real source.

A thing, for Zhuangzi, has a *perspective*; it embodies a way of seeing, a take on things, an assessment of what is what and a prioritizing of what is better and what is worse. Perhaps we can even go so far as to say that, on the most crucial and paradigmatic level, a thing *is* a perspective.[47] Each thing has a view of the world, a distinctive perspectival relationship to all other things. A thing takes in and responds to its particular context in a way roughly analogous to the way a perceiver in a social world feels and responds to that social environment. Moreover, as in the Confucian case, the argument rests on conceiving these perceivers as *social*—which is to say, as also being perceived by others. The world of others that each entity perceives are also not merely inanimate things, but evaluating and perceiving entities. The presence of each one is felt by all the others, and vice versa.

The implications of this assumption become clearest in Zhuangzi's elaboration of his technique of "the illumination of the obvious" (以明 *yiming*): "Nothing is not 'that,' nothing is not 'this.' From 'that' [perspective] [the 'thisness'] is not seen; it is known only to one's own knowing.[48] Thus I say, That emerges from this, and this follows upon that." Here we must pause to note that this "thus I say" makes absolutely no sense unless we assume a perspective-laden, intersubjective concept of "things" here. For what went above, if situated in an ontology of insentience, would lead only to the conclusion that everything can be one person's this and another person's that, but not that these two somehow cause each other or arise mutually. The mutual arising is deduced here solely from the fact that, *since each perspective has not only a "this" but also a "that"* (that is, since each entails not only the affirmation of its own position but, what is really just the simultaneous flip side of the same act, the refutation of the opposite position), *and since by definition each one is only seeing everything from its own perspective*, since it would have no awareness of what lies outside of that perspective, the existence of any notion of "that" at all must mean that any "this"'s own perspective already includes a "that." For if it did not come from its own perspective, it could not come from anywhere, nothing can come from another perspective—and we know that it does come, that we have the concept "that" (i.e., "wrong," "other")—for it is only in its implicit contrast to the "that" that it is a "this" at all. To be a "this" is necessarily to have a contrasting "that," and every "that," if it is be capable of accomplishing the work of contrasting must be a something; but to be a something is to be a "this," a perspective from which the initial "this" is a "that." Hence to be a "this" is always already to also be a "that." This only works because both "this" and "that" are implicitly assumed to be sentient perceivers, on a social model, who see each other from their own perspectives. I see you, and you see me. My world includes only what exists from my perspective, and yet it includes a you, an other, in contrast to which I define myself. Indeed, it necessarily refers to an otherness; its thisness is established only in implicit contrast to a thatness. Here we have the dyadic a priori. Your world is defined by your perspective, and yet it includes a me.

A metaphor may allow us to understand this situation more clearly. Imagine a large booth with a sliding door, such that there are two compartments, only one of which can be seen at any time. Inside each of the two compartments stands a human figure, of which only one is visible or audible at any given time, the other being sealed off in his compartment by the closing of the sliding door. Each of these figures insists that he alone is the real one, and that the other is an android or imposter. The one you can see says, "I am the real one; you can tell if you compare us carefully. Look at me closely, and then take a look at him; that way, having the standard of my genuine appearance, you'll be able to determine that he is a fake." He then slides the door over, concealing himself to reveal the other, so that you may compare them. But of course as soon as the other appears and the first is hidden, this other says just the same thing, adducing himself as the standard by which to judge the falseness of the first one. This process goes on indefinitely. Whichever is present asserts itself as the real, the right, the true, the standard of value by deviation from which all others are to be judged as false and wrong—but inherent in this establishment of a standard is the revealing of the other to show the difference, which puts the other in the position to make the same claim, and so on ad infinitum. The only thing that is agreed on, that is stated from both perspectives, is that one is real and the other is false. This is structurally necessary, even if this process continues forever or is carried to new orders of abstraction. Similarly, for Zhuangzi, all experiences entail the positing of a perspective that is an aggressive assertion of its own rightness and, simultaneously, the positing of an other to which it is to be compared, which is to be judged as false in accordance with itself as standard. But this very counterpositing necessarily gives that other a voice, as it were, for all positing and all perception structurally necessitates this self-assertion. To understand this, it is important to remember the so-called "fact-value fusion" characteristic of early Chinese thought, where "being" and "being named" and "being cognized" are all, ultimately, value terms. That is, for something to come into awareness is for it to be picked out from the whole of existence, and this is done as the result of a distinction that embodies a particular desire, a situation that sets in motion the paradoxes of naming marking the first chapter of the *Laozi*. The implicit theory of perception here is similar to the Gestalt notion, where a figure emerges from a ground due to the interest or desire of the observer. In the *Zhuangzi*, the ultimate conclusions of these premises are drawn. To even mention this other, to even refer to it, to call it to awareness in any form, is to put in the position of focus, which is necessarily the position of self-assertion, the establishment of itself as a standard of value. And since there is no other standard than the standard asserted by some focus, this process continues forever, and can find no final resolution.

The value question then also hinges on this perspectivism, this assumption of sentient points of view that include each other. For their inclusion of each other is a form of negating each other; they include each other *as* their own "other" "that" "wrong" in contradistinction to their own "self" "this" and "right." Moreover, once the opposition between "self" and "other" (this/that, right/wrong) proves to harbor this paradox, then everything flies toward paradox, for this is the most basic distinction we know of. Zhuangzi immediately applies the paradox at a metalevel to the paradox itself, again poking fun at Huizi by quoting his doctrine of "The thing born is the thing dying" (方生方死 *fang sheng fang si*); so if "this" and "that" "birth" each other, they also "die" each other, and vice versa, and if this is right it's also wrong, and if wrong also right.[49] Thus, the sage doesn't pursue this or any other line or argument designed to get to the bottom of things—he just "reflects them in heaven" (照之於天 *zhao zhi yu tian*). Heaven refers to the way things are before being modified, rearranged or tidied up by the purposive activity of humans. It is the way things are when found, before interference according to any one specific purpose. In this context, then, it is identical with "using the manifest, the obvious" (明 *ming*). It means how they are when left alone, in their state of mutual contradiction and contention, their transformation into one another, their drift and doubt. This word for brightness—the obvious or manifest—is here assimilated to the traditional associations of the light coming from the sky. This term is often taken to be the point at which Zhuangzi takes refuge in a kind of intuitionism, thereby discarding his therapeutic skepticism. That is, if this *ming* is translated to mean something such as "illumination" or "enlightenment," we get the impression that Zhuangzi is saying, forget all these logical disputes, which solve nothing, and rely instead on your language-transcending intuition, which alone will show you the truth, reveal the way things really are. My reading of this term yields almost precisely the opposite meaning. I take it to mean the obvious, what is self-evident and clear when confronted with the problem of a multitude of perspectives contradicting each other: namely, this fact that there are a bunch of perspectives contradicting each other. *Ming* then refers to the surface fact that they all affirm themselves and negate each other, that they appear as a complete confusion, an unstable mutual undermining—for after all, "if right were really right, its difference from not-right would be so clear that there would be no dispute at all."[50] This very unstable surface is what is referred to as the "Equalizing Heavenly Potter's Wheel," to be discussed below. Heaven, then, is not the secret hidden essence of things, the harmonious creator behind their present conflicting appearances, but rather that surface of obvious conflict itself, once we cease the futile attempt to try to get to the bottom of it or find out what harmony lies behind it. It is this feature, as we will see, that keeps Zhuangzi from asserting even that it is possible to know what is called Heaven and what is called man, that this "reflection in Heaven" is to be understood as the acquisition of some kind of knowledge that reveals the truth about things and provides a kind of transrational certainty. Quite the contrary, it is the full acceptance of doubt and chaos, and the self-affirmations of whatever is encountered thereby revealed, and then renounced.

This appeal to "obvious fact"—functionally similar to what ancient Skeptics called "the apparent" or "the evident," but with an emphasis not on the few perfectly stable and certain facts of experience but rather in the "radiance of drift and doubt," the very unceasing unstable surface shimmer itself—leads us directly into what I have elsewhere called omnicentrism: "This is also that, that is also this. This has its own this/that and that also has its own this/that. So is there really a this/that or isn't there? When this and that no longer find anything to be their opposites [i.e., come down neither definitively as opposites nor not as opposites, when it becomes no longer coherent as a definitive intelligible identity one way or the other: when everything teeters in the drift and doubt of the question, Is it so or is it not so?], this is called the Axis of Daos. Once the Pivot finds the center, so that it can respond infinitely without obstruction, this/self/right is unobstructed and inexhaustible, and that/other/wrong is equally unobstructed and inexhaustible. This is why I said there's nothing better than using the obvious."[51] I and you are not opposites when I see that the very opposition I/you, which I use to define myself as I and as right, is posited within myself, within my own perspective; "I/you" is a part of "I." I posit you as my own opposition; your wrongness and contradiction of me is my own doing, is part of my system of affirming myself, not its opposite. It is this point that allows Zhuangzi to avoid the tendency to self-enclosed solipsism that sometimes goes with relativism. After all, if what I find true is true only for me, and what you find true is true only for you, there is no shared basis in terms of which we could communicate. Each of us remains trapped forever in our own sealed perspective. But Zhuangzi instead speaks of the "Axis of Courses,"[52] which is a means of interaction and "responding" that relates different perspectives to one another, "opening them up" into one another. Zhuangzi tells us of a perspective from which one can no longer say definitively whether any given "this" and "that"—"right" and "wrong"— are contrasted opposites or not. This is because "this" always both defines itself by its intrinsic contrast to "that" *and* necessarily entails and in that sense includes "that." Is there no contrast between "this" and "that"? That is impossible, because their very identity depends on the contrast. Then is there a contrast between "this" and "that"? That is also impossible, because each implies the other: "this" is really "this plus that" and "that" is also really "this plus that." To be contrasted, we need two *different* things contrasted to each other. But now the same thing—"this plus that"—is found on both sides of the contrast. It is like a magnet that always has both a positive and a negative pole, no matter where you slice it: when you attempt the slice off the negative pole, you only get another one. So everywhere you may go, there is this inescapable division, contrast, opposition between "this" and "that." But precisely because it is everywhere, there is no contrast, in this respect, between one place and another, no "this" versus "that." The contrast between "this" and "that" is everywhere and nowhere. This is the "oneness" of all things which is also not a definitive oneness: there is no difference between its oneness and its non-oneness.[53] We can see things in terms of this oneness or not as we choose,[54] but in either case we flip flop back into this loop of both oneness and non-oneness—which is the real "oneness."[55] Because of the mutual positing of perspectives, staying fully within one's own perspectives necessarily allows one to open outward into interaction with other perspectives, to the accommodation of other viewpoints and other types of "rights" and "wrongs." It is this "not knowing whether it is or isn't a contrast," this "how would I know?"[56] this "finding no sign of him,"[57] this "who?"[58] that Zhuangzi means by "Non-knowing," the Axis of Courses. This "axis" is *the* Course, the Course which is not a Course, the ironically non-guiding guide.

Indeed, Zhuangzi tells us that this Axis of Courses has an endless supply of responses to endless perspectives.[59] Rather than being sealed into one unchanging perspective, it is the flow of the transformation and interaction of perspectives. This is illustrated in the story of the Monkey Keeper.[60] The monkey keeper offers his monkeys three chestnuts in the morning and four in the evening. The monkeys are outraged: they want four in the morning and three in the evening. The monkeys have their own perspective on right and wrong. Wisely, the monkey keeper neither insists on his arrangement nor tries to convince the monkeys to adopt it, nor indeed to recognize that the number of chestnuts is the same either way. Instead, he accommodates them. He "goes by the rightness of the present this." He has, as it were, two perspectives at once. He has his own perspective, at the "center of the circle," the Axis of Courses. And *at any given time* he is *also* temporarily adopting some other perspective, such as he might have encountered at that time—in this case, three in the morning as opposed to four in the morning. This is called "Walking Two Roads," or, as it were, "Doing Both at Once" (兩行 *liangxing*).[61]

This concept of "response" is crucial here, and it will bring us back to the question of dependence (待 *dai*). Chapter 7 tells us, "Just be empty, that is all. The perfect man uses his mind like a mirror, responding but not storing, and thus he can overcome things without being harmed by them."[62] Chapter 4 also glosses this concept of "emptiness" (虛 *xu*), saying not to listen with the ear or the mind, but rather with the qi (氣 *qi*): "The vital energy is an emptiness, a waiting for the presence of things (氣也者虛而待物者也). The Course alone is what gathers in this emptiness."[63] This emptiness, or fasting of the mind, turns out to be equivalent also to "I lost me," as Yan Hui's response shows.[64] It consists not of a blank void, but rather of a responding to things, depending on things, riding things—of not holding to any one perspective as self, this, or right. In the "Xiaoyaoyou" dependence (*dai*) was transformed into freedom by *increasing* the scope of what was depended on, of what one could effective become coherent with, until it included the entire spectrum, until it was "unobstructed" and limitless (*wuqiong*), thus making space for *any* content. This "lost self" "mind fasted" emptiness does not store: it holds onto no completed or definitive perspective (成心 *cheng xin*), no particular identity or concept of right (*shi/fei*). But it is not emptiness in the sense of a constant or definitive blank. It is a space that is always being filled by one or another perspective, but which is unobstructed (*tong* 通) to other perspectives by virtue of the fact that each perspective intrinsically contains its own *fei*, its own negation, which provides the passageway to any other perspective that comes along. This allows it to "respond" to any of the six breaths that happen to appear to it, and thereby ride it unobstructedly where it may go, assuming whatever *shi* (identity—rat's liver, crossbow pellet, and so on) it may bring. This is both to depend (periphery: cast about on whatever wind appears) and not to depend (center: hiding the world in the world so that in spite of all "going away" it is never lost), "being shaken in the endless and *thus* being lodged in the endless" (振諸無竟, 故寓諸無竟 *zhen zhu wu jing, gu yu zhu wu jing*), "turmoil-tranquility" (攖寧 *ying-ning*)), unobstructed like the dimensionless blade through the sinews. To be both sides means to be the eternal "Who?" that blows these different transforming pipings forth—not to be any someone always, for that would be one of the different tones piped forth, but not to be no one either, for that would mean no piping. Rather, to be "Who?"—responding to and depending on anything that comes along (a ceaseless question mark, with realness and reliability [有情有信 *you qing you xin*]) while not storing and not depending on anything (having no definite answer, without evaluative action or form [無為無形 *wu wei wu xing*]).[65] It is to be "coherent" in the sense of "value-creating," "balancing and holding together the two opposite extremes," "grouping together with others," "unobstructed continuity," but "incoherent" in the sense of "having no fixed and identifiable identity."

This (never blank) "emptiness" is Zhuangzi's substitute for the "adequate ideas" of, say, Spinoza—exactly the opposite strategy, it turns out. Rather than holding a comprehensive vision of the whole in one's mind, one keeps one's mind empty like a mirror, so that it may respond and "ride upon" whatever it encounters. This is to depend on whatever one encounters, to have no independent self, but also equally to be independent, since anything will do. This also allows Zhuangzi to avoid some of the contradictions of standard relativism. Relativists who notice the dependence of all assertions on perspective are generally caught in a paradox pointed out already by Plato: they must assert that they can know one thing absolutely, namely, that all is relative. Since they end up asserting some universally valid knowledge independent of perspective—i.e., that all knowledge is perspective-dependent—they are contradicting themselves, and thus relativism stands refuted. Zhuangzi however is not asserting that he knows this.[66] He is merely asserting that this is how things *appear to him from his own present perspective*. Where this perspective comes from and how it could be justified are, by his own admission, unknown and unknowable.

As we've seen above, perspective here means both emotional moods and philosophical positions, as well as any specific identities as such. "This/that"s apply to all of the following dyadic pairs: (1) emotional perspectives (joy/sorrow, etc.), (2) concepts of identity (self/other), (3) value concepts (right/wrong, benefit/harm), and (4) life and death (an extension of now/some other time). The recommendation then seems to be: have the ability to have emotions, to feel your way into various positions and perspectives as expressed by others or even yourself, to live and die; on the other hand, maintain a central point that is still, uninvolved, not fully absorbed into or committed to this perspective, which means, as the image of the pivot or hinge suggests especially, the ability to jump back out of it when the situation changes (通 *tong*), to identify yourself equally with the opposite when the time comes, to know even now that it too will equally be a "this," and hence will be self, right and life, since This includes That, and That includes This. This is to respond without storing. To travel two roads at once. Knowing through not knowing,[71] sayings that don't say anything, the Dao that is not a Dao.[72]

Another extended metaphor may help to make this clearer, which I will offer here with the usual qualification that it is not to be taken too literally or as according perfectly with the case in hand; nonetheless, I think it will prove significantly useful in clarifying what is at issue here. Zhuangzi's view of experience is comparable to finding oneself in a card game, where cards are constantly being issued to one from an unknown source, and one is constantly discarding, but without ever having been explicitly told what the object of the game is. A certain set of rules might suggest that the best thing to do is maximize the high cards you hold while discarding the low cards as much as possible, but it is equally possible, for all you know, that the object is to have the lowest card, or the most cards of the same suit, or same number, or different suit or number. Both the source and the object of the game are unknown. You do not even know how large a deck it is or what the proportions of cards in it are. Occasionally an "instruction card" is issued, that is, a card with instructions printed on it, stating that the object of the game is in fact such and such—to collect high cards, for example. But other instruction cards are issued as well, with contradictory instructions and explanations of the makeup of the deck and the object of the game. Sometimes, after receiving such a card, a player might accept its claims and proceed to order his hand accordingly—having drawn "the object of the game is to collect high cards," he proceeds to do so. If he gets a card that states, "The object of the game is to collect low cards," he quickly discards it; for he already knows it is false, fei. There are even cards that suggest that the collection of instruction cards, or the absence of them, is the true object of the game, and so on.

Now, given this scenario, Zhuangzi's "regarding all things as one" amounts to, not an instruction card that reveals the true state of the deck, namely, that all the differences in the cards are merely illusory (perhaps comparable to the Spinozistic or Advaita Vedanta conception of the One), or that the object of the game is simply to collect as many cards as possible and thus they are all of equal value, or that they all come from a single source and thus are to be valued equally without caring anymore about winning or losing, but rather *a wild card*. It reveals no information about the source of the cards, the makeup of the deck, or the object of the game. Nor is it, more to the point, an injunction to ignore all the instruction cards and instead pay attention to the actual makeup of the cards being issued, in the belief that this will reveal an unbiased picture of the true source and object of the game (comparable to the mystical view that, once reason has been abandoned, an intuitive regard for nature will reveal the truth). Rather, it stays with the "obvious" and inescapable state of things: we don't know the rules, the source, the object of the game, and in fact, every so often someone declares the object to be such and such and we must tally our winnings according to this ad hoc temporary rule, which will be replaced by another in the next round. Given the unknowability of what cards or coming or what hand is better than what, the only thing that will be useful in *any possible case* is the wild card. Whether it is declared at a given time that the object is to collect high cards or low cards, whether there is one source or many, however many different objects of the game may be successively declared, the wild card will always be the best thing to be holding. Note that "best" here is no longer "best in terms of some given instruction card or concept of what the true object of the game is," but one that, due to its uniquely empty status, will be equally useful no matter what the object is *regarded to be* at any given time.

Why is the sage's "regarding things as one" equivalent to a wild card? It is not a claim about any truth or value, like an instruction card, nor the assertion of some intrinsic order to the cards missed by every instruction card, some alternate source of true knowledge. It is merely the acceptance of the apparent fact that new cards keep coming and new concepts of the object of the game keep getting declared, and that the one thing every possible object of the game has in common is that it has something that is considered good in its view or context, and it is to this oneness that the wild card addresses itself. Whatever the particular content might be that is desired in any given case, there is always something or other that can fit into the presently prevailing scenario as desirable; the only thing that will always be desirable, "what all things agree in affirming," will be something that can be anything. It presupposes no knowledge about how things really are or what is really good; in fact, "oneness" here means precisely the same thing as "complete absence of any definite knowledge." The attainment of this view consists not in adding additional facts to our knowledge, but in removing any and all claims to know how things are or are not, even, as Zhuangzi makes explicit, the claim that we do or can know nothing. In good Daoist fashion, it is this sort of a value emptiness that all beings unite themselves in. It is not a claim about the true reality that dwells beneath the flux of deceptive appearances; rather, it is that claim that every appearance so far makes some declaration about what is good and what is bad, on some level, and that we simply do not know what will or won't always be declared good, that apparently there are conflicting claims, and we have no perspective-independent means of adjudicating between them; and thus the only card that will survive all revolutions of perspective, that can persist whatever the appearances do, is not some unchanging truth underlying them, but rather the one thing that, like the mirror, can be anything, and is not restricted to any given determinacy. Zhuangzi's "oneness" view persists and prevails not because it is uniquely true or undoubtable, nor that it escapes the critique of reliance on internal criteria that Zhuangzi applied to all other possible perspectives, but merely for the reason that no five-card draw player ever discards a wild card.

Zhuangzi drives home the true inescapable force of this ironic a priori, in its implications for the meaning of coherence, unmistakably as follows:

> I now want to try to say something about this. But I don't know: will it be in the same category (類 *lei*) as "this"? Or will it not be in the

same category as "this"? But then "being-in-the-same-category" and "not-being-in-the-same-category" are together in the same category! Hence there is nothing to distinguish it from "that."

Nonetheless, let me try to say it. There is a beginning. There is a not-yet-beginning-to-be-a-beginning. There is a not-yet-beginning-to-not-yet-begin-to-be-a-beginning. There is existence (有 you). There is non-existence (無 wu). There is a not-yet-beginning-to-be-non-existence. There is a not-yet-beginning-to-not-yet-beginning-to-be-non-existence. Suddenly there is non-existence. But I have not-yet known whether "there being non-existence" is ultimately existence or non-existence. Now I have said something. But I do not-yet know: has what I have said really said anything? Or has it not really said anything?[73]

Let me restate what has been "said" here. Zhuangzi is suggesting, on the basis of the considerations raised earlier, that, in general and in every possible case, whatever is in any category (類 lei), a member of any class, a thing of any type, is indistinguishable from what is outside that class or category. Like *ming* (name) in the *Laozi*, *lei* is here used as the most inclusive possible term for anything intelligible or assertable. The reason is illustrated in what follows: for any "beginning" or "existence" that might be posited, it is always possible to posit a "not-yet." This is necessary because of the observations about any possible existence as having a beginning, as we saw in the *Laozi*. Here it is stated with a more explicitly a priori implication. As Graham pointed out, in Chinese thought, to be is to exist, to be present in the world, in the context of time, of a before and after. More abstractly, for a category to be definite, to have any content at all, it must begin and end somewhere in conceptual space. "Red" has a meaning because the range of the category "ends" when it reaches the category "green" or any other category. This means whatever is has a beginning, which means that when I posit the existence of X I am also positing the existence of not-yet-X, of not-X.

But the same then applies to the not-yet-X, the not-X, and so on ad infinitum. The conclusions Zhuangzi goes on to draw from this argument— that all categories are then indistinguishable from their negations—may seem to rest on a fallacious confusion of "being in general" with "determinate being." It makes sense to say "The being-there of not-yet-being-there is just another type of being-there," but not, it would seem, "the being-there of green-not-yet-being-here is just another type of green-being-here." And this is what Zhuangzi is implying for *lei,* and for Mt. Tai and an autumn hair, old age and early death, not-me and me, and so on in what follows. But for Zhuangzi any meaningful and assertable being—any intelligibility, any coherence, anything that can be pointed out—is ipso facto a determinate being, with a before and after. To be posited at all is to be posited together with its negation; otherwise, positing has not taken place, nothing has been said, nothing has been pointed out. Even "being in general" makes sense only in contrast to something else—"non-being in general" or even "determinate being." The force of the argument rests again on the previous considerations of "being-here" as a form of "being-this," and the perspectival nature of being-this, to wit, that being-this means "being-the-perspective-of-this-on -all-that"'s. Given this premise, Zhuangzi may say, "To set up any category, any coherence, any quality, is to set up the context of this coherence, the not-this. The context is thus internal to the coherence. The non-alike is like the alike." In terms of our discussion here, the upshot of all this can be stated simply: *cohering-as-this therefore always and necessarily coheres with not-cohering-as-this, and indeed with cohering-as-not-this.* Is cohering-as-this then any different from cohering-as-not-this? The argument rests on the idea of a thing as a perspective and a perspective as a coherence, and on those terms is airtight.[74]

In sum, what has appeared in Zhuangzi's hand is a *wild card.* That is, it is indeed just one more card, one more perspective appearing out of nowhere, but it has some peculiar properties. For it has no *fixed shi/fei* of its own, but for that very reason it *enhances the value of whatever shi/fei is currently operative.* If you are convinced, on the basis of a previously accepted instruction card, that the object of the game is to collect high cards, you can use the wild card to count as a high card. If you think the point is to collect low cards, it can be used as a low card. But even if you change your mind, if you receive a new instruction card and decide to reorder your hand accordingly, the wild card will still be useful, will still enhance your hand's value according to the *new* perspective. This is the Axis of Courses: at any time it can pivot over to become a contributor to the opposite value, the opposite course. The content of this card is simply the point about the obviousness of the transformation of perspectives, their mutual entailment, the way that having a perspective always opens you up to other perspectives, and the undecidability of what is so that goes with it. It is not some intuitive or transcendental "illumination" or "enlightenment" that sees through the surface, but, rather, simple awareness *of the surface itself*: rather than resolving the conflict between perspectives, it notes *this conflict itself.* That is what is "obvious"—that people standing in different places see things differently. What alone is indisputable is that "people sometimes disagree," for this proposition *cannot be contradicted without thereby being further demonstrated* (if I say "I disagree with the proposition that people sometimes disagree," I have demonstrated that people sometimes disagree). This is what allows this one accidental perspective to function and maintain itself as a wild card.

USING THE WILD CARD

We can thus trace the development of the notion of *dao* through three phases:

1. The *daos* of the Confucians and Mohists are courses that, when deliberately practiced, lead to the production of valued states of Virtuosity, valued human attitudes, and valued arrangements of human society and material resources. To produce a desired value, one embraces a set of values and behaves accordingly.

2. The ironic Dao of the *Daodejing* and early "Daoism" is a non-dao, a non-deliberate course of all things that is the real basis of the emergence of all natural processes and the valued states that come with them: life, human virtues, human social harmony. All of these valued things come from *not* deliberately following any one identifiable prescribed course of action, from not embracing any values. Deliberate commitment to a set of values ironically obstructs the actual emergence of the valued things. To produce a desired value, one renounces all deliberate values and allows the spontaneous pre-evaluative process at the basis of all action, virtues and things: "non-action."

3. For Zhuangzi, Dao is the nondeliberate, unknowable emergence not just of valued things, but of all the various courses or ways of knowing and valuing. What it produces is not just natural processes generating valued things, but value-standpoints themselves: it produces *daos*. As such it is neither a particular *dao* nor the exclusion of all *daos*, neither the embracing of a particular standpoint of deliberate endeavor nor the exclusion of all deliberate endeavor. It is the Axis of Courses. The values desired at any given moment are a function of the emergence of a particular perspective from this unknowable source, and that value is accomplished by going along with the perspective so produced while maintaining access to the pivot connecting to all other perspectives from within this one, the Wild Card.

It is this idea of the Wild Card that Zhuangzi then goes on to apply in various ways in the subsequent Inner Chapters. It is the unknowable and purposeless *process of making values, of valuing and revaluing*. The Dao is the ceaseless generation of *new perspectives*. It is the purposeless production of *purposes*. Zhuangzi speaks of the Dao, of Heaven, of the Great Clump, of the Yin and Yang, of Fate—he throws one name after another onto what he has shown can have no single name: the process of producing names, values, perspectives. For Zhuangzi, we may say, a being *is* simply a perspective, and the constant becoming of perspective after perspective, each constitutively unable to know anything outside itself, reveals nothing more or less than the obvious unknownness of what is ultimately so or right or source or purpose. This is the "Illumination of the Obvious," which serves as the Wild Card, by means of which one may now "ride upon" all the transformations in perfect independence and freedom, wherever they may take one.

Zhuangzi sometimes uses "The Heavenly" as a word for this unknowable production of ever new perspectives: for Heaven—the actual openness of the sky, which "rotates" through the seasons, bringing forth the crops of the earth without taking any deliberate action or issuing any commands—means what is produced by no known agent and for no single known purpose. This image of the "Skylike" in all things is useful as a contrast to "the Human," which is used to denote what is done deliberately, for a particular purpose, rooted in an instrumental consciousness that claims to know definitively what is so and what is good: in a word, purposive activity (i.e., activity *guided by a single purpose, which is known beforehand*). But since it is unknowable, or knowable only from a perspective, this spontaneous arising of perspectives cannot properly be identified as "Heaven," either: that is merely a name given to it from one perspective, and Zhuangzi pointedly asks, "How do I know that what I call the Heavenly is not really the Human, and vice versa?"[75] Once again, it is this unknowing, this "how do I know?" that is the real point: the Illumination of the Obvious, which Zhuangzi also calls "the Radiance of Drift and Doubt." This is Zhuangzi's own Course, his Dao.

In chapter 3, Zhuangzi applies this Course to the practical problem of "nourishing life." The question here is how to move skillfully through the practical problems that confront us without harming this spontaneous life process in us, this process of generating perspectives. Another emblematic story takes us into this territory: the cook carving up the ox. The living being is here likened to a knife: something that aggressively takes a position and thereby divides the world (e.g., into *shi* and *fei*, right and wrong). The world stands before it as a dense and impenetrable carcass that must be hacked through, wearing down the blade. But the considerations of Zhuangzi's second chapter tell us that the very dividing edge of the knife is actually "without thickness": it occupies no space, has no fixed position of its own. Similarly, the carcass through which it must wend its way has gaps or channels already present in it: every apparently self-assertive "this" "opens into" (通 *tong*) another, contrary perspective. The story presents a vivid metaphor for the art of "following along" with the affirmations intrinsic to each situation as it arises, like the implicit spaces in the body of an ox through which the blade passes unharmed, thereby artfully untangling the carcass. It is useless to take the knowing consciousness, the understanding, as one's guide: it "never sees all there is to see in the ox," and yet is constructed to issue definitive judgments about what is right and wrong as if it had this comprehensive knowledge. There is always more for it to see, something it has not yet taken into account, other perspectives which it cannot encompass: it is in this sense that it "has no shaping contours," no limits to its vistas. Life, however, always has *some* temporary specific limits and contours: the knife is in a particular aperture, guided along by its contour, at any given time: it is always presented with *some* present perspective. The "This" in each case is what gives it specific contours, specific perspectival guidelines of value, such as the card that the Wild Card matches, doubles, and enhances. This story is also a vivid reminder of the irony of ironic coherence, or ironic "harmony"—it is not a beautiful picnic of joy for all concerned at all times, where all joys converge into some preestablished harmony. In fact it cannot be: there will always be as many *feis* as there are *shis*. it is the ironic harmony of the windstorm, at once "harmony" (*diaodiao*) and "deceit" (*diaodiao*).[76] For though the cook's virtuosity is a delight, in which both he and the ruler (and indeed, Zhuangzi himself and the reader) take pleasure, a seeming harmonic intersubjective convergence of values, the entire story is premised on the existence of someone from whose perspective the whole beautiful scene is presumably not a delight but rather a nightmare of carnage: the ox.

Chapter 3 also includes the crucial assertion: "Whatever 'good' [the flow of life] may do, no reputation can come near it. Whatever 'evil' it may do, no punishment can come near it 為善無近名，為惡無近刑." The exact meaning of this is beautifully illustrated in the two stories that follow the ox-carving story. The first addresses punishment: the one-legged Commander of the Right, though outwardly punished, does not feel punished: being mutilated by punishment is a condition he gladly welcomes in preference to obeying the law, just as the marsh pheasant prefers the hardship of the wilds to the confinement of a cage. Hence his "punishment" is really no punishment to him: following the flow of his life, the punishment does not "get in to do him harm." An exact parallel is given for the case of goodness and reputation in the following story of Lao Dan's funeral. Although he has outwardly gained a reputation for his goodness, he didn't not let this reputation get to him, as his friend soon realizes, thus foregoing the exaggerated mourning of uncomprehending admirers. The flow of his life naturally flowed in a way that his surrounding society happened to call "good," just as the Commander's flowed in a way that was called "evil," but in such a way as to let no reputation or punishment come near them to obstruct them, even when that outward reputation or punishment happened to arise as an unintended by-product.

In chapter 4, the same idea is applied to handling life in the political world. A deliberate plan, conceived in advance, cannot improve either tyrants or political situations. Rather, "the fasting of the mind" is a way of "listening with the vital energies" (equivalent to the perspectival, contoured "flow of the life process" of opening of chapter 3) which "is empty and waits for things," providing the Wild Card responsiveness that both affirms the present "This" *and allows it to transform into other perspectives.* This is, for Zhuangzi, the only viable way to change the world.

Chapter 5 attributes an uncanny effectiveness to this empty inner state (the fasting of the mind, the wild card with no fixed content of its own). A person's physical beauty, social status, and moral virtuosity were thought, in Zhuangzi's time, to have a powerful effect on others, to inspire them, unify them, attract them, transform them. Zhuangzi here tells us of convicted criminals and physically repulsive people—those lacking in both moral and bodily beauty—who nonetheless seem to have just this effect on others. They have no specific attainments—Virtuosities attained through practicing a particular *dao*—but instead embody the unspecifiable axis of all such Virtuosities, which takes no particular form. These are people who have taken on the perspective that "all things are one"—not in the sense of "wearing out their spirits trying to make all things one,"[77] but in the way all perspectives appear as simultaneously mutually exclusive and mutually implicative, which opens them up into transformation and interconnection with one another, all equally connectable and enhanceable by this Wild Card. To be physically whole is Right; to be deformed is also Right. To be a foot is Right; to be a clump of earth is also Right. Power and good reputation are Right; lowliness and disgrace are also Right. All things are, in this sense, one: they are all "Right." This very lack of a fixed distinction between the good and the bad, however, ironically, provides those who embrace it with precisely the powers usually attributed to the "good": the inner emptiness (lack of fixed content or position) of these figures transforms everyone around them, providing them with an uncanny kind of charisma. We find here an exemplary case of ironic coherence: those who are still like still water, empty of any teaching of their own, devoid of any physical or moral attractiveness, are surrounded by followers who are transformed by them, and indeed find that "All beings find themselves unable to be apart from those whose Virtuosity is invisible"[78]—that is, they cannot live without them, are drawn to cohere around them. They are the still, empty, lowly center of social coherence—accomplishing the greater coherence by means of what the previous chapter calls "discombobulated Virtuosity"[79]—an incoherent character. Chapter 5 calls these people who "use their understanding to find the mind, and then use their mind to find the mind of constancy."[80] "Use their understanding to find the mind" refers to the use of reasoning, as exemplified in chapter 2, to find out something important about the mind: that it always has a perspective, and that having a perspective always implies the availability of another, opposite perspective. This understanding of the mind as impossible to pin to any fixed perspective is then used to find the "mind of constancy"—one can view things either so that all, even one's own body, are as different as Chu and Yue are, or one can view them all as one, concentrating on the aspect of being-affirmed-by-themselves that all share; the mind of constancy, of oneness, is always available, and impossible to undermine. The lack of a fixed good and bad accomplishes the good—*any* good. In terms of our metaphor, the Wild Card accomplishes the goals posited by any instruction card (i,e,, any concept of what is good). Thus, the Wild Card is the constant card, the card that is never transferred away—i.e., never discarded. It doesn't achieve the non-ironic coherence of, say, an "instruction card": the permanent basis or goal or rules or values of the game, that are applicable for every hand, remaining unchanging in all situation. It achieves an ironic coherence, being constant only in transforming its value so as to cohere with *any* hand that is dealt. This means it undergoes no death and demise (not discarded by any new situation) and also that it forms the hub around which the community wants to cohere—is not discarded (不離 *buli*) by any living being.

Chapter 6 is in some ways the climax of the Inner Chapters, applying the Wild Card position to the ultimate problems: the transformative power of non-knowing as a kind of utmost knowledge, the Genuine Man who embodies this non-knowing, and the ensuing rightness for him of both life and death. Chapter 7 presents the Wild Card non-knowing as a sovereign response to two kinds of claims to authority: the political and the religious. Questions about how to rule the world are answered repeatedly with recourse to the non-knowing state of mind with no fixed position and no programmatic ideals of its own, and the shaman of Zheng's claims to knowledge of fate are foiled by Huzi's unknowability, his lack of fixed identity, which leads to a summation of Zhuangzi's views on knowledge and identity in the closing story of the death of primal Chaos.

At the beginning of chapter 6, Zhuangzi seems to offer a summing up of his position on knowing:

> "To understand what is done by Heaven and what is to be done by Man, that is the utmost." Understand what is done by the Heavenly: precisely in being the Heavenly, it is the generating of things. Understand what is to be done by the Human: that would mean using what your understanding understands to provide nourishment

for what your understanding does not understand. Then you could live out your Heavenlike-years without being cut down halfway. And that would indeed be the richest kind of knowledge.[81]

"The Heavenly" is here the name for the spontaneous life process, the continual generating of new things and perspectives. It is what deliberate knowing cannot accomplish, and cannot grasp a determinate source for. The role of knowing, then, is merely to recognize its own limits so as to continually "nourish" this uncontrolled and unknown process of generation of perspective on what is true and good, rather than trying to determine or create what is really true or what is really good, to be the master commanding the direction of life. Knowing rests in, and stops at, what it does not know, and this enables the generation of perspectives and responses to continue unobstructedly: the Wild Card, the Obvious, the Radiance of Drift and Doubt.

However, in the next lines Zhuangzi also problematizes this position:

> But there is a problem. For the understanding can only be considered "right" through a relation of dependence on something. But what it depends on is always peculiarly unfixed. So how can I know whether what I call the Heavenly is not really the Human? How can I know whether what I call the Human is not really the Heavenly? Thus only after there is something we tentatively call a Genuine Man can there be anything called Genuine knowledge.[82]

This is a meta-level application of perspectival "drift and doubt" to Zhuangzi's own position, making it clear that the reason Zhuangzi advocates this perspective is *not* because it somehow magically escapes the general problem of relativity to a perspective that he develops so intricately in chapter 2. "Genuine Knowledge" is merely a term to describe the state of mind of a particular type of human, the "Genuine Man." It has no justification, no way to establish itself independently of that perspective. Zhuangzi then goes on in chapter 6 to *describe* what, from his own perspective, he names "the Genuine Man." The source of the arising of this perspective, its "grounding," and its relationship to that source, is as unknowable as that of any other perspective.

THE WILD CARD AGAINST BOTH OBJECTIVE TRUTH AND SUBJECTIVE SOLIPSISM

Nonetheless, Zhuangzi clearly sings the praises of this point of view, this "genuine knowledge." If not because it is objectively true, why does he do so? Because this one perspective, this one way of seeing, which is as unjus-tifiable and groundless as any other, happens to be one that fulfils most of the very tasks that justified or absolute knowledge would set for itself. What are these tasks?

1. Absolute knowledge should remain in force no matter what per-spective is operative; it should be impervious to refutation, able to incorporate any evidence. It should be able to maintain itself and remain true no matter how the perspective on it may shift.

2. Absolute knowledge should have some practical advantages for dealing with the world. Knowing how the world is should make us able to handle it more effectively, whatever our goals might be.

Does Zhuangzi's "genuine knowledge" fulfill the first condition? Yes. "Going by the rightness of the current 'this' 因是 *yinshi*" will remain effec-tive no matter what "this" is operative or dominant at any given time. Each "this" is workable within the context of this "genuine knowledge" perspective without overturning it, and without having to neglect or distort that perspective's data. The monkeys' perspectives neither overturn nor are overturned by the monkey keeper's perspective that sees the oneness (that is, the self-affirmation that necessarily affirms also the opposite from which it is negated, thus enabling the unobstructed transformation—通 *tong*—between all perspectives) in both of the alternatives exercising the monkeys. His perspective remains in force even while allowing theirs to come into and out of operation; it is a "mirrorlike" perspective, which responds but does not store. It can thus operate in, or rather as, any other perspective it might encounter, Walking Two Roads 兩行," i.e., "Doing Both at Once."

Does Zhuangzi's "genuine knowledge" fulfill the second condition? Yes. This is the point illustrated in chapters 3 through 7 of the text: applications to practical skill, nourishing life, politics, physical disabilities, death, and predictive knowledge. The state of mind embodying this viewpoint adopts the value perspective implicit in any "this," any situation that might be encountered, and maximizes the attainment of value therein, as defined by whatever *that* perspective considers good. Note that it implies no first-order value commitment of its own, for none is justifiable outside of its relation to some perspective. It does however entail a second-order value commitment that "considers right" whatever is considered right by the first-order perspec-tive that may arise at any moment. But this second-order commitment is explicitly as arbitrary and ungroundable as any other. It is simply being what it is, "being this," and thereby like all things arbitrarily affirming as right what it considers right. What it considers right is "maximizing rightness by considering right whatever any perspective considers to be right." The concrete content of what it values at any time is provided by the first-order perspective it is encountering, and its "success" in any case is evaluated in terms of that perspective. So, if technical skill is valued as good, this perspective will provide technical skill. If political efficacy is valued, it will provide political efficacy. And so on.

There seems to be one exception, however. What would the holder of the Wild Card do if he drew an instruction card that read, "Discard all wild cards"? That is, what if the Good were defined as "To eliminate all relativism and cling firmly to an absolute commitment"? Could he embrace *this* value, and use the Wild Card to better realize it? Would he *obey* this instruction, and discard the wild card? If so, our story is over. The Wild Card would then fail to preserve itself, and indeed it would perish almost immediately, since every instruction card implicitly makes this kind of demand in some sense.

On the other hand, he might just discard the instruction card. In that case, he has failed to enhance the value of *every shi/fei*. This would be merely his preference, still a dogma like any other. But that may not be inconsistent, since he claims that all positions are dogmatic and unjustifiable, and are necessarily both right and wrong. Thus, he will have no objection to being in some sense, from some perspective, wrong, and simply throwing away what he doesn't like, though it is always in some sense unjust and unjustifiable. He can have no objection to also being "wrong," since the very position that is being called wrong, the one he embraces, stipulates that it is impossible not to be wrong (from some point of view).

A third alternative: he might hold onto both cards, outwardly advocating the discarding of all wild cards, but maintaining his wild card *secretly*. This may seem to be a kind of systematic hypocrisy, but it is also viewed in much Chinese thought as a virtue, under the name of "timeliness." We do find many praises of both timeliness and the ability to "hide" in our text: part of the danger of revealing and broadcasting the Wild Card is that it can then become the target of just this sort of stricture.

All of these are possible responses. But we might consider this instance precisely the place where our metaphor of the Wild Card begins to break down, as all metaphors do somewhere. For if the wild card is really "wild" all the way to the bottom, our gambler should also be able to say, "This is not a wild card." He can then deny that the "Discard all wild cards" card applies to what he is holding. For a "wild card" is still a fixed and specific identity, something known to be thus and so, and thus can be the target of an attack or prohibition. But the "Genuine knowledge" of the Consummate Person has no specific content. Zhuangzi would perhaps remark, "How can I know that what I call a wild card is really a wild card? How can I know that what I call an anti-wild-card card is really so?" When the anti-wild-card

card appears, he would say that the wild card is right now not "a wild card," but merely a further instantiation of the anti-wild-card card. The Zhuangzian relativist, when confronted by an absolutist, would be happy to declare that he, the Zhuangzian, is perhaps really an even more fanatical absolutist than the absolutist. The Course has no name, so any name is the name of the Course. My allegiance to the wild card, he may say, might in fact be a form of allegiance to Confucianism,[83] or to Mohism—or indeed to Allah, or to Christ, or to blind matter, or to evolution, or to the law of the excluded middle, or what have you. He may add: "How can either of us really know what I believe or don't believe?" The only observable difference between the Wild Card functioning in this way and the Anti-wild-card Card is that the Wild Card will still be there, functioning as something else, when the Anti-wild-card Card has been overturned by a subsequent instruction card. Something of this issue informs the many paradoxical forms of rhetoric we find in the later sections of the *Zhuangzi* and its commentaries, as well as many of the metaphysic and epistemological developments in later Chinese thought.[84]

So Zhuangzi's "Genuine knowledge" does most of the things knowledge of objectivity is supposed to do, and provides a rationale for dismissing the relevance of the rest.[85] It remains constantly in force and aids practical effectiveness not as a rulebook does, but as a Wild Card does, which is never discarded because it is found valuable no matter what set of rules might apply at any given time and how they might change. And this is why the *Zhuangzi* of the Inner Chapters can appear to be at times a mystic, at times a skeptic, or a metaphysical monist, or a spirit-body dualist, or an intuitionist, or a theist, a deist, an agnostic, a relativist, a fatalist, a philosopher of language, a nihilist, an existentialist, as well as a poet uncommitted to any particular philosophical position. This perspective allows but also modifies, recontextualizes, each position. Hence, Zhuangzi can be a relativist—but one who privileges and prefers one particular position (the Wild Card). Zhuangzi can be a monist—but one who is also a pluralistic relativist, and a mind-body dualist (for the oneness he asserts is the oneness of *shi/fei* perspective, hence one that always includes a split or division into plurality within itself). Zhuangzi can be a theist—but one who is also a naturalist and a materialist (on a whim altering his name for the agent responsible for all things, when he feels like it replacing "Creator of Things" with "The Great Mass" or even "The Yin and Yang"—the latter being not even a single unified agent). Zhuangzi can be a fatalist—but one who also reserves for himself the power to be the sole determinant of what means what at any given moment. And so on.

Each of these is a position like that of the monkeys, to which he is responding with his Wild Card, affirming each, contributing to whatever that perspective might consider valuable but at the same time facilitating its unobstructed transformation into any other perspective. We may view the rest of the *Zhuangzi* text, and the extended dialogue formed by the voices of all its commentators over the ages, as further applications of the power of the Zhuangzian Wild Card to an ever broader range of divergent perspectives and situations, going by the rightness of each "this," but sustaining itself as the axis of "Heaven the Potter's Wheel," which enhances, develops, and breathes life into each of them with its responsiveness, fully following along with each alternate arbitrary perspective and thereby further maintaining its own arbitrary perspective, and opening them up for interconnection with one another. Such is Zhuangzi's "Course which is not a course," always and everywhere "Doing Both at Once."

Is Zhuangzi then a relativist? Certainly. But he is a relativist of a very distinctive stripe, which can lead to many misunderstandings. Bryan Van Norden, no friend of relativism, has critiqued an earlier version of my interpretation of the *Zhuangzi*. Having profited from Van Norden's careful and forthright criticism, I have tried to refine my presentation here. None-theless, Van Norden's take is possibly representative of a certain common approach to philosophical argumentation, and with it a discomfort with both the logic and the moral implications of the Zhuangzian approach, so it might still be worthwhile to consider his remarks directly. Van Norden raises the following objection:

> [T]he position that Ziporyn attributes to Zhuangzi, that all proposi-tions are necessarily true, does generate Plato's paradox. Imagine (if you will permit me the anachronism) Mozi arguing with Ziporyn's Zhuangzi. Mozi states that there is one correct Way, and it is the Way of Heaven. Ziporyn's Zhuangzi smiles condescendingly and says, "Yes, the Way of Heaven is the correct Way—relative to your perspective!" Mozi replies, "No, it is not just my Way, it is Heaven's Way! The whole point of saying that it is Heaven's Way is to make clear that it does not depend on any one person's perspective or opinion!" Ziporyn's Zhuangzi is now caught in a dilemma: if he says that Mozi is wrong, because there is no such thing as the one, cor-rect perspective of Heaven, he must admit that not all perspectives are right; on the other hand, if he says that Mozi is right, and that there is such a thing as the one, correct perspective of Heaven, then he is not a relativist anymore. Either way, Zhuangzi would end up contradicting his own supposed relativism.[86]

I take it that this contradicting of his own supposed relativism is meant to count as some kind of objection, or as proving that this cannot be Zhuangzi's position, or that if it is, he does not qualify as what Van Norden refers to earlier in the review as a "smart philosopher." But Zhuangzi is under no obligation to observe the rules of a genre of writing we call philosophy. The exceptionless application of the rules of this genre, in fact, is one of the things his writing manages to call into question—including the supposed relation of language and discourse to worlds and things about which they make determinations. One of the points I am trying to make about Chinese conceptions of coherence in this book is that even "the world" in the definitive singular is not really appropriate in this context. The idea of mapping all realities definitively and consistently into a single system of words, symbols, and rules, correlative to a single stable, unchanging, and authoritative perspective, is a remnant of the Platonic dream, whether in science, theology, or philosophy. Zhuangzi manifestly has no problem with contradicting himself. He is not obligated to make an argument, to demonstrate the truth or falsity of any position. On the contrary, he is simply *enunciating* a position, a way of looking at things, and showing what things look like from there. This enunciation can be said to "succeed" to whatever extent it manages to provoke a disclosure of this way of seeing for *some period of time*. That this perspective will not remain in force forever is asserted in advance, is part of the way of seeing being evoked. The coherence of the rest of the world is not apprehended from above, but built from within each particular position. One of the features of this position is that it sees all positions as necessarily involved in contradicting themselves and thus inevitably subject to transformation into other perspectives—as being a "this" which, as such, is always positing a "that" from which it can be viewed as "that." Zhuangzi doesn't only view every position as necessarily right (relative to some perspective); he also views every position as wrong (relative to some perspective). This obviously applies also to this view itself. Now what was the objection supposed to be? The contradicting of itself doesn't make the position go away, or fail to operate. It seems rather to be a necessary condition of its operation, of its being a position at all—and indeed, if anything, merely further exemplifies the claim.

We can now see why this reference to "my" Zhuangzi's supposed condescension is misguided. Like the monkey keeper, there would be no reason for Zhuangzi to say, condescendingly or otherwise, "Yes, it is the correct Way—relative to your perspective." Although *at times* Zhuangzi might say such a thing, it would be more representative to imagine that he would follow along with the self-affirmation of the absolutist view, "responding to it" from the pivot of daos, his own perspective, which means "walking two roads" (兩行 *liangxing*): accepting it fully without argument, himself adopting the unqualified discourse of the one Way of Heaven *for the moment*. Indeed, this is just what we find the *Zhuangzi* text doing, which is perhaps what has caused Van Norden's confusion: it speaks the full-fledged language of the one universal Way of Heaven *sometimes*. Other times it prefers to speak instead "the Great Clod" or "the Yin and the Yang" or "the One Qi" or even "the Creator of Things," or "the torch of slippage and doubt," or "the obvious," or "the shaded light" or "disturbance-peace" (攖寧 *yingning*) or "oneness" or "walking two" or. . . . It is this timeliness, what happens in another moment, that makes the difference between Mozi's "walking one" and Zhuangzi's "walking two" *although at a given time they may say exactly the same thing*. This is the difference between the monkeys and the monkey keepers, although the latter can at times fully agree with the former that "three in the morning" is the *only* truth. The point is that this "agreeing" is by its nature restricted to the moment, the perspective, in which it is performed. Even if the Lord God Almighty declared something to be so, enforcing it with eternal punishment for all who disagreed, and all beings in creation, with the sole exception of Zhuangzi, responded by singing "Holy, Holy, Holy" unceasingly for all eternity, it would still be just a perspective, a this/that, and Zhuangzi would still be "right," that is, "this." This is what I mean by saying that Zhuangzi's position has a kind of "performative" truth to it (another claim that seems to significantly annoy Van Norden). Zhuangzi admits many right perspectives, including the one that each is the *only* right perspective. *Moreover,* each perspective is *also* wrong (*fei*). There simply is no single synordinate cosmos that is under contract to avoid self-contradiction. Van Norden's Mozi is right when he says the perspective of Heaven is the only right perspective, for the only viable criterion of only-rightness is the self-affirmation of a "this"-ness. Mozi's absolutism meets this criterion. Like all other *shi*s, however, it also necessarily posits its own alternative perspectives, its not-this, its *fei*. There is its wrongness. This is more than enough for Zhuangzi. Zhuangzi has his own perspective. It is that all perspectives are right in that they are the self-affirming "this" of some perspective, and that they are wrong in that they are the "not-this" of at least one other perspective. This perspective is also right and wrong in just the same way. Its wrongness allows the rightness of Mozi's absolutism—even his claim, at some given moment, that this must applies to all possible moments. Its rightness, however, is what Zhuangzi wants to talk about—*because he is being Zhuangzi right now, and not Mozi!* It has certain properties: for one thing, a certain way of handling other perspectives, such as Mozi's. So when Mozi says, "My view is right for everyone," it is like the monkeys saying "Three in the morning." Zhuangzi says, "Absolutism, relativism—three in the morning, four in the morning." The absolutism can be followed along with as another self-affirming "this" without difficulty, because it too is a this/that—from Zhuangzi's perspective. The explicit recognition of Zhuangzi's relativism would also be a this/that—from Zhuangzi's perspective. This is what it means to "make them one." Hence, Zhuangzi tells us, "His oneness is one, his not-oneness is also one." Indeed, as we have seen, there *is* a certain sense in which Zhuangzi can be described as not a relativist, in which he puts forward something that is strictly and absolutely indubitable. It has the form of "negation as instantiation," as exemplified in the wild card, structured in the form of assertions such as, "People sometimes disagree" or "Words can raise doubts," as mentioned above: a position that is confirmed even when refuted, of which the refutation of which is a further instantiation: refutation as confirmation, confirmation as refutation. This is itself the "radiance of drift and doubt," the eternally circling "Who?" But this is a strictly empty absolute, threaded through and identical with relativism, absolutism as relativism, and relativism as absolutism: ironic coherence. We will see the full systematic working out of this epistemological move in the Tiantai system in the companion volume to this book: a world that does not add up to a unified one, where each partial perspective is indeed "the only truth for everyone." The Tiantai version, having other goals in mind, expands this acceptance of absolutism to another level: it becomes literally true that there is no truth anywhere except Mozi's truth of the Way of Heaven. There is also no truth other than the Confucian way of ritual, and so on. This is because the reference of these terms turns out to be synonymous, and each can be found to be referring successfully to the facts occurring anywhere and from any perspective. Obviously, this will require a radical reconfiguration of the meaning of words such as "only" and "also"—which is to say, the radical reconfiguration of the very ideas of "sameness" and "difference," the central topic of this book.

CONCLUSION TO CHAPTER FOUR: IRONIC COHERENCE

Taking all of this in, what has become of coherence and omnipresence in the hands of "Laozi" and Zhuangzi? The *Laozi* continues to adhere to the non-ironic conception of value, as it pertained to coherence: balance, togetherness, continuance of life all go together. But intelligibility has dropped out, as a consequence of precisely these requirements. Dao, as the unhewn, is the omnipresent. As such, it is the togetherness of all things, their ultimate coherence. But this emphatically includes also the coherence of the intelligible and the unintelligible, the valued and the unvalued. It includes the coherence of the coherent and the incoherent. It is this coherence that makes things coherent. It is, in effect, the coherence with incoherence that makes things coherent. It is coherence with the unvalued that makes the valued valued. It is the coherence with unintelligibility that makes things intelligible. Hence, ironic coherence: the true coherence (the true value, the true togetherness, the true balance, the true continuance) lies precisely in the unintelligible.

In Zhuangzi, this irony is intensified. The fundamental coherence between value and disvalue now becomes diversified into the individual *shi/fei*s of various perspectives. These are where value comes from: from the positing of value endemic to being some one particular self-affirming being, from being this one in particular instead of that one. That is, from being separate from one another. But beings cohere by means of this separation: it is the *shi/fei* structure itself that, ironically, groups them into a coherent togetherness. Like a wild card, they "cohere" with whatever the "other" is affirming, precisely by being different from the other, by remaining aloof from it. Coherence is here, as in the non-ironic conception, value; and this value is still a balance: the Doing Both at Once of the opposites, *shi/fei*. This value is still a kind of joy in continuing onward without end, of sustainability, derived from grouping with other creatures in opposing pairs. But coherence here is no longer intelligibility. Rather, it is just the opposite, drift and doubt, non-knowing, a Dao that is not a Dao, the absence of all definite content. It is a "radiance," but a radiance of "drift and doubt." It is a coherence, but a coherence of drift and doubt. It is ironic coherence.

What can we say about "sameness" and "difference" on this picture? For the Laozi tradition, we might think that all apparent differences are subsumed into a sameness. Any utensils cut out from the unhewn, say, a cup and a board, are not "really" different, since they are the same stuff. But this is far from what we have discovered the relation between A and B, value and disvalue, amounts to in this text. As we saw, the unhewn (B) is (1) the pure negation of A, making it both the same as and different from A (it is everything A is not, hence if A is differences, B is the *sameness* underlying those differences; but also, B is purely *different* from A), but also (2) the inclusion of both A and B, in another sense making it both same and different (it includes the differentiations that are A, hence it is always *different*; but it is also the greater *sameness* that includes all); (3) neither A nor B, making it neither the same as nor different from itself or from B; (4) the true A, making it more "the same as" A than A itself, in that it is different from every apparent A; and (5) the true B, making it more "the same as" B than B itself, in that it is different from every apparent B. The systematic unintelligibility of B, Dao, namelessness, makes it impossible to attribute simple sameness or difference either to itself, to its relations to things (intelligible coherences, A), or, most importantly, to the relations between things (coherences) themselves.

In the case of Zhuangzi, we can here reconsider the statement posted at the very beginning of this book, which comes from Zhuangzi's chapter 5: "Looked at from the perspective of their differences, your own liver and gall bladder are Chu [to the south] and Yue [to the north]. Looked at from the perspective of there sameness, the ten thousand things are all one." This tells us that things are neither the same nor different. They can be looked at as either same or different, with equal validity. But these are not merely projected opinions about them, but the self-manifestation of perspectives on them, which is what makes them one. But this oneness, even when things are so viewed, is like Laozi's oneness, not something that is in any sense "the same" as itself and "different from" other things. As Zhuangzi puts it in chapter 6, "his oneness is a oneness, and his not-oneness is also a oneness." This is why Zhuangzi does not "labor his spirit to make all things one (一 yi)," realizing that it is all "the same" (同 tong) whether they are viewed as one or not as one. We can now trace the ironies of this "sameness." It is one as one, but it is also one as not-one (其一也一, 其不一也一 qiyiyeyi qibuyiyeyi). The mirror that responds but does not store is not the same as whatever it reflects, nor is it different. Its difference from whatever it reflects (i.e., the fact that it is an empty reflective surface, rather than a definite color) is what allows it to be the same as whatever it reflects. Zhuangzi's wild card is not the same as whatever it is doubling, nor is it different. Its difference from it is what allows it to be the same as it, and vice versa. Sameness and difference are not final and definitive facts. The only sameness and difference we are left with are the drifting unfixed identities of transforming perspectives, which are the same because not the same, different because not different—ironic sameness, ironic difference. Such is ironic coherence.

FIVE

NON-IRONIC RESPONSES TO IRONIC COHERENCE IN *XUNZI* AND THE *RECORD OF RITUAL*

In this chapter we will be considering the encounter between the two types of coherence described in the previous two chapters. In particular, this chapter will deal with ways in which the non-ironic conception of coherence regroups and is reconfigured in response to the challenge posed by the ironic conception. These will take the form of an attempted rebuttal (in the case of Xunzi), and several varieties of compromise that attempt to incorporate the insights of the ironic conception within a system that maintains allegiance to values derived from the non-ironic tradition (in some of the texts that would define the mainstream tradition henceforth, e.g., the more theoretical chapters in the *Liji*: "Great Learning" and "Doctrine of the Mean"). The next chapter will continue this inquiry into the Yin-Yang speculations that grow up in the process of rationalizing the *Book of Changes (Zhouyi)* tradition.

XUNZI AND THE REGULATION OF SAMENESS AND DIFFERENCE

Our first example of post-ironic anti-irony is Xunzi. Xunzi stands somewhat apart from the other post-ironic examples to be discussed (in the following chapter), representing more of a rebuttal of the challenge of irony than a compromise with and an incorporation of it. In this sense he is another exemplary representative of the non-ironic tradition proper, in spite of the fact that Xunzi's version of "Confucianism" is seemingly based on an independent textual tradition: not one of the sayings he attributes to Confucius can be found exactly in the present *Analects,* and the central conception of ritual, as we discussed it above, has completely changed. Ritual is no longer the antithesis of penal laws and coercive corporal punishments, getting its central significance from this contrast, but now unproblematically subsumes and employs them. Its ultimate justification no longer lies directly in the psychological and affective dimensions of a certain type of human interaction, but rather in its pragmatic ability to regulate the objective distribution of material goods and privileges in a way that contributes to collective human strength and the satisfaction of the human desires for these goods and privileges. In my view, the satisfaction of human desires is the only justification of any position developed by any early Chinese thinker. There simply is no conception of value here that is entirely abstractable from some human desires or other. The difference is in *what* desires are taken into account. In Xunzi's case, as in Mozi's, the satisfaction of *material* desires related to the distribution of palpable goods is at the forefront, though Xunzi, unlike Mozi, does make a place for a psychological dimension of desire to be fulfilled. The ultimate justification for his program, however, is accomplished independently of any appeal to these psychological satisfactions (in harmony, in affection, in "feeling at ease," and so on) per se. But ultimately Xunzi's goal is not a compromise and integration of ironic elements, but a full spelling-out of and further unfolding of the non-ironic tradition in such a way as to handle the ironic objections. To do so, Xunzi incorporates a much more "Mohist" approach to the central problems of the tradition—the appeal to material consequence—than the earlier, pre-ironic non-ironic tradition had. Indeed, Xunzi writes very much in response to the challenges presented by the "ironic" tradition. Still, I think Xunzi's explicit discussion of the issues so far raised as it were in passing in the *Mencius* gives us a good barometer of the meaning of coherence within the non-ironic tradition. The reason I classify Xunzi straightforwardly as a representative of the non-ironic tradition, rather than as an example of the non-ironic assimilation of ironic elements—the compromise positions to be discussed in the rest of this chapter and the following chapter—can be stated simply. Xunzi does not regard the highest and most comprehensive coherence as unintelligible, that is, as only coherent in the ironic sense, and then attempt to derive or situate practical non-ironic mini-coherences within it, as we will see the compromise positions doing. Rather, the overall coherence remains non-ironically coherent, intelligible. The whole that subsumes all smaller coherences can be discerned and known. As we shall see, this highest coherence is not Heaven, which is indeed not coherent or knowable for Xunzi, but rather the totality of usable coherences, harmonized into systematic order. It is true that this does not include all the ways of grouping that can be found in nature; Xunzi does accept the ironic critique that rejects a perspectiveless, synordinate whole. But he does not, like the ironic tradition, go on to acknowledge that this whole, as the greatest coherence, is a cipher of unintelligibility that must be brought into relation with his discourse, decisively altering how all smaller coherence must be conceived. What cannot be spoken of, he passes over in silence: "[I]t is only the Sage who does not seek to understand Heaven." Rather, he posits a non-ironic greatest possible whole, which is knowable and describable, and relates unproblematically and without any flip-flops to the smaller levels of coherence contained within it. Xunzi's term for it is Greatest Coherence (大理 *dali*), and he is willing to state clearly and unambiguously what it is. The accessible aspects of Heaven are merely an aspect of this Greatest Coherence.[1] On this crucial point, Xunzi does not compromise, does not accept the ironic critique.

As the introduction of this term may suggest, in the works of Xunzi Li has already become a common and important term with its own special usage, no longer merely a borrowing, as it were, or a still-startling and living metaphor creatively applied to a more abstract discussion. In fact, it is in the *Xunzi* that we first see a huge quantitative increase in occurrences—the character appears a total of 106 times in the text, as compared to the total of seven appearances in the *Mencius*—and perhaps we can surmise that it is Xunzi and his school who first make it a genuine technical term with its own stable set of associations. We will discuss these usages in more detail in the first chapter of the companion volume to this book. But we can get at his understanding of coherence as such, which will underwrite and overdetermine those usages, through his more central interest: the question of ritual.

The application of the conception of coherence that stresses harmony as a joining of differences ("harmony" as opposed to "sameness") is essential to Xunzi's notion of the unity or coherence of ritual principles as the cornerstone of universal coherence. And what is ritual? Xunzi tells us:

> Man is born with desires. When desire goes unsatisfied, there cannot fail to be seeking. When seeking is done without proper measure and divisions, there cannot fail to be contention. With contention comes disorder, and with disorder poverty and failure. The Former Kings hated this disorder, so they created the system of ritual and rightness to make the divisions, so as to nourish and satisfy man's desires and satisfy man's seeking. This allows the desires not to be frustrated by [lack of] goods, and goods not to be depleted by [unchecked] desires. The two maintain each other so that both flourish. This is the origin of ritual.[2]

Note here the beginning of the discussion with the flat assertion: man is born with desires. Here again we see the *givenness* of human desire, without an inquiry into its source or meaning, as the premise for all further discussion. Everything else that is said is founded on this premise.[3] These desires are an indispensable factor in the creation of ritual. Xunzi states, "Ritual has three sources. Heaven and earth are the source of life. The ancestors are the source of species-similarity (*lei*). Rulers and teachers are the source of order. . . . If any of these three is lacking, there is no way to bring peace (安 *an*) to human beings. Thus ritual is a way of serving heaven above and earth below, of honoring the ancestors and of exalting the rulers and teachers."[4] Here we see Xunzi combining the givenness of the desires of life from heaven and earth, the coherence of a group of humans in species similarity, and the deliberate contrivances of rulers and teachers to create order out of these two types of demand. The human source attributed to species-similarity is to be noted here. Xunzi seems to be asserting that what things are grouped in what ways is itself an achievement of an inherited culture, the ancestors. The groupings and identifications of things that are relevant here are those that exist *within* the system of ritual, that is, what objects are used in what way and "as" what within the inherited grammar of the culture, as a function of our own grouping as a coherent social body deriving from a single set of ancestral antecedents; there is no other kind of grouping that can be meaningfully discussed. In the *overlap* of these three separate forms of coherence, as it were, the rituals emerge.

It is in this context that Xunzi steps forward as the first in the tradition to assert definitively that what concerns him is not reducible to any available categories of "sameness" and "difference," and to give to this supremely important but resistant to sameness-and-difference something the name "Li"—the still distant ultimate target of our reflections here, to be taken up explicitly in the companion volume. Xunzi tells us that the "coherence of ritual" (禮之理 *li zhi Li*) (i.e., the value-bearing coherence, or "*constructive* patterns,"[5] of these coherences as an object to be recognized) is "profound . . . vast . . . lofty,"[6] and goes on to state pointedly that it is beyond the understanding of sameness and difference (同異 *tong yi*) analyzed by the logicians. It emerges, as we shall see, when the demands of given human desires, the conditions of human grouping, and the deliberate choices of modes of grouping fashioned by the sages, combine coherently.

For comprehending this "Li of ritual," an alternate form of understanding of sameness and difference is required, which Xunzi spells out very explicitly:

> For what reason do we have the use of ideas of sameness and difference? I say: because of our natural organs.[7] For all creatures of the same type (纇 *lei*) and the same condition will apprehend objects with the natural organs in the same way. Thus they will compare

and map the similarities together until they can communicate with each other, which is how they agree upon names in common so as to come into agreement with each other (相期 *xiang qi*). The eye differentiates the colors and coherences (色理 *seli*) of visible forms and bodies. The ear differentiates the clarity, turbidity, harmony and dissonance, and the odd unclassified instance, of sounds and tones. . . . The mind has a function of confirming knowledge. In confirming knowledge, it traces the ear and knows which sounds are acceptable, traces the eye and knows which forms are acceptable. But the confirmation of knowledge can only determine acceptability after the natural organs have matched and registered the types of the things. . . . Thereafter the things are named accordingly: those that are the same are given the same name, those that differ are given different names. . . . Different actualities are given different names, same actualities are given same names.[8]

Thus far, it sounds as if Xunzi is offering a straightforward "realist" account of the application of names; to wit, there are real samenesses and differences in the world, apprehended as different and the same by the senses according to isomorphism of shape or continuity of locality, which are named accordingly; this, however, seems to contradict the just-quoted assertion that *lei*-types have their *source* in the ancestors, which on this interpretation must be dismissed as some kind of anomaly. Note, however, that even thus far we are told that all this depends on the sameness of the organs of the members of a single species of living being, namely, humans, thereby pushing the question to a meta-level, as it were. The coherence at the bedrock of the distinction is not that of things, but of perceivers-and-things. A similar group of observers and a set of objects yield a coherent set of sameness and differences. A different set of samenesses and differences may be picked out by another group. Xunzi does not here tell us what the extent or criteria of the *lei* he has in mind here are. All humans? All animals? All Confucians? All Chinese? All sages? For the question of sameness and differences is begged here: What determines what group of perceivers counts as "the same type"? Do they have to be again distinguished as such by someone, some organs that pick out their sameness and differences? They will presumably, by the same principle, be picked out as being of the same type of perceivers only by a group of perceivers that is itself sufficiently of one type to see this first group as all belonging to one group—and so on ad infinitum. Or is it the very fact that their natural faculties apprehend objects in the same way that is the criterion that classifies them as being of the same type and disposition? Does their seeing sameness and differences in the same way simultaneously classify them as the same, either definitionally or as a second act of self-viewing and self-classifying? What if their natural organs sometimes apprehend in the same way and sometimes in a different way from one another? Are they then sometimes of the same type and sometimes not? So far, Xunzi has left these questions unresolved, and with it the question of to what extent he can be considered an ontological realist. But then Xunzi continues:

> Names have no fixed appropriateness; they are restricted by agreement through the act of naming. When the agreements are fixed to the point of becoming customary, then they are called appropriate. If they differ from this agreement, they are called inappropriate. Names refer to no fixed actuality; they are agreed upon to name an actuality, and when these agreements are fixed to the point of becoming customary, they are called names for real things. But names do have a fixed standard of what makes them good names: when they are direct and easy, and do not drift, they are good names.[9]

This passage might be interpreted simply as a "soft" nominalism, claiming that, although there are real-kinds in the world, what particular sound or symbol is used to designate them is merely a matter of custom.[10] This interpretation has been adopted at times to maintain consistency with Xunzi's apparent realism. But in fact, as we have begun to see, Xunzi is deeply committed to a kind of species relativism as well, and the priority of human desires and values in determining the appropriate forms of coherence, of sameness and difference. This apparent tension can be resolved if we recall the picture of "overlapping" sources of ritual mentioned above. On the one hand, Xunzi gives the sage the role of actually creating the order in the universe, making kinds exist. On the other hand, he often speaks of genuine "similarities," not only similarities between human desires, as stressed by Mencius, but similarities in objects perceived by the senses (without, as in Mencius, the qualification that these similarities are merely "adduced" (ju) abstracted from a larger, perhaps dissimilar, whole), on the basis of which distinctions can be made. Xunzi also speaks straightforwardly of natural facts unaffected by human response to them (as in the "Discourse on Heaven"), and of inborn propensities that are just the fact of the matter (as in the "Discourse on Ritual").

The problem is exacerbated by a further consideration of Xunzi's pronouncements on *lei*-groups, which appear to further support his "realism": his concept of actual "feeling and response" taking place in nature, which objectively provides a grouping of real things. A real *lei*-group is one among whose members there is a natural mutual feeling and response. All things "of the same type," we are told, move each other:

The origin of types of things necessarily has its appropriate beginnings. The arrival of praise or blame always corresponds to one's
own qualities. When flesh decays it gives birth to worms, when
fish dry up they produce maggots. When a man is careless and
arrogant, disasters begin for him. . . . Evil and corruption of one's
person invite resentment of others. If you lay out firewood, all other
things being equal, the fire will go to the driest. If the ground is
level, the water will naturally move toward dampness. Trees and
plants grow together according to species, birds and animals dwell
together according to type: *all things follow their own kind.* (物各從
其類也 *Wu ge cong qi lei ye*).[11]

We should note here not only that things in general are assumed to group
together by type spontaneously and as it were voluntarily, but also that this
is unhesitatingly assumed to be a universal trait of everything, even abstract
psychological entities such as virtues, which belong to a "kind" with good
reputation and good fortune and thus spontaneously attract it.[12] An entity
is not an independent and inert substance; it is a social being, attracted to
its own type, existing in a reciprocal regard with other things of that type
and spontaneously moving toward them. Things interact by a process of
feeling or noticing each other and responding (感應 *ganying*).[13] They are
not autonomously active: they wait for the external stimulus or arousal. But
at the same time they are not inertly passive: they respond. In a word, they
are parts of a "social" totality. This pervasive assumption suggests a notion
of causal interaction that is neither free nor coercive. To be stimulated by
the ideal member of one's own kind is both to be moved from outside, to
be conditioned, and to be moved from within, to express one's own intrinsic
character, revealing the category to which one belongs.[14]

As noted, this applies equally to concrete objects and to components
of the personality, to virtues. Here even the moral behavior and its psychological consequences are viewed as part of a system of natural, seemingly
"objective" correspondences: "The exemplary person purifies his person and
those who are likewise join with him. He speaks good words and those
who are of the same [resonating] type (*lei*) respond. When a horse neighs
horses respond. When a cow moos cows respond. This is not because of any
knowledge or wisdom; it is just the way things go."[15]

This seems to be another strong assertion of real coherences existing
objectively in the world, without reference to human perspective. How do
we reconcile this to the apparent nominalism of Xunzi's discussion of naming, and his claim that the exemplary man is the *source* of similarity-types,
that he actually creates the order of the universe through ritual? There
seems to be a real tension here. Indeed, it is on precisely this point that

the interpretations of Xunzi have been most divided, highlighted profitably in the wake of Kurtis Hagen's recent book, *The Philosophy of Xunzi: A
Reconstruction*. Hagen's book throws down the gauntlet to what has been
the dominant interpretation of Xunzi in English, what he calls the "realist"
interpretation, holding "not merely that there is a reality independent of our
thoughts about it, but that there is a privileged description of this reality,
that concepts can and should mirror it, and that there is a uniquely correct
way of being in it. In particular, properly chosen moral concepts capture
eternal truths revealing the one true way."[16] Hagen finds some version of this
view informing the Xunzi interpretations offered by Goldin, Ivanhoe, Puett,
Kline, and Van Norden.[17] Hagen rejects this interpretation and instead,
drawing in part on observations from Lee Yearley and Antonio Cua among
others, proffers what he calls a "constructivist" interpretation, "one that
stresses the importance of formulating constructive social constructs. The
distinctions made by the sages have no absolute status. Rather, categories
are judged according to values, such as harmony and social stability, which
are in turn justified by their critical role in facilitating the satisfaction of a
substantial number of our desires." Importantly, this also implies for Hagen
that "there may be more than one way to achieve success in constructing
a moral world."[18] As will be obvious by now, my view is in close agreement
with Hagen's overall position, as stated here, but with a few small adjustments which are, I think, of some consequence. The questions at issue in
this debate are (1) whether moral standards are "discovered" or "invented,"
and (2) whether there is "one" right set of standards or "many." My approach
here, of course, is premised on the rejection of *both* of these dichotomies in
principle: my claim is that the key Chinese thinkers of the classical period
recognize no distinction between "discovering" and "inventing," that they
have no categories that would sharply distinguish the "realist" discovery of
facts and regularities from the "nominalist" (or "conceptualist") projection
of the same, and that "one" and "many" are inapt categories to apply to an
ontology rooted in the notion of coherence, which is definitionally neither
one nor many, and indeed is expressed in a language for which an either-or
between one and many has no semantic force. The neither-one-nor-many,
neither-inside-nor-outside of coherence applies *also* to the question of "who
made morality" and "how many right moralities are there?" Xunzi, in fact,
is a particularly useful thinker to examine for determining in exactly what
way this can be so.

  For the solution to this apparent tension can be found by closely
examining Xunzi's treatment of the relations of man and nature. He tells us:

> By using a single general type (*lei*) we can accomplish manifold
> practices, by using "one" we can practice ten thousand. Whatever
> begins is brought to completion, and whatever ends is begun again,

like the endless turning of a circle; without this the empire falls into decay. *Heaven and earth are the beginning of life; ritual and rightness are the beginning of good order; the exemplary person is the beginning of ritual and rightness.* Deliberate activity, threading cases together [into unified types], accumulating, working to improve—these are the beginning of becoming an exemplary person. *So heaven and earth produce the exemplary person, and the exemplary person orders heaven and earth. The exemplary person forms a triad with heaven and earth, is the unifier* (總 *zong*) *of the ten thousand things, the father and mother of the people. Without the exemplary person heaven and earth are not ordered, ritual and rightness have no consistency, above there is no true ruler or teacher, and below no true father or son: this is called utter chaos.* The relations between lord and minister, father and son, elder and younger brother, husband and wife—these bring to completion whatever begins, and begin again whatever ends; [thereby] they share the same coherence with heaven and earth, and live as long as ten thousand generations: this is called the great foundation. Thus that which is operative in funerals and sacrifices, the relations in court and in the army is one. [That which is evident in] exalting and debasing, killing and giving life, giving and taking is one. To treat a ruler as a ruler, a minister as a minister, a father as a father, a son as a son, an elder brother as an elder brother, a younger brother as a younger brother: One. To treat a farmer as a farmer, a scholar as a scholar, a craftsman as a craftsman, a trader as a trader: One. . . .

Mineral objects [lit. fire and water] have material force (*qi*), but no life. Plants [grass and trees] have life, but no awareness. Animals and birds have awareness, but no sense of rightness (義 *yi*). Man has material force, life, awareness and *also a sense of rightness*, and thus is the most precious thing in the world. He is not as powerful as the ox, not as fast as the horse, and yet he employs the ox and horse as servants. And why? I say, because humans are able to gather together, and the others cannot. How is it that humans can gather? I say, by dividing. How does division proceed? By means of this sense of rightness. So if the sense of rightness is used to divide there will be harmony, and where there is harmony there is unity . . . power . . . strength . . . and thus the ability to conquer other creatures. . . . His ordering of the four seasons, tailoring the ten thousand things, universally bringing benefit to all is due to nothing besides his attainment of right divisions.[19]

This passage is rich with implications for the present discussion. First we have an assertion of the utility of "coherence," and of the general categories that unite particulars. What sort of coherence? The answer comes soon enough: The coherence that is seen in all the contrary and relative ritual role relations, such that these apparently contrasted principles are all asserted to be one. Here again we see our dyadic pendulum swings joined by a center. To treat a ruler as a ruler—i.e., to behave subserviently, etc.—and to treat a minister as a minister—i.e., to behave authoritatively, etc.—are one. Here already we see how the reciprocal role mode of thinking leads directly into a rhetoric that unites opposites. From noting that the principle of appropriate division is applied equally in various situations to produce diverse ritual commitments, we get the assertion that "exalting and debasing, killing and giving life, giving and taking: these are one." In other words these opposite behaviors are one in their appropriateness in their particular situations, thereby creating a greater coherence among the roles, leading to unity, strength, and the satisfaction of desires. Coherence is a unity that presupposes differences and divisions, and that must include human desires among its terms. Man's ability "to gather together with his kind" means specifically to do so with a deliberate graded hierarchy leading to an effective unified coherence that is useful in creating the strength to overcome nature and the distribution of goods, which makes maximal satisfaction of human desires possible. All beings have material force, and all attract each other, as we have seen; but their mutual pull, even in the case of animals with awareness, is not organized by self-conscious and deliberately orchestrated rightness and role divisions; it is at best mere mobbing, and thus lacks organizational power. As Xunzi says elsewhere, "What makes humans humans is that they can make distinctions . . . birds and beasts have fathers and sons among them but not the intimacy of father and son; they have male and female but not the division of male and female. Thus the way of man always involves making distinctions."[20] The animals group, but they do not make deliberate role distinctions, so they cannot group in the ritually proper way which is most effective for social cohesiveness and unity, distribution of resources and collective strength.

Putting these points together, we discover that the solution to the apparent tension between nominalism and realism is quite simple. Xunzi sees real coherences existing in nature, real divisions in the world, real similarities and differences. The problem is that these coherences themselves do not cohere. There are too many of them, too many alternate, equally *real* ways in which things group.[21] This chaos and conflict between alternate coherences is for Xunzi anti-value ("evil") itself. Evil, in Xunzi's thought, means something like "disorder, inconsistency, internal conflict—whatever obstructs a cohesion around a single purpose, that allows for strength and unity to overcome nature and obtain the satisfaction of desires." The apparent conflict between nominalism and realism with respect to natural kinds admits of a similar solution. What matters is the broadest unity of the whole, organized around the satisfaction of the human desires. To cohere with value, to be genuine coherences, certain of these coherences in nature must be picked out from among the others, and regulations must be decreed by those in authority, just as is the case of established fixed weights and measures for use within a single coherent community. The community becomes genuinely coherent as a community by this very procedure, just as the world is made genuinely coherent-for-them by the same gesture.

This idea can be clarified by means of an example. According to the way animal species are grouped by modern biology, a whale is not a fish, but rather a mammal. This is because certain features are chosen as the criterion for grouping; for example, the way the offspring in any species are produced and nourished. In modern Chinese, a whale is named with a two character term 鯨魚 *jingyu*. The second character, *yu*, a term usually translated with the English word *fish*. (And indeed this radical appears in the first character as well.) The term is applied to many animals which swim in water, with or without the general "fishlike" shape (*zhangyu*, for example, means octopus), and the use of the term with a modifier certainly suggests that whale is here regarded as a particular member of the larger class of beings called *yu*. This is based on another type of criteria for grouping, for example, behavior and habitat. Both of these types of similarities exist in nature; there is a group of animals who nurse their young, which may be considered as one set, and there is also a group that swim in the water, which may also be considered one set, depending on which criteria we choose. These two groups overlap. But both are based on genuine similarities and differences that really exist in nature. For Xunzi, a community must choose and enforce which set of real similarities and differences it will endorse with its naming procedures, and which it will ignore. The ultimate justification for doing so is not because one way of grouping is truer than another. There can be no question of greater or lesser reality between these alternate forms of coherence. The justification is the same as that for setting standards for weights and measures in the marketplace; so that commerce and interaction can proceed smoothly and with minimal contention—in other words, "coherently." This involves three further levels of "coherence": (1) coherence among whichever of these real coherence can cohere into a single synordinate coherence, (2) coherence of the human social group, and (3) coherence between these two coherences, which is to say, whichever set of coherence is consistent with this human value. That is, the coherences among all the real coherences in the world that are to be chosen are the ones which (1) best cohere with one another into a single overarching synordinate coherence, and (2) best cohere with someone's conception of the promoting of human value, (3) noncontentious, synordinate coherence in the social group.

Thus, in Xunzi we see the tension between nominalism and realism given an ingenious solution. There is an overabundance of real divisions in the world known to the senses, real spontaneous groupings between things. They are out there, but the sage regulates by choosing which among them are to serve as standards, like weights and measures used in the marketplace, by regulating the proper use of language. Jane Geaney, in her study of the epistemology of the senses in early Chinese thought, notes in her own terms that "the poles of idealism versus realism do not seem important in Warring States philosophical texts. Whether things, such as colors, are out there or in the sensing subject is not in question."[22] This is Geaney's way of noting the point about the inapplicability of both nominalism and realism to early Chinese thought, which has been central to our discussion so far. We are now beginning to see why this is so. Geaney suggests a useful way to describe this situation in the case of the *Xunzi*: she compares the Xunzian theory of sense perception to the notion of "aspect perception." "The notion that looking and listening are aimed at organizing things in a particular way resembles the continuous 'seeing as' and 'hearing as' of aspect perception."[23] This notion of "seeing as" fits between the poles of nominalism and realism, encompassing both to a certain degree: the object out there really *can* be seen this way, *as* this thing, but need not be; the subject is the decisive factor that determines what the object will be seen as, and yet also cannot freely see the object in any way at all: the possibilities of what it can be seen as are limited by the objective conditions. No object is seeable in either only one way or in an infinite number of ways; it is always multiply seeable, within a certain given and finite range. The "types" are real, but also null and void without the participation of man. Hence, Xunzi states plainly, "Laws cannot stand on their own; types cannot function by themselves (類不能自行 *lei buneng zixing*). When they attain the right person they exist, when they lose the right person they vanish."[24] Even the types, the groupings of things in nature according to their feelings and responses, depend on man for their actualization, indeed only really exist when selected out and ratified by the right person, "their" person (其人 *qiren*).[25]

This same solution is crucial also to Xunzi's ethics and theory of human nature, also his cosmology. Just as in the case of Mencius, he neither claims that all the pre-deliberate ways of grouping are good nor bad. He selects among them. However, his standards are different. For Mencius, those aspects of the inborn human endowment which lead to harmonious grouping of the group in actual fact, which do not involve limited resources and competition, which are spontaneous, which distinguish this group from others, and which can be attained without requiring any external contingent help, are called its "universal" class-criterion, the Nature. Xunzi also chooses those aspects of both the human group and the world that lead to harmonious grouping (order) and circumvent competition within the group, as well as handling the problem of distribution of the scarcity of goods. However, for him these must be legislated in the use of particular words like weights and measures, and the system of ritual, and must be done deliberately and administratively, by means of commands, rewards, and punishments. For natural kinds in objects, however, Xunzi introduces the category of *ganying*, actual feeling and response, and his theory of ritual, and thus of the human grouping, also implies some reliance on a related idea.

Keeping this in mind, and understanding his implicit definition of evil (= disorder, internal conflict of purposes), allows us also to clarify another point that has puzzled readers of Xunzi: on the one hand he tells us that human nature is evil (in that chapter of that name), but at the same time he admits (in the "Regulations of the King" chapter, quoted above) that man is born with a sense of rightness (義 *yi*). This has led some interpreters to suggest that one or the other of these chapters must not be Xunzi's own work. But if "evil" simply *means* internal conflict, then it is easy to reconcile "Man's nature is evil" and "man is born with an innate sense of rightness and justice." Man is born with *many different conflicting desires and inclinations*. Among these, there is the sense of justice—indeed, Xunzi could equally admit all the Mencian "sprouts" without interfering with his thesis in the least. The point is that an inborn nature that consists of both good and evil spontaneous inclinations, taken as a whole, *is itself evil*. That is, it is in conflict with itself, cannot attain unity of purpose, coherence, needed for the satisfaction of desires. Human nature is evil *because* man is born with the spontaneous inclination for justice *and* other spontaneous inclinations that stand in conflict with it. Human nature is *incoherent*.

The desired coherence, for Xunzi, has the temporal or developmental aspect we have alluded to above: it is justified by the fact that it leads to continuance, like the "Good" in the "Great Commentary" (to be discussed below) and the "harmony" in the *Guoyu* passage, such that what begins reaches completion and begins again. This assertion might originally give us pause, but once again the father/son model makes it clear: the father is a beginning who is brought to completion as a father by having a son, who brings the cycle to a new beginning, becomes a father in turn. This dyadic cycle is the motor of stability and preservation. Indeed, this type of dyadic coherence of opposites is the basis of the order and stability of the cosmos itself: "Heaven and earth join through [rites], the sun and moon are bright through them, the four seasons are ordered through them, the stars and constellations proceed through them, the rivers flow, the ten thousand things manifest, love and hate are measured, joy and anger are regulated through them. . . . Are not rites the most perfect?!"[26]

We see in this passage also Xunzi's performative, nominalistic side, which is stated more radically in his works than almost anywhere else: the exemplary person literally is the unifier of the world and all things, he is what gives them their order, in spite of the fact that he is himself one of them. He has in fact had to struggle to attain this position as organizing, unifying center by means of his own deliberate conscious activity. He unifies all the opposites, by perceiving the unified types that harmonize them. The exemplary person is the unifier (*zong*) and third participant (參 *san*)with heaven and earth of the cosmos; his role, as the executor of ritual divisions, is to create social unity, ("the ruler is he who is skilled at making people group together" [君者善群也 *junzhe shan qun ye*]),[27] hence he is the focus of the whole, he embodies in that sense the whole, by comprehending it and executing it. Without him it would not be a truly coherent whole at all, although there would be a chaos of real, alternate coherences. Anyone may become this center of the cosmos who both forms its focal point and transforms it; but only a few ever do so.

Xunzi's approach to this question, and his accentuation of the performative nominalism already implicit in Mencius, can perhaps best be regarded as a response to the thoroughgoing perpsectivism of the Inner Chapters of the *Zhuangzi*. I call this a perspectivism rather than a straightforward nominalism because, although Zhuangzi seems to be rejecting all natural kinds, making them all wholly perspective-dependent, he too is really, as we have seen, by this very move asserting rather the overabundance of natural kinds. This is again premised on the notion that subjective responses are genuine parts of reality that must also be factored into any account of coherence. We have seen that Zhuangzi's view, as expressed in the "Inner Chapters," seems to be that each perspective makes its own "this-that" distinction, necessarily, and this means that in the world there are an infinite number of real this-that distinctions, groupings, coherences. These can never cohere into any single synordinate coherence, for it is in the nature of the case that various perspectives will form mutually contradictory ways of grouping the coherences they find present to them. At the same time, however, each single perspectival way of grouping the world does make its own "single synordinate" coherence of all the coherences it finds; the others are grouped as its "other," and this categorization is internal to its regarding of itself as "this." With this we come to what I have called the dyadic a priori and the ironic use of coherence. But we should note Xunzi's response, in defense of the non-ironic sense of coherence. In effect, Xunzi accepts Zhuangzi's point that the world is full of an overabundance of mutually contradictory but equally "real" coherences. He simply privileges coherence with one perspective above the others, the coherence with the desires of the sages, who select among these coherences a group that can form a single synordinate global coherence. In his argument about the use of words, and hence of ways of dividing up the world, we have the implications of a sort of social-pragmatic version of Kant's transcendental unity of apperception. That is, Xunzi holds that unless some regulation of the ways of cohering is made, so that they form a single synordinate system, there is no way even to compare, contrast, reject alternate views; one's words are used with different meanings from those understood by one's interlocutors, just as Zhuangzi had urged, and this chaos makes all other possibilities literally meaningless. As in Davidson's principle of charity, a massive agreement must be assumed for there to be any meaningful difference, or even anything meaningfully meant by "a different way of carving up the world, a different perspective."

Returning to the controversies around Hagen's constructivist reading, we can perhaps now make some headway. One of the central issues of the dispute between the constructivist and realist readings was the question of whether for Xunzi there was one unique system of Dao, or, as Hagen suggests, the possibility of many such systems. The debate finds a focal point in the interpretation of the following passage that begins the "Dispelling Obsessions" chapter (or in Hagen's translation):

> Human problems all derive from obsession with a single corner of things which obscures the Greatest Coherence. When ordered, these all return to the norm, but when doubts arise over alternatives between them, there is confusion. *In the world there are not two Daos, and the Sages are not of two minds.* Nowadays the feudal lords all have differing governments, the philosophers all have differing theories, so that there is inevitably agreement and disagreement among them, some well-ordered and others in chaos.

> 凡人之患，蔽於一曲，而闇於大理。治則復經，兩疑則惑矣。
> 天下無二道，聖人無兩心。今諸侯異政，百家異說，則必或是
> 或非，或治或亂。

Defenders of the "realist" view suggest that the phrase "in the world there are not two Daos" should be taken to mean that in Xunzi's view there is really only one unique system of moral norms, objectively built into reality, contra Hagen's claim that "there may be more than one way to achieve success in constructing a moral world." But we can now see, I think, that this whole controversy is based on a false premise, namely, that "one" and "not-one" are being conceived on a same-different model rather than a coherence model. The phrase in question can certainly be interpreted, taking advantage once again of the lack of tense and other ambiguities in the Chinese, to mean not "There is only One Dao in the universe," but rather "In the political world, at any given time, there should be not be two competing and unintegrable Daos." The point is not just to read *tianxia* in its more restricted sense as referring to the existing social polity, and supply the implicit "at any given time," which perhaps would support Hagen's point nicely; it is rather that "two" here does not mean numerically distinct, but rather unintegrable. The whole point of this chapter, after all, is that *apparently diverse* and even *contradictory* virtues and values can all be integrated into the Greatest Coherence. Is "the Way of Heaven" one Dao, and 'the Way of Man" another Dao? How about "Inclusiveness" and "Separatism"? Xunzi tells us that *both* are parts of the Greatest Coherence, whereas Daoists and Mohists had mistakenly taken them as two separate and opposed Daos, each clinging to his own obsession and missing the rest. The question of one or many Daos actually becomes moot on a coherence model. Whatever new standards might be created at future times, even unforeseen and apparently sharply in contradiction to previously existing ones, will be "part of" the same Dao, that is, in continuity with the Dao of the past, *not* because they replicate or instantiate any selfsame essence of moral rightness or map onto any preexisting template, but because they *cohere* with the past rightnesses, thereby forming one fabric with it. In other words, even if "different," future "daos" would be part of the one Dao. As I've indicated above, this does not mean that any and every set of norms would qualify: Xunzi does have a standard, which he specifies clearly. The ultimate justification for the ritual system is its contribution to the satisfaction of human desires, by increasing collective human strength and ordering the distribution of desired rewards within the human community. In his existing situation, he sees only one way in which this has been achieved: the ritual system. He has no reason to speculate on the question that exercises the combatants in the realism/constructivism debate beyond this point. But where X is justified wholly in terms of its contribution to Y, X remains a negotiable term whenever something else can perform the same contribution to Y. If X is only valuable because of its value to Y, then in principle X is replaceable by something else with the same value to Y. Xunzi gives no reason to *rule out* that something other than the present ritual system might do the same work (i.e., harmonizing diverse virtues, making man coherent with world, increasing human strength and satisfaction). He simply says that the ritual system in fact does so, and no other proposal currently before him does so; nor, inasmuch as he claims that the existing ritual system does the job beautifully, does he call for any attempt to invent any other way of doing so. But my point here is that if he did, and if any such system did emerge in the future that satisfied those conditions, remaining coherent with the previous (ritual) means of doing so, that future "other" system would ipso facto *not* be something "other"; it too would therefore be another coherent part of the "one" Dao.

OMNIPRESENCE AND COHERENCE IN XUNZI

Xunzi's treatment of the problem thus also brings into sharp focus the question of the "universal universal," the encompassing category of categories or coherence of coherences, much more explicitly than in the case of Mencius. This again is no doubt due to the challenge posed by the "ironic" treatment of coherence in the Daoist traditions. In his writings we find very explicit invocations of the principle of holism as a unifier of opposites, as we have seen to some extent already, but the whole is usually conceived of as radically disjoined from the extremes, that is, from any partial perspective. Whole and part are contrasted once and for all, with value residing solely in the former; all value of the latter must come from their subordinated relation to the former. The idea that "the whole" or all-inclusiveness is identical to value has become explicit here, perhaps due to developments in Mohism and Daoism. Hence: "He who misses even once out of a hundred shots is not to be considered a good archer. . . . He who does not connect all categories and kinds and cannot unify benevolence and rightness cannot be called good at learning. For learning is most definitely learning how to unify. . . . Only after one makes it complete and comprehensive can he be called a true learner. The exemplary person knows that what is not whole and pure is not to be considered beautiful. . . . Thus the exemplary person values his wholeness (君子貴其全也 junzi gui qi quan ye)."[28] This wholeness is now also a criterion by which to adjudicate between various doctrines; as in the "Tianxia" chapter of the Zhuangzi, which may date from roughly the same time, and as we see already in incipient form in Mencius's discussion of Yang and Mo, the true doctrine is the whole doctrine, the one that is most all-inclusive, and false equals partial: "Impartiality begets clear-sightedness, partiality begets darkness."[29] "The ten thousand things are one corner of the Way, and any given thing is just one corner of all things. The ignorant take one thing or one corner and think they know the Way, but they do not. Shenzi had insight into staying behind, but none into going ahead; Laozi had insight into contracting but not into expanding; Mozi had insight into equality but not into inequality."[30] Once again we have dyads, two endpoints meant to describe a whole, and the imputation that the lesser doctrines had understood only one side of the pair. We have here an alternative to the "appearance versus reality" model for epistemology. We may call it a whole/part epistemology. The question to be adjudicated when confronted with conflicting claims is not which is true and which is false, but rather which is more complete. In Xunzi's case, there may be some claims which have no place in the whole, which are not even partial truths, which cannot be integrated into the whole and must be eliminated completely, although he clearly makes an attempt to be as all-embracing as possible in his inclusiveness. In general, as we have seen, Xunzi attempts to regard any view that he sees as just plain false, as unassimilable to the whole, to be in a certain sense meaningless, that is, as a misuse or misapplication of words, as in the case of Mencius's doctrine that human nature is good. This misuse of words is directly analogous to the disregard for ritual: it means not heeding the regulations for language use prevailing in a certain community, standards of use that need to enforced just as weights and measures in the marketplace do, and as ritual forms do. Anything that can fit into these linguistic and ritual forms, integrated into this whole, is a partial truth, a partial good.[31]

We can see Xunzi's appropriation and modification of ironic motifs also, perhaps most obviously, in his description of the mind:

> By means of what does man know the Dao? By means of his mind. By means of what does the mind know? By means of its emptiness, unity and stillness. The mind is always storing something, and yet there is something about it we describe as empty. The mind is always a multiplicity, and yet there is something about it we describe as unified. The mind is always moving, and yet there is something about it we describe as still. Once born, man has awareness, and with awareness there is a harboring of intentions. To harbor an intention is to store something, and yet there is something in it we describe as empty. What we call its emptiness is the fact that it does not disrupt future receptions with what it has already stored up. When the mind arises there is awareness, and with awareness there is [knowledge of] differences (yi). Differences are known through the simultaneous awareness of more than one thing. Such simultaneous awareness is a multiplicity. But there is something in it we call a unity. What we call its unity is the fact that it does not allow the apprehension of this one to disrupt its apprehension of another one. The mind dreams when we sleep, goes its own way when it is relaxed, calculates when put to work, so the mind is always moving. But it has something in it that is called a stillness. What we call its stillness is the fact that it doesn't allow dreams and confusion to disrupt its awareness.

Xunzi here appropriates the ideas of emptiness, unity, and stillness, which play so central a role in the ironic conception of coherence in the *Laozi* tradition and in the *Zhuangzi* (and indeed, even in the pre-ironic Daoism of the "Neiye"). Xunzi's conception is quite consistent with that of the *Laozi*: the emptiness, unity, and stillness of the mind are not the negation of fullness, multiplicity, and activity, but rather the conditions that allow them to exist. The value of each of these comes from its allowing of coherence among the multiple activities with which the mind is filled, allowing them to continue unhindered and undisrupted.[32] The further coherence between stillness and activity, and so on, is the true locus of the mind's value and ability to sustain its function. But note the way Xunzi continues, reworking these ideas to fit his conception of the knowable intelligibility of the non-ironic Greatest Coherence:

> One who seeks the Dao but has not yet found it calls these emptiness, unity and stillness. But when they are put into practice, the emptiness of one who tarries in the Dao becomes penetration, the unity of one who serves the Dao becomes thoroughness, and the stillness of one who contemplates the Dao becomes clarity. To know the Dao clearly, and put that knowledge into practice, is to realize the Dao from within. Such emptiness, unity and stillness is then called the Great Clarity. All things that take shape can be seen in it, whatever is seen can be made sense of [lun, i.e., put in proper order by means of discourse], whatever sense is made of things never loses its proper place [in the total system]. Then one can set in one's room and yet see the four seas, dwell in the present but make sense of the long ago and far away, distantly view all things but know their real inclinations, personally examine order and disorder and yet penetrate their proper measures, manage and integrate heaven and earth so that he finds the talents and uses of all things, mould and carve the Greatest Coherence [制割大理 zhige dali] so that all of time and space is included in it.

We can perceive here a criticism of the original Daoist use of these ideas: to speak only of emptiness, unity, and stillness is typical of someone who is merely seeking the Dao, but has not yet begun to put into practice. When it is put into practice, it entails an active and pragmatic shaping of things, putting them into order, making of them into a Greatest Coherence. Emptiness, unity, and stillness are not to be taken as undermining any attempt at an ultimate intelligible coherence of things, as they are in the original ironic texts. Rather, for Xunzi, recognizing this fact about the mind, and with it the way in which all items are made to cohere into a whole, is only a first step premising the further shaping of all things into a total system, a non-ironic intelligible coherence that embraces everything.

This applies to the order of the cosmos as well, and to the relation between humans and the rest of the world: "Heaven has its seasons, earth has its riches, man has his ordering; herein lies their ability to participate together [as one whole]. . . . Only the sage does not seek to understand heaven."[33] The model of a whole here is one in which the parts do not replace each other or interpenetrate; each is always just what it is, plays its own role, restricted to its own sphere, defined in one way only, given a single significance determined by the place within the whole, and indeed this is precisely what makes them function together as a whole. Each part is just a part. However, since this separation is what makes the whole a whole, Xunzi still speaks, somewhat ironically, of this mutual neglect as "mutual participation." Man deals only with those parts of the whole that directly pertain to his own role therein, but thereby he plays an essential role which holds it together. "Heaven can give birth to creatures but it cannot distinguish them; earth can bear people up but it cannot order them. All creatures and humans in the world await the sage to attain their correct divisions."[34] Man's role is to complete and order the whole cosmos, which is done, however, precisely by keeping to his own distinctive role. This apparent paradox is of course made possible by the initial definition of "unity" as a harmonious coherence of differences, including human desires, on a social model. In this we may wholeheartedly concur with Yang Changzhen's conclusion, in his excellent monograph on the ontology of *lei* in the *Xunzi*: "For Xunzi, *lei* is treated initially in the humanistic sense of 'clan-type' (族類 *zulei*); hence the grouping of people or things into species-types perhaps need not be limited to that which is built on the foundation of an [abstract] universal, but rather can be based on a concrete interconnection or mutual containment. For example, if we take a particular family as a type, it is very difficult to find a single abstract point shared by all the members of the clan which defines them as a single family, but we can say they belong to a single clan-type on the basis of mutual containment seen in the intimacy between the father and the son or the role divisions between the husband and the wife as displayed in their life together. . . . Xunzi's conception of *lei* is close to that of members of a single clan group—'family resemblances' or 'mutual containment'; in this way, similarity and interconnection are conceived of as changeable, and the scope of the species-type so formed is also changeable. In different situations, or with respect to different goals or contexts, the same components can count as different categories or different types (with different interconnections). . . ."[35] The negotiable quality of the ad hoc categories is of particular importance here; they are neither arbitrary nor absolute.

This is not to say that all organizational subsets are lacking here. They are simply put in their proper places, like everything else. Hence, in a passage already quoted in part above, Xunzi says, "Ritual has three sources. Heaven and earth are the source of life. The ancestors are the source of species-similarity (*lei*). Rulers and teachers are the source of order. . . . If any of these three is lacking, there is no way to bring peace (*an*) to human beings. Thus ritual is a way of serving heaven above and earth below, of honoring the ancestors and of exalting the rulers and teachers. So the king honors his ancestors as equals of heaven, the feudal lords dare not destroy their ancestral temples, the high officials maintain constant ancestral sacrifice. This is how they honor their distinctive origin. To honor one's origin is the beginning of virtue."[36] Note how the significance of family allegiance has been preserved as an element or moment within the whole here, but one that no longer has the power to undermine that whole by being made into a whole unto itself, with its own claim to ultimate value. Xunzi makes a place for "differentiation" (別 bie), which Mozi rejects in favor of "universality" (兼 jian); but unlike the case with Confucius and Mencius, this differentiation remains subordinated to the universal at all times, and has no value apart from this relation.

Noticing the extent of nominalism and pragmatism in early Chinese argumentation, many commentators have pointed out that we seem to be dealing here less with a correspondence theory of truth than a coherence theory, and perhaps with an indifference to the question of truth as such, at least as it has been understood in European philosophy. On the basis of the above discussion I think we can now say that the non-ironic tradition can be described as embracing a coherence theory of truth, but with the additional condition that this coherence must always include human desire as one of the items that must cohere—not only propositions, facts, or beliefs. This leaves ambiguous which desires are to be included, one of the meta-questions which allows for the ironic/non-ironic split. But what counts as true will be what coheres not only with perceptual data and conceptual commitments, but with some chosen coherent set of human desires.

This question of value is what is most crucial for determining the relation of these terms to the ultimate Confucian concerns. For the most central implication of the issue at hand in the context of the Confucian thinkers revolves around what Edward Slingerland, discussing the "paradox of wu-wei," the paradox of trying not to try, has characterized as a tension between self-cultivation internalism and externalism. Internalism (Slingerland gives Zhuangzi, Laozi, and Mencius as examples) here refers to the view that "at some level . . . we already *are* good, and we merely need to allow this virtuous potential to realize itself." The externalists (including Xunzi and the *Analects*, in Slingerland's view), on the other hand, claim that "we do *not* possess the resources to attain wu-wei on our own and that wu-wei is a state acquired only after a long and intensive regime of training in traditional, external forms."[37] Slingerland has done a great service to the field by pinpointing this issue as one of the central fault lines of the tradition, reappearing in various forms again and again in quite disparate contexts. Its relevance to our present concerns is not hard to discern; it should be obvious that we have here a reversed and moral version of the "sameness" and "difference" problem, and with it the nominalism/realism problem, discussed earlier. The question here is not whether we project categories onto the world, but whether the social demands for ethical or ritual behaviors are projected from the social world onto our selves. The nominalism/realism question concerns whether our cognitive categories correspond to anything real in the external natural objects of knowledge to which they apply. The internalist/externalist problem concerns whether the social world's ethical categories correspond to anything real in the spontaneous constitution of our natural selves. In both cases, the question is whether the match of internal and external is something arbitrarily imposed or something natural and inevitable. In both cases, I have tried to show, the answer is "both and neither," that is, that these two dichotomous categories are misconceived and inapplicable to the question at hand. Slingerland concludes that the internalist/externalist tension is never resolved, and in fact it is by definition irresolvable. I want to suggest here that this state of affairs calls for us to devise if possible a new set of categories for dealing with the problem, one that does not begin with the premise that internal and external are necessarily mutually exclusive categories. For with that definition the problem can never be solved, and we have the kind of endless circling around it described by Slingerland. But rather than assume that the notorious failure of all the thinkers in the tradition to solve this problem was a result of negligence, ideological bad faith, or insufficient rigor, I would suggest that it was not felt as a problem for them, due to their orientation to a different set of assumptions. For all of them, I have tried to show, what is "internal" and what is "external" are not simple unambiguous matters of fact, unrelated to the ethical act of naming them, but rather are fluid terms that come to be alternately defined in the process of assuming a particular ethical attitude, conceived as a way of making one's desires cohere.

In sum, we have in both Mencius and Xunzi and selecting out of real coherences into a greater coherence with human value, a process neither nominalist nor realist. This coherence is a harmony, not a sameness; it is not the application of the same pattern or principle to different instances, but the finding of maximal coherences with maximal human value. This is the essence of the non-ironic concept of coherence in early China.

TWO TEXTS FROM THE *RECORD OF RITUAL (LIJI)*: "THE GREAT LEARNING" AND "THE DOCTRINE OF THE MEAN"

We have seen an attempt to answer to and an incorporation of some aspects of the ironic tradition by the non-ironic in the epistemology of the *Xunzi*. More thoroughgoing, probably somewhat later, syntheses of Daoist and Confucian ideas, again in the service of Confucian ultimate values, can be found in many places in the *Liji*. I classify these differently because the impact of the ironic tradition is much deeper here than it had been in the *Xunzi*—the ironic ideas have now come to influence even the way in which coherence is conceived, and its structural relationship to ultimate values and to omnipresence. The most notable of the examples from the *Liji* are, unsurprisingly, the chapters subsequently to have the greatest impact on Neo-Confucianism: "The Great Learning" and "The Doctrine of the Mean."

"The Great Learning" begins with a summary of its teaching in three phrases: "The Way of the Great Learning lies in 1) illuminating the virtue of illumination (明明德 *ming ming de*), 2) forming an intimacy with the people (親民 *qinmin*), and 3) finding rest in the ultimate value (止於至善 *zhiyuzhishan*)."

Here we have spelled out three of the aspects of non-ironic coherence already discussed: (1) intelligibility (illumination, manifestation, *ming*), (2) human grouping (forming an intimacy with the people), and (3) balanced equilibrium (finding rest) as value (the good). By making the power of manifestation (i.e., the power to make something coherent in the sense of intelligible) manifest, the coherence of the social group is accomplished, as predicated on recognizing and abiding in the highest good. By finding this ultimate value in oneself, perceiving it, one makes it visible to others, perceptible outwardly and intelligible to them as a model, which influences the group, causes it to cohere. This ultimate value is the power of manifestation itself, of making intelligible. By showing this power to show, by making coherent this power to make coherent, the social group is made coherent. The emphasis on stillness as a condition for proper knowing of this value, which immediately follows in the text, is reminiscent of the proto-Daoist texts from the *Guanzi*. The coherence of the social world is then spelled out in terms of the priority of levels of micro-coherence, each of which is a precondition for the coherence of the next level. This chain of conditions ends with the famous *gewu* (格物, usually translated "investigation of things"), the locus of some of the most intense hermeneutic controversies among Neo-Confucians. But in light of the present discussion we would do well to note that the term *ge*—variously interpreted as "to arrive," "to rectify," and "to investigate"—can perhaps most simply be understood as meaning "to frame," "to put into a framework or grid," that is, "to contextualize," to make one element "reach" another and therefore allow their mutual adjustment (rectification), as well as the further manifestation of their implications (investigation). Contextualizing things in terms of their relation to their coherence with human desires allows for the extension of knowledge (further intelligibility of coherence) and the integration or sincerity (誠 *cheng*) of the intentions, from which follow the balancing of the mind, the cultivation of the person, the ordering of the family, the governing of the state, and the intelligibility of the full coherence of the world.

The term *cheng*, translated as sincerity, integrity, or realness, calls for further comment. An Yanming has pointed out, the way this term bridges the gap between what he calls "ethical *cheng*" (rooted in a combination of the sense of trustworthiness [信 *xin*] and realness [實 *shi*]) and "cosmic *cheng*" in the "Zhongyong," finally pointing to a "universal *cheng*" which functions as "a general principle responsible for all kinds of consistency, correspondence, regularity and predictability in both humans and Nature."[38] The gap left, on our earlier analysis, by the absence of either a deity or a set of universals or immaterial laws of nature that would be universally applicable to underwrite the predictability of natural phenomena is here filled by *cheng*. The derivation of predictability and regularity not from a multilocal metaphysical entity but from *cheng* brings with it important consequences for our understanding of coherence. In the sense of integration of a set of diverse intentions, suggested by Graham, the relation of *cheng* to "coherence" is obvious. We might even understand this term as denoting a kind of coherence of one's spontaneous tendencies at the stage where they are still too small and incipient to be seen, what we might translate as "Unseen Coherence." This connection between *cheng* and coherence was not lost on the Neo-Confucians in relating the term to Li. By contextualizing things with respect to our own ultimate values or normatively deepest desires, in which we abide or find our balanced equilibrium (benevolence when one is a ruler, respect when one is a minister, filiality when one is a son, compassion when is one is a father, good faith when one is a friend, as the text explains "finding rest"), our knowledge of the order of priorities that allow that desire to find fulfillment is extended. The comprehension of this sequence allows us to sincerely desire the steps that are means to the attainment of these ultimate desires, thereby integrating our intentions, making them coherent in the non-ironic sense of consistent with one another. The text explains the extension of knowledge so succinctly that some Neo-Confucians felt something had fallen out of the text here: it simply quotes Confucius as saying that while he is no better than anyone else at deciding legal cases, what is really worthwhile is to make legal cases unnecessary. This is done by knowing their source, knowing that what will really allow the people to be free of contention are the Confucian values of exemplary rulers and ritual respect for the people's interests. The implication is that knowing this connection (coherence) the ruler will be genuinely motivated to rule virtuously, not deceiving himself, sincere as one is in "liking a beautiful color," because he sees that it is immediately connected to his desire for noncontention among his people (ostensibly because this accords with the "highest good" of their coherence, but also because it makes his rule secure).

The term *cheng* is of course the centerpiece of the other *Liji* text just mentioned, the "Doctrine of the Mean." Here the Daoist ironic sense of coherence as unintelligibility, the primary importance of the constitutively unseeable, is brilliantly incorporated into non-ironic discourse by means of a witty twist. The text begins:

> What Heaven decrees is called human nature. The guidance of this nature is called the Dao. The practice of this Dao is called education. The Dao is that which cannot be departed from for even a moment. What one can depart from is not [one's true] Way. Hence the exemplary person is cautious over the unseen, and apprehensive over the unheard. For nothing is more evident than that which is hidden, nothing more manifest than what is subtle. Thus the exemplary person is careful over his aloneness [i.e., what no one else can see or hear]. When the emotions have not yet emerged, it is called Central Balance (中 *zhong*); when they have emerged, but all hit the mark, it is called Harmony (和 *he*). . . .

The constitutively unseeable is now reinterpreted as the innermost value commitment of the person, his true ultimate orientation, his sincerity, which although never manifest *simpliciter*, manifests itself indirectly in all his outward deeds without exception, can never be departed from for a moment, and hence is the most evident thing of all—the intelligibility of the unintelligible, or the coherence of the incoherent. This central equilibrium is what one cannot help doing, what one is doing at all times, whether apparently engaged in any action or emotion (X), *or* in its opposite (non-X)—what is constant and common to all contrasted dyads, equally present in joy or in anger, in sorrow or in happiness. It is the "Center," which here plays the role of the omnipresent and what transcends any particular observable intelligible coherence, but which also holds the extremes together, the ironic "coherence" that is itself "incoherent" in the sense of "unintelligible." The ironic Laozian *problematik* of the seen and the unseen is appropriated into the purposes of the non-ironic tradition here with dazzling skill. The harmony shown in outward activity is merely a manifestation of the unseeable Balance, that is, the value commitment in which one sincerely finds his ultimate rest.

We should pause here to consider this conjunction of "Centrality" and "Harmony" in further detail. For here we have the most crucial elements of our definition of Li explicitly joined. "Center" is translated "central balance" here, but perhaps the term *pivot* or *center of gravity* would give a better sense of what is meant. "Pivot" of course recalls Zhuangzi's "Pivot of Dao(s)" (道樞 *daoshu*), which, it will be recalled, was the point at which "shi and fei are no longer opposites, and can thus respond without cease." This entailed a sense of omnipresence as the union of opposites; what is co-present in all apparently opposed items, and thus is never absent. We may regard the "Zhongyong" as an adaptation of this sense of centrality into the older Confucian notion of centrality as the Mean in the ethical sense, namely, the avoiding of two extremes (for example, Mencius's idea of Confucianism as a mean between Yangist egoism and Mohist altruism). A "center of gravity" suggests both the Confucian/Mencian notion of the "pole star" model of order, where an exemplar creates a pattern around himself through the emulation that comes when it is made visible and valued, and the Laozian twist on this, the lowly invisible center, the non-Dao Dao, toward which all things converge as water flows downward.

Indeed, this "center-periphery" paradigm—already sketched out in the empty hub of the wheel image of the *Laozi* 11, and the "pivot of Dao(s)" formulation in the *Zhuangzi*—may be said to present the real alternative to the two-tiered metaphysics of the occidental type, which contrasts the intelligible realm to the empirical realm, or the unchanging law to its temporal expressions. This center-periphery model does some of the same work as the occidental two-tiered metaphysic, but with crucial differences in its implications. The Center is a "neither/nor" with respect to the extremes, and in this sense transcends them, but by doing so it plays the role of "connector" between them, as the "cause of their coherence" and of the "non-empirical (unseen)"; all these can be said also of Platonic forms or universals, the intelligible realm of immutable forms or laws, in much occidental metaphysics. The Form "red" is neither this nor that red thing, is nonempirical, and yet it is what makes them each red and what connects all red things by making them members of the same class. But in the case of the center-periphery model, this determiner is itself strictly indeterminate, except as a value, for it is what ensures the continuance of life, of continuity, of coherence itself. It is perhaps no accident that the only Platonic Form that comes close to sharing this characteristic is the Form of the Good. The implications of this model have perhaps been best summarized by Qian Mu's image of the pendulum, cited at length in chapter 2.

The separation of man and heaven, and yet their ultimate coherence, is played out here in the context of the term *cheng,* in a line of thought that also appears in the *Mencius* (4A12): "The Dao of Heaven is to be *cheng*; the Dao of man is to become *cheng*." The term here might be translated as "real," "sincere," "integrated," or again coherence, if we keep in mind that we use this term here with a special emphasis on the subjective value and desire dimension which we've already asserted to be inseparable from the meaning of this term, and subtract from it the meaning of non-ironic intelligibility, substituting the newly appropriated subjective form of ironic intelligibility as hiddenness that is indirectly expressed in all actions, and hence omnipresent in that sense. We thus translate it simply as "unseen coherence," that is, hidden coherence, as opposed to explicitly manifest intelligibility. The text continues, "To be invisibly coherent is to hit the mark/be balanced without trying, to attain the goal without thinking, to effortlessly match the Dao; this pertains to the sage. To become internally coherent is to choose the good and hold to it firmly." When one is already fully coherent, with things contextualized and the priorities of means and end recognized, so that all one's intentions are consistent with one's ultimate concern, the good can be accomplished without deliberate effort. The appropriate application of effort then lies in recognizing this ultimate concern and making all one's desires cohere with it: becoming sincere. The text then connects this sense of coherence with the sense of intelligibility: "When intelligibility (illumination, manifestation, *ming*) proceeds from unseen coherence it is a matter of the inborn nature. When unseen coherence proceeds from intelligibility (i.e., from knowledge), it is called education. If there is unseen coherence, there will be intelligibility; if there is intelligibility, there will be unseen coherence. It is only those with perfect unseen coherence who can fully realize their inborn nature. Those who can fully realize their own inborn nature can fully realize that of other people. Those who can fully realize the inborn nature of human beings can fully realize the inborn nature of things, and thus can participate in the nourishments and transformations of heaven and earth, thus forming a triad with heaven and earth. . . ."

This connection between unseen coherence as unceasing orientation toward the ultimate concern and its manifestation into full intelligibility is quite similar to that expressed in "The Great Learning." The text goes on to make explicit a further similarity, which lies in the extension of this coherence to the social group, which is transformed into a truly coherent whole by virtue of the coming to intelligibility of this unseen coherence; one's sincerity takes on visible form, and inspires the group to cohere. But then comes a metaphysical twist to unseen coherence, which goes beyond anything found in "The Great Learning": "Unseen coherence means self-completion [spontaneously coming into full being, becoming perfect as oneself, 自成 *zicheng*]. Dao means self-guidance [auto-guidance, spontaneous nondeliberate directedness]. For unseen coherence is the end and beginning of each thing. Without unseen coherence there is no thing. This is why the exemplary person values unseen coherence. Unseen coherence not only brings the self to completion, but also brings things to completion. Completion of oneself is benevolence; completion of things is wisdom. These are the Virtuosities (*de*: "virtues") of the inborn nature, the Dao of joining inner and outer. . . ." Unseen coherence is the real being of any being; its having a true beginning and end, completing fully and properly the process initiated by its beginning, and moreover, as the reversal of the terms suggests (i.e., "end and beginning" rather than "beginning and end"), allowing that thing to continue and perpetuate itself, to begin again after each ending, to be "ceaseless," something that persists constantly, which one can never for a moment be separated from. It is the inner equilibrium that implies not only balance but continuation and self-perpetuation, as we've seen before and will see again as a central component of coherence in the non-ironic tradition. Without unseen coherence, there is no thing as such at all; whatever is is what it is because it is coherent as that thing, and only to that extent. If it loses this coherence, it ceases to be that thing. This is the realness of the thing, and everything is real in some sense, even if only as a real fake. Here this unseen coherence as the unseen inner ceaseless commitment to ultimate value takes the place of the Dao of the Daoists as the ground of all particular being, the universal universal, and the intelligible regularity of their course. Like that ironic Dao, it is unintelligible in itself, but visible in everything. But it is finally knowable through a subjective attentiveness to one's own true value orientation, one's sincerity, which thus becomes the point of contact between the metaphysical and the empirical, the solution to the skeptical epistemology of the ironic tradition.

The text goes on to describe this coherence in more detail: "Perfect Unseen Coherence is ceaseless. Because it is ceaseless, it is long-lasting. Because it is long-lasting, it is manifested. Because it is manifested, it is far-reaching. Because it is far-reaching, it is broad and thick. Because it is broad and thick, it is lofty and bright. Its broadness and thickness allow it to bear up all things [like the Earth]; its loftiness and brightness allow it to cover all things [like Heaven]. It is long-lasting without limit. Thus it does not show itself and yet is manifest, does not move and yet transforms, does nothing and yet brings things to completion. The Way of Heaven and Earth can be summed up in one phrase: as things they are not-two, and thus they produce things unfathomably. The Way of Heaven and Earth is broad, thick, lofty, bright, far-reaching and long-lasting."

All the themes of the text come together here, showing that inner coherence is the key to the long-lastingness and far-reachingness, the bearing up and covering of all things conventionally associated with Heaven and Earth separately. The ceaseless production of things, the continuance of life, is the result of inner coherence, of the not-twoness of the apparently contradictory aspects of heaven and earth, like the extremes in Qian Mu's pendulum; they are connected by their coherence with the Center, the inner coherence, the non-twoness, and this is what allows them to continue to exist, to reproduce themselves ceaselessly. Hence, the text ends up by no longer speaking about "the Way of Heaven" as lofty and bright, covering all things, and the "the Way of Earth" as broad and thick, bearing up all things, but converges them into a not-two "Way of Heaven and Earth," which has all these contrary characteristics, all of which are ultimately reducible to this inner coherence, this sincerity, integrity, realness that is present everywhere indirectly but never explicitly expressed. Here we see the full integration of the ironic notion of coherence into the non-ironic, conceived on the model of the unseen not-yet-expressed point of equilibrium in the swing between contrary expressions or intelligible coherences.

Each of these texts effects a compromise of the ironic and non-ironic tradition from the side of the non-ironic, and indeed it may be said that all late Warring States thinking is preoccupied with coming to terms with this tension in one way or another. But the most systematic and broadly influential compromise between ironic and non-ironic conceptions of coherence is the one I would like to concentrate on below, the one that lies in the systematic application of the terms Yin and Yang, as they develop in the commentaries to the *Zhouyi* toward the end of the Warring States period (third century BCE).

SIX

THE YIN-YANG COMPROMISE

Yin and Yang have become English words, now standing as perhaps the most broadly recognized of all Chinese terms among nonspeakers of Chinese. Ask an American on the street about Chinese philosophy, and he or she will likely say something about Yin and Yang. Press a little harder, and you may hear something such as, "There are two sides to everything," or "We have to take the good with the bad," or "It means there is an equal goodness of good and bad, each in its own way."[1] What is problematic about these simplifications is not only that they ignore the great variety of ways in which these terms are used through the tradition (and indeed even in the pre-Qin texts, where the concepts are not yet fully formed or universal, they admit a wide variety of implications), but, more centrally, that even when they do take on a more stable usage, these Chinese terms are in general notably less contentless and formal than their English equivalents: they are not defined *solely* in terms of each other (as, e.g., positive and negative, the former meaning originally anything "posited" as a point of reference and the latter defined simply as its opposite), and they are not applicable to any and every opposition. They have a more specific and less unrestrictedly relative content. They cannot be reversed by redefining the system of coordinates (as "this" and "that" can, à la Zhuangzi) unless the scope of reference is expanded. That is, what is called Yin may indeed also be called Yang, just as what is called "that" may also be called "this," and this will necessarily involve positing a complementary Yin as its context, just as the assignment of the name "this" to the former "that" necessarily posits a new corresponding "that." In the Zhuangzian view, though, this new "that" may be precisely what was formerly called "this." But in the Yin-Yang systems, the corresponding Yin to the newly defined Yang will have to be something other than the item originally called Yang. Any item can indeed be called either Yin or Yang, but which is Yin and which is Yang in the context of a particular dyad is now fixed. We may view this as the distinctive rewriting of the ironic Zhuangzian this-that which makes it possible to incorporate it into non-ironic systems of coherence. We will return to this perhaps still confusing point, which may be regarded as the central deep-structural inno-vation of the Yin-Yang compromise, its main strategy for incorporating and denuding the Zhuangzian relativism, after giving a more detailed exposition of the general contours of the system, below.

Originally, Yang and Yin refer to sunny and shaded sides of a hill or a ravine, or sunshine (or, in one version, a flag illuminated by sunshine) and shade generally, as part of three sets of meteorological contrasts known as the six *qi* (sun, shade, heat, cold, wind, and rain)—an image that suggests contrast, alternation, and inseparability, but certainly no interchangeability or, necessarily, equality.[2] In the Inner Chapters of the *Zhuangzi*, the dyadic term *Yin-Yang* appears as a stand-in for fate, the creator, the cause of one's destiny,[3] and again as the determinant of one's physical health, put into a dangerous disequilibrium, described as an "inner heat," caused by excessive worry.[4] In a later chapter, one of those which Graham dates to the late third or second century BCE, they appear as the two basic cosmic forces, parallel (and more than just parallel) with earth and heaven.[5] This last usage comes close to that found in the lists of parallelisms, probably of late Warring States or early Han provenance, which attempt to exhaustively categorize all phenomena into these two classes, Yin and Yang. An example of this can be seen in the document entitled "Chen" ("Balance" 稱) one of the "Four Classics of the Yellow Emperor" recovered from the Ma Wang Dui tomb, where the pairs matched to the predicative Yang-Yin dyad include not only, respectively, heaven and earth, spring and autumn, summer and winter, day and night, father and son, man and woman, but also large states and small states, success and failure, marrying and mourning, controlling and being controlled, speech and silence, and giving and receiving.[6] Graham comments on this passage, "Throughout the chain A is superior to B but the two are mutually dependent; it does not . . . lead to 'Good/Evil.' As has long been recognised, China tends to treat opposites as complementary, the West as conflicting."[7]

And yet the exact nature of this "complementarity," and how it is supposed to relate to the "superiority" of one member to the other on which it is predicated, leaves much room for further discussion. Graham here combines two aspects of the Yin-Yang pairing that are often contrasted or tracked in their development across time. Lisa Raphals, for example, in tracing the development of specifically gendered associations of the terms, points out three distinct emphases constructing the development of various versions of the Yin-Yang polarity: the pair as complementary (the "cyclic polarity" found in the "pulse" of natural alternating process, such as day and night, summer and winter, and so on), as oppositional (as in unchangeable gender distinctions), and as hierarchical (where in addition to fixed roles we have a fixed value association of superior and inferior to each of the terms).[8] Zhang Dainian is covering some of the same ground in his distinction between Yin-Yang as aspects of Qi and Yin-Yang as definite "essences" (性質 xingzhi).[9] The former, where the two terms are adjectival descriptions of a shifting *state* of some third thing (Qi) which can be either yin or yang, is close to Raphals's sense of the complementarity that attends to the pairing when it is related to any alternating, "pulsing" process. What is interesting about these taxonomies is that the categories with which they must deal are so fundamental that they cannot help but lead to implications at the reflexive metalevel, leading to splaying and recombining of the possibilities that undermines any way simply to keep them neatly separated—as Raphals and Zhang both admirably demonstrate in their historical overviews of the relevant material. For if some form of the Yin-Yang structure informs the broadest conceptions of contrast in the tradition, it seems that they might also inform the contrast between varying forms of contrast. We might construe the hierarchical as either complementary or oppositional; the official ideological line, of course, is that hierarchy is itself a version of complementarity, while it is often viewed critically as intrinsically oppositional. But even opposition itself can be either complementary or hierarchical, and for that matter the complementary might be oppositional. Indeed, the obvious question when reading a statement such as Graham's, claiming that the pair is generally, in "Chinese correlative thinking," complementary (though hierarchical) *rather* than conflictual, is: "But are 'complementarity' and 'conflictual' complementary, or in conflict?" The latter seems to be assumed in the way the statement is framed, but this, in the sweeping breadth of abstraction implied by Graham's own hypothesis, could not have been assumed by the thinkers in questions, which introduces a troublesome abyss between the form and the content: an alien method is being applied to the material, one that assumes a discontinuity between opposites. If the thinkers in question really considered opposites complementary, they must have considered "complementarity" and "conflict" complementary, and this type of "complementarity" would clearly be a different concept from one that is taken to be in conflict with "conflict." But this is precisely the question that is at issue in the contrast between the ironic and the non-ironic tradition. The ironic tradition holds, in a nutshell, that conflict itself is a form of complementarity, or that conflict and complementarity are complementary: incoherence is itself the inevitable outcome of all coherence, since the relation between a content and its opposite is a necessary component of coherence, which renders that coherence unintelligible. The "complementarity" of Yin and Yang cannot be stated and taken care of so glibly or easily, and at the same time, the understanding of conflict and of hierarchy evoked by means of Yin-Yang associations must also be rethought in accordance with the nature of this peculiar form of complementarity. All we have said when we say they are complementary is that somehow or other they need each other (to exist? to flourish? to function properly? to function at all? to function optimally?). But this may or may not also involve or even require conflict and tension or hierarchy, all of which, in turn, might depend on acknowledgment of this complementarity in some form. Complementariness may be understood either ironically or non-ironically, and the same can be said of conflict and hierarchy.[10]

To excavate the specific vectors of implication embedded in these notions as concomitants of the Yin-Yang dyad, I will concentrate mainly on the doctrine of Yin and Yang that appears in the commentaries to the *Zhouyi*, since in my view these represent a mature synthesis of pre-Qin speculations on this matter, one that not only seems to be representative of a wide range of contemporaneous thinking, but was of course hugely influential. These commentaries date to the late Warring States period. The *Zhouyi* text, of which these commentaries are a rationalization, was originally a manual for divination. It is worth noting in this context that, although it has been claimed that the earliest stratum of Chinese history shows no evidence of a founding creation myth, it does show extensive interest in prognostication.[11] In its earliest form, this seems to have been done with turtle plastrons and the shoulder bones of oxen. A project of some kind was proposed by the king: How about if I go hunting at X? How about if I attack Y? We see here again the givenness of human desire as the irreducible starting point of all inquiry, as in the other texts we have considered. The answer was, initially, a binary yes or no, either "it will go well" or "it will go badly," good fortune or misfortune. Put into the terminology we have been using in this book, the events of the future will either *cohere* with your desire or they will not. Your project will flourish and continue, causing events to cohere around it, or it will fail to do so. Your desire and project will either be the defining initiation that draws a context around it, becoming the sustainable center of a coherence, or it will fail to do so. These simple yes-no answers later come to complexify into a more contoured depiction of a situation across time, and the shifting play of coherences and contexts in that process. For example, the situation might go from yes to no, or from no to yes, or from yes to more yes or too much yes, leading into no, and so on. Yes is the unbroken line, the firm, later read as the Yang; no is the broken line, the yielding, the Yin. The Warring States text "Great Commentary" (大傳 *dazhuan*, also known as the 繫辭 傳 *xicizhuan*) speaks of the two basic forms (Yin and Yang) producing the four basic "images" (四象 *sixiang*) (1.11) often interpreted as the four possible two-line combinations: two Yin lines ("old Yin"), two Yang lines ("old

Yang"), a Yin line over a Yang line (a Yang-to-Yin transition, "young Yin")
or a Yang line over a Yin line (a Yin-to-Yang transition, "young Yang"). The
combination of a Yin and a Yang line is now seen as a structural analogue
to a transition, introducing an element of temporal process embodied as a
structural form. These situational symbols are taken here to represent the
four seasons, usually construed as young Yang (spring), old Yang (summer),
young Yin (autumn), and old Yin (winter). Yang is the force of life breaking through the frozen stagnation of winter, and it is at its most vital and
pure in the spring, when it is as yet not fully apparent. Plants start growing,
animals start moving again: specific things become apparent as centers of
integration; things emerge into coherence, fulfilling their incipient projects,
from an incoherent (Yin) background of aimless, nonarticulated inertia. It
is motion, activity, life that attracts our attention against an unmoving and
inert background, that takes on the form of the fulfilling of a coherent desire
and the formation into a recognizable being. Yang is here the desire-laden
emergence into intelligibility, coherence, fulfillment, and integration of an
environmental context into the project of living and desiring.

These two line symbols are further expanded into eight three-line
trigrams. The structural peculiarities of these are then assigned eight arche-
typal meanings: heaven, earth, thunder, abyss (plummeting water), mountain, wind, fire, lake (still water). Heaven is represented by three Yang lines,
earth by three Yin lines. Thunder, the stirring up of activity and life, by
one yang line under two yin lines—a rumbling under the stagnant earth,
the process as yet unseen and just beginning, for the trigrams are read from
bottom to top. Plummeting water (or abyss) is a Yang line between two Yin
lines—the current in the stream, an active power surrounded on both sides
by yielding water. The mountain is one Yang line atop two Yin lines—here
depicting literal highness as well as temporal posteriority, Yang activity as
trees and vegetation on top of a big pile of lifeless rock and dirt. These
three trigrams, with one Yang line and two Yin lines, are identified as Yang
trigrams. The remaining three, with one Yin line and two Yang lines, are
identified as Yin trigrams. The first of these feminine trigrams is wind, one
Yin under two Yangs, hence, reading upward, a gentle yielding that grows
into a persuasive determinative force. The second is fire or clinging, one Yin
between two Yangs, suggesting the vigorous activity, heat, and energy of a
flame which is nonetheless weak and dependent in the middle, needing to
"cling" to its fuel. The last is the still water of a lake or swamp, one Yin
on top of two Yangs, suggesting the still passive surface covering a depth
full of activity.

The eight trigrams are also construed as a family, with Heaven and
Earth as the father and mother, the three Yang trigrams as sons, and the
three Yin trigrams as daughters. The fact that the total valence of a trigram

is determined by the element that is quantitatively in the minority is of great significance for understanding the notion of "coherence" in this system. As the Great Commentary says, "The Yang trigrams have a majority of Yin lines; the Yin trigrams have a majority of Yang lines" (2. 4). This summary of the principle embodied in the diagrammatic system notes an important point: the determination of the character of a trigram or hexagram as a whole is not mechanical or quantitative, but structural and holistic: it is not a mere adding together of parts, but a question of how the parts are arranged. Its basis is explained in the same passage: "The Yang trigrams have one ruler (Yang line) and two subjects (Yin lines)—this is the way of the exemplary person. The Yin trigrams have two rulers (Yang lines) and one subject (Yin line)—the way of the petty person." The many are ruled by the few, as Wang Bi explained this point. The structural analogy used to explain the holistic emergence of the intelligible coherence here (e.g., Yangness emerging from a whole consisting of a majority of Yin elements) is a sociopolitical one of leading and following, suggesting one possible root for this holism, that is, in conceptions of social relationships.

A trigram with only one Yang line thus takes Yang as its ruler, and thus is characterized (when functioning as a part in a larger structure, e.g., a hexagram) as Yang in character. A more literal rendering would be, "Situations quantitatively dominated by receptivity or subservience, the responsiveness that brings things to completion, may nonetheless holistically function as active and creative, as actively initiating new existences." Here we see the adumbration of the nesting of coherences which is characteristic of this way of thinking, and the manner in which the valences of each member change with each context. This is what I will be identifying as the incorporation of the primary insight of the ironic tradition, the insight into the instability and unintelligibility that necessarily come with coherence (since coherence always involves contextualization), into a system of non-ironic coherence.

The complete divination system of the Book of Changes is formed when these eight trigrams are further combined into sixty-four hexagrams, representing all possible combinations of two alternate valences in six places. The arrangement of these sixty-four hexagrams underwent several changes in ancient times. The present version, called the Changes of Zhou, starts with Qian, six Yang lines, representing heaven or pure Yang. Tradition and recent archeological evidence tell us, however, that the older arrangement, prior to the Zhou, began with Kun, six Yin lines, representing Earth or pure Yin. It is tempting to take the placing of Qian at the front as a concerted reply from the non-ironic tradition to the ironic tradition, which places the source of all being in the hyper-Yin motherliness of Dao, à la Laozi. In any case, the present arrangement is the one rationalized by the late Warring

States commentaries, and can be understood as a non-ironic incorporation of the ironic tradition's discovery of the importance of Yin.

This endeavor to accomplish a rationalization of precisely this kind of text deserves some comment. Ancient mythology generally consists of stories accounting for the origin of the world as a whole, of mankind, and of the overall human condition. In many ancient cultures, when the veracity or moral wholesomeness of the old myths became susceptible to doubt, these myths were either rejected as false (as in Plato, for example) or efforts were made to reinterpret them in terms as allegorical representations of newer philosophical and moral ideas (Philo and the Christian Fathers treat the Old Testament this way, and the Neoplatonists do the same for Greek myth). In the Chinese case, these rationalizing energies were devoted not to reinterpreting myth, but to reinterpreting the ancient art of prognostication. We may detect here an interest in particular situations, the ways they emerge and transform, and the optimal human responses to them, rather than objective knowledge about a once-and-for-all "way things are," and this interest in ever-new encountered situations as a form of "ultimate concern" is something we find in much of later Chinese thought. To say it again, the irreducible givenness of human desire, and its ineradicability from any reading of the existing coherences in the world, is crucial here. In the commentaries to the *Zhouyi*, man is depicted as a microcosm of natural forces, above all the Yin and the Yang, the receptive and the creative (the dark and the light, the female and the male, the completing and the initiating forces), which combine in various ways to form certain prototypical situations, each of which calls for a particular response from man by which it can be brought to its ideal completion, that is, can fully manifest the value implicit within it. This value was both moral and utilitarian. The "Great Commentary" looks upon the ceaseless production of life, or of change as such, the unending generation of new situations and beings, as an ultimate good. This process is a function of the interaction of the forces of Yin and Yang, and man's moral activity as both rooted in and aimed toward the participation in this process of life. Here the naturalness and spontaneity of Confucian morality—including both "benevolence" and the ritual system—is once again affirmed, but no longer on the basis of human inclinations themselves, but rather in terms of the root and implication of these tendencies within the natural world as a whole; man is a microcosm of the universal process of life.

The pair Yin-Yang does not appear in its later sense in the earliest strata of the text of the *Zhouyi* proper; instead, there is talk of the firm and the yielding (剛柔 *gang* and *rou*) as descriptions of the configurations of the unbroken and broken lines of the hexagrams. Sometime thereafter the proto-scientific, meteorological, and medical notion of Yin and Yang came to attach itself to this dyad, melding together with earlier philosophical speculations, yielding eventually the well-rounded syncretic metaphysical doctrine of the Great Commentary, which unites the currents of earlier thought in the service of mainly Confucian (non-ironic) ultimate values.

By this time, Yang has become a complex concept used to denote the principle of visibility, of brightness, of maleness, of initiation, of creativity, of vigor, of starting something, while Yin denotes invisibility, darkness, femaleness, following, harmonizing, bringing to structured completion what Yang has started. Two primary models can be said to interact here: night and day in the diurnal rotation, and male and female in sexual intercourse. The sense of visibility versus invisibility, and of the process of alternation, where each begins when the other reaches an extreme, comes from the day and night model. The sense of vigor and receptivity, of initiation and completion and of motion and stillness comes from the sexual model. Both imply a combination of qualitatively opposed terms in a balanced harmony that is productive of life and its continuance, a theme we already encountered again and again, going back to the *Guoyu* passage. The turning of day and night makes the soil fecund, the sexual congress of male and female produces offspring. Yang is light and male, Yin is dark and female. Yang initiates and makes models and Yin imitates or executes them; Yang rules and Yin follows. The connection between these various correlated meanings may be hard to locate for modern readers. We might think more concretely of the male and female genitals engaged in sexual activity; the convex phallus is put forth, out there, makes itself felt, known, seen; the concave hidden depths of the vagina and womb are dark, unseen, responding to this imposition of a shaping definition by completing the impulse, rallying around the intruding penis as the people are to rally around the king, forming a coherent and (re)productive whole. The Laozian implication that life is started by the unsung, unseen mother and the depths of her mysterious gate is trumped by an extension of the metaphor; life begins with the "putting forth" and activity of the father, and is merely brought to completion by the receptivity, responsiveness, and hidden stillness of the mother. Note also that "visibility" is itself a marker of coherence, not only in the sense of intelligibility, but also in the primary "sticking together" sense; for manifestation or disclosure in its most basic signification means that two things that were formerly isolated are now joined into a greater whole. In the dark, that rock and I had no explicit relation, but in the light, when I see it, we are unified in a common world. The subject and object are joined in perception, in manifestation, in light. Yang is thus sticking together, intelligibility and value: coherence. And yet the whole Yin-Yang system is a way of acknowledging that this coherence must also "cohere" with its contrary, the unintelligible isolation of Yin. This is how the ironic coherence of the unintelligible is domesticated here.

The first section of the "Great Commentary" lays out these themes as follows:

> Heaven is exalted and earth is lowly; so the positions of Qian and Kun are fixed.
>
> [All things] become manifest by [progressing from] the lowly [to] the exalted; so the positions [of the hexagram lines are arranged to denote] noble and base.
>
> There is a constancy to motion and stillness; so firm and yielding are decided.
>
> Characteristic regions gather according to type (*lei*), and things divide by their groupings; so good and bad fortune are generated. . . .
>
> The sun and moon proceed in their cycles, day alternating with night. The Way of Qian forms the male, while the Way of Kun forms the female.
>
> Qian's knowability is the great beginning; Kun's action brings things to completion.
>
> Qian is knowable because of its ease; Kun is capable because of its simplicity. What is easy is easy to know; what is simple can easily follow. What is easy to know will allow [the knowers] to come close and feel intimate with it; what can easily follow will have accomplishments. What has close intimates can endure; what has accomplishments can be vast. Ability to endure is the worthy man's Virtue, while ability to be vast is his vocation.
>
> In this ease and simplicity, then, the coherences (Li) of all the world are attained. When the coherences of the world are attained, one can find one's place among them.

In this passage, we have first an appeal to nature and the "great coherence" of heaven up there and earth down there, a direct rejection of the ironic tradition's skepticism on such points. This is used to justify the priority and higher value of Qian, pure Yang. The ironic tradition's emphasis on the lowly as the true beginning of things is incorporated in the following line, if I am reading it correctly (i.e., as indicating a progression from lowly to exalted, as the reversed order of the words would suggest), as already built into the hexagram system. "Constancy" (常 *chang*), used in the sense of "sustainability" and denied to any intelligible coherence by the first line of the received *Laozi*, is affirmed in the next line, as depicted in the firm and yielding lines the hexagrams; these are constant—i.e., reliably omniavailable—coherences that are knowable through the hexagrams. In the next line we have a direct statement about the coherence of things and their spontaneous groupings, applies, as in the *Xunzi* passage on *ganying*, to good and bad fortune as forming part of a single group with the activities that bring them about, hence *ganying* here according to similarity, not contrast.

The next three lines of the text I have translated here give the basic definition of Yin and Yang as understood in this system: day and night, male and female, and beginning-through-knowability and completion-through-activity. This is explained in the following passage, and we find here again the social model of coherence already proposed in the *Mencius* and elsewhere: Qian (yang) is what makes itself known (the text later says, "makes images"), strongly reasserting the "intelligibility" aspect of coherence. These are bright, exalted, and seen; they attract intimates by virtue of the easiness of their intelligibility. In this we have again a covert reference to the givenness of human desire; what is easy to know gives pleasure, making creatures feel attracted to it and group around it. This is immediately connected with endurance, the ability to maintain itself, sustainability. Yang is here coherence as intelligibility which is also coherent with desire, and makes things cohere with it by inspiring them to imitate it, approach it, and complete what it has started, the latter being the role of Kun or Yin (as the text later says, it "imitates the images" of Qian). The next section, immediately following the one translated above, asserts the role of the sages who created the *Zhouyi* text, thereby establishing the ultimate determinant of the text's authority in this coherence with tradition.

For our purposes, it will perhaps be most convenient to narrow our attention to one particular angle on these meaning-clusters (and thereby of course unavoidably oversimplify), and speak of the root sense of the two terms as meaning *Starting and Finishing*, with all the temporal and axiological implications thereof (i.e., "Finishing" already implying a note of negativity, bringing things to an end, cessation, death). "Starting" here, however, must be understood in accordance with the passage just cited; it means to begin things by making an ideal visible. We can restate both "begin things" and "make an ideal visible" in terms of coherence: Yang means to create coherences by displaying something intelligible and desirable, where both "displaying" and "desirable" are understood as precisely coherence with human awareness and desire. Yang is thus coherence in the sense of intelligibility and sticking together with human desire. The thrust of the *Zhouyi*'s refutation of the ironic tradition of the *Laozi* is to assert that it is ultimately this intelligibility, the manifesting of an image which attracts, which coheres with human desire and makes humans cohere around it in emulation, which begins the existence of all things. The implication is that to exist is to be coherent; what makes them coherent, hence existent, is this orientation to a basic value. It is Yang, not Yin as in the *Laozi*, that is truly creative. (This was true, in fact, also of the pre-ironic Daoism of the *Guanzi* texts, which also esteem Yang rather than Yin.)[12] Yin's role, in a nutshell, is to finish what Yang has started. In the language we have been using so far in this book, this means Yang is a coherent something, a valued something, around which a complementary context most responsively gathers, the latter being Yin. Yang, valued coherence, needs Yin, the unintelligible with which it must cohere. Coherence must cohere with incoherence. But the Yin-Yang system provides an ingenious way to keep this insight from bleeding into the ironic effacement of the intelligibility of coherence. For in this conception a complete, rather complex axiological meta-structure is implied.

In this text, value equals a particular relationship between Yin and Yang (which is to say, the Yang-Yin relationship is *not* itself primarily a value-antivalue relationship). That is, *a situation is "good" when Yang is master, is first, is controlling, is above, and Yin follows it, supports it, completes it, assists it.* This is how harmony between them is defined, and this is value, which is, as we have seen, one of the defining aspects of coherence in the non-ironic tradition. When this harmony is disturbed, it is first-order anti-value. However, this disequilibrium itself can be a value, if contextualized appropriately, either temporally or situationally. This possibility for turnaround would seem to be related to the unpredictable judgments of the lines in the hexagrams (in the earlier strata of the text), which often come in the wrong place and time—i.e., with Yin in "ruling" or "initiating" positions—and yet are judged to be auspicious, challenging exegetes to come up with explanations of why this transgression of the general rule was justified, harmonious, legitimate in this particular case. This is not the place to speculate about why the hexagrams first began to be interpreted in this way; but it does seem evident that the author of the "Great Commentary" was familiar with this stratum of the text, and his conception of the working of Yin and Yang was strongly influenced thereby. This introduced a complexity and elusiveness to the value attached to the configurations of Yin and Yang that may not have emerged on purely rationalistic or a priori grounds. The impossibility of a hard and fast rule that would always define, before the event, which kind of Yin-Yang situation would equal "Good" is perhaps the most obvious feature of the overlapping set of rules that are applied to the interpretation of the lines. Hence, the text says, "The transformations simply go where they go; no essential rule can be made for them" (唯變所適,不可為典要 *weibiansuoshi, bukeweidianyao*).

This is not to say that there are no hermeneutic rules; on the contrary, there is an *overabundance of conflicting rules*. For example, the six lines of the hexagram are interpreted as two trigrams, the bottom or "inner" trigram representing the private sphere or what is not yet publicly manifest, and the top or "outer" the social manifestation of the same impulse. But the six lines are also interpreted as three pairs, representing, from bottom to top, earth, man, and heaven. They are also taken as the temporal development of a situation running from bottom to top, from incipience to full flourishing. They are also taken as representing relative lowliness or exaltation of rank within a bureaucratic hierarchy. Sometimes they are taken as four stacked interlocking trigrams. Each trigram as a whole has its own symbolic implication, which may come to bear in the lines appended to each line therein, but sometimes the lines are interpreted individually without reference to which of the trigrams it may form a part of in any given hexagram. The positions of the six lines are given alternating Yin-Yang valences, with the odd numbered positions (1, 3, and 5) regarded as Yang and the even numbered positions (2, 4, and 6) as Yin. If a Yang line is in a Yang position, or a Yin in a Yin position, it is called "correct" (正 *zheng*)—hitting the mark, balanced and playing the right role for that position. The lines in the second and fifth positions are called "central" because they are in the center of the inner and outer trigrams, respectively, also generally a desirable state of affairs. In terms of Yin-Yang relations between the lines, opposite valences in 1 and 3, 2 and 4, or 3 and 6 are said to "correspond" (相應 *xiangying*), which is again auspicious. At the same time, opposite valences in proximal positions are regarded as giving "support," which can also be a determinant of positive value.

From this very simplified overview of the kinds of rules that apply in interpreting the lines of *Yijing* hexagrams, and used to explain the gnomic statements appended to the images of the divination text, it should be obvious that in many cases the alternate rules and schema will conflict. A line may be "correct" in terms of the same-valence of its position, but fail to correspond with the same rank in the other trigram, or lack support, and so on. Which of these will be the determining rule applied in any given case is the question that presents itself here. It should be immediately obvious that the overabundance of conflicting, alternate sets of rules is an exact equivalent of the overabundance of coherences in the real world accepted in their various ways by Mencius, Xunzi, and Zhuangzi. It is not that there are no rules; there are too many rules, and they form no single consistent set. The solution in the *Zhouyi* is precisely the Confucian solution, apparent in Mencius but most explicit in Xunzi: the overabundance of coherences in any given case is narrowed down by reference to the decisive coherence: the authority of *tradition*. It is coherence with the past, in particular with the authority of the sages, that is adduced as the basis for deciding which of the many alternate rules comes to be applied in any given case. The sages composed the text; they chose among the possible rules the ones that cohered most effectively in that particular case, and we are to follow this ruling because of our own coherence with the tradition founded by these sages. It might be said that the argument is ultimately pragmatic and crypto-Darwinian: these interpretations are proven effective in that they have allowed the tradition to continue to the present day, down unto us; a performative understanding of authoritative conservatism. In any case, it is clear that we have here a parallel situation: too many alternate sets of coherent rules, from among those which were in each case chosen by authoritative sages who effected a maximal social coherence with the surrounding world, and with whom we also aspire to cohere.

Nonetheless, value is consistently conceived as a kind of coherence relation between Yin and Yang, varying according to the context of each hexagram, but gravitating around—and deriving nuance by deviating from—the standard mentioned above, namely, value is for Yang to rule and initiate things, and for Yin to follow, be subordinate, and thereby bring things to completion. This notion of value is predicated on the assumption that creativity or the production of life is itself ultimate, noninstrumental value, combined with its sustainability, continuity and continuation, which we have seen posited as a defining mark of harmonious coherence all the way back to the *Guoyu* passage.

This ultimate value is defined as follows: "The great virtuosity of Heaven and Earth is generation" (天地之大德之謂生 *tiandi zhi da de zhiwei sheng*) (II.1). And again, "Constant generation and regeneration is what is meant by Change" (生生之謂易 *shengsheng zhiwei yi*) (I.5). The crux of the value theory operating in the "Great Commentary," bringing us to the level of ultimate value, is indicated in the following well-known passage: "One Yin and one Yang—this is called Dao. Its continuance is the Good. Its completion is human nature. The benevolent see it and call it benevolent; the wise see it and call it wise; the ordinary folk use it every day and yet are not aware of it. Thus the way of the exemplary man is rare indeed. It manifests as benevolence, but is concealed in all processes [or activities of the ordinary folk]. It drums the ten thousand things forward and yet does not worry itself as the sage must. This is the ultimate of flourishing virtue and great vocation!"

Here, we are given a strict definition of the Good, of value per se. Mencius had defined the Good as "the desirable," what coheres with given human desires. The *Zhouyi* commentary also defines value as a kind of coherence—in this case, a relation between Yin and Yang, the dark and the bright, the female and the male, the intelligible figure and the unintelligible context that forms its background, and with which it must cohere. We have already seen that an equal measure of Yin and Yang is in fact not considered good; good should have less of creativity (which is in itself the more positive half of the dyad) than subservience (which is the negative half), but placed in a ruling position from which it can utilize and ride upon the negative. Hence we should be careful not to take this "One Yin and one Yang" as signifying a quantitative equality.

I would therefore interpret this passage as follows: "The process of alternation of the emergence of intelligible coherences and the necessary incoherence with which it must cohere, of the active and the structive, of beginnings and finishes, such that they are always leading to each other, implying each other and mixed with each other, is called the Way. When this alternation occurs in a proportion that is consistent with its own continuance, so that it does not get caught in a dead-end of unceasing dominance of either one side or the other, this harmony is called goodness, or value. What completes this harmony, both in the sense of being its pinnacle and of being the agent of its completion in the universe, is human nature. This principle of value is most obvious in what is called benevolence and wisdom, which is why the Way may one-sidedly be called benevolent or wise by those focused on these qualities, but it is the source and foundation of all activity in the cosmos, in a less obvious form, even in the daily activities of the common folk."

What, then is non-ironically valued coherence here, and what is its relation to disvalued unintelligibility with which it must nonetheless cohere? Valued coherence is a proportion between Beginnings and Finishes, between the active and the responding structive, or, we may say, between the apparently positively valued (Yang, coherence in the first-level, naive sense, which brings things into being) and the *apparently* negatively valued (Yin, first level, naive incoherence, which brings things to their finishes), a proportion that allows both to continue to exist in a proportion that will allow them to continue to exist, and so on ad infinitum. It so happens that this proportion is one that usually involves the (nonquantitative) dominance and primacy of the apparently positive over the apparently negative, at the same time, perhaps, as the quantitative dominance of the apparently negative. But this is of value only because it allows *both* to flourish. Beginnings and finishes should be arranged such that beginnings and finishes, that is, the creation of things and situations, continue to occur afterward, so that, in other words, *no finish is final*. The dominance of a finish, Yin, would spell the end of both beginnings and finishes, for to finish is to bring a coherence into incoherence. Likewise, the total dominion of beginnings (Yang) that never lead anywhere, are never picked up, given structure, brought to completion, would also disturb the formation of things, the process of beginning and finishing, of making coherent. For to finish is also to make fully formed, to make fully coherent.

This gives us a clear understanding of how Yin is both negative in itself (the finish, death, the end of all being) and a part of the necessary process of creation of things (since "finish" here has both the sense of "to make an ending" and "to bring to its final form"—to complete or perfect, to bring to its *proper* end). It brings us to a way of understanding a form of "complementarity" that could be complementary with, and not in conflict with, "conflict." The complementarity of Yin and Yang presupposes their conflict. They are both conflicting opposites and two necessary parts of a single process, and there is no conflict between these two levels. Yin, as "finishing," is both negatively valued (in conflict with Yang and with the whole process) and positively valued (complementary to Yang and the whole process).[13]

The implication is that a dominance of Yin would kill off both Yin and Yang, and this alone is the source of its ultimate disvalue. The continuance of both is the determinant of what sort of relationship between them is desirable. Humanity's role is to make sure that this proportion prevails, lest the cosmos go askew, veering into a dominance of Yin that would end the alternating process of Yin and Yang. This, and not the eradication of Yin, nor even its suppression in every situation, is the aim of moral endeavor. Moreover, and crucially, there exist situations where the dominance of Yang would endanger the continuing flourishing of both, when it would lead to a monopoly that would eradicate Yin or itself. In these cases, the dominance of Yin is identical to value. The "one thread" running through all value is then: the relationship that will allow relationships to continue to exist.[14]

The implications of all this for the way the order of things in the world is to be conceived is nowhere more stunningly portrayed than in another of the classical "Wings" to the *Book of Changes,* the "Shuogua" ("Explanations of the Trigrams"). This text, particularly its concluding statements about the ways the trigrams help to classify things in the world, seemed to its earliest Occidental readers to be the pinnacle of ridiculous nonsense.[15] But it is here that we can see on display the cash value of the conceptions of coherence we have been discussing in this book, how they affect the understanding of groupings of things in the world, and how the notions of sameness and difference must be reconceived in order to understand them.

This short text attempts to sum up the implications of the system of trigrams and hexagrams comprising the *Zhouyi.* Here, we are told, is how the sages devised that system:

> Viewing the transformations of Yin and Yang [in the sky, i.e., Heaven],
> they established the trigrams. Developing the further implications

of the hard and soft [of the Earth], they produced the individual lines. Harmonizing it to make it comply [和順 *heshun*] with the [human] Dao and its Virtue, they separated into coherent groups what was appropriate to each [理於義 *li yu yi*]. Fully exhausting this coherence they plumbed the depths of Human Nature, until it reached the Decree [Fate]. In ancient times when the sages created the *Changes*, they were attempting to comply with these coherences of human nature and its Decree, and so they established the Dao of Heaven, calling it Yin and Yang; established the Dao of Earth, calling it the soft and the hard; and established the Dao of Man, calling it Benevolence and Rightness. Encompassing all three primal powers and applying this doubleness to each, they exchanged the six lines [in all possible ways] and made them into the hexagrams. Dividing Yin from Yang, alternately applying the soft and the hard, they transformed the six positions [in various ways] and made them into the visible figures.

A two-termed "pendulum range" is here observed in three parallel realms: Heaven, Earth, and Man. Each has its own Dao, its "course," by means of which it proceeds. In each case, a dyadic alternation is observed as what is necessary to its sustainability. Heaven alternates between dark and light, night and day, Yin and Yang. The terrain of the earth alternates between soft and hard (e.g., mountains and waters, obstructions and passages). Human action alternates between the accepting lovingness of Benevolence and the judgmental severity of Rightness. It is the *overlap* of these three subsystems that yields the final system: those elements of the natural processes of celestial and earthly oscillations that can be made to "harmonize and comply" with the human course of benevolence and rightness, the course and its virtuosities, by means of the hexagram system. This is what is meant, it seems, by "separated into coherent groups what was appropriate to each [理於義 *li yu yi*]." That is, a "Li"-grouping emerges wherever the oscillation of the moral-pragmatic needs of *man* and the oscillations of the light and dark of the sky and the obstruction and passages of the earth overlap and coincide; we can imagine this as a kind of interference pattern of three types of waves, perhaps along the lines of the "double-slit experiment" used to demonstrate the wave-function of photons. Where these three types of oscillation "sync up," we have a Li, that is, a valued coherence.[16]

The eight trigrams are then presented in four contrasted pairs: Heaven/earth, mountain/lake, thunder/wind, water/fire. Here we have the simplicity of a one-dimensional back-and-forth, as it might be represented by a single line, multiplied into four simultaneous oscillations. The eight trigrams are then a three-tiered version of Qian Mu's pendulum, oscillating in these four simultaneous dimensions. A typical function is then attributed to each of these configurations, derived from the structure of forces depicted in the line-structure of the trigrams. Thunder instigates. Wind scatters. Rain (plummeting water) irrigates. Sunlight (fire) warms. Mountains steady. Lakes please. Heaven rules. Earth stores. More abstractly, the trigram for heaven is vigor, for earth is compliance, for thunder is instigation, for wind is infil-tration of influence ("entering"), for plummeting water is endangerment, for fire is brightness or attachment, for mountain is steadying, for lake is pleasing. These proliferations are what tend to drive outside interpreters to despair. One would try in vain to derive these qualities directly from the line structures. There is nothing intrinsically "scattering" to be discovered, for example, in the structure of the Sun 巽 trigram (one yin under two yangs), and if there were, this would perhaps make it difficult to find the same for "infiltrating influence." But both of these pertain to wind (which scatters things, and also gently enters wherever an opening is provided). Similarly, one could not find both "danger" and "irrigation" in the line-structure for plummeting water. But plummeting water is both dangerous and irrigating. What will be identified as the essential quality of each trigram is, of course, a matter of context. The entire field of "natural forces" is assumed to form a single self-sustaining, life-giving whole, which is balanced into a coherence according to these four types of oscillation. Within that whole, there are positions to be filled, describing the eight extremities. The coherent whole of natural objects is comprised of thunder, wind, water, fire, mountains, lakes, heaven and earth, which form the circumference of a fourfold oscillations. The coherent whole of natural activities of those objects is comprised of instigating, scattering, irrigating, warming, steadying, pleasing, ruling, and storing. Alternately, on the more abstract plain, the coherent whole of natural activities is comprised of vigor, compliance, instigation, infiltration, endangerment, illumination, steadying, and pleasing.

The text doesn't stop there. The coherent whole of "the animal king-dom," is comprised of horse, cow, dragon, chicken, pig, pheasant, dog, and sheep, arranged as the same eight places. In the coherent whole of "the human body," we have head, stomach, foot, hindquarters, ears, eyes, hand, mouth. We may describe these as "horizontal" coherences. Human bodies exist in the world, as one coherent whole. As a coherent whole, it must be a balancing of these eight circumferential forces, the extremities of its system of oscillations. The animal kingdom also exists in the world, as a coherent whole. As a coherent whole, it must also be a balancing of these eight circumferential forces, these extremities of the system of oscillation that makes something balanced, coherent and self-sustaining. Human bodies and the animal kingdom, however, are themselves items in a larger whole. All such items presumably form a similar system of eight points.

But it is clear also that we can continue to divide down. Among animals, the horse is Qian 乾, heaven. But among horses, we are then told, good horses, thin horses, and mottled horses are Qian; good neighers, horses with a white hind leg, and prancers are also Zhen 震, thunder; horses with lovely spines, eager hearts, drooping heads, thin hooves, or shambling steps, on the other hand, are Kan 坎, trigram of plummeting water. Horse is the Qian element of the coherent whole which is known as "animals"; but the good, thin and mottled are the Qian element of the coherent whole which is known as "horses."

But how are we to understand the "vertical" coherences—all the items that are grouped under one trigram? What puts all the items identified within these groups as Qian together? Horses run fast: they are the vigorous, heavenlike, among animals. Oxen plow the fields and are easily domesticated: they are compliant, earthlike, among animals. Dragons rumble up from below (out of the water), thunderlike, among animals. Dogs are loyal, steady, staying with their masters: mountainlike, handlike. Head, like heaven (Qian) commands and rules, and is up above. Stomach, like earth, stores, nourishes, complies (i.e., is dependent on and responds to its food) and is directly underneath. Hands steady and stop things. Mouths bring pleasure. And so on. So far these would seem to be relations of *parallelisms of position and function*. Each item in the vertical class functions, within its respective horizontal sphere, in a parallel way, although this does not necessarily entail isomorphism of internal structure or the possession of an identical essence. An analogous function exists between head and heaven: they are on top, and they initiate action. They have a further relation of isomorphic relation: they are both round. Either of these connections, or any other type, is sufficient to qualify an item for inclusion in a vertical class. To this limited extent, at least, we might think that the vertical coherences are thus like the members of a class, or instantiations of a form or universal, for instance, the trigram's paradigmatic function ("ruling, storing, steadying," etc.) But it must be noticed how the nesting horses within horses affects this schema. An individual good-neigher would not have either Qian or Zhen as its "essence," that which makes it what it is on some kind of mimesis model, *simpliciter*. The very fact that it "is" Qian or Zhen is itself determined by context: the same neighing horse is Qian if being considered next to a cow, and Zhen if considered next to a mottled horse. Are we to think of that structure of Qian-ness and Zhen-ness *both* structuring that creature simultaneously? Are they both somehow "within" it? The resemblance that joins the vertical coherence is itself a function of the horizontal coherences, and do not form a single synordinate system. In other words, this neighing horse "resembles" a head, or has the "same" structure of Qian-ness as a head has, only within certain contexts; in other contexts, it is the same as a foot (the Zhen of the body). Sameness is a function of coherence, not the other way around.

It should be noted also that sameness of structure is not even the sole criterion for inclusion in a vertical coherence. Rather, as in the case of the hexagram interpretations, we have an overabundance of possibly applicable rules, some of which apply in some cases and some in others. Sometimes it is similarity of structure, sometimes of function, and sometimes not similarity at all, not something that is the same in all these members. For example, the Dui 兌 hexagram is "lake" among natural objects, "pleasing" among forces, "sheep" among animals, and "mouth" among body parts. Why? How do these items fit together? It should be obvious that we are not here talking about a group of items each of which instantiates the same structure, the same universal, the same form. Not at all. Rather, in this case, it would seem that "mouth" and "sheep" come together because "lamb" is "pleasing" to the human "mouth." That is, a harmonizing relation, rather than a resemblance relation: a coherence. Zhen, the trigram of thunder and vigorous instigation of movement, is also "a large road"—something static that facilitates movement. It harmonizes with vigorous movement, but does not resemble it. Kan, the trigram of plummeting water, is also channels and ditches: not downward flowing water, but what contains, harmonizes with downward flowing water. These are relations not of resemblance, but of coherence.

In addition to parallelism of position and function (the most frequent relation), and harmonizing relations of coherence, we also have what seem to be even more whimsical associations based on the visual appearance of the diagrammed trigram—a technique that appears frequently in the hexagram interpretations as well. This seems to be the thought, for example, behind associated Sun, trigram of wind and influence, with persons with large whites of the eyes and broad foreheads. The trigram sort of looks that way, if viewed in a certain manner. There are also more abstract interpretations involved: Kan, trigram of plummeting water, is associated with the moon, presumably simply because it is one Yang line between two Yin lines, and hence figures a bright thing in the midst of darkness.

One could continue to speculate in this vein, but it would be folly to try to explain the rationale for all the vertical associations made in the "Shuo Gua." I certainly do not claim to understand what is going on everywhere in this text. But it is clear from the above considerations that what is going on in these classifications is not the identification of a single selfsame essence instantiated in various particulars. This is an exemplary case of what has been called "correlative thinking," into which we can now perhaps gain some further insight. Hall and Ames are certainly right to emphasize the ad hoc and often poetic nature of these groupings. What I want to stress here is the way this affects what we mean by coherence, its impact on ideas of sameness and difference, and—more distantly—how this will influence the later development of formal concepts of order, such as those associated with the term *Li*. As in the case of interpreting the individual lines of the hexagrams, we have here an overabundance of mutually incompatible rules, which can never add up to a single synoptic view. All the items in a particular vertical class associated with a particular trigram do not bear the same relation to one another, and some of them bear no apparent relation to one another other than the chain formed by making this association. Here again, we might think of Wittgenstein's idea of family resemblances, where A may resemble B and B may resemble C without A resembling C. But what we have here is not only a nontransferable relation that nonetheless forms a group, but the absence even of a univocal form of relation as the link between any two members. That is, we have not family resemblances, but *family coherences*. (Cf. the Godfather metaphor in ch. 2). Item A coheres with item B in one way or another—due to resemblance, parallelism of function, visual resemblance, or harmonic relation. Item B coheres with item C, due to another one of these criteria. A and C are then members of the same class without necessarily resembling each other, but also without necessarily cohering directly with one another. What makes them cohere is their *various* coherent relations to the central term, the literal trigram itself, *and* the decision of the sages to make this particular association among all that were available—the second-order coherence with the tradition itself.

Considering the multiple classifications of, say, horses above, we noted the context-dependence of each item's identity as bearing a particular trigram as its character. That is, it is not that item I belongs to class C because I has the essence of C-ness to it, but rather that being put coherently into class C brings out the I character of this item. Horses are not first Qianlike and then included in the class Qian. Rather, by being put in parallelism with other Qian items, and assuming a position within the coherent whole of the animal kingdom, horse manifests Qian-ness. Combining this consideration with our point about family coherences, we can now draw an interesting conclusion of broader application. The coherences that determine the relevant identity of any item are only locally applicable. These identities themselves, in fact, are therefore only locally applicable. The horse does not stay Qianlike in all contexts; it becomes Zhenlike in some of the contexts included in the totality of all contexts. It is only locally coherent. Its global coherence is restricted to seeing the totality *as a totality only*, and in connection with the disambiguating decisions of the sages in making these particular connections. We have here a new containment of the ironic notion of coherence, a way of combining it with the non-ironic notion of coherence, one that would become dominant in later Chinese thought.

Considering the whole as whole, things remain coherently what they are: a horse in this context, with the entirety of connections viewed at once, is to be understood as emblematic of Qian-ness in the animal kingdom. But this does not mean the real essence of horse has been identified. In any subset coherence, the horse will cohere differently, and thus exemplify a different character. Its horseness is dependent on its coherence with the tradition of sagely action. We will have much to say about the various combinations of local coherence and global incoherence in subsequent Chinese thought, in particular in its relation to the development of various notions of Li, to which we will turn in the companion volume to this work.[17]

We should now be in a position to understand the point made above about the limited reversibility of Yin and Yang, as opposed to the this-that of the *Zhuangzi*. I can perhaps clarify this idea by recourse to a homely metaphor. In American football, we have the offensive team of one side and the defensive team of the other on the field at any time. The offensive team is, in the context of this opposition, Yang, while the defensive team is Yin; that is, all plays are "initiated" by the offensive team, and responded to or "completed" by the defensive team. The defensive team must accord with, cohere with, the definition of the situation defined by the initiations of the offensive team. Here we have a relation of conflict, which is nonetheless understandable as one of initiation and response, of coherence and contextualization. But there are also nested relations of complementarity that fall under this rubric. Within the offensive team, we may perhaps say that the quarterback is Yang and the receivers are Yin. Within the quarterback himself, the nervous system is Yang and the bones and muscles are Yin. Expanding outward, we may say that both teams on the field are Yang, and the crowd of spectators in Yin. Expanding farther, the entire stadium of teams and spectators is Yang, while the home television audience is Yin. And so on. The point here is that once we have defined the context, there is no question about which item is Yang and which is Yin, in spite of the fact that, for example, a receiver on the offensive team is simultaneously Yin and Yang; he is Yin with respect to his quarterback, and Yang with respect to the defensive team. So we can perhaps say, à la Zhuangzi, that "there is no thing that is not Yin, there is no thing that is not Yang." But we cannot really take the next Zhuangzian step, which would say, "When the quarterback is Yang, the receivers are Yin; but when the receivers are Yang, the quarterback is Yin." This might be true in the very limited sense that if we were to fix the context in question as "the subjective experience of the receiver himself," but in any case it remains true that once we have defined the scope of relationship under discussion, the roles of Yin and Yang are objectively fixed and knowable. Thus does the Yin-Yang compromise adopt and adapt the ironic problematic of multiple contextualization inherited from the *Zhuangzi*, after reasserting the preeminence of Yang over Yin, while acknowledging the necessary presence of the latter, as a domestication of the challenge of the *Laozi*.

YIN-YANG THEISM IN DONG ZHONGSHU:
THE METASTASIS OF HARMONY AND IRONY

We have seen that the Yin-Yang paradigm has embedded within it an incorporation of aspects of the ironic conception of coherence. This leads to some interesting consequences, particularly when these aspects work against what seem to be attempts to reestablish non-ironic coherence in its purest form. I have already briefly discussed the impact of the anthropomorphic theism of Mozi as a determinant of his non-ironic conception of sameness. In general, we may say that theism, the reference to a single unequivocal final arbiter of value and identity, is the ultimate guarantor of non-ironic sameness, a well-nigh inevitable concomitant of the theory of universals or Forms that reiterate a true sameness. Han Confucianism marks the reappearance of a henotheistic conception of Heaven in the works of Dong Zhongshu, which served as a basis for Han Confucian imperial ideology. As Makeham has argued, Dong develops a theory of language that can perhaps be described as essentialist; things in the world have a single identifiable essence, and even a uniquely proper name with an etymological connection to this essence. These essences and even names are decided by Heaven, rooted in Heaven's will, and remain the same for this thing in multiple instances as a result of this grounding in the authority of Heaven. As Makeham correctly states, Dong's theory of naming is based on three propositions:

> 1. That it is Heaven's will (*tian yi*) which is the ultimate source of all "correct" names. 2. That names are the criterion for deciding "what is" (*shi*) and "what is not" (*fei*) the case. 3. That only sages or sage rulers are capable of apprehending which name is intrinsically appropriate to a given actuality.[18]

Heaven creates the actualities of entities. These have a certain, fixed essence. It is, however, the sage who discerns these essences and coins an appropriate name for them, usually involving a pun which obliquely points to that essence. The sage is still the "midwife" for the appearance of appropriate names in the world, and here the older reference to human existence as a determinant of coherence remains in effect. But ultimately, the essence of the entity is already fixed and coherent before the intervention of the sage, or of any human being. It remains the same essence, whole and entire, in every appearance of that thing. This is a consequence of the theory of Heaven as that which makes things what they definitively are.

This would seem to point toward a full-fledged theistic non-ironic theory of sameness, perhaps a more refined version of the Mohist system, adjusted to promote Confucian rather than Mohist ethical values. But that is not what we find in Dong's work. Rather, the power of the incorporation of ironic coherence into the notion of harmony embedded in the Yin-Yang paradigm is already too powerful; we can observe what appears to be an almost reluctant skewing of Dong's thought away from an intended non-ironic sameness theory into a non-ironic incorporation of ironic harmony. The value opposition of Yin and Yang comes to the fore in Han Imperial Confucianism, and Dong is himself perhaps the prime exemplar of this trend. The Yin-Yang structure sits uneasily with his theism as the structural determinant of his thinking. This leads to some very intriguing results. For example, Dong very clearly wishes to promote a non-ironic theory of Yin-Yang as explanatory coherences underlying the regularities of the world in a law-like way, allowing for predictability and control. One aspect of this is an intensification of a kind of essentialistic moral reading of Yin and Yang, so that they stand in axiological opposition. As Robin Wang has argued, this is a decisive moment in the transformation of the meaning of the two terms. Yang is good, while Yin is bad.[19] As Dongian essences, they should remain definitively so valued, identified, and named by the sages as such, so that the will of Heaven can be apprehended in them. Dong spells this out in chapter 43 of his main work, *Chunqiu Fanlu*, entitled "Yang Is Exalted and Yin Is Base." This title announces the principle of hierarchy between the two poles, enunciated also in the very first line of the "Great Commentary," cited above. Dong equates Yang with the creative force, as correlated with the Han calendrical ideas that associated Yang qi with the warmth of summer and the flourishing of agricultural products, hence with life as such. Dong states, "When Yang starts to emerge, all things start to emerge; when Yang flourishes, all things flourish; when Yang is in decline, all things are in decline. . . . From this point of view, [we know] to value Yang and disvalue Yin . . . to depend on Yang and not on Yin, which means not to allow Yin to succeed." Here we see a tendency to place all value in Yang per se, and all anti-value in Yin. He goes on, "[This distinction of Yin and Yang is evident] in superior and inferior positions, in great and small, in strong and weak, in worthy and unworthy, in good and evil; all that pertains to evil belongs to Yin, all that pertains to good belongs to Yang." This would seem to take Yin and Yang as a perfect value dualism, a strict dichotomy between good and bad, as two separate fixed and reliably reiterable "same" essences. Indeed, this would be the most axiologically dualistic use of the terms in the tradition.

But what is remarkable is that even here the nuances of complementarity in these two terms is inescapable. Dong continues:

> Yang is kindness (德 *de*, "virtuosity," here the leniency of a ruler) and Yin is punishment. Punishment opposes kindness, and yet it is consistent with kindness [順 *shun*, lit. follows kindness, the term used of Yin in the *Zhouyi*, to follow and complete what Yang has started]. It is also a kind of temporary measure (權 *quan*). Although we call it a temporary measure, its value always resides in bringing the normal standard (經 *jing*) to completion.[20] Thus Yang proceeds in going with the current, Yin in going against the current. Yin is what goes with the current in spite of going against it, and goes against it in spite of going with it. Thus Heaven uses Yin as its temporary measure and Yang as its normal standard. . . . The normal standard is used at the point of flourishing, the temporary measure only at the end. From this we see that Heaven makes the normal standard eminent and hides the temporary measure, puts kindness first and punishment last. Thus I say, Yang is heaven's kindness, Yin is heaven's punishment. Yang qi warms and Yin qi cools, Yang qi gives and Yin qi takes, Yang qi is benevolent and Yin qi is cruel . . . Yang qi loves and Yin qi hates, Yang qi gives life and Yin qi kills. . . . Thus Heaven favors benevolence and keeps it near, but hates cruelty and keeps it far, meaning that it maximizes kindness and minimizes punishment. Thus we put the normal standard first and the temporary measure last, we value Yang and devalue Yin.[21]

Thus, we see that even here, where an *attempt* is made to create a total disjunction and dichotomy of value between Yin and Yang, placing all value in Yang, the intrinsic complementarity of the two terms ends up bringing about a placement of value in a certain relationship between the two, as before, and not the total elimination of the Yin. Instead, value is here in prioritizing Yang, maximizing Yang, but still including Yin as an element in the totality. The possibility of a total absence of Yin is never even mentioned, either because it is simply assumed to be impossible, or because it is better to have a little Yin than no Yin at all. But because Dong assumes Heaven to be the source of both value and of fact, these two possibilities in the end amount to the same thing.[22] Rather than call such a relation either complementary or hierarchical, we would perhaps do better to call it hierarchical as complementary, rather than hierarchical as conflictual. This may or may not conflict with Raphals's use of these terms, inasmuch as she is careful to define them in terms of relative emphasis rather than exclusion, and notes repeatedly that they are "overlapping."[23] In the case of Dong's usage here, it would be hard to say whether he is emphasizing hierarchy over complementarity, or vice versa. In fact, my point is that he seems to regard complementarity and hierarchy as aspects of one another, as *themselves* complementary, and when he emphasizes one he emphasizes the other. What he attempts to downplay is *conflict*, and even more, *irony*, which is a single item's conflict *with itself*. But he ends up unable to exclude the irony that is built into the provenance of the categories of Yin and Yang even in his attempted disparagement of Yin, which ends up being at times preferable to Yang—ironically enough.

Dong's calendrical and geomantic model for understanding Yin and Yang, typical of Han thought and played out in another way in Yang Xiong's system, to be discussed below, leads to a further development of the idea of Centrality and Harmony, explicitly linking them with Li, as will often be the case in the development of this term, to be examined in the companion volume to this work. Here again we see the force of the conception of coherence as harmony. In chapter 77 of the same work, entitled "Following the Way of Heaven," Dong writes:

Following the Way of heaven in order to nourish one's person is called the Way. Heaven has two Harmonies, which complete its two Centers. When the year establishes its Centers, its function is endless. That is: the function of the Center of the North joins with Yin, and only then do things begin to move what is below. The function Center of the South joins with Yang, and only then does its nourishment begin to beautify what is above. The motion below cannot be produced without the Harmony of the East, namely, the Mid-spring (Spring Equinox, literally Center of Spring). The nourishing above cannot be completed without the Harmony of the West, namely, the Mid-Autumn (Autumn Equinox, Center of Autumn). So then what does the beauty of Heaven and Earth reside in? In the place of these two Harmonies, which accomplish and complete the activities of the two Centers when the latter return to them. Thus the East generates and the West completes, and thus the Harmony of the East is generated. What the North brings forth is completed by the Harmony of the West, and thus what is nourished by the South grows. What arises cannot be generated unless it reaches the Harmony. What is nourished and grows cannot come to completion unless it reaches the Harmony. What is completed in Harmony must have Harmony also at its inception. What is begun in Centrality must have Centrality also in its ending. The Center is what makes for the all the ends and beginnings of Heaven and Earth. And Harmony is what makes for all the generations and completions of Heaven and Earth. For generally speaking, there is no greater virtuosity than Harmony, and no Way more correct than the Center. The Center is the unobstructed Coherence of the beauties of Heaven and Earth (中者天地之美達理也 *zhongzhe tiandizhimeidali*), and what the Sage preserves and holds to. The *Odes* say, "Neither firm nor yielding, he spreads forth his governance in all its excellence." Is this not referring to the Center? For this reason, the virtuosity of he who can use Centrality and Harmony to coherently order (Li) the empire (以中和理天下 *yi zhonghe li tianxia*) will flourish, and the longevity of he who can use Centrality and Harmony to nourish his person will reach its ultimate of his allotted span.

The quotation from the *Odes* brings us a coded reference to Yin and Yang, here interpreted through their calendrical and geomantic associations, with some typical Dongian punning, to present an equation of Li with centrality as such, the point of balance that harmonizes the extremes of Yin and Yang. In this sense, in spite of his exaltation of Yang, the real ultimate value of Dong's system is not Yang but Centrality, which he explicitly links with Li, a particular kind of coherence between the apparently valued and the apparently disvalued, the Yang and the Yin. Here as before, the criterion for what counts as Li is that it must be a coherence (in this case, between Yin and Yang, and also between their concrete forms as the four seasons and the four directions), with which humans can cohere (knowing it, using it to order the empire and the body) to bring about a further coherence (sustainability, continuance, longevity, flourishing).

But we may note here that the ironic implications of Centrality have been completely eliminated here. The Center is perfectly identifiable, intelligible, coherent in its own right; none of the paradoxes associated with the Daoist union of opposites or the *Doctrine of the Mean*'s appropriation of that paradoxicality enter the picture here. Rather, equating the process of the seasons and the corresponding array of the directions as Heaven's deliberate way of creating life, he conceives of Centrality as an identifiable, describable midpoint balancing the two extremes, assimilating Centrality to Harmony as such. Harmony is an adequate representation of Centrality. Instead of the neither/nor of Centrality, which makes it an ironic conception, we have the both/and of Harmony. We will see echoes of this in Song Neo-Confucianism; Zhu Xi's opposition to Hu Hong's theory that human Nature is neither Good nor Evil may be said to rest on a similar idea. For Zhu Xi, the Nature can be described definitively as Good because the both/and is at least a *more* adequate representation of the neither/nor than an either/or would be, and since both/and (harmony, balance, coherence) is the definition of the Good, the unknowable Nature (Centrality) may be legitimately described as Good. For Dong, the center is the solstice, the beginning of life, conceived as central in accordance with the analogy to spatial Yin-Yang configurations. Centrality begins what is completed by Harmony, so that Centrality and Harmony permeate one another. The Center here becomes just a name for incipient Harmony, and as such is stripped of all its ironic implications. It is the source of coherence in the straightforward sense of harmony, the creation and sustaining of life in the turning of the seasons, as Heaven's deliberate work. As such, this coherence and this Centrality have a definite, fixed, always-the-same non-ironic identity.

We may say, then, that the Yin-Yang correlations of space and time, combined with an ultimate theistic grounding, produce an effacement of the ironic implications of Centrality, although some remnants of ironic ideas of coherence continue to play a role in the application of Yin-Yang ideas to specific ethical issues. When this theistic grounding is removed, however, we find another Han Yin-Yang system that makes much of the irony of the largest coherence, yielding a very different expression of Yin-Yang cosmology: Yang Xiong's *Taixuanjing*.

AN ALTERNATE YIN-YANG DIVINATION SYSTEM: YANG XIONG'S *TAIXUANJING*

I noted that the ultimate guarantor and standard for coherence in the *Zhouyi* system, which determines which of the overabundance of rules are to apply in any case, was tradition, the judgment of the sage kings, just as it had been for Xunzi and Mencius. Yang Xiong's *Taixuanjing*, composed in the mid-Han, was an attempt to construct a new systematic and comprehensive application of the Yin-Yang idea from scratch, without the benefit of tradition as the ultimate arbiter of coherence. Yang met with many objections to his presumption in attempting to construct this nontraditional one-man show, devising a set of symbols and his own commentaries to them to create a new and better *Zhouyi*, as if he were claiming to be a sage himself. Nonetheless, it is quite instructive to see how he attempted to give coherence to his system without being able to appeal to a tradition that would allow for the coexistence of many alternate sets of rules. Yang makes up his own rules, and in so doing creates his own way of domesticating the ironic insights of the *Laozi* especially, in a way that can be understood non-ironically, and provide a systematic set of kinds that exist in the world, universal archetypes not of things, but of spacetime situations, as in the *Zhouyi*. This in turn will disclose for us a further set of nuances to the conception of coherence operative in this tradition, working with ideas calendrical and geomantic models such as those of Dong Zhongshu and expanding the notion of the Li as Center. In this context, incorporating the ironic—unknowable—nature of the Center, Yang gives a new non-ironic account of how real classes of beings in time and space are conceived as grouping, and what kinds of general inductions can be made about them.

Yang's system was in a sense made to order; it began with Zhong (中 "The Center," corresponding to Zhongfu 中孚, and also representing the winter solstice) and ending with Yang (養 "Nourishment," corresponding with Yi 頤), and was designed to work on a system of multiples of three,[24] yielding eighty-one tetragrams. The exaltation of the concept of The Center is to be noted here; it has become in effect synonymous with the Dao, in accordance with the type of non-ironic incorporation of ironic thinking we found in "The Doctrine of the Mean." As we shall see, the Center is here equated with "The Mystery" (玄 xuan), the name of the system as a whole, and indeed of the whole of the cosmos, the greatest possible coherence, which is here given the ironic name: the unknowable, the unintelligible, the dark, the incoherent. Eighty-one is the number corresponding to a complete day in the Taichuli 太初曆, modified from the eighty of the Sifenli 四分曆 so as to correspond to the Huangzhong ("yellow bell"), the fundamental pitch, which bore the number eighty-one as the result of its derivation through the sanfensunyi 三分損益 pitch-generation system, which made a number easily divisible by three extremely desirable.[25] Moreover, these eighty-one tetragrams, by further interaction with multiples of three, correspond closely to the Santongli 三統曆 calender, as we shall see below.

In Yang's system, each tetragram corresponds to four and one-half days in the calendar, and to the hexagram assigned to it in the guaqi system. The name of the tetragram names the phase of agricultural activity characteristic of that chunk of time, in the language of a relation between yangqi 陽氣 and yinqi 陰氣. To understand how this works, however, it is crucial first to note that the tetragrams differ from the hexagrams of the Yijing in that they are, according to Yang, to be conceived as numbers.[26] As Nylan and Sivin point out, we can view each tetragram as a four-place, base-three numeral, which will yield a perfectly regular counting of eighty-one (ten thousand in base three) successive numerals. Hence, as Yang himself states in the commentaries, the place in the sequence of any imagined tetragram can be quite simply calculated.[27] Here we have perhaps the closest approximation of an attempt to truly quantify coherence in the Chinese tradition, which, as I said before, is generally regarded as vaguely quantitative (i.e., involving a balance, a reference to proper measure) but not numerically quantified. The tetragrams are not graphic diagrams of a particular configuration of interaction Yin and Yang forces, which can then be analyzed to reveal the deep structure of that situation, as the hexagrams of the Zhouyi are purported to be. Rather, they are a way of denoting eighty-one places within a total sequence, and their meaning derives entirely from the systematic connection of this sequence. Their sequential order is perfectly regular and calculable, and is all that is represented by their structure.

It is for this reason that the individual lines of the tetragrams are not interpreted, as the lines of the *Zhouyi* are. Rather, each tetragram has nine Appraisals (贊 *zan*). There are precisely nine of them not only as an extension of the base-three system of these tetragrammic "numerals" themselves, but also so that the total number of Appraisals amounts to twice the number of days in a year.[28] Two Appraisals correspond to each day, and this is their fundamental referent: a particular place in the annual cycle. Thus, as noted above, each tetragram represents a block of time: four and one-half days. The character of this stretch of four and one-half days is to be gleaned not so much from the structure of the tetragram as from the name and text Yang has affixed to it, which in turn derive from its place in the annual cycle. Eighty-one phases of the yearly cycle of the potentiality, nascence, origination, flourishing, and decline of life are described in these texts, so that, if read in succession, they produce a kind of prose-poem on natural process in general and on the cycle of the agricultural year in particular. The nuancing of these descriptions comes in the nine Appraisals, which must be interpreted with reference to several sets of variables at once. Since two Appraisals correspond to each day, they divide neatly into mornings and evenings, the former being Yang and auspicious and the latter being Yin and inauspicious.[29] Moreover, the sequence of the five phases is correlated to the sequence of the appraisals (water, fire, wood, metal, earth; this works nicely in that successive tetragrams will also follow the sequence of the phases, since they come nine Appraisals later; thus both the Appraisals and the tetragrams are able to follow the regular order of the phases, each tetragram sharing the phase of its first Appraisal). Each of the phases, in turn, corresponds to one of the four directions in space (with Earth for the center).[30]

All these groups of nested triads (Appraisals, Households, Departments, Provinces, Regions) are meant to describe a set of nested bell-shaped processes of incipience, zenith, and decline. We may see in this Yang Xiong's adaptation of Laozi's bell-shaped straw dog progression from namelessness to name to namelessness into a "Great Coherence" non-ironic system. These three phases in each process are applied systematically to heaven, earth, and man simultaneously. The three phases of growth and decline take different forms in each of these three loci: in Heaven, representing the temporal dimension of growth, they are Beginning (始 *shi*), Middle (中 *zhong*), and End (終 *zhong*). In Earth, representing the spatial dimension (on the model of a growing plant), they are Below (下 *xia*), Center (中 *zhong*), and Above (上 *shang*). In Man, they are Reflection (思 *si*), Felicity (福 *fu*), and Calamity (禍 *huo*).[31] These three triads are thought to be parallel or mutually explicating. The first item in each of these triads ("Beginnings" for Heaven, "Below" [i.e., underground, the Yellow Springs] for Earth, and "Reflection" [i.e., thoughts occurring in man prior to action] for Man) is associated with the "Mystery," the unseen aspect, and corresponds to the first three Appraisals in any tetragram. The next three refer to the group Middle, Center, and Felicity, and the last three to End, Above, and Calamity.[32] As Yang's "Revelation" commentary ("Taixuan gao") puts it, "Heaven completes by three stages: beginning, middle and end. Earth gives form in three stages: bottom, center and top. Man becomes manifest through three stages: reflection, felicity and calamity. Joining above and joining below, they go in and out of the nine empty [places, i.e., the Appraisals]. . . . The Mystery in Heaven is its invisibility, in earth what is unformed, and in man what is in his heart. Heaven's profundity lies in the west and north [Yin directions], where it accumulates transforming seed-essence (精 *jing*). Earth's profundity lies in the Yellow Springs, where it hides the blossoming of the material soul. Man's profundity lies in his thought and fore-planning, which contains the perfected seminal-essence."[33] The first stage is hidden in each, the unseen thought or initial impulse. The last phase goes too far, brings the process in general to an end. The center is the balance, the felicity, the value. The nine Appraisals, taken together, are thus meant to describe the complete cyclical process or situation indicated by the tetragram's name: the first three pertain to its commencement, the next three to its culmination, and the last three to its decline. This basic shape, of a three-part process of unseen incipience, glorious zenith, and excess-created self-overcoming, is clearest and most explicit in the sequence of the nine Appraisals to each tetragram; but the same general pattern can be seen, more loosely applied, as characteristic of all the nested triads making up the eighty-one tetragrams, as we shall see below. Here we have a general blueprint of the process of "becoming manifest" or "becoming intelligible"—of becoming coherent, and the manner in which it is rooted in the profundity of the Mystery, the Center, that lies at its bases, and which temporally precedes and follows it.

There are two important sets of nodes in this total sequence. The winter solstice comes at the first tetragram ("Center," water, four solid lines),[34] while the summer solstice comes right in the middle, with tetragram 41 ("Response," earth, four singly broken lines). Similar structural symmetries result for the other significant dates in the calendar, vernal and autumnal equinoxes, and the beginnings of the four seasons, one of which comes every ten tetragrams (1, 11, 21, 31, 41, 51, 61, 71, 81). Each is named and given a text that characterizes its place in the yearly cycle.[35]

It will be noticed that the entire system of tetragrams is based on an intricate intermingling of the calendrical cycle, with all its relevant correspondents (seasonal phases of change, diurnal cycles, etc.) and the geographical-administrative form that provides the four lines of each graph, the four "places" of each "number." Spatial and temporal concepts are further integrated through the directional and astronomical associations of the numbers and times, and through the "Below, Middle, and Above" connected with Earth, which is also rife with administrative-hierarchical overtones.[36] This division of the tetragrams thus derives from the superimposition of the spatial model of ruling influences (with three subordinates under each ruling member of the hierarchy) on the temporal calendrical cycle.

Now, to understand the general implications of this system, and the notion of spatiotemporal coherence operative in it, we have to note the special features of the kind of space and time, and of the categories, employed here. We noted that the structure of the tetragrams is based on a geographical/administrative model. However, Yang does not seem to make any attempt to associate particular tetragrams with particular locations in the empire; we are not told the exact name of the particular town that would correspond to a particular Household as diagrammed by a particular tetragram, although one can imagine that this might have been done. The eighty-one tetragrams do not represent eighty-one particular locations in the Han empire (in spite of correlation with the five phases, which have a directional component). It is not, however, correct to say, as Xu Fuguan does, that the spatial designations that underlie the four-line structure of the tetragrams "actually have no function."[37] On the contrary, the spatial model of the tetragrams provides a particular structural paradigm according to which we are to understand the relations between the various tetragrams—which is to say, between the various times. In the Representations (太玄梡 "Taixuan nie") commentary, Yang says, "Holding the *gui*-tablet and wearing the *bi*-pendant, ordering thereby all the feudal lords—this is represented by the 81 tetragrams."[39] The reference to ritual objects of authority here stresses the notion of rule through charismatic inspiration, which we will discuss in some detail below. Yang's Illumination (太玄瑩 "Taixuan ying") commentary says, "Regions, provinces, departments, households, coming to 81 locations, drawn above, between and below one another to express [all within] the four seas—the methods of the *Xuan* illuminate them. One ruler (辟 *bi*), three Dukes (公 *gong*), nine Ministers (卿 *qing*), 27 Grand Masters(大夫 *daifu*) and 81 Senior Servicemen (元士 *yuanshi*), the few ruling the many, the absent (無 *wu*) ruling the present (有 *you*)—the methods of the *Xuan* illuminate them."[40] Here we can see how closely these geographical units used as organizing principles in the *Taixuan's* tetragram system are linked with areas of administrative control, and how they fit into an administrative hierarchy of a very specific and concrete kind.[41] This suggests that the primary ordering function of the spatial model embodied in the tetragrams is to be understood on an administrative, rather than a geometrical or even geographical, model. The spatial classifications are designed to indicate a relationship between the tetragrams that is analogous to the relationship between the members of the ruling bureaucracy. The eighty-one phases of the year are thus related to one another as eighty-one local feudal lords, and are related in turn to the "larger" geographical units represented by the Departments, Provinces, Regions, and the Mystery as these local magistrates are related to their superiors in the hierarchy, all the way up to the emperor (represented by the unseen Mystery [*xuan*] itself).

The conception of spatial order operative here is thus that of *administrative space*. The paradigm underlying this type of space is very different from that of mathematical space. This is important to note in our current context, for it is here in the complex numerology of the *Taixuan* and of other derivatives of the *Zhouyi* that we seem to find the closest equivalent to the number mysticism of the Pythagoreans, which we are claiming underwrites the Platonic theory of forms, the two-tiered metaphysic of the intelligible versus the empirical world, and the concept of natural law and principles. It is here that we can see most clearly the parting of the ways. For the numerical system with which Yang creates his blueprint for all existence has built into it an undermining of the static *partes extra partes* absolutism of the intelligible world of laws and principles, where a principle *rules* its exemplifications exceptionlessly and unchangingly. For Yang's numerical system is built upon the notions of administrative space and calendrical time, rather than geometrical space and arithmetical (i.e., adding one plus one, moment after moment, in identical units) time. Once again we must make the contrast between harmony and sameness. For administrative and calendrical spacetime is a system of harmonically grouping coherences, while geometrical and arithmetical spacetime is constructed of abstract identical units of absolute sameness.

On the temporal side, then, the whole is not so much *constituted* by its parts as it is *completed* by its parts, a relation similar to the *sheng* 生 and *cheng* 成, associated with Yang and Yin respectively in the Great Commentary to the *Zhouyi* as just discussed The quality that names the whole also names the "unseen" (玄 *xuan*) incipience, which inspired the whole progression, even its decline. It is in this sense that Yang says, "The absent (無 *wu*) rule the present (有 *you*)," as quoted above. The absent, the Daoistic non-being, is here understood temporally as the *not-yet*-apprehendable incipient impulse, corresponding to "Beginning" in the realm of Heaven (cyclical calendrical time), to "Below" (unseen, as a still lowly but promising official, or a seed in the ground) in the realm of Earth (administrative space) and to Reflection (思 *si*) (which has *not yet* manifested as action) in the realm of human action. The unseen contemplation of an action is what "rules" it, "inspires" it, initiates the character that will be fully realized by the whole action per se, including its completion and decline, its transition into something else, the next phase. We might think here again of the handling of the idea of the unseen and its relation to the seen in the "Doctrine of the Mean" as modeled on the center-periphery paradigm. Yang takes this intermelding of spatial and temporal forms of coherence a step farther, giving it a systematic exposition. He also gives us a very detailed and clear example of what it means to say that coherence is rooted in harmony rather than sameness.

Here we have the mutual influence and inclusion implied by the very idea of succession; the fact that these different times grow out of one another, succeed one another, form parts of one total process, further ensures their mutual penetration and inclusion. But this mutual inclusion is in Yang's case even more extreme than in the case of linear time where the asymmetry of past and future arguably suggests the inclusion of the past in the future, but not the future in the past. For here we are dealing with agricultural cyclical time, wherein every moment is part of both the future and the past of every other moment, thus contributing to its constitution and in turn being constituted by it. In fact, it is not even exactly accurate to speak of a causal relationship between the parts here at all; it is not exactly that the spring "causes" the summer that succeeds it. What accounts for the existence of the summer is in a very real sense *the whole year*—in Yang's language, the Mystery, the totality of the eighty-one tetragrams. It is the entire sequence, worked out as a progression of conceptual/temporal *spaces* represented by four-place numerals, that determines the value of any of the numbers in the sequence, and the character of the corresponding space. The time before and after it is infinite in the sense that a circle is infinite: it has no beginning or end. What comes after has also come before, and all this determines what a particular time will be like; all of it is constitutive of that time's character.[42]

To sum up, the spatiotemporal coherence here is of a kind that leads almost inevitably to a conception of the mutual influence and inherence of the "parts" in one another. This is due to the following special features: (1) The space here is *administrative space,* which already implies a degree of mutual inclusion and subjectively motivated interaction among parts, unlike geometrical space; and (2) the time is *cyclical time,* which, as exemplified in the tetragrams, exhibits an even greater degree of such mutual inclusion and implication than linear time, where opposite qualities represent the culmination of one another, such that time is a structure of mutually inclusive round-trips, leading into one another and progressing and fully expressing themselves by negating and overcoming themselves.

Yang Xiong's most general and intriguing statement of the meaning of his own system is perhaps the following:

The Mystery (玄 *xuan*) is what, while remaining unseen itself, unfolds the ten thousand Kinds (萬類 *wan lei*) and yet reveals no form of its own. Taking up and molding (spatial) nothingness (虛無 *xuwu*), it gives rise to the determinate turning of the compass [i.e., the circular motion of the sky]. Connecting the divinities, it fixes definite models. Penetrating and joining the past and present, it divides and develops the Kinds. It unfolds and arrays Yin and Yang, and puts forth material force. As these now divide, now join, Heaven and Earth are complete. The heavenly configuration and the sun rotate, and the hard and soft succeed one another. Running full circle back to their point of origin, the beginning and end are set. Now being born, now dying, the inborn nature and extrinsic givenness (性命 *xingming*) [of each] become clear.

Looking up, we observe the images, looking down we see the conditions of things (情 *qing*). Examining their inborn natures and understanding their extrinsic givenness, we can trace their beginnings and perceive their ends. The three powers [heaven, earth, and man] follow equally the same rule, the mutual chafing of the thick and the thin [Yin and Yang]. The circular [heaven] never rests, the square [earth] gathers and hoards. The exhalation is the flowing body [heaven], the inhalation is the coagulation of palpable form [earth].

Thus that which "closes up" all of Heaven is called the spatial aspect, and that which "opens up" this spatial aspect is called temporal aspect (是故闔天謂之宇, 闢宇謂之宙 *shi gu he tian wei zhi yu, pi yu wei zhi zhou*).[43]

By now we can perhaps discern the sense of this description, especially the cryptic final sentence. The ironic tradition's unintelligible coherence is drafted into service here as the *xuan*, darkness, which gives the entire system its name, denoting both the uttermost unseen beginning and the comprehensive coherence of the whole cyclical system of particular coherences. Each particular coherence shares this cyclical structure of beginning as not-yet being intelligible as such and then returning to it, and also in that all eighty-one tetragrams are the playing out of this very process for the coherence named in the first tetragram, the Great Coherence: Xuan itself. The individual coherences in this way share in the overall incoherence (or ironic coherence) of the whole, or the Dao. But when all is said and done, Yang remains a partisan of the non-ironic tradition in that he presents a system that makes this incoherence fully intelligible: the *Taixuanjing* itself. It is knowable accurately in this coherent, systematic form. The exact nature of this coherence is indicated by the final statement about the coherent relation between temporal and spatial coherence.

Thus, "The closing up of heaven is the spatial aspect; the opening up of this spatial aspect is the temporal aspect." In other words, spatiality is the structural aspect of temporality, and temporality is the interconnective (active, developmental, self-overcoming) aspect of spatiality. Together, they yield a systematic picture of a coherence in the non-ironic sense, but one which has thoroughly internalized the ironic sense of coherence: the Mystery, the unintelligible, the Center, is the unintelligible togetherness of the whole, the structure of coherence between incoherence and coherence (Yin and Yang, the unseen beginning and the manifest outcome). This structure itself has now been enlisted as the coherence of all the determinate things, their specific "principles": all these principles are one principle, the Mystery itself (ironic, i.e., unintelligible, coherence), but expressing itself as specific, individual principles, each of which is non-ironically coherent. Although this may seem to place Yang's system among the "ironic incorporations of the non-ironic" systems to be considered in Part Two, since the ultimate principle is incoherent while the lower-level principles are coherent, this is only apparent. For by systematizing the relation between the two sides, and tracing the triadic structure of the unintelligible into each intelligible principle, so that the unintelligible is completely expressed in and as the coherent individual principles (as for example in the "Doctrine of the Mean"), the relation has been reversed. The lower-order coherences are not merely pragmatic, approximate patterns, as in, for example, the "Community Words" dialogue from the *Zhuangzi* (which we will discuss at length in the companion volume); rather, they now partake of the unshakeable absoluteness of the Mystery itself, the ironic unintelligible coherence, which is beyond question because it is beyond apprehension.

CONCLUSION AND SUMMARY

Toward Li

In the preceding pages, we have attempted to draw attention to an emergent conception of coherence in early Chinese thought, which comes to play a crucial role in accounting for the presence, value, sustainability, and intelligibility of things. We have delineated two intertwining variants of this conception, the non-ironic and the ironic. In both we identify coherence as a founding, fundamental category, from which sameness and difference are negotiable, non-ultimate derivatives.

Why are things what they are, as they are, able to continue being what they are, and having the values they have? Because of the ways they cohere. If they cohere differently, they are different things, have different identities. In the non-ironic conception, harmonizing in a certain way allows things to manifest in a particular way, and it is in this that their value lies. To be seen, known, shown as having a certain identity (coherence as knowability) derives from a relation to a particular context, most centrally a context of human desires and the discerning, exemplary eye of a sagely person steeped in coherence with a tradition of other such persons. In the ironic conception, the total coherence of all things, from which their identities and value and sustainability indeed do derive, undermines any visibility, identifiability, definitive identity (coherence as knowability) of either any of the parts or of the whole itself; true coherence for any X always means coherence also with the totality, which itself being unframed in any larger context must be incoherent (since coherence as intelligibility requires coherence as framing), and also always means coherence with X's own negation, the before-X and after-X when X is not, the non-Xness that grounds X and constantly saturates X. Hence true coherence undermines coherence; true coherence is incoherence. These reflections will put us in a position to see how "centrality" and "coherence" converge into the meaning of 理 Li, and how this sort of notion developed through various partial prefigurements in Confucian and Daoist thought. Let us review our conclusions briefly:

In the *Analects*, we find that Confucius has no "constant teacher," and yet finds his teacher everywhere. He himself is the "center," which here means the determinant of the coherence, the "pattern," the "principle," the value. But he neither subjectively creates this value ex nihilo nor acts as a mere passive mirror of an objectively existing truth. The value he creates is a coherence, a readable converging, of aspects available everywhere, combined by the selective filter of Confucius's own responses and evaluations. His discernment is a selective frame which creates/finds coherence, the value-endowed style of culture, which is omniavailable, present in more than one place, not strictly reiterable except in the special sense of being continuable. We have here already the sprout of a model of a form of omnipresence that is neither nominalist nor realist, neither idealist nor materialist, manifesting in a cognition that is neither objective nor subjective.

In the *Mencius*, we have the selective definition of which of the inborn capabilities of the human animal are to be properly named "the Nature," with a more explicit set of criteria: precisely those spontaneous human tendencies that allow for coherence, that is, those that are appealing (valued) and discernible to other humans, and that create cohesion among humans, are to be called the Nature. These are the desires that can be satisfied independently of external material conditions, that allow for the other (for example, material) desires to be equally nurtured and developed, the enjoyment of which is increased rather than decreased when shared, and so on. The material desires are to be called "the Decree" because they are not conducive to coherence in this sense: they isolate, they create strife because their satisfaction depends on external material resources which may be in short supply, their enjoyment is decreased when shared, and so on. The class name "Human nature" is here also neither objective nor subjective, neither nominalist nor realist; and here again we have a "center" embodied by a living human agent, the sage, whose manifestation of these virtues makes him the hub, the center, around which this style of being, humanity, converges. The presence of this center literally actualizes the coherence "humanity."

In Xunzi, we have a seeming conflict between a nominalistic and a realist theory of naming, which is resolved once again by recourse to a human center, in this case the tradition of the sages and exemplary persons who literally give order to the cosmos through mandated ritual. But this too is neither creation nor passive reflection of coherence: there is an overabundance of real distinctions, groupings, coherences in the world, among which the sages serve as a selective filter, enforcing their standardized names in the same way that weights and measures are to be enforced in the marketplace. Omnipresence is here the "great coherence," the value present in all parts of the organized whole which results from the exemplary man's selective ritual regulations of which of the really occurring groupings of nature may be grouped into a valued whole, that is, a whole that maximizes the satisfaction of human desires.

In the Laozi tradition, we have the advent of ironic coherence: a togetherness that is necessarily also unintelligible, unreadable. When all is together, nothing is discernible, and this is the ultimate cohering, also the ultimate value, from which lesser values/coherences emerge. Since everything that is valued in any way is rooted in something that is not so valued, and since all intelligibility emerges only in coherent connection with a surrounding context which cannot also be intelligible without requiring a further context, the whole can be neither valuable nor intelligible: it must be incoherent. Since all specific coherences depend on their contextualization within a coherent whole for their coherence, each and every coherence is similarly undermined, or rendered provisional, negotiable, ironic, by the ultimate incoherence of the whole. That is, all things have coherence in the sense of inescapable togetherness, but for that very reason lack coherence in the sense of value and intelligibility. Further, it is this coherence-due-to-incoherence and incoherence-due-to-coherence that truly provides such value and intelligibility that things do have, and which is thus the true, ironic, coherence. The motif of the center is here transformed from the exemplary center of Confucianism, the model that inspires those around it to modify themselves because it is seen and valued, to the invisible center, which creates togetherness and value precisely by not being seen, not being valued. To be valued is to inspire imitation, which is to inspire competition, which is to create strife, which is to undermine ultimate coherence. To be seen is to be cut out from a background that is unseen, which means again a loss of the greatest coherence. Coherence is "ironic" in that the true coherence (value, togetherness, the unhewn or devalued from which the valued grows, which is inseparable from the valued, which accounts for the cycle of reversal from value to anti-value, and which is omnipresent in both the valued and the devalued) is by definition incoherent (undiscernible, invisible).

In the writings of Zhuang Zhou, we have an overabundance of perspectives, each positing its own standard of rightness (是 shi), which are filtered down to practical application in any given case not according to tradition or sagacity, but by virtue of the mere fact that each perspective is in fact a perspective, a "this." It is self-limiting simply by being a this as opposed to that, by defining things from its own limited perspective, situation and needs, by its own arbitrary finitude. At the same time, every perspective transcends itself toward other perspectives: being a "this," it necessarily posits a contrasting "that," but the "that," to be capable of serving as a contrast, must also be a something, and to be a something is to be a "this," hence to be another perspective. Zhuang Zhou's "wild card" perspective "responds but does not store": it reflects and affirms the "rightness" presented by each new situation, but does not consider it in conflict with the opposite perspective, the opposed *shi/fei*. *Shi* is "this," which is coherence, value, intelligibility; but in positing its own negation which in turn negates "this," every coherence is also necessarily an incoherence, which again affirms Laozi's ironic coherence: value which is togetherness which is unintelligibility: the torch of drift and doubt. The "togetherness" here comes in not as an overriding convergence of all things in a single vision (as in Xunzi's "Great Coherence") but resides in a new application of the motif of the center, already prefigured in Mencius's discussion of "not clinging to the center." Zhuang Zhou introduces the idea of the pivot of Tao, which is also the pivots of Taos: the point where opposed *shi/feis* are not opposed, not mutually exclusive, precisely because of their mutual positing, and hence, in not "storing," they flow freely into one another. The center allows one to "travel two roads at once": this special kind of value bilocality is Zhuang Zhou's distinctive contribution to the problematic of coherence, universality, and omnipresence in Chinese thought.

In *Liji* texts such as the "Yueji," "Daxue," and "Zhongyong," as also in the Yin-Yang systems of the commentaries to the *Zhouyi* and Yang Xiong's *Taixuanjing*, we find a domestication of the ironic notion of the coherence and center—the unseen, the unmanifest, the unintelligible—as a creator of observable order and consistency. Overall coherence works through local pockets of invisibility or ironic coherence: the as-yet-unseen sprouts, the unmanifest but constant Unseen Coherence (誠 *cheng*), which reveals itself in all individual affects and actions but never shows itself *simpliciter*, the least manifest aspect of a hexagram-situation, the Yin side of a Yin-Yang dyad, which however works toward and is subordinated to the manifestation and purposes of the Yang. The role of the unintelligible, the background, the unreadable togetherness in which value is rooted is here acknowledged and integrated into the system of Great Coherence. For Yin-Yang represents a coherent and valued cohesion between ironic coherence-as-unintelligibility, value as necessarily non-explicit (Yin) and non-ironic coherence-as-intelligibility, value as explicit (Yang).

Our focus on these issues sets the stage for the emergence of the word *Li* as a fundamental philosophical concept, in which much of this intertwining is enfolded. The development of the pre-Neo-Confucian conceptions of Li will be explored in *Beyond Oneness and Diffence: Li (Coherence) in Pre-Neoconfucian Chinese Thought* (Albany: State University of New York Press, forthcoming).

NOTES

INTRODUCTION

1. The companion volume is *Beyond Oneness and Difference: Li (Coherence) in Pre-Neoconfucian Chinese Thought*, forthcoming from State University of New York press.

2. Already appearing in the literature of the field is a new round of heated disputation on the translation of Li as "coherence" in Neo-Confucianism, adopted by Peter Bol in his monumental book, *Neo-Confucianism in History* (Cambridge: Harvard University Press, 2008). In a review appearing recently in *Dao: A Journal in Comparative Philosophy*, Philip Ivanhoe has made strenuous objections to this usage, his extreme distaste for this choice forming the central polemical thrust of the review (*Dao* 9 [2010]: 471–75). Ivanhoe's objections to the term seem to be rooted in the claim that the term coherence, prima facie, fails to indicate "what it is that coheres," *why* this coherence takes place, and the strong sense of a *standard of value* embedded in this demand for and account of cohering, which for Ivanhoe, quite reasonably, are the heart and soul of Li for most Neo-Confucian thinkers. The Li for these thinkers are indeed coherent among themselves, and are the source of all coherence of other things in the universe, but to say that they are themselves "coherence" would be, for Ivanhoe, to confuse what they are with one of the things they produce or with a characteristic they possess. For these reasons Ivanhoe strongly prefers the traditional translation "principle," while also admitting that it has some (though far fewer) problems of its own. Ivanhoe thinks that Li are closer to what we call "moral principles" in English than to anything that could be denoted by a weird and "thin" term such as coherence, unless we are giving it new meanings ad hoc, in which case, he says, we should just admit we are coining a new word rather than translating Li with the existing English word *coherence*. Though a full response to these concerns will have to wait for the explicit discussion of Li (though not primarily as the term is used in Neo-Confucianism) in the companion volume, it is worth noting here that, appearances to the contrary, I am in broad agreement with Ivanhoe's remarks about direct translation of Li with the word *coherence* in most contexts. The obvious subtext of this conflict, though, lies in questions about (1) whether the logical priority of "what coheres" to "the cohering," and the ultimate metaphysical nonidentity between the two, is an inescapable metaphysical fact or merely a stubborn inheritance of certain cultural traditions; (2) whether "moral principle" is itself a coherent notion outside of the metaphysical traditions that root it in, say, a fixed and determinate intelligible realm exempt from the transience and relativities of empirical events, or a mathematical model of unchanging and derelativized truth, or an objectivism derived from grappling with (and perhaps rejecting)

the idea of a separate intelligible realm, or a transcendent God who in some sense rewards obedience and punishes disobedience to specific rules of behavior or belief. One reason for the interest in a word such as "coherence" as a substitute translation most likely lies in the obscurity of what "principle" could possibly mean when disconnected from its thick traditional associations with such premises as these. Indeed, "coherence" may be considered an attempt to answer just this question. Ivanhoe does not deny that principles are about creating and instantiating certain forms of coherence, moral or intellectual. For whatever else it is, a "principle" is supposed to be some single something that applies to, explains, is instantiated in, or controls a multitude of individual somethings, a way of talking about how and why these many somethings cohere with one another; in its moral sense, further, it must have something to do with an indissoluble bond between the moral agent and the demand placed upon her, with consequences that concern either the relations of the agent to herself, the relations between her various faculties or aspects, or the relations between herself and something beyond herself, whether world or truth or the source of the demand. The question is whether the principles that are implicated in these coherences are also something more than these coherences, a separate cause thereof, ontologically independent of them. "Coherence" is at the very least an attempt to provide some actual content to these dimensions of "principle," useful because the latter term reads, to many thoughtful people, like at best a no longer intelligible dead metaphor, a coinage whose face has been worn away by use, and at worst a hypostatized remnant of a questionable metaphysic. To say something is so, and should be so, "because of a principle" is a meaningless pleonasm; it is like, to borrow an example used by Nietzsche, the doctor in Molière explaining why a certain substance could cause sleep: "Because it possesses a certain property, whose character is to be causative of sleep." "Because of a principle" tells us nothing more than "because of some reason," without telling us what that reason is. Clearly, though, the Neo-Confucians mean something more than this when they say that it is Li that makes something as it is and tells us also how it should be, and this is where a term such as "coherence" begins to be so useful. For "coherence" as an English word can indeed be used to *explain* why something is what it is (because of the way it joins and interacts with other things, or as what emerges as newly intelligible if and only if some set of other things comes together in a certain way), can *demand* that something be a certain way (coherence demands that it be this way rather than that way; if it fails to be this way, it will fail to connect and interact and function in the demanded way), and indeed, can *give value* to something being as it is (value in the simplest sense as a relation between a desire and a desideratum, which must accord and interact in some specified way, usually called the desire being "fulfilled" or "satisfied" by the desideratum). That the evaluative normativity of the word *coherence* must often be adjusted upward when used to help track the implications of certain key Chinese terms is indeed, as Ivanhoe insists, of crucial importance; to do so in an immanent manner, which derives a specific conception of value from the more directly accessible implications of "sticking together" and "intelligibility," and even how this in some cases comes to approximate something more closely resembling a "transcendent" than an "immanent" function (as these are conceived according to traditions that regard them as mutually exclusive opposites), will be central concerns of the following pages.

3. Whitehead, *Process and Reality*, 259.

4. For a fuller exposition of the premises behind this unpopular epistemological position, see my *Being and Ambiguity: Philosophical Experiments with Tiantai Buddhism* (Chicago: Open Court, 2004).

CHAPTER ONE. ESSENCES, UNIVERSALS, AND OMNIPRESENCE

1. Chenyang Li, for example, has argued persuasively that Confucian theories of language presume a pragmatic orientation, which grounds reference in connotation and prescription, rather than unambiguous semantic truth. See his "Language: Pragmatic versus Semantic," in *The Tao Encounters the West: Explorations in Comparative Philosophy* (Albany: State University of New York Press, 1999), 63–87.

2. Robert Eno's exposition of this point, in relation to the Zhuangzi, remains, for my money, the most efficient and powerful explanation of the issue available. See Robert Eno, "Cook Ding's Dao and the Limits of Philosophy," in *Essays on Skepticism, Relativism, and Ethics in the Zhuangzi*, ed. Kjellberg and Ivanhoe (Albany: State University of New York Press, 1996), 127–51.

3. Hall and Ames, *Thinking from the Han*, 132–35. Hansen too, who has developed the anti-truth-and-belief position extensively, brilliantly, and in my view convincingly, is willing to acknowledge, in a footnote, that "assertability is not independent of the way the world is" (Chad Hansen, *A Daoist Theory of Chinese Thought*, 392). Again, the question is how to think about the way in which this dependence on "the way the world is" may then be understood.

4. See Li Chenyang, 11–33.

5. To avoid misunderstandings, let me state in advance that one of the results of this study will be to support the contention that Li—and other candidates for equivalency to "Truth," such as Dao—is in the end importantly different from any Western notion of Truth.

6. Indeed, on these grounds one might almost imagine a history of this idea in Greek thought, paralleling the present work, entitled, *Ironies of Universality in Greek Thought*.

7. Lucien Levy-Bruhl, *How Natives Think*, trans. Lilian A. Clare (London: Allen and Unwin, 1926), 77.

8. Ibid., 128.

9. Ibid., 127.

10. Stephan Korner, *Metaphysics: Its Structure and Function* (New York: Cambridge University Press, 1984), 7–8.

11. See Hansen, *A Daoist Theory of Chinese Thought*, 30–54, and passim.

12. See Whitehead, *Science and the Modern World* (New York: Macmillan, 1925), 19–38, for a good overview of the importance of mathematics to Western thought.

13. Ibid., 62.

14. In particular, he suggests that immediate experience is characterized by "Causal Efficacy," which is prior to the division of units into absolute separation of simple location characteristic of what he calls "Presentational Immediacy."

15. Whitehead, *Process and Reality*, 76–77. Whitehead's sometime collaborator Bertrand Russell makes a similar suggestion, this time specifically pointing to China as an alternative: "The influence of language on philosophy has, I believe, been

profound and almost unrecognized. If we are not to be misled by this influence, it is necessary to become conscious of it, and to ask ourselves deliberately how far it is legitimate. The subject-predicate logic, with the substance-attribute metaphysics, is a case in point. It is doubtful whether either would have been invented by people speaking a non-Aryan language; certainly they do not seem to have arisen in China, except in connexion with Buddhism, which brought Indian philosophy with it." Bertrand Russell, *Logic and Knowledge* (London: George Allen and Unwin), 330.

16. Whitehead himself, of course, endeavors to provide just such an alternative. But it is noteworthy that even Whitehead finds it necessary to posit a type of entity, which he calls "Eternal Objects," which are universally applicable, "ingressing" in every actual occasion, albeit with the important qualification that they may be prehended with various degrees of intensity or emphasis, or even negatively prehended, i.e., definitely excluded from relevance. Still, we have here a set of interrelated but genuinely plural entities that are necessary conditions for each and every portion of actuality, in a manner that is somewhat reminiscent of the Kantian transcendental categories. Whitehead also has his own distinctive version of the Universal Universal, which he calls creativity or, sometimes, Eros as such, which he explicitly compares to Spinoza's absolute substance. It has been suggested, understandably, that these aspects of Whitehead's thought represent a continued beholdenness to the categories of Greek thought. Certainly, Whitehead's continued interest in mathematical standards of knowledge would be relevant in this connection, and it would appear to be in the interest of making a place for the special status of mathematical truths that he makes these apparent concessions. But it raises the further question: what would the alternatives to worldviews assuming simple-location and universals, which bear no relation to Greek thinking look like?

17. The high value placed on mathematical truths in Plato and Aristotle is typically linked to the ontological privileging of the limited over the unlimited, which makes some version of the doctrine of simple location almost inevitable. Form in the Aristotelian sense is explicitly conceived as a kind of limiting of an otherwise infinite, unlimited matter, formless and indeterminate potential as such. Limitation itself is equated with essence, what makes any existence be what it is. As such, separation into simple locations is in a sense the most fundamental ontological fact about all beings.

Given this premise, Aristotle's solution to the problem of universals is quite ingenious: the universals are "forms" that are also quintessentially *active,* indeed "actuality" itself. It is precisely form, self-limitation, which makes relations, which bridges limitations, the agent that creates unities among the diverse under the category of teleology, i.e., the subordination of diverse parts (organs) to a single whole (organism) and of diverse means to a single end. It is in the actual, the acting, rather than in the potential, the unseen power to so act, that the connections between things lie. (In this connection it is clearly no accident that there is a special form of autotelic wholeness that pertains to actuality for Aristotle. Active form is the kind of motion which is its own aim, where "doing X" and "having done X" can be simultaneous. Hence, for Aristotle, "building a house" is not an active form in the way "seeing an object" is, since one cannot be building a house and have built it at once, whereas one can see and have seen a given object simultaneously. (Having seen it does not mean one cannot be presently seeing it.) The teleological notion of actuality implies a certain interpenetration of past and present, an overcoming of the disjunction of ends and means. However, with this stroke the second-level return of the problem of relation—i.e., among essences, among substances, among natural kinds, among forms—becomes the recurrent stumbling block that again and again seriously problematizes the Aristotelian picture of nature. We see this idea of teleological, self-moving form reappearing in Hegel, for example, in his own version of these problems, supplemented by an attempt to remedy the second-level relation problem by making the essences themselves relational (as Whitehead also does for his Eternal Objects). Hegel had inherited this problem from Kant, and his solution, of which we will say more in a moment, may be viewed as an extension and modification of the approach taken by Kant. Kant's transcendental solution attributes the unification of the discrete units of the sensual manifold to the a priori faculty of the transcendental unity of apperception, and the application of its twelve derivative categories.

We may perhaps feel some sympathy with Nietzsche's sarcastic ridicule of this solution, which he viewed as failing to give any real explanation at all to the problem. It amounted, he thought, to asking how it is that the absolutely discrete could nonetheless be meaningfully unified, and answered by positing a faculty of unification, as if (to cite this zinger again) one asked why a medicine caused sleep and answered that it did so because of its property of sleep-causing. But this is perhaps not entirely fair to Kant; he is obviously not trying to provide a "cause" of the possibility of causality, but rather the impossibility of conceiving any alternative, *given that we are already "conceiving" anything at all*. Nonetheless, it is clear that there is a thorny problem here of a more general nature, a troubling circularity, in that indeed the question is posed only by presupposing prior acts of unification, or universality.

18. Now, I am not claiming that all doctrines that posit some sense of the Omnipresent necessarily derive from the prior investment in some concept of universals or natural kinds. Historically this would be a very questionable claim. If we tried to tally up, very schematically and inadequately, the history of Occidental ideas of the Omnipresent, we would have to start with the pre-Socratic ideas of a single element that serves as the *arche* (ἀρχή) or beginning of the others, their principle, to which they were reducible and from which they emerged—water, fire, air—and which was in that sense omnipresent. At this point no explicit notion of universals has yet come upon the scene. Indeed, when Anaximander proposed that the *arche* was not any particular element but instead "the limitless," a truly abstract category but one that points in the opposite direction from the tradition of universals that was about to open up, we might almost spy the possibility of a Greek Daoism. This was not to be, however: with Pythagoras things change, for there we are told that number, ratio, the limit, is the omnipresent principle of all existences, and here we begin to get the thread of the tradition as we have presented it above. From there it is a short step to Anaxagoras, who suggested that mind, *nous*, is the real cause of all things, which Socrates is made to report, in the *Phaedo*, was what turned him away from natural philosophy and toward his inquiry into definitions and unchangeable universals. Not long before, Parmenides had given the most abstract possible definition of the Omnipresent, Being, and concluded that this implies an opposite

that is Non-present—Nonbeing. Being is everywhere, and other than Being there is nothing else. Wherever you look, there is Being and only Being; but strangely, this comes with a caveat therefore *not* to look in some places—i.e., wherever there is "nonbeing." This should not be possible to do, but it is presented rather as something that it is forbidden to do. With this we are forced into the doctrine of the dichotomy between illusion and reality: it *seems* possible to speak about nonbeing, but that is merely an error, which must be avoided. The ontological claim is converted into an epistemological, even ethical, demand. With this comes the claim that all motion and change are illusory. From then on, I would claim, the conception of the Omnipresent was split down the middle to follow the two courses just outlined. For Plato it is perhaps the form of the Good, but on the other side, for example in the *Timaeus*, matter—formless, chaotic, valueless, and ultimately evil matter—is equally omnipresent, but in the opposite way, as it were. The same could be said for Aristotle's Form and Matter; both are indeed present everywhere in the empirical world, but in opposite senses. Here we have as it were the combination of both senses of Omnipresence, but held apart as the two opposite extremes in an eternal dichotomy. Do we not see some form of this problem reemerging with each fresh attempt to confront this problem in the long annals of Occidental philosophy?

19. Baruch Spinoza, *Treatise on the Emendation of the Intellect*, in *The Essential Spinoza: Ethics and Related Writings*, ed. Michael L. Morgan, trans. Samuel Shirley (Indianapolis: Hackett, 2006), 187; emphases added.

20. Hilary Putnam puts it this way: "Peirce's views are much more in line with the tradition of metaphysical realism (or as Peirce called it elsewhere . . . 'scholastic realism') than with the pragmatism of James or Dewey. For James and Dewey, there is no such thing as Nature's own language; *we* make languages, guided by our interests, ideals, and by the particular 'problematic situations' (as Dewey would say) that we find ourselves in. . . . [N]either of them supposed that *that to which inquiry would converge* is independent of *us* . . . there is no such thing as discovering Nature's own categories, for James and Dewey. For Peirce, Nature has a set of 'joints' which a group of determined inquirers will discover if they pursue their inquiry long enough. . . ." Kenneth Laine Ketner and Hilary Putnam, eds., *Reasoning and the Logic of Things: The Cambridge Conferences Lectures of 1898 by Charles Sanders Peirce* (Cambridge: Harvard University Press, 1992), 73. Putnam himself, and Rorty, seem to be squarely in the nominalist Jamesian/Dewayan tradition.

CHAPTER TWO. WHAT IS COHERENCE?

1. See Chad Hansen, *Language and Logic in Ancient China* (Ann Arbor: University of Michigan Press, 1983), 30–54, and *A Daoist Theory of Chinese Thought*, 30–54 and passim.

2. See the discussion of recent sinological interpretation of Li in *Beyond Oneness and Difference*, the companion volume to this work.

3. Han Xiaoqiang, "Maybe There Are No Subject-Predicate Sentences in Chinese," *Dao: A Journal of Comparative Philosophy* 8 (2009): 277–87.

4. A. C. Graham, "Relating Categories to Question Forms in Pre-Han Chinese Thought," in *Studies in Chinese Philosophy and Philosophical Literature* (Singapore: Insti-

tute of East Asian Philosophies, 1986), 382–83. The case of the Mohist is obviously quite relevant to the question at hand. For here we have the closest case in the tradition of an attempt to give an abstract and comprehensive "logical" treatment to the question of how predicates attach to multiple instances, the equivalent of the problem of universals. I have nothing to add to Graham's analysis of the Mohist's, except to note the relevance of his analysis in the present context.

5. Ibid., 431.

6. Ibid., 136.

7. Ibid., 138.

8. Ibid., 140–41.

9. Ibid., 140.

10. Hall and Ames, *Thinking from the Han*, 124.

11. Ibid., 273.

12. Ibid., 273–74.

13. Ibid., 112.

14. Michael Puett, *To Become a God* (Cambridge: Harvard University Press, 2004), 150–60 and passim.

15. Hall and Ames have famously drawn the distinction between aesthetic order and rational order, which is supremely relevant here. The notion of coherence here may be viewed as an extension and modification of what they call aesthetic order, attempting to sharpen and expand the implications and concrete applications of this concept. See David Hall, *Eros and Irony: a Prelude to Philosophical Anarchism*, and Hall and Ames, *Thinking Through Confucius*.

16. See Chenyang Li, "The Confucian Ideal of Harmony," *Philosophy East and West* 56, no. 4 (October 2006): 583–603; Li Chenyang, "The Ideal of Harmony in Ancient Chinese and Greek Philosophy," *Dao: A Journal of Comparative Philosophy* (2008) 7:81–98; and also Li Chenyang, "The Philosophy of Harmony in Classical Confucianism," *Philosophy Compass* 3, no. 3 (2008): 423–35.

17. See Alan K. L. Chan, "Harmony as a Contested Metaphor and Conceptions of Rightness (*yi*) in Early Confucian Ethics," in *How Should One Live? Comparing Ethics in Ancient China and Greco-Roman Antiquity*, ed. R. A. H. King and Dennis Schilling (Berlin/Boston: Gruyter, 2011), 37–62.

18. *Guoyu* (Shanghai: Shanghai guji chubanshe, 1978), 515–16.

19. Indeed, harmony *he* is often used as a gloss of virtue 德 *de*, which signifies the consistently accomplished virtuosity in the practice of a Dao such that it begins to have the power to influence others to follow it spontaneously themselves. The fifth chapter of the *Zhuangzi* (14/5/47), for example, states 德者成和之修 (*dezhe cheng he zhi xiu*), which in context means "Virtuosity is really just an ornamental form giving a definite shape to the fullness of the harmony within," but is often read out of context almost as a full-on definition, meaning something like, "Virtue is the cultivation which accomplishes harmony." In either case, a strong linkage between Virtuosity and harmony is axiomatic. More directly, a later chapter of the *Zhuangzi* states point blank: "Virtue means harmony" (*fu De heye* 夫德和也), followed, not insignificantly for our purposes, with, "Dao means coherence" (*dao li ye* 道理也) (ch. 16). Virtue is also at times conceived as the harmonious combination of Yin and Yang *qi*.

20. The importance given to the notion of "continuance" here and in what follows deserves some consideration. For continuance implies preexistence; something that was already there is continued, helped to move along into the future. Qian Mu, in one of his arresting offhand generalizations, suggests that traditional Chinese thinking in general tends to emphasize "raising and nourishing" (養育 *yangyu*) rather than "creativity" (創造 *chuangzao*). The latter suggests the production of something from nothing, while the former is concerned with developing and expanding something that is already there. Where this given something comes from originally is not so central a concern. As Michael Puett has recently shown in detail, this is a highly oversimplified picture of the attitude toward creation in early Chinese texts. Even so, Qian's remarks do seem to point out something important at least about the dominant, mainstream Confucian tradition as it emerges through the centuries. More importantly, even the sort of "creativity" entertained in early texts refers to cultural innovation, and is not to be confounded with the radical idea of *creation ex nihilo*, true emergence of something from nothing. This idea does not seem to have been thinkable to the ancient Greeks either, and indeed it is challenging to make sense out of it even for theologians who are scripturally committed to it. *Laozi* 40, which is also found among the Guodian fragments in a slightly variant form, comes closest to what looks like a strong statement about creativity of something entirely new, from nothing: "Reversal is the motion of the Dao. Yielding is the function of the Dao. The ten thousand things are born from Being. Being is born from Non-being." But the context both of this little chapter and of early Chinese thought as a whole militates against reading this as any statement about creation—or even emergence—from "nothingness" in the strong ontological sense. Indeed, the Guodian version omits the second "Being," so that the line reads: "The ten thousand things are born from Being, [and are] born from Non-being." This pairing of Being and Non-being is more obviously in keeping with the anti–ex nihilo thinking of the text as a whole. But even in the context of the received *Laozi* read as a whole, "Non-being" is clearly synonymous with "the Nameless," and "name," as we shall see in the full discussion of the *Laozi* to follow, has a very special meaning in this context: it refers inexorably to human values. The connection between "reversal," "yielding," and this statement about emergence from nothingness further suggest that this emergence of "something" from "nothing" is one of many examples of the reversal of mutually producing opposites, and indeed, value opposites. In *Laozi* 2, in fact, also found in the Guodian fragments, "being" and "nothing" are listed among a set of value opposites that are said to be "mutually producing." In any case, it is worth noting that even this much discussion of nothingness is too much for later Confucians at least to take; Zhang Zai in the Northern Song points out, for example, that the "Great Commentary" of the *Book of Changes* constructs a parallel cosmological theory that pointedly omits any reference to "Being" and "Non-Being," the latter, in Zhang's view, being a mark of the typical error of the Daoists.

    Laozi 25, also represented in the Guodian corpus, is perhaps the other place where some readers might smell something like hardcore creation ex nihilo by a genuinely preexisting metaphysical absolute. But considered carefully, the context militates against this reading. The claim appears as part of a proto-ironic couplet:

"stands alone without changing, but flows all-around without being endangered. . . ." The structure here is like the other forked paradoxes of the Laozi tradition, such as "doing non-doing," *wei wu wei*, "practicing non-practice," "speaking non-speaking," and so on. Preexistence here is half of a paradox. "Stand" (立 *li*) is opposed to "proceed" (行 *xing*), and "alone" (獨 *du*) is opposed to "all-around" (周 *zhou*), while the two rhymed phrases are consonant in meaning: unchanging and unendangered. The claim about the "confused completeness" (混成 *huncheng*) preceding heaven and earth is expanded here with these two contrasted phrases: this preexistent confused completeness—whatever precedes clarified separation—stands and yet proceeds, is secluded in aloneness but is involved everywhere, and it is these two paradoxes that underwrite its constancy and unendangerability. Although we have a notion of preexistence in what seems a full metaphysical sense here, the required sense of real transcendence that we might expect is actually only half of a paradox: it preexists only because it is continually going away everywhere, and stands alone only because it ceaselessly finds itself involved. It is precisely a transcendental preexistence in the literal sense that is being denied here. The Dao can only act as prior by being non-prior: it guides by not guiding. We will undertake a detailed exploration of this general structure of rhetoric and thought in the discussion of the *Laozi* below.

Given what we will find about the relation between Dao and Li, we can suggest here the Li are going to be preexistent in a certain sense, but also in need of continuance in the same way, and indeed that like the Dao in these passages, they have a paradoxical or ironic preexistence, which is posited only, as it were, retrospectively. We will be seeing that the constructions of transcendent realities in both the ironic and the non-ironic traditions evade both a pure Realism—which would posit a strong, literal preexistence of universals and norms—and pure Nominalism—which would regard them as created ex nihilo by human beings.

21. On Dong Zhongshu's realism, see John Makeham, "Names, Actualities, and The Emergence of Essentialist Theories of Naming in Classical Chinese Thought," *Philosophy East & West* 41, no. 3 (July 1991): 341–63. I agree with Makeham's reading of Dong as advocating an essentialist—i.e., realist—theory of naming, which in my view is dependent on his notion of Heaven as intentional, providing a single meaning of things in advance. However, I disagree with Makeham's reading of the "Four Chapters" of the *Guanzi*, which, as I will try to show below, I see as neither essentialist nor nominalist.

22. *Mozi suoyin*, Chinese Studies, Ancient Chinese Texts Concordance Series, Chinese University of Hong Kong (Hong Kong: The Commercial Press, 1994), 10.3.83/84/6–7. See Graham, *Later Mohist Logic, Ethics and Science*, 334–36.

23. Here again I am in broad agreement with Li Chenyang, who sees the Mohist attitude not as a total departure from the harmony model, but simply as stressing the "sameness" component more heavily within it. See Li Chenyang, "The Ideal of Harmony," 90.

24. It is worth considering the coupled, more mischievous, implication: that the dominant tradition in European thought, in the wake of the problem of universals, sees even rule breaking, creativity, innovation, and harmonizing as instances

of repetition, instantiation of a universal, the iteration of a rule or law or principle or pattern.

25. Fung Yu-lan, *Selected Writings of Fung Yu-lan* (Beijing: Foreign Languages Press, 1991), 289.

26. A. C. Graham, "Kung-sun Lung's Discourse Re-read as Argument About Whole and Part," in *Studies in Chinese Philosophy and Philosophical Literature*, 193–215.

27. Bou Mo, "A Double-Reference Account: Gongsun Long's 'White-Horse-Not-Horse' Thesis," *Journal of Chinese Philosophy* 34, no. 4 (2007): 493–513.

28. Im Manyul, "Horse-parts, White-parts, and Naming: Semantics, Ontology, and Compound Terms in the White Horse Dialogue," *Dao* 6 (2007): 167–85.

29. Hansen translates, " 'White' does not fix anything as white; that may be left out of account. 'White horse' says 'white' fixes something as white. What fixes something as white is not white" (*Language and Logic*, 165). I believe this is a slight misunderstanding of the key line: what can be "left out of account" in the first sentence is "what is whited," not the white that whites it. It means that "white" per se does not specify any whited thing, and precisely because it is by definition unspecified, white cannot be what is doing the whiting of the white horse. Bou Mo renders it, "It is adequate to ignore being white when it is not fixed on any [concrete] white things" (Bou Mo, 497). But this contradicts the following line, which does not "ignore" the nonfixing white, but rather makes a determination about it, namely, that it is different from the white which specifies what is white.

30. Yiu-Ming Fung, "A Logical Perspective on 'Discourse on White-Horse,' " *Journal of Chinese Philosophy* 34, no. 4 (2007): 515–36.

31. Chung-ying Cheng, "Reinterpreting Gongsun Longzi and Critical Comments on Other Interpretations," *Journal of Chinese Philosophy* 34, no. 4 (2007): 548.

32. Qian Mu, *Hushang xiansi lu* (Taipei: Dongda tushu gongsi, 1988), 42–44.

33. Qian's own way of thinking here clearly reflects the influence of Cheng-Zhu Neo-Confucianism, along with its interpretation of the version of coherence that takes shape in the Yin-Yang theory of *Yijing* speculation (to be treated later). As such, it is most closely fitted to what we will be calling the non-ironic sense of coherence, or perhaps the non-ironic incorporation of the ironic.

34. With the identification of the terms *Li* and *Center* in Tiantai, we have the bridge to the Neo-Confucian usage of the term *Li* to denote this kind of centrality. We will return to this in our discussion of Tiantai in the companion volume and also when we briefly discuss the status of Li in Neo-Confucianism in its Conclusion.

35. See Li Chenyang's contrast to Pythagorean mathematical notions of harmony in his "The Ideal of Harmony," 92–94. The importance of this early divergence for the ensuing traditions is well formulated by Li (96) with reference to Plato: "Whereas for ancient Confucians as well as ancient Daoists harmony is 'deep harmony' without a pre-set order, Plato's harmony is to conform to a firm, pre-set, rational order imposed onto the world from outside. . . . Plato's harmony resembles Pythagorean harmony in an important way, even though they differ in other aspects. They are both conformist harmony, seeing harmony as complying with a pre-given, perfect order in the world." This is indeed the crux of the matter, precisely the point this book and its sequel are endeavoring to elucidate.

CHAPTER THREE. NON-IRONIC COHERENCE AND NEGOTIABLE CONTINUITY

1. The assertion that *ke* 可 means not "able to" but "acceptable," in a pre-moralized sense, is sometime used to attempt to avoid the full straightforward implications of this amazingly uninflected statement, making it instead a contentless tautology. But it is quite clear that *ke* cannot always mean "morally acceptable" in Mencius; indeed, in the famous "bear paw and fish" passage (6A10), the two are explicitly contrasted: "If people desire nothing more than life, then why don't they take every opportunity in which they CAN (*ke*) stay alive?" (如使人之所欲莫甚於 生，則凡可以得生者，何不用也？). The point is that sometimes a person is *able* (*ke*) to stay alive, but regards it as morally unacceptable, and chooses to die instead—and this presented explicitly in terms of "what one desires more." If *ke* means "morally acceptable," the point is completely lost.

2. See Van Norden, *Virtue Ethics and Consequentialism*, 29–64.

3. Nivison, *Ways of Confucianism*, 106–107.

4. Ibid., 274.

5. Van Norden, 6.

6. For an extensive discussion of various interpretations of this passage, see Philip J. Ivanhoe, "Which Analects? Whose Confucius," in *Confucius and the Analects: New Essays*, ed. Bryan Van Norden (Oxford: Oxford University Press, 2002).

7. Philip J. Ivanhoe, "Heaven as a Source of Ethical Warrant in Early Confucianism," *Dao: A Journal of Comparative Philosophy* 6 (2007): 212.

8. Ibid., 217, note 11.

9. Chen Derong makes a similar idea, suggesting that *tian* is initially the "palace" in which *Shangdi* resides, and even that the use of *tian* rather than *shangdi* is a sign of reverence by way of avoiding the tabooed name of the deity, much as an emperor's name was also tabooed. See Chen Derong, "Di and Tian in Ancient Chinese Thought: A Critical Analysis of Hegel's Views," *Dao: A Journal of Comparative Philosophy* 8 (2009): 13–27.

10. Behuniak, *Mencius on Becoming Human*, xxiii.

11. Ibid., 94.

12. Franklin Perkins, "Reproaching Heaven: The Problem of Evil in Mengzi," *Dao: A Journal of Comparative Philosophy* 2 (2005): 293–312. Perkins is able to make this point even while assuming that Human Nature is, for Mencius, straightforwardly good—benevolent—in a way that Heaven is not. I will argue for a similar ambiguity to that he finds in Heaven even in the case of Human Nature, as we will see below.

13. Like almost all recent discussions of the uniquely Confucian conception of ritual, the one offered here owes much to points first raised in Herbert Fingarette's groundbreaking book, *Confucius: The Secular as Sacred*, although ultimately there are obviously enormous disagreements between my understanding of Confucian ritual and Fingarette's.

14. It should be noted that with Xunzi, this conception changes decisively, and punishment is fully accepted. But the Confucius cited by Xunzi is not the Confucius of the *Analects*; in fact, not a single exact quotation attributed to Confucius by

Xunzi can be found in the *Analects*. Xunzi's Confucius not only approves of physical punishment, but himself applies the death penalty to Shao Zhengmao for purely political reasons. The veracity of this story has been doubted by Zhu Xi, Qian Mu, and many other Confucians, for it is found in no source before Xunzi and does not sit well with the antipunishment position of the *Analects*.

15. See Li Chenyang, "Li as Cultural Grammar: On the Relation Between Li and Ren in Confucius' *Analects*," *Philosophy East and West* 57, no. 3 (July 2007): 311–29. The metaphor of "social grammar" for li actually appears earlier in Hall and Ames, *Focusing the Familiar* (Honolulu: University of Hawaii Press, 2001), 70. My discussion here is closer to Li's development of this trope, stressing the ritual grammar of social behavior more than propriety as a manifested through social role divisions.

16. The referent of this line is ambiguous. It could also mean, "It is to be followed in great and small matters alike, and [therefore] there exist some things [i.e., those not prescribed by ritual] which are not to be done." My interpretation here is not conclusive, but it seems to give more pointed relevance to this remark in relation to the proclamation about harmony and ritual at the beginning of this passage, and sets up a balanced contrast with the following sentence. a structure (adumbrating "the Center" or the Mean between extremes) so often found in the *Analects*.

17. See Arthur Waley, *Analects*, 22, and Bryan Van Norden's excellent overview and supplements to the arguments for textual interpolation here, in Van Norden, *Virtue Ethics and Consequentialism in Early Chinese Philosophy*, 86–89. I am obviously strongly in agreement with Van Norden's conclusions on this point, both in terms of textual questionability and the rejection of the claim, well documented in his discussion, that "rectification of names" is to be regarded as central to an interpretation of the *Analects*.

18. Li Chenyang, 317.

19. Kwong-loi Shun, "Mencius and Jen-Hsing," *Philosophy East and West* 47 (January 1997): 3.

20. See Kim-chong Chong, "Mengzi and Gaozi on *Nei* and *Wai*," in *Mencius: Contexts and Interpretations*, ed. Alan Kam-leung Chan (Honolulu: University of Hawai'i Press, 2002), 103–24, for a detailed and rigorous examination of this issue. Chong's conclusions about the criteria for what counts as human nature, and as internal, partially overlap with my contentions in this chapter, although they obviously differ sharply in other respects (misconceiving and overstressing, in my view, the difference between the classification of types of desire in Mencius, and above all the significance of 7B24). But Chong most usefully demonstrates that the Mencius/Gaozi debate on internal and external functions as a problematizing of these concepts themselves, of what it means to be internal and external, rather than as an assertion of a definitive theory about what really is internal and what external (which Chong, however, seems to see Mencius offering elsewhere). Irene Bloom's essay in the same volume, "Biology and Culture in the Mencian View of Human Nature" (91–102), presses a parallel point somewhat closer to the view presented here, arguing that Mencius's concept of "the Nature" cannot be construed in terms of mutually exclusive categories of innate versus acquired or of nature versus nurture. I argue here that the same can be said of the parallel categories of "internal" and "external."

21. Both Graham and Van Norden offer an interesting alternate reading of *sheng* in this passage, meaning not "the innate" but "life" or "being alive," the basic condition of life per se. Graham, *Disputers*, 119; Van Norden, *Virtue Ethics and Consequentialism*, 284–87. This is also plausible, and makes good sense of what is coming in 6A4 ("food and sex"), and also of Mencius's counterargument.

22. Following the interpretation of 6A4 suggested by Nivison, *The Ways of Confucianism*, 156–57.

23. Kwong-loi Shun gives an excellent and illuminating overview of various traditional and modern attempts to interpret this passage in his *Mencius and Early Chinese Thought*, 203–207. In addition to clarifying the complexities of the issues at stake in this passage, Shun's overview demonstrates the quandaries any interpreter faces in trying to read it as straightforwardly normative or straightforwardly descriptive, highlighting the problems involved in bringing the assumption that these two categories are mutually exclusive and exhaustive, to early Chinese thought. Hence Shun's closing comment on the passage: "[I]t is quite possible that Mencius himself did not draw a clear distinction between the two dimensions of 'ming^a,' and hence did not clearly distinguish between the two lines of thought sketched in these two interpretations." The current work may be viewed as an attempt to understand the implications and presuppositions of this "not clearly distinguishing."

24. Tang Junyi, *Zhongguo zhexue yuanlun: yuanxingpian* (Taipei: Xuesheng shuju, 1989), 38–46.

25. *Mencius and Early Chinese Philosophy*, 200.

26. For a good expansion on the implications of the notion of "similarity" in Mencius's notion of *renxing*, which is indeed "similar" to the view put forward here, see Roger Ames, "The Mencian Conception of *renxing*: Does it Mean 'Human Nature'?" in *Chinese Texts and Philosophical Contexts: Essays Dedicated to Angus C. Graham*, ed. Henry Rosemont Jr. (La Salle: Open Court, 1991).

27. See the fuller discussion of this term in the analysis of the "Doctrine of the Mean" in chapter 5, below.

28. My understanding of this passage is largely consistent with that put forth by Alan K. L. Chan, "A Matter of Taste: *Qi* (Vital Energy) and the Tending of the Heart (*Xin*) in *Mencius* 2A2," in *Mencius: Contexts and Interpretations*, ed. Alan K. L. Chan (Honolulu: University of Hawai'i Press, 2002), 42–71, particularly its stress on the continuity and mutual influence between the vital energy and the mind.

29. See for example Chen Guying, *Guanzi sipian quanshi; jixia daojia daibiao zuo* (Taipei: Sanmin, 2002), 3–26. For more on the Guodian Laozi, see Ding Yuan-zhi, *Guodian zhujian Laozi shixi yu yanjiu* (Taipei: Wanjuanlou tushu youxian gongsi, 1999), and Wei Qipeng, *Chujian Laozi Jianshi* (Taipei: Wanjuanlou tushu youxian gongsi, 1999).

30. I tentatively accept the separation of these two portions, the adjudication of what sections belong to which stratum, presented by Chen Guying. See ibid., 125–58.

31. Zhang Dainian, *Zhongguo zhexue shi shiliao xue* (Beijing: Sanlian shuju, 1982), 581.

32. William Baxter has noted linguistic and rhetorical similarities between these *Guanzi* texts and the received *Laozi* (without having a chance yet to take

into account the Guodian discoveries), which further suggest a close connection between these texts. See his "Situating the Language of the *Lao-tzu*," in Kohn and LaFargue, eds., *Lao-tzu and the Tao-te-ching*, 240–43. Baxter concludes that "it is linguistically quite plausible to date the bulk of the *Lao-tzu* to the mid or early fourth century, a view that agrees with much of the traditional scholarship" (249). Harold Roth, working with Baxter's conclusions, gives an extensive argument for dating the "Neiye" at least to a time earlier than the *Laozi*, representing an earlier stratum of Daoism. See Harold Roth, *Original Dao: Inward Training (Nei-yeh) and the Foundations of Daoist Mysticism* (New York: Columbia University Press, 1999), 11–30. This is a conclusion with which I concur, if we are talking about the received *Laozi* text. My suggestion here is that the Guodian fragments of *Laozi* may be roughly contemporaneous with the "Neiye." However, I interpret this relation differently from Roth: see the following footnote. W. Allyn Rickett gives a good overview of the scholarly debate on the dating of the "Neiye," concurring with Roth that "the bulk of the material is quite early . . . probably no later than the beginning of the fourth century B.C." See W. Allyn Rickett, *Guanzi: Political, Economic, and Philosophical Essay from Early China*, vol. 2 (Boston: Cheng and Tsuim, 2001), 32–37. However, I do not think the rest of the four *Guanzi* texts can be as early: rather, with the possible exception of the first part of the "Xinshu shang," I think they are all products of the later Jixia academy, possibly from around Xunzi's time. I agree with some of Machida's objections to the earlier dating, and see the bulk of the material, as he does, as what I would call "compromise" works incorporating non-ironic materials into an ironic framework (see chapter 5). But I do not think we have to date all these materials to so late a point in time as Machida does. See Machida Saburô, "Kan Shi shi hen ni tsuite" (originally published 1961), in his *Shin Kan shisôshi no kenkyû* (Tokyo: Sôbunsha, 1985), 358–61. Specifically, the usage of terms and the approach to exposition alter noticeably among these texts; in particular, we can see the primitive use of Li still in force in the "Neiye" and first part of "Xinshu shang," but a far more elaborated concept, bleeding into the later nominal usage and attempts at systematic definitions, in the other sections. I realize that his argument, like all arguments about dating ancient texts, is to some degree circular: this usage cannot be that early, because this usage cannot be that early. All such speculations must be taken with a grain of salt. But it will perhaps enable us to organize this material effectively for the moment.

33. See A. C. Graham, *Disputers of the Tao* (LaSalle: Open Court, 1989), 95–106. Roth, on the other hand, takes the Confucian-friendly passage as a later interpolation that is inconsistent with the overall program of the text. His argument from linguistic usage is worth considering, but inconclusive, and the bulk of his argument is derived from "philosophical reasons," which beg the question, for Roth assumes that a sharp differentiation between "Confucian" and "Daoist" orientations was in place from the beginning. See Roth, op. cit., 30–31.

34. The fragment of chapter 5, for example, lacks the first two lines ("Heaven and Earth are not Benevolent; they treat the ten thousand things as straw dogs. The sage is not Benevolent; he treats the people as straw dogs") of the received version. Chapter 19 calls for the destruction and discarding of "skill" and "profit" (巧利 *qiao*, *li*), where the received version calls for the destruction and discarding of "Benevo-

lence" and "Rightness" (仁義 *ren*,*yi*). Chapter 18 does include the claim that the Confucian virtues emerged only after the Great Course fell into disuse, which in the received text forms one of many angles from which these virtues are attacked. But like the Mawangdui texts, the Guodian version of 18 has the additional character 安 *an*, in this sentence (hence, 大道廢安有仁義 *dadaofei anyourenyi*, and so on), which might be read as a loan for 焉 *yan*, thereby meaning "in this"—i.e., due to this, due to the disuse of the Great Course—benevolence and rightness arise, which would be consistent with the received text. It is more natural, however, to read the *an* as a question word, thereby yielding the meaning, "If the Great Dao fell into disuse, how could there be any such thing as benevolence and rightness?" This would be consistent with the *Guanzi* texts, which seem to suggest that true benevolence and rightness are natural and even inevitable results of practice of the Great Dao, and can only exist on that basis. But even the statement that "the Confucian virtues arise when the Great Dao disappears" is structurally quite different from the call to discard these virtues, and is compatible with a quite different philosophical position.

35. Reading *yi* for *yin*, as suggested by Wang Niansun, and adopted by Chen Guying. See Chen, 95.

36. Hong Ye, et al., editors, *Zhuzi jicheng* (henceforth ZZJC), vol. 5, 269. My emphasis. Compare "Techniques, Part One": "The Great Dao can be dwelt in securely, but cannot be spoken of (大道可安而不可說)."

37. ZZJC, vol. 5, 270.

38. These are the verses rejected by Roth as later interpolations, and indeed they are reminiscent of many of the compromise texts we will be considering below. For the sake of argument, however, I want to try to make sense of them from within the position of the rest of the "Neiye."

39. We may note in this context a telling passage in the "Shuyan" chapter of the *Guanzi*. The text in one place states "What has qi lives, what lacks qi dies." A bit later it says: "If attained one necessarily lives, if lost one necessarily dies: what is it? It is only Nothingness (惟無 *wei wu*)." This suggests the same interchangeability between Dao and qi that we have seen in the "Four Chapters." Moreover, as Guo Moruo points out, the two characters are quite close in their ancient form. Although 氣 and 無 no longer display any morphological similarity, in ancient texts the two characters were often written as 炁 and 无 respectively.

CHAPTER FOUR. IRONIC COHERENCE AND THE DISCOVERY OF THE YIN

1. It is primarily in order to maintain the strong presence of "non" as a separable and cross-referencing unit that I will translate 無 *wu* as "non-being" in this chapter, in spite of all the excellent objections that have been made concerning how misleading this translation is, with which I generally agree. The term means simply "not having," or at best "absence."

2. One is tempted to speculate that this is post–Zhuang Zhou Daoism, i.e., that ironic Daoism is a Zhuangzian invention and that the present version of the Laozi represents a post-Zhuangzian restructuring of older, pre-ironic Daoism in a way consistent with Zhuangzian irony.

3. This application of Yin-Yang language is of course in close consonance with Hall and Ames's remark that Yin and Yang are "no more than a convenient way or organizing 'thises' and 'that's" (*Thinking from the Han*, 190, cited already in chapter 2), and its application to Laozi is in close harmony with Graham's discussion (see especially *Disputers*, 223), and Van Norden's reading of Laozi as endorsing an embrace of the Yin (see "Method in the Madness of the *Laozi*," in Csikszentmihaly and Ivanhoe, eds., *Religious and Philosophical Aspects*, especially 198–200 and 210, note 38.

4. Hall and Ames, *Thinking from the Han* (Albany: State University of New York Press, 1998), 75–76.

5. See Bai Tongdong, "An Ontological Interpretation of *You* (Something) and *Wu* (Nothing) in the *Laozi*," *Journal of Chinese Philosophy* 35, no. 2 (2008): 339–51. Isabelle Robinet makes a similar point in her "The Diverse Interpretations of the Laozi," in Csikszentmihalyi and Ivanhoe, op. cit., 138–40.

6. Robinet gives a particularly fine elaboration of the double meaning of "the One" in the text (ibid., 137–38).

7. Tang Junyi, *Zhongguo zhexue yuanlun: Daolunpian* (Taipei: Taiwan xuesheng shuju, 1986), 368–81.

8. I parse the first three characters as a full sentence, in accordance with the 也 *ye* particle in the Mawangdui versions. I use "course" for Dao because it combines both a prescriptive and a descriptive sense well, as well as connecting with "discourse" as dao connects with speech. A course can also be a program of study, as can a dao. "Guiding course" is a fuller translation used to bring out all these senses.

9. The term *name* is enormously complex in this text. It involves all the senses lurking in the term in early Chinese thought. These include: the normative description of a position or role (as in 正名 *zheng ming*, 型名 *xing ming*), fame and reputation, what is evident to the community (how one affects one's community), and what is divided out from the whole by cutting it in certain ways. It should be noted that, like Dao, it is already a normative term in usual parlance, which however is beginning to get a new, less explicitly normative sense, an ambiguity with which *Laozi* plays. I will discuss this in some detail below.

10. Or perhaps, in accordance with an interpretation to be suggested below, this could be read: "Its fame can be made eminent, but in that case it will not be enduring fame." Or, more to the point: "Its value can be valued, but then it will not be enduring value," which I believe is the real import of this line.

11. Chapter 52 indicates strongly that "the beginning" and "the mother" are two ways of referring to the same thing: "The world has a beginning, which can be treated as the mother of the world." This "treated as" (以為 *wei*), also found in Chapter 25 concerning the term *mother*, suggests that this is a figurative way of referring to the unnamed beginning, a convenient way of taking it as an object and taking the appropriate attitude toward it, which involves some kind of decision on the part of the one who refers to it in this way. Hence, "it can be referred to, if you wish, as the mother. . . ."

12. Here again I punctuate with the Mawangdui texts, taking this to be a deliberately paradoxical recommendation to be both at all times; indeed, as we shall

see below in discussing "desires" and "purposive action" in this text, this is another way of saying "Do nothing but fail to do nothing." The term *have no desires* appears again in chapter 34 (although Gao Heng, for example, suggests it be amended), and recommendations based on the premise of having desires appear throughout the text, most explicitly and notoriously perhaps in 36 (If you want [欲 *yu*] to shrink something, first expand it . . .).

13. I interpret *miao* and *jiao* as a parallel and contrasting dyad. Their basic meaning is "hard to see" and "easy to see." The character *miao* as we have it in the Wang Bi version, with the woman radical, did not exist before the Han, and does not appear in the *Shuowen*. The Mawangdui texts have the eye radical (眇), meaning small and hard to discern. The radical on *jiao* is inconsistent among the received texts (the Mawangdui texts have the interesting combination, 所嗷 *sojiao*, which could mean something such as, "what is cried for," which it is tempting to take as a reference to the "Mother" of the previous line; but I have opted for the interpretation offered here instead). I assume that the early versions had no radical (probably for either character), in which case this *jiao* would be identical to the one appearing in chapter 14, 皦 meaning "bright," even "dazzlingly brilliant," or in this context, fully evident. This is not far from Wang Bi's interpretation, which relates them to hard to see beginnings and manifest outcomes, in accord, one feels, with his interest in the *Book of Changes*, but not inconsistently with the temporal sense of development of chapters 63 and 64, and the character *jiao* used in Wang's text, meaning that toward which things tend. More on the relation of smallness, beginning, invisibility, and desire below.

14. Here again I adopt the Mawangdui reading: 異名同謂 *yiming tongwei*.

15. See Hansen, *Daoist Theory*, passim.

16. *Wenzi*, "Daoyuan," juan 1 (Taipei: Zhonghua shuju, 1978), 7.

17. *Zhuangzi yinde* (In *Zhuzi yinde; Laozi, Zhuangzi* [Taipei: Zongqing tushu chuban gongsi, 1986]; the citations correspond to those in the Harvard-Yenching concordances; numbers given for all subsequent Zhuangzi quotations will refer to this source) 2/1/21–22. This is to be contrasted to the use of the term as it develops in later syncretic works, for example, the *Yinwenzi*, where we find the following characterization: "There are three levels of meaning to the word 'name' (*ming*). . . . First, the description of objects, such as square, round, black or white. Second, the names used in blame and praise, such as good, evil, noble and base. Third, comparative designations (*kuangwei*), such as wise and stupid, love and hate" (*Yinwenzi; Guanyinzi* [Taipei: Zhonghua shuju, 1979], 2). I am not at all certain what this passage means, but it is clear that more concentrated and nuanced thought on the meaning of names has taken place here, and aspects of meaning formerly far in the background have been brought into the foreground.

18. It should be noted that, as in the case of the notion of *wuwei*, there is a Confucian provenance, or at least precedent, for this overcoming of Confucian ideals, e.g., *Analects* 8:19, where Confucius says of Yao's virtue that it was "so vast that the people could give no name to it." Perhaps this belongs to a time in the history of Confucianism before the adoption of the originally Mohist notion of "Exalting the worthy," as a source of emulation; it can equally be read as a seed of self-overcoming at the upper crust of Confucianism, a final twist providing nuance to what came

before. Again, the relation between the purposive action of the aspirant-sage and the effortless action of the sage provides a good model for this relationship.

19. To have a name is to become well known, esteemed, a model, to show off a hard-to-get thing—which excites others to emulate one, to wish to occupy the same place, to contend, to become thieves (ch. 3: "Don't display the desirable and you will keep the people's hearts from disorder"); thus, it is crucial to have no name (fame) in order to maintain one's name (i.e., the accomplishment for which one deserved fame in the first place, the achievement of the good governance of the people, or the maintenance of their constancy and life free from the impetus for mutual extermination.) If one got credit for achieving this constant governance and nurturance, the achievement of the same would soon be undone, for this name/credit would inspire the people to emulate oneself, to struggle to become equally eminent and in possession of hard-to-get goods; then one would have no achievement after all, as the state would be in chaos. This is a paradigm for the way in which having no name allows one to keep one's good name. Thus, the Course both has a "name" and is "nameless"—and its "name" (fame, merit, achievement) is eternal and great for this very reason.

20. It is worth noting that, if this is the primary meaning of "named" and "nameless" here, it is really not so far from simply "existent and nonexistent." The *Wenzi* quote already drew a connection between this pair and the pair "Formed and formless." When something is not yet formed, just an incipient process, it has no name *yet*; once it reaches completion, it is given a name. The unhewn wood is nameless for this reason; it is *not yet* a utensil to be used in a social setting, it has as yet no social value. But consider the definition of *you* and *wu* implicit, for example, in the following passage, from a late chapter of the *Zhuangzi*: "Viewing the question from the point of view of merit (*gong*), if we call something 'existent' because it has it, there is nothing that is not existent; if we call something 'non-existent' because it lacks it, there is nothing that is not non-existent. When one knows that (the two are like) east and west (which) are opposites that cannot lack one another, the limits of merit are fixed" (*Zhuangzi* 43/17/31–33). *Gong*—merit or causal effectivity, i.e., the state of having an effect on other things—is here equated with being. To be is to have an effect. Not to be is to have no effect. Thus, since anything named has some effect—even if it is an imaginary entity, one supposes the argument would run, it is playing a role in this conversation—it is to that extent existent, while to the extent that it lacks merit or effect on its "fellows" it lacks being. In this sense, then, it would seem that there may not be so great a difference between "The nameless" and "non-being"—and indeed, we shall see throughout the text that these are used almost interchangeably. "Being" and "being named" and "having value" are, in other words, more or less convertible terms in this text. And it is here that the derivation of the name "Namelessness" as a designation for the Dao and the One, given in *Laozi* 14, fits into the picture.

21. The causal relation between these two assertions (know X *by* holding to anti-X) is suggested by ch. 52: "Having known the mother, use it to know the sons; having known the sons, return and hold fast (守 *shou*) to the Mother." The two verbs *to know* and *to hold to* are identical in these two passages, and the relation between the symbolic poles seems to be the same as well. Hence, we may assume that in

this passage as well, knowing the masculine *enables* one to hold to the feminine, and conversely that holding to the feminine *enables* one to know the masculine. They are mutually reinforcing.

22. The apparently incongruous parallel of "model" with ravine and valley here, together with the fact that the Tianxia chapter of the *Zhuangzi* lacks this line (reading, instead, "Know the bright/honored, hold to the disgraced. . . ." and omitting the lines in between) has led some to conclude that this passage is a late interpolation. See Yi Shunding's note quoted in Zhang Yangming, *Laozi jiaozheng yishi* (Taipei: Weixin shuju, 1973), 149. However, against this view, besides the fact that the Mawangdui texts have this whole passage, and in another order, so that the *Zhuangzi* text could not be restored simply by removing a chunk in the middle anymore, we must note that "model" in fact forms a perfect parallel with "ravine" and "valley" *if we keep in mind the magnetic center paradigm*. A model is held up and seen by all, and they are spontaneously attracted to it, move toward it. This is exactly the function of the ravine and the valley in the *Laozi*: all things move toward it spontaneously. The difference is that the valley and ravine are low and unseen, while the model is "elevated" and displayed. Laozi's magnetic center is invisible, but both images underscore the paradoxical nature of the master that is no master.

23. The Mawangdui versions of the second (Wang Bi) chapter provide further insight into the meaning of sustainability as entailing the joining of value opposites: "The mutual production of being and nonbeing, the mutual completion of difficult and easy, the mutual formation of long and short, the mutual filling of high and low, the mutual harmony of tone and voice, the mutual following of front and back—**these are all sustainables**" (Henricks translation, from Robert G. Henricks, *Lao-tzu Te-Dao Ching* (New York: Ballantine Books, 1989], 190. The words in boldface are lacking in the standard edition of the text. I should note to that I take all these pairs to be value laden, and not merely descriptive opposites. The first term in each pair is always the more positively valued. This is obvious in all cases except the difficult *yin/sheng* pair, but Scott Cook's researches into the use of these terms in classical musical theory, especially in the "Yueji" chapter of the *Liji*, point to a valuation of *yin* over *sheng*. See Cook, "Yue Ji: Introduction, Translation, Notes, and Commentary," *Asian Music* XXVI, no. 2 (Spring/Summer 1995): 19–24.

24. Graham, *Disputers*, 223.

25. E.g., "Work on it when it is not yet existent, order it before it is disordered. A tree the size of one's embrace begins as a minute sprout. A nine-story tower begins with a heap of mud. A journey of a thousand miles begins under one's feet. . . . Thus the sage desires to be without desires, and does not value hard-to-attain goods" (64).

26. E.g., "Disaster is what good fortune leans on. Good fortune is what disaster hides in. Who knows the ultimate point [of this reversal—again, we see here the failure to obtain an final answer, the mystery]. Neither side is the proper side, for any proper side reverts immediately to its opposite, the anomalous, and good reverts to monstrosity" (58).

27. Here we see the social analogy again, and indeed the point of contact between *Laozi* and Confucius that we might perhaps regard as the starting point of the former's doctrine, taken from the latter and built upon, via a clever *bon mot*, to form a new system of thought. All "things," as we saw in the discussion of Confucian-

ism, return to the sage ruler, who "does nothing" (*Analects*, 15:4). They are inspired by him, and therefore come flocking to him. The Great Course also does nothing. And, in another sense, as discussed earlier, all things "return" to it. "Take emptiness to its furthest reaches, hold deeply to stillness. All things arise together, and I use this to watch their return. However manifold the things are in their flourishing, each returns to its root. This returning to the root is what I called 'stillness.' This is called return to the fated, which is [all that can be] called 'sustainability.' To know this sustainability is called discernment, and not to know it is to invite disaster. To know it is to be accepting, and thus to be all-embracing, kingly, heaven-like, to follow the course, and thus to long endure. This is to be unendangered even at the end of one's physical life" (16).

28. Philip J. Ivanhoe, "The Concept of *de* ("Virtue") in the *Laozi*," in Csik-szentmihalyi and Ivanhoe, op. cit., 242.

29. "When we look and cannot see, we nonetheless give it [this experience] a name: slight. When we listen and cannot hear, we nonetheless give it a name: faint. When we grasp but cannot get a hold, we nonetheless give it a name: minute. These three cannot be further determined, and so they are combined into a single concept, a unity. The top side of [this one] is not bright, the bottom side is not dark. Seeking and searching, we still cannot name it, and so return to no thing. This is called the formless form, the thingless image. This is called vague and indistinct (荒忽 *huanghu*)."

    This passage is crucial in explaining the connections between Non-being and Oneness, between the two prongs of the name and the namelessness of the Dao. A dao, in general, is a course of study, standards, lore, and practices to be followed in order to create value. In general, value emerges from valuelessness by means of a dao, a course of endeavor. It is in this sense especially that a dao is a creator, a beginning of existent (named, known, *valued*) things. The text seems to be quoting (in suitably archaic diction) a revered platitude applicable to any dao in 21: "The aspect of great virtue (i.e., virtuosity, mastery of that dao) is to follow a dao and only that dao." But if we seek the course by which anything emerges, the begin-ning of any (valued) thing, or the end (where the course is aiming to go), or the consistent rule that applies to them (the dao as a way and a rule), or their ultimate value—if we *desire*, that is, to get to the bottom of any given event in any of these senses—we come at last to a point where it is too faint to trace, where we come to nothing, to the limits of our senses, where we lose the valued and the named in the nameless valuelessness from which it emerged and to which it eventually returns. Hence, the text continues, in 21, to point out where a paradox comes into this injunction to follow the dao and only the dao: "But the Dao is precisely the kind of thing which is vague and indistinct [and hence impossible to follow]. How vague! How indistinct! And yet precisely in this vagueness there is an image [i.e., something to follow and emulate, a name]. . . ." The search in this sense has failed, has yielded nothing. But nonetheless, we have experienced this failure, and *we give it a name*: faint, vague and indistinct (*huanghu*), dark, mysterious, "nameless," formless form, thingless image, etc. All these terms are names for the failure to find a name, for the failure to find the source of value, which may alternately be described as a finding of the source and origin of value in the state of valuelessness. In tracing the emergence of value backward, we come to a place where it is no longer graspable as value, where it is no value at all. These names (vague, dark, slight, formless, etc.) are the determinations that inevitably come from finding no determinations, answers that are no answers. But since names are values, these names for the nameless are the values of the valueless.

30. "Those who attained the One: Heaven attained the One so as to be limpid, earth attained the One so as to be settled, the spirits attained the One so as to become efficacious, the valley attained the One so as to be full, all things attained the one so as to live, lords and kings attained the One so as to be the enduring standard of the empire. . . . If Heaven lacked that by which it is limpid, it would be in danger of splitting. If Earth lacked that by which it is settled, it would be in danger of caving in. If the spirits lacked that by which they are efficacious, they would be in danger of being exhausted. If the valley lacked that by which it is full, it would be in danger of running dry. If things lost that by which they live, they would be in danger of being extinguished. If lords and kings lacked that by which they are an enduring standard, they would be in danger of falling. *Thus the valued takes the devalued as its root, the exalted takes the lowly as its base. . . .*" (39). Oneness is here construed not merely or even primarily as unity, but more crucially as lowliness.

31. The two most powerful attempts to classify the strains of thought in the text are surely those of Angus Graham, op. cit., and Liu Xiaogan, in his *Classifying the Zhuangzi Chapters*. These two scholars agree that most of the traditional "Outer" and "Miscellaneous" Chapters are not the work of Zhuang Zhou. They differ in that Liu considers them all the work of actual followers of Zhuang Zhou, and in the way they divide the remaining chapters according to philological, stylistic, and philosophical characteristics. Liu divides the remaining chapters into three distinct groups: the "Transmitters," the "Huang-Lao School," and the "Anarchists." Liu holds that the work of the "Transmitters" most closely resembles that of the "Inner Chapters" of Zhuang Zhou, and come closest to him in time. Liu considers this group responsible for chapters 17–27 and 32. The "Huang-Lao School," who synthesize Confucian, Daoist, and Legalist ideas, are responsible for chapters 12–16, 33, and the latter part of 11. The work of the "Anarchists" can be found in chapters 8–10, 28–29, 31, and the first part of 11. Graham's categories are the "School of Zhuangzi," the "Syncretists," the "Primitivists," and the "Yangists." Within the "School of Zhuangzi" writings, closely comparable to Liu's "Transmitter School," to which Graham attributes chapters 17–22, he further distinguishes a "Rationalizing" and an "Irrationalizing" strain, and in both cases considers a significant philosophical departure from Zhuang Zhou to have occurred here, a position I share, as will become apparent below. Liu, on the contrary, seems to approve of the traditional consensus that, for example, the Qiushui (Autumn Floods) chapter is a faithful systematic exposition of the ideas of the Inner Chapters, a view which I reject (see Liu, 98–99). Graham's "Syncretists" are represented by chapters 12–14, the end of 11, 15, and 33, corresponding approximately to Liu's category of Huang-Lao. Graham's "Primitivists" are represented by chapters 8–10 and the beginning of 11, and his "Yangists," which he considers non-Daoist, are represented by chapters 28–31; these two categories together correspond to Liu's category of "Anarchists."

32. The rhetorical framing of this chapter suggests the hypothesis that the Inner Chapters were perhaps written by Zhuang Zhou as a response to his archfoil and archfriend, the logician Huizi (Hui Shi), perhaps intended for the latter's eyes in particular, almost as a private joke. We are told, after all, that Zhuangzi considered Huizi the only one who really understood his words, the one for whom alone he spoke or wrote. (67/24/50–51). The chapter begins with a vast fish that transforms into a vast bird and is then ridiculed for his high flying by smaller birds gazing up at him from the ground. It ends with two dialogues between Zhuangzi and Huizi, which closely parallel the structure of the relationship between Peng and the little birds. Another story of a confrontation between Zhuangzi and Huizi (45/17/84–87) supports the view that the large-and-small-bird trope symbolizes Zhuangzi's view of their relationship. There, Zhuangzi, after hearing that Huizi believes him to be after his official position, tells the story of a tiny creature who screeches at a vast one uncomprehendingly. The rhetorical trope there ("In the southern region there is a bird, and its name is. . . ." and so on) closely parallels the opening tale of Peng and the little birds, with Huizi compared to the latter and Zhuangzi himself to the former.

33. ZZJS (1/1/17).

34. "I have lost me" introduces an asymmetrical doubleness that reminds us of the *Laozi*. For it implies both that I am still here and that I am gone, I am absent and present, both at once: "I" lost "me" (吾喪我 *wu sang wo*), I am both that which loses (the one who is left behind after the loss), and that which is lost. The ambiguity of identity is encoded into the grammatical difference of the two words used for "self" here: unlike *wu*, *wo* can be paired as a dyad with *bi*, signifying the contrastive self, the self as opposed to others, or ourselves, my party, as opposed to other parties. It is my self as taking a definite position among and against other positions, or as having certain characteristics among or against other characteristics. It is the defined, the definite self that is lost. This both/and equivocation on the question of the existence of the self (the "true lord," the "one who blows the breath," etc.) is a central theme running through the chapter. Zhuangzi generally ends his discussions with a double-pronged question: "Is there really X? Or is there really no X?" In my view, this is meant to imply neither that there is X (e.g., a true ruler) nor that there is not, but simply to come to rest precisely at the uncertainty and the question itself (leaving the ultimate self-consistent level out of the discourse altogether and resting content in the paradox). That in itself is his conclusion, that balanced teetering of yes and no.

35. 3/2/8–9.

36. Hence the peculiar punning double characterization of the harmony: 而獨不見之調調、之刁刁乎 *erdubujianzhidiaodiao,zhidiaodiao*. The first reduplicated *diao* means "harmony" or "mutual adjustment," while the latter reduplicated *diao* means "deceitful and cunning." This coherence is both harmonious and deceitful, in harmony and in chaos, and moreover, as suggested by the homophony, its harmony is its chaos and its chaos is its harmony. We see the same idea often in the Inner Chapters, perhaps most pithily in the formulation 攖寧 *yingning*, "tranquil turmoil," in chapter 6.

37. 4/2/13.

38. 4/2/14–15. *Qu* here echoes the "*xian qi zi qu*" 咸其自取 of a few lines back, referring again to the wind sounds. The relation between the self and the passing moods is thus likened to that between the wind and the sounds from the various holes; to "pick themselves out" is perhaps a way of indicating the interdependence indicated by the citation to which this is a note. I pick them out, but the I who picks them out (distinguishes them, individuates them) is nothing but them, the passing moods, the sounds from the holes. Hence, this line could perhaps also be translated, "Without them there is no me, without me they have nothing to pick themselves out from"—i.e., nothing from which they are distinguished, nothing to which they are related or the parts of which they are—but this sounds confusing in English.

39. 16/6/29.

40. As should be clear from the above, I regard this statement not as indicating that the "true self" has lost the "false self," but rather that the self, the ruler, is simultaneously present and absent, is indeterminable as either definitively present or definitively absent; this situation itself describes both the so-called false self and the so-called true self.

41. 4/2/15.

42. 4/2/23–24.

43. 4/2/23–24.

44. 4/2/26–27. My interpretation of the infamous *yiming* is, I realize, rather unusual. I take *ming* to mean, not "illumination" or "enlightenment" or anything like that, all of which seem to me vague and useless readings that moreover have Zhuangzi suddenly begging the question in a weirdly emphatic way, but rather simply, "what is evident, clear, obvious." I hope the justification for this reading, and why I view it as superior to the other, will emerge in the following pages.

45. 5/2/47.

46. 4/2/33–34.

47. See Chenyang Li, "Chapter 1 Being: Perspective Versus Substance," in *The Tao Encounters the West: Explorations in Comparative Philosophy* (Albany: State University of New York Press, 1999), 11–33 for a detailed discussion of Zhuangzi's thought as a thoroughgoing metaphysic of perspective, compared to Aristotle's metaphysic of substance. Li's approach to Zhuangzi has much in common with my take here, although there is perhaps some danger of "stacking the deck" in choosing a comparison of precisely Zhuangzi and precisely Aristotle as counterparts who are in a similar sense representative of their respective ontological traditions.

48. I read this line as implicitly taking the "this" from the previous sentence as its subject. Another possibility is that, following Chen Guying, who cites Yen Lingfeng and Chen Qitian, the first *zhi* may be replaced with 是 *shi*, resulting in: "what appears from one's own perspective of this-ness alone is known to one." See Chen Guying, *Zhuangzi jinzhu jinyi* (Taipei: Shangwu yinshuguan, 1989), 61–62.

49. 4/2/28–29. My construal of a jump in levels is based not only on the Huizi quote (see ch. 33, 93/33/71–72), but also on the *suiran*, "However," which otherwise seems quite superfluous.

50. 7/2/90–91.

51. 4/2/31.

52. 4/2/27–31. Since the Chinese language lacks plural and singular forms, this translation is controversial.

53. 5/2/37, 16/6/19–20.

54. 12/5/6–7.

55. 16/6/19–20.

56. 6/2/64–65.

57. 4/2/15.

58. 3/2/9.

59. 4/2/31.

60. 5/2/38–40.

61. 5/2/40.

62. 21/7/32–33.

63. 9/4/27–28.

64. "Before I heard this, I was Hui, but now that I've heard it, I have never begun to be Hui, can this be called emptiness?" Confucius answers, "You've got it!" 9/4/28–29.

65. As Zhuangzi is quoted as saying, strikingly, in a later chapter, "Without praise or blame, now a dragon, now a snake, changing together with the seasons and unwilling to be or do any one thing exclusively, now above, now below, taking harmony as the measure, floating along in the ancestor of all things, taking things as things without being taken as a thing by things. . . ." (51/20/6–7).

66. 6/2/64–66, 15/6/3–4.

67. 5/2/39–40. I take Graham's reading of *tianjun* 天鈞. See his *Chuang-tzu,* 54: " . . . stays at the point of rest on the potter's wheel of Heaven." I translate in a way that preserves both the sense of equalizing and the concrete image of the potter's wheel, to which I attach great importance.

68. Following Guo Songtao, as cited in Chen Guying, op. cit., 795.

69. 75/27/9–10.

70. Qian Mu quotes Cao Shoukun as follows: "Huainanzi's 'Yuan dao' says, 'The potter's wheel turns in circles, makes a full revolution and then starts again. . . . This corresponds with the sense of turning in circles. 'To travel two roads' indicates that no matter how it rotates, to the right or to the left, it always returns to the one [central] point" (Qian Mu, *Zhuangzi zuanqian* [Taipei: Dongda tushu gongsi, 1986], 15). Elsewhere, Qian Mu has this to say about the Zhuangzi's heavenly potter's wheel and omnicentrism: "All phenomena in the world are spinning around, in constant motion, and all depend on having a center. But all things in the world are one center. Not understanding this, we want to make ourselves the center. [Thus far Qian is speaking unicentrically, but he continues:] One's self is indeed a center, but we ought not to annul all the other centers by only acknowledging this one center. By the same token, we ought not to annul the center that is our self just because of the presence of the many other centers. This is what Zhuangzi calls 'walking two.' Two means self and other. Walking two doesn't mean two forming opposites, which leads to contradiction and conflict. Rather, the two refer to a center and a periphery, which can rotate unimpededly. Each thing in the world is a center and each has a periphery, and all can rotate unimpededly. . . ." (Qian Mu, *Zhongguo sixiang shi* [Taipei: Xuesheng shuju, 1985], 42–43.)

71. 6/4/31–32.

72. 5/2/60–61. It is noteworthy that Zhuangzi thus arrives at this last Laozian slogan from a starting point in a value theory that is in a certain sense the precise opposite of Laozi's. That is, while Laozi (and Xunzi) assume that what one posits as value (*shi*'s) is a marker of the opposite of what one oneself actually is, of one's present position, Zhuangzi assumes the opposite: this, what you are (*shi*), is what you assert as right and good (*shi*). For Laozi, you *shi* only what you are not (*fei*) (e.g., the country is in chaos, so we value good order and loyal ministers, etc.), and moreover, what gets *shi*-ed *thereby* ceases to be *shi* (to deliberately value something undermines its efficacy as a value, for reasons I elaborated in the previous chapter). Laozi's practical paradoxes of value proceed from this assumption; *shi* and *fei* are bound together from the beginning since any *shi* arises out of its corresponding *fei*, as being arises out of non-being. For Zhuangzi, on the contrary, you affirm only what you are; value is assumed to be intrinsic to position and wholly perspective-dependent. Note also that for Zhuangzi value is primary and anti-value as it were a secondary, though simultaneous and necessary, correlate, whereas for Laozi anti-value has both temporal and ontic priority. Moreover, Laozi would seem to have a more stable vision of second-order value in view (constancy, stability, continuance), whereas Zhuangzi has brought the very question of a value perspective per se into question, and develops a theory that is applicable in principle to any imaginable system of values. However, these two positions converge in a most interesting way. For Zhuangzi, value and anti-value get bound together because the existence of any position implies the positing of its antithesis as an outer circumference of otherness and opposition, and this other point in turn regards the first point as other. Each is first a value to itself and an anti-value to the other, and anti-value gets included in value by means of the mutual inclusion of perspectives, most strikingly manifest in the transformation of perspectives experienced moment after moment (as emotions, for example). Laozi's paradox of desire is lacking here: for Zhuangzi, they do not desire what they are not, but rather simply affirm what they are; their anti-value becomes identical to themselves only via the mediation of the Other who is also a self-affirming other-negating self, by a kind of double mirroring effect; if two moments confront each other, trying to adjudicate which one is real, they find that they are standing in the same spot, they are both *shi*. And yet, as the text says of Zhuang Zhou and the butterfly, "there must be some distinction between them." This "some" distinction is precisely analogous to the "Who?" discussed earlier; it deliberately stops short of saying precisely *what* the distinction might be; it does not want to claim that we can really tell which is which, but only that they each contain the moment of noticing that there is another perspective negating them, contending for the throne of identity—this is all that matters, the contention itself. So it is enough simply for there to be "some" distinction. The distinction is not eliminated, leaving us with a Brahman-esque undetermined Oneness, but is, rather, simply included from *whichever* perspective one happens to be standing in at the moment, and one is always standing in some particular perspective or other. The intersubjective element is thus much more central in the Zhuangzian account, with its background of contending debaters. But in both cases we wind up with the view that the true value is a value that is also anti-value. In Zhuangzi's case, this is a general principle

applicable to any value position equally: to negate and reject is an act of intimacy, to disvalue something is an act in our economy of valuation. The interpenetration of value and anti-value provides constant access to value, in an infinity of guises, surrounded by a temporarily assumed anti-value that is no longer an opposite, but rather another guise of value, an empty space into which one may move tomorrow. In other words, only value that is not "a given value to the eternal exclusion of its corresponding anti-value (where one positive content or dao is preferred to any other)" is true Value. In Laozi, value roots itself in anti-value, organizes itself around anti-value, returns to it, so as to maintain itself; a prescription is offered for a stable alloy of the two, where any posited desideratum acts as a goad to desire and thus undermines value. In other words, only value that is hidden in, rooted in, oriented toward anti-value is true Value. Both thinkers can thus say, "The true Dao cannot be posited as a dao (a system of value, a perspective, etc.); whatever daos are posited as objects of knowledge are not the Dao."

73. 5/2/47–51.

74. We may note here an important ambiguity in the concept of *lei*, and the notion of "feeling and response" (感應 *ganying*) that goes with it: do things cohere because they are of the same type, or because they are of a balanced pair of opposite types, leading to "harmonious" coherence? Xunzi, introducing the notion of *ganying*, opted for the former answer, which is characteristic of the classical "non-ironic" notion of coherence. We find the same point made, and identified directly with non-ironic "heavenly coherence," in the late "Yufu" ("The Old Fisherman") chapter of the *Zhuangzi*: "Things of the same type follow one another, sounds of the same tone respond to one another—this is fixedly Heaven's coherence" (同類相從, 同聲相應, 固天之理也 *tonglei xiangcong, tongsheng xiangying, gu tian zhi li ye*) (86/31/12). The *Guoyu* passage, however, in stressing "harmony" over sameness, seems to stress a particular type of difference which however forms a larger coherence, a second-level *lei*, in forming harmonies, and the Yin-Yang tradition, as we shall see, takes a similar approach, nesting levels of sameness and difference on the model of sexual response within a species—what coheres harmoniously is what is the same but different in a particular way. In a story about Zhuangzi in a later chapter of the *Zhuangzi*, however, we find a crucial application of the "ironic" scrambling of the notion of *lei* we have just cited from the *Qiwulun*. Graham has cited this passage as perhaps telling of Zhuang Zhou's "conversion" from Yangism to Daoism. After observing a number of creatures of different species, each of which exposes itself to danger by forgetting itself in the pursuit of some perceived profit, and further noting that his fascination with them was another meta-example of the same foolish behavior, Zhuang Zhou exclaims, "Alas! Things truly fetter one another; for different (literally, two) types call one another forth (物固相累 二類相召也 *wu gu xiang lei, er lei xiang zhao ye*)" (54/20/64). Feeling and response happens across "types" (*lei*) here. This may be read as an insight into the impossibility of fixing the limits of things in a single type, once coherence is seen to include both harmony and contextualizing contrast, or even mutual harm. As soon as beings start looking outside themselves for benefit, giving free rein to their "eye desires," there is no way of limiting what will affect what, and what properly belongs to what *lei*. In fact, in spite of the superficial declaration

of the existence of "different kinds" here, this story is profoundly consistent with the Inner Chapters position that there are no uniquely privileged natural kinds.

75. 15/6/3–4.

76. See note 35, above.

77. 5/2/37.

78. 德不形者,物不能離。14/5/47.

79. 支離其德者。12/4/86.

80. 以其知得其心,以其心得其常心。13/5/9.

81. 15/6/1–4.

82. 15/2/3–4.

83. See for example Zhuangzi's claim that "Great Benevolence is not benevolent" and so on in chapter 2, where Zhuangzi claims the Confucian virtues by denying their Confucian forms. Cf. also the discussion on filial piety in chapter 14.

84. In my opinion, the epistemological quandary posed here does not receive a fully satisfactory solution until the advent of Tiantai Buddhist theory, which extends to their utmost some of Zhuangzi's points on knowing, identity, and the relativism/absolutism interchange.

85. A third criterion for absolute knowledge might be suggested, especially pronounced in, say, modern scientific method: it should be able to predict what will happen in the future accurately. Can Zhuangzi's perspective do this? The answer is no. But his emphasis on transformation and perspective suggests a skepticism about the possibility of this type of knowledge from any perspective whatsoever: none can survive the transformation not of phenomena, but of perspectives on phenomena. The confirmation of data in the future presupposes that the perspective on it has not changed. From another perspective, which arises in the future or from another present viewpoint, where the defining terms are otherwise determined, the confirmation will not be valid. This is perhaps the thrust of the story of Liezi and the shaman, which stands as the climactic point in the Inner Chapters. The shaman could successfully predict the future, but Huzi's display of transforming identities and perspectives undermines the meaning and effectiveness of this kind of knowledge. There is a related criterion for genuine knowledge, which has become more central in the modern world than in previous times: the ability to create effective technology. Can Zhuangzi's "Genuine knowledge" do this? Again, no. But here again an implicit critique of such a criterion can perhaps be derived from the text. Technology is a means to an end. Ends are goals, and according to Zhuangzi, the goals or values are themselves dependent on perspectives. The transformation of perspectives into other perspectives is, for Zhuangzi, just what is "obvious," and indeed implicit in there even being a perspective: a "this" implicitly posits a contrasting "that," which is itself another "this" from which the first "this" is seen as a "that." The presence of any one perspective already brings with it alternate perspectives. There has never been and can never be only a single perspective, or a single set of values, in the world. But the establishment of technologies to facilitate the easier attainment of a particular set of goals and values will tend to fix those values and their perspectives in place; they will be an obstruction to the free flow of perspectival transformation that Zhuangzi prizes as the true meta-goal that allows for the rightness of any and every

perspective to operate. The technologies will serve to attain the values posited by some perspectives and not others, and hence will be inferior to Zhuangzi's "Genuine knowledge," which will facilitate the attainment of the values of any perspective, and allow for the free transformation from one to another.

86. Bryan Van Norden, "Review of Scott Cook, editor, *Hiding the World in the World*," *China Review International* 12, no. 1 (Spring 2005): 3.

CHAPTER FIVE. NON-IRONIC RESPONSES TO IRONIC COHERENCE IN *XUNZI* AND THE *RECORD OF RITUAL*

1. Here and throughout this discussion I will be translating Li as coherence without further ado. But the full justification for and implications of this usage will be spelled out in detail in the companion volume to this work.

2. *Xunzi yinde*, 70/19/1–3.

3. There has been some controversy over whether or not Xunzi admits of any other standard higher than that of desire. Van Norden, in a classic essay, notes the distinction between 欲 *yu* and 可 *ke* in the *Zhengming* chapter (111/22/6–12), which he translates as "desire" and "approval" respectively (with 可以 *keyi* in the same passage transforming into "what is proper"), the latter specified by Xunzi as the operation specifically of the mind, and able to keep one from "pursuing" (求 *qiu*) things that one nonetheless desires. Van Norden reads this as the introduction of a faculty of morality that is not rooted in or reducible to any kind of desire, citing three reasons for the distinction: the incommensurability of the two (citing Xunzi's claim that *ke* can trump *yu*); the nonenjoyment of what is approved in the early stages of moral cultivation (in Xunzi but not in Mencius); and an alleged phenomenological difference between the experiences of *yu* and *ke*. Even Van Norden knows the third reason is rather weak, so I will not address it here except to say that if the appeal is to the personal experiences of his readers, I am unable to corroborate the phenomenological difference so described. I am in agreement, however, with David Wong, who, though admitting that Van Norden has pinpointed an important point in the text here (see Watson's translation for an instance of how it can be overlooked), argues persuasively that if Xunzi admits that approval can override desire, this can only be in the "weak" sense of deferring short-term to long-term interests. As Wong notes, "The only basis for approval of an action given in his philosophy is desire—that the action is best, given the agent's long-term interests, even if it is not dictated by her immediate desires. Even if the mind can override emotions and desires, it does so in their interests, so to speak" (David B. Wong, "Xunzi on Moral Motivation," in *Virtue, Nature, and Moral Agency in the Xunzi*, 141. Wong cites only a tiny portion of the passages from Xunzi's text that support this contention; T. C. Kline's attempt to salvage a stronger sense of separation between approval and desire, appealing to Xunzi's technical definition of *yu* as innate rather than acquired ("Moral Agency and Moral Motivation in the Xunzi," in ibid., 161), fails to address the role of *yu* in Xunzi's accounts of the origin of morality (his solution to Nivison's "paradox of Virtue") and the glaring absence of any further invocation of this faculty of *ke*-approval above and beyond the desires in the rest of Xunzi's theoretical and psychological theories, or in the very lists of primitive terms, which Xunzi seems

to regard as exhaustive delineations of all the irreducible building blocks he needs to build these theories, from which Kline draws this definition. That "approval" appears only at the end of the process of cultivation, and must be created out of spontaneous desires rather than being innate does not undermine Wong's point, but rather corroborates it; otherwise, we are left with no motivation for the creation of the sense of approval by the sages or its acquisition by the aspiring Confucian. Kline's further attempt to disengage some forms of motivation from inclusion under the term *desire* seems to me nothing more than linguistic legislation; I take it Wong means by desire what most speakers of English mean, namely, "wanting something," whether for oneself or another, innate or acquired. It certainly doesn't seem to help Van Norden's case either that in one of the few other places where Xunzi adverts to this allegedly crucial category of a special moral faculty of approval, in the "Dispelling Obsessions" chapter, he seems to explicitly ground its efficacy in desire, *yu* 人孰欲得恣而守其所不可以禁其所可. This could be read in several ways: "Who would *desire to* attain satisfaction at the cost of holding to what he disapproves and preventing what he approves?" or "What person would *allow his desires to attain satisfaction* at the cost of. . . ." The first reading directly grounds approval in desire as such. But even the second reading, which would seem at first to be compatible with Van Norden's point, implies, in the form of a rhetorical question, that it is a simple empirical fact that *no one would do this*—not just the sages, the select few who think through the big picture, but *everyone* would simply and intuitively not do this, which is hardly consonant with Xunzi's views. Even in the passage originally cited by Van Norden, Xunzi goes on to say, "When someone adopts something, it is not purely what he desires that comes to him, and when he rejects something, it isn't only what he hates that he loses," and then goes on to "do the math" to show that in "following what one approves" rather than what one "desires," one gains the satisfaction of two by sacrificing one—a good deal and a net gain framed entirely in terms of the desire.

4. 71/19/13–15.

5. I owe this term to Kurtis Hagen's translation of Li; in some important ways it handily covers the way I understand this term, if we remember to keep in view both senses of "constructive": of positive value, and involving human effort and choice. See Hagen, *The Philosophy of Xunzi*, 41–42, and passim. More on "constructivism" below.

6. 71/19/30–31.

7. 天官 *tianguan*. I translate *tian* as "natural" here in the sense outlined in Xunzi's "Tianlun," i.e., the value-free "given" that is acquired without any deliberate human effort or intention.

8. 83/22/15–21.

9. 83/22/25–84/22/27.

10. This view, epitomizing the "ultimately realist but accommodating a soft-nominalism" reading of Xunzi, is nicely summed up by Bryan Van Norden's view: "[T]he distinctions among things in the world picked out by the (arbitrarily chosen) words of Chinese are themselves objective." "Mengzi and Xunzi: Two Views of Human Agency," in *Virtue, Nature, and Moral Agency in the Xunzi*, ed. T. C. Kline and Philip J. Ivanhoe, 132, note 61 (Indianapolis: Hackett, 2000).

11. 1/1/13–15.

12. The Mohist Canons, representing the most empirical of all ancient Chinese observers of nature, assert the same thing when attempting to explain the optical phenomenon of reflection: "It is inherent in things of one kind that they call each other up. If the energies are the same they act together, when a sound correlates it responds." Graham's translation, from A. C. Graham, *Later Mohist Logic, Ethics, and Science* (Hong Kong: Chinese University Press, 1978), 373.

13. Xunzi uses the term to describe the spontaneous relation of the sense organs to their objects, very similarly to Mencius's description of the senses. See 53/22/2–3: "What is harmonized from what is inborn, and feels and responds when the quintessence joins with external things, what is so of itself without deliberate effort is called the Nature."

14. It should be stressed that this does *not* entail any ignorance of the difference between animate and inanimate realms. Indeed, Xunzi himself elsewhere notes those differences, and specifies the animate as having this quality: "Whatever is born between heaven and earth *which belong to the category having blood and breath* there is none without awareness, and whatever has awareness loves its own kind. For example, whenever a great animal or bird loses its herd or companions, before long it will return to search for them" (74/19/98). The fact that this characteristic is the fundamental and as it were most intuitively comfortable way of explaining phenomena does not mean that one cannot distinguish between groups that do this most paradigmatically and others in certain rhetorical contexts; indeed, in this context the animals are a larger category than the one Xunzi really wants to discuss: mankind. The argument is that mankind too, as an aware creature with blood and breath, will behave in this way. Less obviously interrelating entities were not relevant in this context. When attention was turned to such entities, however, this category of spontaneous social grouping (of which there may be many types) was simply what was available, and deviations therefrom had to be explained in terms of it.

15. 7/3/24–25.

16. Kurtis Hagen, *The Philosophy of Xunzi: A Reconstruction* (Chicago: Open Court, 2007), 8.

17. As Eric Hutton has pointed out in his review of Hagen's book, however, this is perhaps partially a distortion, as many of the above-named scholars do in fact admit that Xunzi allows for a human role in the creation of moral values. Most do admit, at least that the existing institutional forms of moral regulation are the creation of specific human interventions. Hagen's point, however, as he says in his response to Hutton, is that this human role still seems to be merely a matter of application and translation of preexisting moral "norms" into particular social forms, rather than the actual *creation* of these norms. See Eric L. Hutton, *Hagen, Kurtis, The Philosophy of Xunzi: A Reconstruction*, reviewed in *Dao: A Journal of Comparative Philosophy* 6 (2007): 417–21, and Hagen's response in the same issue.

18. Ibid.

19. 28/9/63–29/9/73; emphases mine.

20. 13/5/26–28.

21. This is of course quite in keeping with Hagen's sense of "constructivism," of which the present remarks may be considered an elaboration.

22. Jane Geaney, *On the Epistemology of the Senses in Early Chinese Thought* (Honolulu: University of Hawaii, 2002), 35.

23. Ibid., 44.

24. 44/12/2.

25. We will see a further development of this notion of "asness," modified as in the *Zhuangzi* so as to annul the qualification that limits the possibility of "seeing as" within a finite range, when we turn to Tiantai Buddhist epistemology in the companion volume.

26. 71/19/26–28.

27. 29/9/75.

28. 3/1/51.

29. 8/3/44.

30. 6/17/50–52.

31. But as we shall see, in the Tiantai case later, it is also possible for the category of "falsehood" to drop out completely, in a sense combining these two aspects of Xunzi's epistemology, so that all inaccurate or distorted views are *necessarily* partial truths.

32. See Aaron Stalnaker, "Aspects of Xunzi's Engagement with Early Daoism," *Philosophy East and West* 53, no. 1 (January 2003): 87–129, for a more detailed discussion of some of these points, reaching similar conclusions.

33. 62/17/7–10.

34. Yang Changzhen, *Xunzi lei de cunyoulun yanjiu* (Taipei: Wenjin chubanshe, 1996), 155. Yang's note on this point explicitly cites Wittgenstein's notion of "family resemblances," which is quite relevant here.

35. 71/19/13–16.

36. Slingerland, 12.

37. An Yanming, "The Concept of *Cheng* and its Western Translations," *Dao: A Journal of Comparative Philosophy* IV, no. 1 (Winter 2004): 128.

CHAPTER SIX. THE YIN-YANG COMPROMISE

1. As can be found, for example, in the discussion of Chinese religion in Bahm, *The World's Living Religions* (Carbondale: Southern Illinois University Press, 1964), 157.

2. The earliest uses of this dyad separated from the context of the six qi seem to stress the sense of alternation and process rather than the static image of the two sides of a mountain. See for example the *Shujing*, "Zhouguan": "These are the three Kung. They discourse on the principles of reason, and adjust the States; harmonizing also and regulating the operations of Yin and Yang" (modified from the translation of Legge, *The Shoo King* [Taipei: Southern Materials Center, 1985], 527). In the *Shijing*, "Kongliu" (in "Da ya") we find: "He surveyed the light and shade (yin and yang), viewing also the course of the streams and springs" (Legge, *The She King* [Taipei: Southern Materials Center, 1985], 488). The latter citation is ambiguous, and probably refers both to the static contours of the topology and the temporal progressions of day and night, the motion of shadows as the sun moves.

3. *Zhuangzi yinde* (In *Zhuzi yinde*; *Laozi, Zhuangzi* [Taipei: Zongqing tushu chuban gongsi, 1986]; the citations correspond to those in the Harvard-Yenching concordances), 17/6/56. But ultimately this perhaps reduces to simply the physical forces of health, as in the next citations; both are simply the determining conditions of one's physical existence, which is the main thing here.

4. Ibid., 10/4/36–38, 17/6/49.

5. Graham, *Disputers of the Dao* (La Salle: Open Court, 1989), 328, citing *Zhuangzi*, 72/25/67.

6. *Huangdi sijing*, in *Laozi Wangbizhu* et al. (Taipei: Tianshi chubanshe, 1982), 321.

7. Graham, 331.

8. Lisa Ann Raphals, *Sharing the Light: Representations of Women and Virtue in Early China* (Albany: State University of New York Press, 1998), 167.

9. Zhang Dainian, *Zhongguo gudian zhexue gainian fanchou yaolun* (*On classical Chinese philosophical terms*) (Beijing: Zhouguo Shehuikexue Chubanshe, 2000), 84–85.

10. Some echo of this distinction can be found in Zhang Dainian, ibid., passim.

11. By "earliest stratum," I mean works up to and including the *Analects* and the *Mozi*. For later creation myths, see Paul Goldin, "The Myth That China Has No Creation Myth," *Monumenta Serica* 56 (2008): 1–22.

12. See Chen, *Guanzi sipian quanshi*, 70.

13. It is also worth noting that this conception can be boiled down into an *immanent* axiology, i.e., that an attempt is made to derive value simply from existence as such, without applying a heteronomous valuation from without, which would in principle designate some portion of being as good and another portion as bad. This is equal to saying also that it is tautological, or that it leads to an infinite regress. It rests on the base assumption that being (or rather, continuous creation) is good as such. But this differs from Western (e.g., Neoplatonic or medieval Christian) conceptions of the convertibility of the concepts of Being and Good, for it is predicated wholly on the conception of process, of the repeated beginnings and finishes of particular things in the unceasing productivity of heaven, with the introduction of the possibility of evil coming with the necessary presence of "finishing" in the process of creation itself.

14. There are many instances of such a situation in the hexagrams themselves. For example, Hexagram #24, Return (復 *Fu*), is one of the most auspicious overall hexagrams in the system, and is traditionally regarded as the reassertion of the power of Yang. It consists of one Yang line, on the bottom, and five Yin lines. The "ruling line" of the hexagram, the fifth from the bottom, which should "ideally" be occupied by a Yang line, is here occupied by a Yin line, which moreover does not have the virtue of "responding" with the second line, since the latter is also Yin. Structurally, this hexagram doesn't have much going for it, according to the general rules applied to hexagram interpretation. And yet it is highly auspicious and moreover emblematic of a Yang situation because the single Yang line comes "at the beginning," is perfectly playing its pure role of initiation, a turning point (associated with the winter solstice) where a small bubbling up of Yang force is enough to ensure subsequent "responses" and "finishes" from the Yin elements present (structurally, this response would come especially from the fourth line), and thereby to serve the process of

continuance. Another example is the final hexagram, #64, Before Completion (未 濟 *Wei Ji*). Here *every* line is in the "wrong" place. But this too is one of the most auspicious of hexagrams, since its disequilibrium implies of state of incompletion that will function, holistically, as an initiation for later completion. The total hexagram is thus Yangish, although it is quantitatively equally Yin and Yang and structurally perfectly wrong, with a Yin ruler. Here we see a non-ironic incorporation of the ironic implications of coherence: it is still value, it is still intelligibility, it is still a kind of sticking together or harmony of elements, but now value and intelligibility reside in the harmony between valued intelligibility and non-valued unintelligibility.

15. Legge's amusingly outraged comments on the "silliness" of this "drivel" are still well worth consulting.

16. We will have more to say about this important usage of Li in *Beyond Oneness and Difference: Li (Coherence) in Pre-Neoconfucian Chinese Thought*.

17. This is not the place for a detailed examination of how this habit is played out in specific later thinkers who utilize the Yin-Yang dyad. But as a further clue to the axiological ambiguities of the terms *Yin* and *Yang* as they manifest in the later dominant tradition, let us take a look at Zhu Xi's remarks on their relationship from the *Zhouyi Benyi*, which after all represents a culmination of Sung Neo-Confucianism and the standard of Confucian orthodoxy throughout the subsequent dynasties of imperial Chinese history: "Yin and Yang are the foundation of creation, and cannot exist in isolation from one another. Moreover, their process of growth and decline has its constancy, which cannot be augmented or decreased by man. However, Yang controls generation while Yin controls destruction, and thus the categories corresponding to them are divided into the good [for Yang] and the evil [for Yin]. Thus the sage, in creating the *Yi*, because of their mutual dependence illuminated them [Yin and Yang] by means of vigor [Yang] and compliance [Yin], benevolence [Yang] and righteousness [Yin], with no bias to either side of these dyads. But with respect to their effect on growth and decline and the division of good and evil between them, the sage always added a sense of promoting Yang and suppressing Yin. This is the means of aiding transformation and nurturance [of all things] and forming a triad with heaven and earth. Its meaning is deep!" (Zhu Xi, *Zhouyi benyi*. [Taipei: Guangxue she yinshu guan, 1975], 51–52, commentary to the first line of the Kun hexagram). Zhu Xi is here carefully straddling the question of value opposition in the two fundamental components of the world function. He seems to be saying here *both* that Yin and Yang are equally necessary to the universal process of creation, that neither can be lacking, *and* that the sage recommends suppressing one and promoting the other, that one is good and the other evil. Here we see a coexistence of the union of opposites and their eternal opposition, both of which are asserted to be absolutely necessary to a correct understanding of the nature of the world and the correct ethical attitude thereto. A place is being made for both earnest moral value and endeavor, and also the union, in some as yet unclarified sense, between the ground of value and that of anti-value. (Nevertheless, Zhu Xi maintains that human nature can and must be called good, as against Hu Hong's position that it is neither good nor evil, but is the source of both. The subtleties of the distinctions between the two views are quite intricate, and can be profitably compared to the Shanjia/Shanwai disputes within Tiantai, which addressed many similar issues. An

introduction to this controversy by Conrad Shirokauer can be found in W. T. Chan, *Chu Hsi and Neo-Confucianism* [University of Hawaii, 1986]). As we would expect from the above discussion, Zhu acknowledges two orders of value here. At the primary level, Yang is value and Yin is disvalue. At the secondary level, the balanced proportion of value and disvalue is Value, and again this "balanced proportion" is defined with respect to the continuance of the relation. Zhu would like to keep these two levels equally weighted, and praises the sagely author of the text for his ability to handle this ambivalent attitude toward disvalue (as both necessary and worthy of suppression) so virtuosically, keeping both in sight at all times. Yin in particular is both something negative in itself and an integral part of something positive, which can never be excised. It should be noted also that, where the original conception would seem to have left these two levels intertwined, so that the *dominance* of Yang is defined as value, at least in theory, Zhu separates them into a *balance* of Yin and Yang on the first level, compensated for by an *opposition* of the two on the other level. In effect, we have here the creation of a balanced and complementary coherence between the complementarity and the conflict of Yin and Yang.

18. Makeham, op. cit., 350.

19. See Robin Wang, "Dong Zhongshu's Transformation of Yin-Yang Theory and Contesting of Gender Identity," *Philosophy East and West* 55, no. 2 (April 2005): 209–31. Wang makes the interesting argument that Dong actually transforms the early relation of "harmony" (和 *he*) between Yin and Yang to one of "imposed unity" (合 *he*), thereby shifting away from a more flexible and otherness-respecting "harmony" paradigm to something similar to what we have here been calling a paradigm of "sameness." It seems incontestable that the alteration of the form of unity is crucial to the attempted suppression of irony in Yin-Yang in Dong's thought, which goes with the centralization of the intention of Heaven and of the empire, and the "single-meaning" non-ironic view of role and meaning.

20. Following Su Yu, I read *jing* for *quan*. See Lai Yenyuan, ed., *Chunqiu Fanlu jinzhu jinyi* (Taipei: Taiwan Shanwu yinshuguan, 1987), 292.

21. Ibid., 289–91.

22. I differ slightly here from Robin Wang's interpretation of this turn in Dong's thought. Wang sees the association of Yin with punishment as being, on the one hand, another insult to the value of the Yin and on the other hand the introduction of punishment into Confucian authoritarian ideology. I agree with the first part of this but not the second, with which it seems incompatible. Wang seems to lean toward taking punishment to be a reshaping of what is Yin (and hence in a certain sense anti-Yin), rather than punishment itself being an activity of a Yin character, which I see as Dong's position here. The rehabilitation of punishment and coercion into Confucianism was actually already in place in Xunzi's thought, as we've seen; what Dong has done is rather to give a differently constructed *positive* value as the indispensable "yin" aspect of perfection. Since punishment was by this time the de facto lever of Han realpolitik, this amounts to an extremely strong, though perhaps somewhat wink-winked, affirmation of the essential power and importance of the Yin. That this was the fatal last piece in the puzzle that made Confucian a force of unbreakable authoritarian oppression, as Wang suggests, is of course undeniable.

23. For example, see *Sharing the Light*, 151: "Most discussions of yin-yang do not distinguish these overlapping aspects of polarity. . . . By hierarchical polarity,

I mean a polarity that emphasizes the hierarchical distinction between sub- and superordinate. By complementary polarity, I mean a polarity that emphasizes the need for balance between the two terms."

24. In the Diagrams commentary ("Taixuan tu"), Yang says, "The Mystery encompasses equally the three ways—the way of heaven, the way of earth and the way of man—but uses the character of heaven [*xuan*, Mystery, black, as opposed to earth's yellow] to name it. . . . The Mystery has two methods: one is to arise in threes, one is to produce in threes. To arise in threes is the system of the regions, provinces, departments and households [the spatial nesting by threes]. To produce in threes is to divide Yang material force into three layers [the solid, once broken, and twice broken lines]" (Zheng, 358). Zheng Wangeng, *Taixuan jiaoshi* (Beijing: Beijing Shifan daxue chubanshe, 1989).

25. See Xu Fuguan, 347–48, for a discussion of the importance of the number three in the *Santongli*, as the triad of heaven, earth, and man, and in the *sanfensunyi* harmonic system. In this system, a fifth above the fundamental pitch was generated by "decreasing" the length by one-third, and a fourth above by "increasing" it by the same amount. The other main pitches were generated by repeating this process of "increasing and decreasing by thirds" (i.e., *sanfensunyi*). These tones in turn corresponded to the members of the bureacratic hierarchy, a fact that is of great importance for Yang's adoption of the system of multiples of three, as we shall see below. See *Hou Hanshu*, "Lulizhi," (*Zhonghua shuju*), vol. 11, 2999–3002. For a detailed explanation of the mathematical implications of the harmonic system, see Wang Guangqi, *Zhongguo Yinyue shi* (Hong Kong: Taiping shuju, 1963), 1–65.

26. Nylan and Sivin, in their excellent introduction to the *Taixuan* (op. cit., 79), translate Yang's revelant remarks in the *Hanshu* as follows: "Those who study the Changes must peruse the diagram (卦 *gua*) in order to tell [which text to consult], but those who study the Mystery determine [the text] by counting (数 *shu*) the lines. The reason that the [tetragram corresponding to] each Head [i.e., tetragram text] in the Mystery is fourfold is that it is not a diagram but a number (数 *shu*)."

27. Ibid., 79–81. Let a solid line equal 0, a singly broken line equal 1, and a doubly broken line equal 2 (in other words, count the breaks in each line). The number of any tetragram can be generated by the formula: Household# + 3(Department#) + 9(Province#) + 27(Region#) +1 = 81 Tetragram#.

28. 81 tetragrams x 4 1/2 days equals 364 1/2 days. This falls 3/4 of a day short of the 365 1/4 day solar year. The discrepancy is compensated for by Yang's addition of two extra Appraisals. The ad hoc nature of this system, aggravated by the fact that these two additional Appraisals, attached to no tetragram, had to be added to make it work out perfectly, has been criticized by several later commentators. The Ming commentator Ye Ziqi lists eight features of the *Taixuan* that either do not make sense or are inferior to the structure of the *Changes,* among which he counts the lack of any explicit and detailed correspondence between the lines of the tetragrams and the Appraisals, and also the forced addition of the two extra Appraisals. Nonetheless, Ye held the work in very high regard, and wrote a detailed commentary on it. See Zheng Wangeng, *Taixuan jiaoshi,* 429–32.

29. When divining, it is generally auspicious to be given a tetragram corresponding to a month in the calendar that comes later than the month in which one is actually divining, and inauspicious if the period denoted by the tetragram has

already passed. Nylan and Sivin, 68, suggest a rationale: warned as to the prevailing influences in advance, one has time to adjust and prepare for what is to come. Having drawn a particular tetragram, a number of factors determine which of the nine Appraisals are relevant. First and foremost is the time of day at which the divination was made: morning (Appraisals 1, 5, and 7), evening (3, 4, and 8) or "Median" (2, 6, and 9). Which of these are auspicious will depend on which are Yin and which Yang (evening and morning) in that particular tetragram (since the positions of these alternate with each tetragram).

30. Here we see one of the prime concrete forms of time/space correlation (in addition to the directions of heavenly motion), indeed one that was already in place long before Yang.

31. Xu Fuguan, 350.

32. See Zheng, 378, note 4, and Xu Fuguan, 350.

33. Zheng, 376. The Appraisals are also read as representing the bureaucratic hierarchy, with the fifth line as the ruler, in the center, and increasingly distant ministers and petty persons as one moves farther from this central imperial radiance. See Nylan and Sivin, 60–62, for a fuller analysis of the structure of the Appraisals, complete with helpful charts.

34. Note also that the winter solstice returns with the last tetragram, #81 ("Nurture"), which consists of four twice-broken lines, another perfect opposite to the tetragram for the summer solstice.

35. See chart in Nylan and Sivin, 82. But the content of the particular Appraisals is never explained or justified, after the manner of the lines in the *Zhouyi*, in terms of the structural symbolism of the individual tetragram—neither in terms of the administrative-geographical significance of the four places nor the putative symbolism of heaven, earth and man represented by the three types of lines. Rather, the nine Appraisals describe in various ways the situation that is *also* characteristic of the place in the total sequence of the yearly round denoted by the tetragram, construed as a four-place, base-three number. This is the only basis of the correspondence of the two.

36. In the "Diagram" commentary ("Taixuan tu") Yang says, "One Mystery covers the three Regions, the Regions unify the nine Provinces, which branch out to bear the Departments, which divide and regulate the many Households. All events take place within them (*shi shi qi zhong*)." The places of tetragrams are indeed meant to encompass the spatial setting of all events in the Empire. In addition, Yang correlates the five phases, the stages in the process of growth, with five virtues, (corresponding to the four virtues of the Changes, i.e., Origination, Penetration, Benefit, and Perseverence [*yuan heng li zhen*]), each of which also brings with it a particular spatial direction and a season: "Wang . . . ("nothingness") is the north, the winter: not yet having form. Zhi ("straight extension") is the east, the spring: having palpable substance (*zhi*) but not yet having visible pattern (*wen*). Meng ("bearing up") is the south, the summer: the growth of things, so that all can bear [fruit?] (?). Qiu ("maturity") is the west, the autumn: things all form their images (*cheng xiang*) and are completed. When that with palpable form reverts to formlessness, it is called Ming 冥 ("darkness"). Thus the myriad things have their nothingness in the north, their straight extension in the east, their bearing up in the south, their

maturation in the west, and then their darkness in the north" (Zheng, 330). Here the temporal sequence of the process of growth and decline described in the round of the tetragrams is given a particular spatial correspondence. This correspondence is common in writings of this time, and its astronomical significance is obvious. As Yang says elsewhere, "As soon as the sun reaches its southernmost point (and starts heading back north, i.e., on the summer solstice), things begin to die; as soon as it reaches its northernmost point (and starts heading back south, on the winter solstice), things begin to come to life. When the dipper points north, things decline; when it points south, they revive" (Zheng, 264). The temporal turning of the seasons is precisely the spatial motion of the heavenly bodies, and these in turn are the phases of growth and decline that make up the year. This is the process, in all its aspects, intricately described in the 81 X 9 "gnomic images" (as Nylan and Sivin put it, 83) of the tetragrams and their Appraisals. Hence, the system does indeed provide some kind of specific interrelation between calendrical time and administrative/geographic/astronomical space.

37. Xu Fuguan, 349.

38. Zheng, 346. The rhetoric of ritual emblems of authority here stresses a particular aspect of the administrative structure: the charismatic moral influence of the ruled by the ruler, about which we shall say more below.

39. Zheng, 281. We will have much more to say below about the word here used for ruler, *bi*. Sima Guang (1019–1086) comments on this whole set of geographical and administrative designations as follows: "The Mystery represents [the domain of] the Son of Heaven. Fang represents [the domain of] the Regional Earls (*fangbo*). Zhou represents [the domain of] the Provincial Governors. Bu represents the individual states (*guo*), and Jia represents individual families. The higher control the lower, the few rule the many, and thereby the ruling network is set" (Zheng, 2).

40. It should be noted, however, that the official titles cited by Yang himself as corresponding to his four administrative-geographical units (i.e., *gong*, *qing*, *dafu*, *yuanshi*) are derived from the idealized Zhou system (as found, for example, in the "Wang zhi" chapter of the *Liji*). The first two of these official titles were the mainstay of the Han administrative system: there were indeed three *gong* and nine *qing*, introducing the system of multiples of three, which, as we shall see, is in a sense what primarily interests Yang in this nomenclature, but the 27 *dafu* and 81 *yuanshi* did not seem to be in place. Thus, the *Taixuan* system cannot be said exactly to represent the administrative system of his time, nor, presciently, as Wang Fuzhi seems to allege, to derive from Wang Mang's land reform system. For Wang Fuzhi's accusation, see Zheng, 433. The fact is, of course, that the *Taixuan* was written before Wang Mang actually usurped the throne. Moreover, according to Shen Zhanru's study of Wang Mang's reforms, only the middle two terms, *zhou* and *bu*, correspond to Wang's land system. Of these, only *bu* was an addition to the original Han system (Shen Zhanru, *Xin Mang quanshi* [Taipei: Zhengzhong shuju, 1977], 179). Wang Fuzhi's charge must be considered a bit of disparaging hyperbole designed to discredit Yang's system. The model for the system is an ideal (albeit putatively formerly existent) geographical/administrative order, referring primarily to the territory of the Zhou empire but also in principle to the slightly modified geography of the Han.

41. The mutual penetration of the tetragrams is quite complex; their influence jumps across intervening spaces in several simultaneous patterns. The structure of the tetragrams—which is really just a graphic representation of their places in cycles of rise and fall of various scales—points to special connections between certain of these times: those that represent times a half-year apart from each other turn out to be modified inversions of one another, indicating their special resonance and responsiveness, based on their perfect contrariety, as is explicated in Yang's "Polar Oppositions" ("Taixuan chong"). In "Interplay of Opposites" ("Taixuan cuo") commentary, Yang sketches out another, more complicated system of such correspondences, pairing specific tetragrams according to their oppositions and resonances. This pairing is a result of the special relationship of particular phases in the yearly cycle, e.g., the winter solstice and the summer solstice. Different moments in time (i.e., "parts of the whole") are also related by the divination process: the morning or evening on which one is divining proves to have an unexpected special relationship to the 4 1/2 day period represented by the tetragram one draws.

42. Zheng Wangeng, 261.

BIBLIOGRAPHY

WORKS CITED

Allan, Sarah. *The Way of Water and Sprouts of Virtue*. Albany: State University of New York Press, 1997. Print.

An Yanming. "The Concept of Cheng and Its Western Translations." *Dao: A Journal of Comparative Philosophy* IV, no. 1 (Winter 2004): 117–36. Print.

Bahm, Archie J. *The World's Living Religions*. Carbondale: Southern Illinois University Press, 1964. Print.

Bai Tongdong. "An Ontological Interpretation of You (Something) and Wu (Nothing) in the Laozi." *Journal of Chinese Philosophy* 35, no. 2 (2008): 339–51. Print.

Behuniak, James. *Mencius on Becoming Human*. Albany: State University of New York Press, 2005. Print.

Bergson, Henri. *An Introduction to Metaphysics*. Trans. Mabelle L. Andison. Totowa: Helix, 1975. Print.

Black, Allison Harley. *Man and Nature in the Philosophical Thought of Wang Fu-Chih*. Seattle: University of Washington Press, 1989. Print.

Bol, Peter K. *Neo-Confucianism in History*. Cambridge: Harvard University Press, 2008. Print.

Bou Mo. "A Double-Reference Account: Gongsun Long's 'White-Horse-Not-Horse' Thesis." *Journal of Chinese Philosophy* 34, no. 4 (2007): 493–513. Print.

Chan, Alan Kam-leung. "Harmony as a Contested Metaphor and Conceptions of Rightness (yi) in Early Confucian Ethics," in *How Should One Live? Comparing Ethics in Ancient China and Greco-Roman Antiquity*, ed. R. A. H. King and Dennis Schilling (Berlin/Boston: Gruyter, 2011), 37–62.

———, ed. *Mencius: Contexts and Interpretations*. Honolulu: University of Hawaii Press, 2002. Print.

Chan, Wing-Tsit. *Chu Hsi and Neo-Confucianism*. Honolulu: University of Hawaii Press, 1986. Print.

Chen Derong. "Di and Tian in Ancient Chinese Thought: A Critical Analysis of Hegel's Views." *Dao: A Journal of Comparative Philosophy* 8 (2009): 13–27. Print.

Chen Guying 陳鼓應. *Guanzi Sipian Quanshi; Jixia Daojia Daibiao Zuo* 管子四篇詮釋；稷下道家代表作 ("The 'Four Chapters' of the *Guanzi*, with Exegesis: Representative Works of the Jixia Academy Daoists). Taipei: Sanmin, 2002. Print.

———. *Zhuangzi Jinzhu Jinyi* 莊子今注今譯 ("*Zhuangzi*: A Modern Commentary and Modern Translation"). Taipei: Shangwu Yinshuguan, 1989. Print.

Cheng Chung-ying. "Reinterpreting Gongsun Longzi and Critical Comments on Other Interpretations." *Journal of Chinese Philosophy* 34, no. 4 (2007). Print.

Cook, Scott. *The Term "Li" in Chinese Treatises on Literature and the Arts*. MS. Unpublished.

———. "Yue Ji: Introduction, Translation, Notes, and Commentary." *Asian Music* XXVI, no. 2 (1995): 19–24. Print.

Csikszentmihalyi, Mark. *Material Virtue: Ethics and the Body in Early China*. Leiden: Brill, 2004. Print.

———, and P. J. Ivanhoe, eds. *Religious and Philosophical Aspects of the Laozi*. Albany: State University of New York Press, 1999. Print.

DeWoskin, Kenneth J. *A Song for One or Two Music and the Concept of Art in Early China*. Ann Arbor: Center for Chinese Studies, University of Michigan, 1982. Print.

Ding Yuanzhi 丁原植. *Guodian Zhujian Laozi Shixi Yu Yanjiu* 郭店竹簡老子釋析與研究 ("Explanation, Analysis and Research into the Guodian Bamboo Strips of the *Laozi*"). Taipei: Wanjuanlou Tushu Youxian Gongsi, 1999. Print.

Eno, Robert. *The Confucian Creation of Heaven: Philosophy and The Defense of Ritual Mastery*. Albany: State University of New York Press, 1990. Print.

Feng Yulan. *Selected Philosophical Writings of Fung Yu-Lan*. Beijing: Foreign Languages Press, 1998. Print.

Fingarette, Herbert. *Confucius the Secular as Sacred*. New York: Harper and Row, 1972. Print.

Frege, Gottlob. "On Sense and Reference." In *Translations from the Philosophical Writings of Gotlob Frege*, trans. Max Black, ed. P. T. Geach and Max Black. Oxford: Oxford University Press, 1952. Print.

Geaney, Jane. *On the Epistemology of the Senses in Early Chinese Thought*. Honolulu: University of Hawaii Press, 2002. Print.

Goldin, Paul. *Rituals of the Way: The Philosophy of Xunzi*. Chicago: Open Court, 1999. Print.

———. "The Myth That China Has No Creation Myth." *Monumenta Serica* 56 (2008): 1–22. Print.

Graham, A. C. *Chuang-Tzu: The Seven Inner Chapters and Other Writings from the Book* Chuang-Tzu. London: Allen and Unwin, 1981. Print.

———. *Disputers of the Tao: Philosophical Argument in Ancient China*. La Salle, IL: Open Court, 1989. Print.

———. "Kung-sun Lung's Discourse Re-read as Argument About Whole and Part." *Studies in Chinese Philosophy and Philosophical Literature*: 193–215. Print.

———. *Later Mohist Logic, Ethics, and Science*. Hong Kong: Chinese University Press, 2003. Print.

———. *Studies in Chinese Philosophy and Philosophical Literature*. Albany: State University of New York Press, 1990. Print.

———. *Two Chinese Philosophers: The Metaphysics of the Brothers Ch'eng*. La Salle, IL: Open Court, 1992. Print.

Guo Qingfan 郭慶藩. *Zhuangzi Jishi* 莊子集釋 ("Collected Explanations on the *Zhuangzi*"). Taipei: Muduo Chuban She, 1983. Print.

Hagen, Kurtis. *The Philosophy of Xunzi: A Reconstruction*. Chicago: Open Court, 2007. Print.

Hall, David L. *Eros and Irony: A Prelude to Philosophical Anarchism*. Albany: State University of New York Press, 1982. Print.

———, and Roger T. Ames. *Focusing the Familiar: A Translation and Philosophical Interpretation of the* Zhongyong. Honolulu: University of Hawaii Press, 2001. Print.

———. *Thinking from the Han: Self, Truth, and Transcendence in Chinese and Western Culture*. Albany: State University of New York Press, 1998. Print.

———. *Thinking Through Confucius*. Albany: State University of New York Press, 1987. Print.

Han Xiaoqiang. "Maybe There Are No Subject-Predicate Sentences in Chinese." *Dao: A Journal of Comparative Philosophy* 8 (2009): 277–87. Print.

Hansen, Chad. *A Daoist Theory of Chinese Thought: A Philosophical Interpretation*. New York: Oxford University Press, 1992. Print.

———. *Language and Logic in Ancient China*. Ann Arbor: University of Michigan, 1983. Print.

Hegel, Georg Wilhelm Friedrich. *Elements of the Philosophy of Right*. Ed. Allen W. Wood. Trans. Hugh Barr Nisbet. Cambridge: Cambridge University Press, 1991. Print.

———. *Hegel's Science of Logic*. Trans. A. V. Miller. Atlantic Highlands, NJ: Humanities International, 1989. Print.

———. *Lectures on the Philosophy of Religion*. Ed. J. Glenn Gray. Trans. J. Burdon. Sanderson, Ebenezer Brown Speirs, E. S. Haldane, and Bernard Bosanquet. New York: Humanities, 1974. Print.

———. *The Phenomenology of Spirit*. Trans. Arnold V. Miller and J. N. Findlay. Oxford: Clarendon, 1977. Print.

———. *Hegel's Logic: Being Part One of the Encyclopaedia of the Philosophical Sciences*. Trans. William Wallace. Oxford: Clarendon, 1975. Print.

Henricks, Robert G. *Lao-Tzu Tao Te Ching*. New York: Ballantine, 1989. Print.

Hong Ye 洪業, Nie Chongqi 聶崇岐, Li Shuchun 李書春, and Ma Xiyong 馬錫用, eds. *Zhuzi Jicheng* 諸子集成 ("The Complete Classical Philosophers") (*In Eight Volumes*). Shanghai: Shanghai Shudian Chubanshe, 1996. Print.

Ivanhoe, P. J. "Heaven as a Source of Ethical Warrant in Early Confucianism." *Dao: A Journal of Comparative Philosophy* 6 (2007). Print.

———. "Review of *Neo-Confucianism in History* by Peter K. Bol." *Dao: A Journal of Comparative Philosophy* (2010): 471–77. Print.

Jiao Hong 焦宏. *Laozi Yi* 老子翼 ("Wings to the *Laozi*"). Taipei: Guangwen Shuju, 1962. Print.

Kant, Immanuel. *Critique of Pure Reason*. Trans. J. M. D. Meiklejohn. London: Dent Library, 1969. Print.

Kaufmann, Walter, ed. *Existentialism from Dostoevsky to Sartre*. New York: Meridian, 1963. Print.

King, R. A. H, and Dennis Schilling, editors. *How Should One Live? Comparing Ethics in Ancient China and Greco-Roman Antiquity*. Berlin/Boston: Gruyter, 2011.

Kjellberg, Paul, and P. J. Ivanhoe, eds. *Essays on Skepticism, Relativism, and Ethics in the Zhuangzi*. Albany: State University of New York Press, 1996. Print.

Kline, T. C., and P. J. Ivanhoe. *Virtue, Nature, and Moral Agency in the Xunzi*. Indianapolis: Hackett, 2000. Print.

Knaul, Livia. "Kuo Hsiang and the Chuang Tzu." *Journal of Chinese Philosophy* 12, no. 4 (1985): 429–47. Print.

Kohn, Livia, and Michael LaFargue. *Lao-Tzu and the Tao-Te-Ching*. Albany: State University of New York Press, 1998. Print.

Kojeve, Alexandre. *Introduction to the Reading of Hegel*. Trans. Raymond Queneau. New York: Basic, 1969. Print.

Kong Yinda 孔穎達. *Zhouyi Zhengyi* 周易正義 ("The Book of Changes, with Corrected Meanings"). Taipei: Zhonghua Shuju, 1986. Print.

Korner, Stephan. *Metaphysics: Its Structure and Function*. Cambridge: Cambridge University Press, 1984. Print.

Kripke, Saul A. *Naming and Necessity*. Cambridge: Harvard University Press, 1980. Print.

Lai Yenyuan 賴炎元, ed. *Chunqiu Fanlu Jinzhu Jinyi* 春秋繁露今注今譯 ("Modern Annotation and Translation of [Dong Zhongshu's] *Luxuriant Dew of the Spring and Autumn Annals*"). Taipei: Taiwan Shanwu Yinshuguan, 1987. Print.

Lakoff, George. *Women, Fire, and Dangerous Things: What Categories Reveal about the Mind*. Chicago: University of Chicago Press, 1987. Print.

Laozi Wangbizhu, Boshu Laozi, Yiyin, Jiuzhu, Huangdi Sijing 老子王弼注，帛書老子，伊尹，九主，黃帝四經 ("The Laozi with the Wang Bi Commentary, The Silk Manuscript Version of the Laozi, the Yiyin, the Nine Masters, and the Four Scriptures of the Yellow Thearch"). Taipei: Tianshi Chubanshe, 1982. Print.

Lau, D. C. *Lao Tzu Tao Te Ching*. Middlesex: Penguin, 1963. Print.

Legge, James, trans. *The She King: The Book of Poetry*. Taibei Shi: Southern Materials Center, 1985. Print.

———, trans. *The Shoo King*. Taipei: Southern Materials Center, 1985. Print.

Leibniz, Gottfried. *Discourse on the Natural Theology of the Chinese (Monographs of the Society for Asian and Comparative Philosophy, No. 4)*. Trans. Henry Rosemont and Daniel J. Cook. Honolulu: University of Hawaii Press, 1977. Print.

Levy-Bruhl, Lucien. *How Natives Think*. Trans. Lilian A. Clare. London: Allen and Unwin, 1926. Print.

Li Chenyang. "Li as Cultural Grammar: On the Relation Between Li and Ren in Confucius' Analects." *Philosophy East and West* 57, no. 3 (2007): 311–29. Print.

———. "The Confucian Ideal of Harmony," *Philosophy East and West* 56, no. 4 (October 2006): 583–603.

———. "The Ideal of Harmony in Ancient Chinese and Greek Philosophy," *Dao: A Journal of Comparative Philosophy* (2008) 7:81–98.

———. "The Philosophy of Harmony in Classical Confucianism," *Philosophy Compass* 3, no. 3 (2008): 423–35.

———. *The Tao Encounters the West: Explorations in Comparative Philosophy*. Albany: State University of New York Press, 1999. Print.

Li Disheng 李滌生, ed. *Xunzi Jishi* 荀子集釋 ("*The Xunzi*, with Collected Explanations"). Taipei: Xuesheng Shuju, 1979. Print.

Liang Qichao 梁啟超. *Mojing Jiaoshi* 墨經校釋 ("Text Criticism and Explanations of the *Mohist Canon*"). Taipei: Xinwenfeng Chubanshe, 1975. Print.

Liji Yinde 禮記引得 ("Index to *The Record of Ritual*"). Shanghai: Shanghai Guji Chubanshe, 1983. Print.

Liu Xiaogan. *Classifying the Zhuangzi Chapters*. Trans. William Savage. Ann Arbor: Center for Chinese Studies, University of Michigan, 1994. Print.

Lynn, Richard John. *The Classic of Changes: A New Translation of the* I Ching *as Interpreted by Wang Bi*. New York: Columbia University Press, 1994. Print.

Machida Saburô 町田三郎. "Kan Shi Shi Hen Ni Tsuite" 管子四篇について. In *Shin Kan Shisoshi No Kenkyu* 秦漢思想史の研究. Tokyo: Sobunsha, 1985. Print.

Mair, Victor H., ed. *Experimental Essays on Chuang-tzu*. Dunedin, FL: Three Pines, 2010. Print.

Makeham, John. *Name and Actuality in Early Chinese Thought*. Albany: State University of New York Press, 1994. Print.

———. "Names, Actualities, and The Emergence of Essentialist Theories of Naming in Classical Chinese Thought." *Philosophy East & West* 41, no. 3 (1991): 341–63. Print.

Manyul, Im. "Horse-parts, White-Parts, and Naming: Semantics, Ontology, and Compound Terms in the White Horse Dialogue." *Dao: A Journal of Comparative Philosophy* 6 (2007): 167–85. Print.

Mozi Suoyin. Hong Kong: Chinese Studies, Ancient Chinese Texts Concordance Series, Chinese University of Hong Kong, The Commercial, 1994. Print.

Munro, Donald J., ed. *Individualism and Holism: Studies in Confucian and Taoist Values*. Ann Arbor: Center for Chinese Studies, University of Michigan, 1985. Print.

———. *Images of Human Nature: A Sung Portrait*. Princeton: Princeton University Press, 1988. Print.

———. *The Concept of Man in Contemporary China*. Ann Arbor: University of Michigan Press, 1977. Print.

———. *The Concept of Man in Early China*. Stanford: Stanford University Press, 1969. Print.

———. "The Yang Hsien-Chen Affair." *The China Quarterly* (1965): 75–82. Print.

Needham, Joseph, ed. *Science and Civilisation in China*. Comp. Ling Wang. Vol. 2. Cambridge: Cambridge University Press, 1954–2008. Print.

Nietzsche, Friedrich. *Twilight of the Idols and The Anti-Christ*. Trans. R. J. Hollingdale. Middlesex: Penguin, 1983. Print.

———. *Beyond Good and Evil: Prelude to a Philosophy of the Future Friedrich Nietzsche*. Trans. R. J. Hollingdale. Middlesex: Penguin, 1977. Print.

———. *Daybreak: Thoughts on the Prejudices of Morality*. Trans. R. J. Hollingdale. Cambridge: Cambridge University Press, 1982. Print.

———. *The Gay Science*. Trans. Walter Kaufmann. New York: Vintage, 1974. Print.

———, and R. J. Hollingdale. *Thus Spoke Zarathustra*. Middlesex: Penguin, 1969. Print.

Nivison, David S. *The Ways of Confucianism: Investigations in Chinese Philosophy*. Ed. Bryan W. Van Norden. Chicago: Open Court, 1996. Print.

Nylan, Michael. *The Canon of Supreme Mystery By Yang Hsiung: A Translation with Commentary of the* T'ai Hsüan Ching. Albany: State University of New York Press, 1993. Print.

Peirce, Charles S. *Reasoning and the Logic of Things: The Cambridge Conferences Lectures of 1898*. Ed. Kenneth Laine Ketner and Hillary Putnam. Cambridge: Harvard University Press, 1992. Print.

Perkins, Franklin. "Reproaching Heaven: The Problem of Evil in Mengzi." *Dao: A Journal of Comparative Philosophy* 5 (2006): 293–312. Print.

Peterson, Willard. "Another Look at Li." *Bulletin of Sung-Yuan Studies* 18 (1986): 14. Print.

———, Andrew H. Plaks, Yu Yingshi, Chen Ta-Tuan, and Frederick W. Mote, eds. *The Power of Culture: Studies in Chinese Cultural History*. Hong Kong: Chinese University Press, 1994. Print.

Pfeiffer, Franz. *Meister Eckhart*. London: J. M. Watkins, 1924, 1947. Print.

Puett, Michael J. *The Ambivalence of Creation Debates Concerning Innovation and Artifice in Early China*. Stanford: Stanford University Press, 2001. Print.

———. *To Become a God: Cosmology, Sacrifice, and Self-Divinization in Early China*. Cambridge: Harvard University Press, 2002. Print.

Qian Mu 錢穆. *Hushang Xiansi Lu* 湖上閒思錄 ("A Record of Leisurely Lakeside Thoughts"). Taipei: Dongda Tushu Gongsi, 1988. Print.

———. *Zhongguo Sixiang Shi* 中國思想史 ("A History of Chinese Thought"). Taipei: Xuesheng Shuju, 1985. Print.

———. *Zhuang Lao Tong Bian* 莊老通辨 ("Comprehensive Discernments Concerning Zhuangzi and Laozi"). Hong Kong: Xinya Yanjiusuo, 1957. Print.

———. *Zhuangzi Zuanjian* 莊子纂箋 ("*The Zhuangzi*, with Compiled Commentaries"). Taipei: Dongda Tushu Gongsi, 1986. Print.

Raphals, Lisa Ann. *Sharing the Light: Representations of Women and Virtue in Early China*. Albany: State University of New York Press, 1998. Print.

Rickett, W. Allyn. *Guanzi: Political, Economic, and Philosophical Essays from Early China—A Study and Translation*. Vol. 2. Boston: Cheng and Tsui, 2001. Print.

Rosemont, Henry, ed. *Chinese Texts and Philosophical Contexts: Essays Dedicated to Angus C. Graham*. La Salle, IL: Open Court, 1991. Print.

Roth, Harold D. *Original Tao: Inward Training (Nei-Yeh) and the Foundations of Taoist Mysticism*. New York: Columbia University Press, 1999. Print.

Russell, Bertrand. *Logic and Knowledge: Essays, 1901–1950*. London: Allen and Unwin, 1956. Print.

Schopenhauer, Arthur. *The World as Will and Idea*. Trans. R. B. Haldane and John Kemp. London: Routledge and Kegan Paul, 1964. Print.

———. *The World as Will and Representation*. Trans. E. F. J. Payne. 2 Vols. New York: Dover, 1969. Print.

Schwartz, Benjamin I. *The World of Thought in Ancient China*. Cambridge: Belknap of Harvard University Press, 1985. Print.

Shen Zhanru 沈展如. *Xin Mang Quanshi* 新莽全史 ("A Complete History of the Xin Dynasty of Wang Mang"). Taipei: Zhengzhong Shuju, 1977. Print.

Shi Yisan 石一參, ed. *Guanzi Jinquan* 管子今詮 (*The Guanzi, with a Modern Interpretation*). Changsha: Shangwu Yinshuguan, 1938. Print.

Shun Kwong-Loi. *Mencius and Early Chinese Thought*. Stanford: Stanford University Press, 1997. Print.

Shun Kwong-Loi. "Mencius and Jen Hsing." *Philosophy East and West* 47 (1997): 3. Print.

Sivin, Nathan. "The First Neo-Confucianism: An Introduction to Yang Hsiung's 'Canon of Supreme Mystery' (T'ai Hsuan Ching, C. 4 B.C.)." *Chinese Ideas about Nature and Society: Studies in Honour of Derk Bodde*. By Michael Nylan. Ed. Charles Le Blanc and Susan Blader. Hong Kong: Hong Kong University Press, 1987. Print.

Slingerland, Edward G. *Effortless Action: Wu-wei as Conceptual Metaphor and Spiritual Ideal in Early China*. Oxford: Oxford University Press, 2003. Print.

Spinoza, Baruch. *The Essential Spinoza: Ethics and Related Writings*. Ed. Michael L. Morgan. Trans. Samuel Shirley. Indianapolis: Hackett, 2006. Print.

Stalnaker, Aaron. "Aspects of Xunzi's Engagement with Early Daoism." *Philosophy East and West* 53, no. 1 (2003): 87–129. Print.

Strawson, Peter Frederick. *Individuals: An Essay in Descriptive Metaphysics*. London: Routledge, 2006. Print.

Sun Yirang 孫詒讓. *Mozi Jiangu* 墨子閒詁 (*The Mozi, with Substitutions and Glosses*). Taipei: Taiwan Shangwu Yinshuaguan, 1983. Print.

Tang Junyi 唐君毅. *Zhongguo Zhexue Yuanlun: Yuandaopian* 中國哲學原論：原道篇. Vol. 3. ("Essays Tracing the Sources of Chinese Philosophy: Tracing the Origins of Dao.") Taipei: Xuesheng Shuju, 1986. Print.

———. *Zhongguo Zhexue Yuanlun: Yuanxing Pian* 中國哲學原論：原性篇 ("Essays Tracing the Sources of Chinese Philosophy: On the Origins of Theories of Human Nature"). Taipei: Xuesheng Shuju, 1989. Print.

———. *Zhongxi Zhexue Sixiang Zhi Bijiao Lunwenji* 中西哲學思想之比較論文集 ("A Collection of Essays on Comparative Topics in Chinese and Western Philosophical Thought"). Taipei: Xuesheng Shuju, 1988. Print.

Tu Wei-Ming. *Confucian Thought: Selfhood as Creative Transformation*. Albany: State University of New York Press, 1985. Print.

Van Norden, Bryan. "Hiding the World in the World: Uneven Discourses on the Zhuangzi (review)" *China Review International* (2005): 3. Print.

———. *Virtue Ethics and Consequentialism in Early Chinese Philosophy*. New York: Cambridge University Press, 2007. Print.

———, ed. *Confucius and the Analects: New Essays*. Oxford: Oxford University Press, 2002. Print.

Waley, Arthur, trans. *The Analects of Confucius: Translated and Annotated by Arthur Waley*. New York: Vintage, 1938. Print.

Wang Fuzhi 王夫之. *Du Sishu Quanshuo* 讀四書全說 ("Complete Explanations for Reading the Four Books"). Beijing: Zhonghua Shuju, 1975. Print.

———. *Zhuangzi Tong, Zhuangzi Jie* 莊子通，莊子解 ("Comprehending the Zhuangzi; Explanations of the Zhuangzi"). Taipei: Liren Shuju, 1984. Print.

Wang Guangqi 王光祈. *Zhongguo Yinyue Shi* 中國音樂史 ("History of Chinese Music"). Hong Kong: Taiping Shuju, 1963. Print.

Wang, Robin. "Dong Zhongshu's Transformation of Yin-Yang Theory and Contesting of Gender Identity." *Philosophy East and West* 55, no. 2 (2005): 209–31. Print.

Wang Shumin 王淑岷. *Zhuangzi Jiaoquan* 莊子校詮 ("*The Zhuangzi*, with Collations and Explanations"). Taipei: Academia Sinica, 1988. Print.

Wei Qipeng 魏啟鵬. *Chujian Laozi Jianshi* 楚簡老子柬釋 ("Selections and Explanations of the Chu Bamboo Strip Version of the *Laozi*"). Taipei: Wanjuanlou Tushu Youxian Gongsi, 1999. Print.

Wenzi 文子. Taipei: Zhonghua Shuju, 1978. Print.

Whitehead, Alfred North. *Adventures of Ideas*. New York: Free Press, 1967. Print.

———. *Process and Reality: An Essay in Cosmology*. New York: Cambridge University Press, 1929. Print.

————. *Science and the Modern World: Lowell Lectures*. New York: Macmillan, 1925. Print.

Wittenborn, Allen. "Li Revisited and Other Explorations." *The Bulletin of Sung-Yuan Studies* 17 (1981). Print.

Wu Kuang-Ming. *Chuang Tzu: World Philosopher at Play*. New York: Crossroad, 1982. Print.

————. *The Butterfly as Companion: Meditations on the First Three Chapters of the Chuang Tzu*. Albany: State University of New York Press, 1990. Print.

Xu Fuguan 徐復觀. *Liang-Han Sixiang Shi* 兩漢思想史 ("History of the Thought of the Former and Latter Han Dynasties"). Hong Kong: Xianggang Zhongwen Daxue, 1975. Print.

Xunzi Yinde 荀子引得. Shanghai: Shanghai Guji Chubanshe, 1986. Print.

Yang Changzhen 楊長鎮. *Xunzi Lei De Cunyoulun Yanjiu* 荀子類的存有論研究 ("An Investigation of the Ontology of Types in the *Xunzi*"). Taipei: Wenjin Chubanshe, 1996. Print.

Yang Xiong 楊雄. *Fayan* 法言. Taipei: Zhonghua Shuju, 1983. Print.

————. *Taixuanjing* 太玄經. Taipei: Taiwan Zhonghua Shuju, 1983. Print.

Yinwenzi; Guanyinzi 尹文子; 關尹子. Taipei: Zhonghua Shuju, 1979. Print.

Yiu-Ming Fung. "A Logical Perspective on 'Discourse on White-Horse.'" *Journal of Chinese Philosophy* 34, no. 4 (2007): 515–36. Print.

Yuan Shuya 苑淑婭, ed. *Zhongguo Guannian Shi* 中國觀念史 ("History of Chinese Concepts"). Zhengzhou: Zhongzhou Guji Chubanshe, 2005. Print.

Zhang Chun, and Feng Yu. *The Four Political Treatises of the Yellow Emperor*. Honolulu: University of Hawaii Press, 1998. Print.

Zhang Dainian 張岱年. *Zhongguo Zhexue Shi Shiliao Xue* 中國哲學史史料學 ("On Historical Materials in the Study of Classical Chinese Philosophy"). Beijing: Sanlian Shuju, 1982. Print.

Zhang Yangming 張揚明. *Laozi Jiaozheng Yishi* 老子斠證譯釋 ("*The Laozi*, with Critical Translations and Explanations"). Taipei: Weixin Shuju, 1973. Print.

Zhang Zhan 張湛. *Liezi Zhushi* 列子注釋 ("*The Liezi*, with Explanatory Commentary"). Taipei: Hualian Chubanshe, 1969. Print.

Zheng Wangeng 鄭萬耕, *Taixuan jiaoshi* 太玄校釋 ("Text Critical Edition of the *Taixuanjing*, with Explanations") (*Taixuanjing*, Critical Edition). Beijing: Beijing Shifan daxue chubanshe, 1989. Print.

Zhu Xi 朱熹. *Zhouyi Benyi* 周易本義 ("*The Book of Changes* in Its Original Signification"). Taipei: Guangxue She Yinshu Guan, 1975. Print.

Zhuzi Yinde. Laozi, Zhuangzi 諸子引得: 老子莊子 ("Indices to the Philosophers: *Laozi* and *Zhuangzi*"). Taipei: Zhongqing Tushu Chuban Gongsi, 1986. Print.

Ziporyn, Brook. "Anti-Chan Polemics in Post-Tang Tiantai." *Journal of the International Association of Buddhist Studies* 17, no. 1 (1994): 26–65. Print.

————. *Being and Ambiguity: Philosophical Experiments with Tiantai Buddhism*. Chicago: Open Court, 2004. Print.

————. *The Penumbra Unbound: The Neo-Taoist Philosophy of Guo Xiang*. Albany: State University of New York Press, 2003. Print.

————. "The Self-so and Its Traces in the Thought of Guo Xiang." *Philosophy East and West* 43, no. 3 (1993): 511–39. Print.

Zuo Qiuming 左丘明. *Guoyu* 國語. Shanghai: Shanghai Guji Chubanshe, 1978. Print.

INDEX

a priori, 162

Absolute Idea, 42

absolutism, 191, 193–95

abstraction, 39–40
  the abstract and the concrete, 42

administrative space, 260

aesthetic vs. rational order, 275n15

alternate belief systems, 1–2

ambiguity, ontological, 22

Ames, Roger T., 20, 53–58, 60–62
  on aesthetic vs. rational order, 275n15
  correlative thinking and, 53, 57–58, 247
  Focus and Field model, 55–56
  on Heaven, 100
  on irony as characterizing the Daoist attitude toward existence, 140
  nominalism and, 54–56
  on Yin and Yang, 54, 284n3

Analects of Confucius, 92–94, 103, 112, 266. *See also* Confucius
  coherence and Heaven in, 94–103

analytic-synthetic distinction, 25

animality, 29, 37–38

anti-value, 151, 154–56, 267, 293n72

Aristotle, 22, 37, 43, 272n17

aspect perception, 210

assumptions, questioning, 1

availability, 136. *See also* omniavailability

Axis of Courses, 182

Bai Tongdong, 141

balance, 65–66, 83, 84, 221–23, 302n17. *See also* Yin and Yang

Baxter, William, 281n32

behavior, grammar of, 104–5, 108. *See also* grammar

benevolence, 100, 118–20, 139, 241, 244, 282n34

Bo Mou, 73

Book of Changes. See *Zhouyi*

categories, 14, 24, 38. *See also* same and different
  transcendental, 34

center-periphery paradigm, 224, 261

centrality, 79–80, 82, 134, 223–24, 253–55

change. *See also* Zhouyi 周易 (*Book of Changes*)
  and "unchanging," 21

cheng 誠 (sincerity/integrity/realness), 221–24

Cheng Chung-ying, 75–76

Chong, Kim-chong, 280n20

clarity, 149, 150, 217. See also *ming*

class-logic vs. mereology, 32–33

classes. *See under* Mencius

coherence, 265–68. *See also* Li; *specific topics*
  impossibility of, 140–41
  vs. law, rule, principle, and pattern, 63
  meanings/notions of, 10–11, 23, 62, 148–50
  unseen. See *cheng*

"common notions" vs. universals, 40–42

communicability and grammar, 108–14

complementarity, 65, 229–32, 243, 252–53

conceptualism, 24

315

conflict and complementarity, 231–32
Confucian notion of centrality, 224
Confucian ritual, 103–10, 112, 128, 195, 199–200, 279n13
Confucian values and ethics, 90, 92, 156, 219–22, 224, 235, 236
Confucian virtues, 92, 135, 139, 283n34
Confucianism, 285n18, 302n22
  Bryan Van Norden and, 92
  centrality and, 224
  coherence and, 86, 134, 135, 137, 142
  Daoism and, 132, 135, 136, 183
  Han, 250
  harmony and, 69
  on human nature, 78
  Mencius and, 219, 224, 240
  Mohism and, 92, 171, 183, 195, 251
  as moral communication, 113
  Xunzi's version of, 199–200
Confucius, 64, 266. See also *Analects of Confucius*
  coherence and, 89–94, 96, 97
  on Heaven, 95, 97, 98, 100–103, 106, 107, 109
  human nature and, 114
  on language, 111
  Mencius and, 94–98, 110, 120, 123, 127–28, 130, 135
  mourning and, 106, 108–10
  omniavailability of value in, 89–94
  omnipresence and, 92–95, 127–28, 130, 131
  opposition to death penalty, 103
  on Rectification of Names, 111
  on rulers, 112
  value system/orientation, 106, 110, 127–28
  on virtuosity and benevolence, 105, 120, 132, 139
  Xunzi and, 240, 279n14
  on Yao's virtue, 285n18
  Zai Wo and, 106–10
consequentialism, 90–91, 112

constancy. See also *yi*
  mind of, 187
constraints, 45
constructivism, 45, 206
context, 152
contextualization, 140, 221–22, 234, 249
  art of, 55, 60
continuance, 66, 84, 115, 195–96, 276n20
continuity vs. discontinuity, 58–60
correlative thinking, 47, 53–54, 57–59, 231, 247
  Angus Graham and, 53, 57, 231
  Hall and Ames and, 53, 57–58, 247
  Lévy-Bruhl on, 47
cultural grammar, 97, 104–5, 109, 111, 113. See also grammar
cyclical processes, 77–78, 81–82, 211, 257–61

Dao, 223–24
  irony of the term, 154
  Li and, 277n20
  meanings, 142, 160
  as omniavailability of value, 135
  Zhuangzi on, 183–84
dao, notion of
  development through three phases, 183
Daodejing 道德經 (Laozi 老子), 183
Daoism, 283n2. See also *specific topics*
  Confucianism and, 132, 135, 136, 183
  Mencius and, 115, 127–28, 135–36, 224
  types of, 132, 133, 137, 140–43. See also proto-Daoism
Daoist attitude toward existence, 140
Daoist use of terms that signify coherence, 140–41
Decree, the, 78, 117, 118, 120–22, 126–27, 130, 244, 266
deontological ethics, 91
deontology, 90–91

dependence, 163, 168. *See also* independence and interdependence

desire, types of, 148–50. *See also* eye desires; stomach desires

determination, 42, 44–47
 as negation, 44

Dewey, John, 44

dialectical view of reality, 21

distinctions, making, 51

Doctrine of the Mean (中庸 *Zhongyong*), 221–23, 254, 261

Dong Zhongshu, 88, 250–55

doubleness, 146

dyadic a priori, 140

emptiness, 144, 150, 157, 177–78, 216–17

essences, 6, 13. *See also* universals
 doctrine of, 6–7, 35–36
 individual vs. universal, 23–24

essentialism, 13–14

eternal modes, 40–41

ethics, 90–92, 113, 126, 156, 210–11. *See also* Confucian values and ethics; *specific topics*

evil, 78–79, 185, 208, 211

externalism vs. internalism, 219

eye desires, 148–51, 154, 156–59

fact/value distinction, 53

fact-value fusion, 173

"facticity," 20

false self and true self, 291n40

family coherences, 248

field, 54–55

Focus and Field model, 54–55

form and matter, 160–61

formless matter, 38, 161

Forms, 37–38

Fung Yu-lan, 73–74

Gaozi, 115–17, 135

Geaney, Jane, 210

Gestalts, 83–84

God, 99

gong 功 (merit), 147, 286n20

Gongsun Long, 72–75, 170

Good, 78

Graham, Angus C., 52–53, 73, 75, 132, 169, 230–31, 289n31
 Chad Hansen and, 52–53, 73
 coherence and, 53, 222
 correlative thinking and, 53, 57, 231
 on *Laozi* text, 152
 on Yin and Yang, 230–31

grammar, 104–9, 111, 112
 Chinese, 50–52, 95
 and communicability, 108–14
 meanings and nature of, 113
 rules of, 104–7

Granet, Marcel, 57–59

Great Commentary, 232–37, 239, 241
 doctrine of the, 236

Great Learning, 221, 225

Greatest Coherence, 143, 201, 213, 214, 217, 267

Greek thinking, 4

groupings, 63, 70, 84, 87, 89, 202, 209–12, 221, 266

Guo Xiang 郭象, 11

Hagen, Kurtis, 206, 213, 298n17

Hall, David L., 20, 53, 57, 58, 60–62
 on aesthetic vs. rational order, 275n15
 correlative thinking and, 53, 57–58, 247
 Focus and Field model, 55–56
 on Heaven, 100
 on irony as characterizing the Daoist attitude toward existence, 140
 nominalism and, 54–56
 on Yin and Yang, 54, 284n3

Han Confucianism, 250

Han Xiaoqiang, 51–53

Hansen, Chad, 51–53, 55
 anti-truth-and-belief position, 271n3
 on assertability, 72, 73, 271n3
 on indexicals, 169
 mass-noun hypothesis, 33, 50–52, 72

Hansen, Chad (*continued*)
 nominalism and, 55–56
 White Horse Dialogue and, 71–72
harmony, 77, 79, 111–13, 247
 Centrality and, 223, 253–55
 coherence and, 70–71, 77, 79, 81,
  84, 85, 111, 120, 139, 149, 201,
  218, 220, 290n36
 defined, 66–67
 Dong Zhongshu on, 253–55
 ironic, 166, 185, 251
 as joining of differences, 65–66, 123,
  124, 201
 knowing, 149
 Li on, 278n35
 Mencius and, 123
 metastasis of irony and, 250–55
 non-ironic, 139
 Plato's, 278n35
 vs. repeatability, 63–71
 ritual and, 110
 rules of, 67–68
 sameness and, 64–70, 112, 113, 124,
  157, 201, 260, 261, 294n74
 singing, 67
 social, 67
 sustainability and, 149
 value and, 110, 139
 virtuosity and, 275n19
 Yin-Yang and, 236, 239, 241, 244,
  250–55
Hartshorne, Charles, 46–47
Heaven, 100, 175. *See also* Way of
  Heaven
 in *Analects*, 94–103
 as collective body, 95
 definition and nature of, 97, 98
 is neither personal nor impersonal, 98
 Mencius on, 95, 98, 100
 Zhuangzi on, 183–84
Hegel, Georg Wilhelm Friedrich, 39,
  41–43, 46
hierarchical polarity, 231–32, 251–53,
  259–60
Huang-Lao Daoism, 132
Huizi 惠子(Hui Shi 惠施), 290n32

human nature (*xing*), 78, 114
 Mencius on human nature, 68, 100,
  115–17, 119, 120, 122, 124–26,
  130, 210, 216
 Xunzi's theory of, 210–11
Hutton, Eric, 298n17

I Ching 易經. See *Zhouyi* 周易
idealism, 8
 vs. realism, 210
idealist derivation of the Omnipresent,
  39
idealist omnipresence, 161
Ideas, 24, 35, 37, 38
identifying, 2. *See also* same and
  different
identities, 7–8, 56
"Illumination of the Obvious," 172, 184
independence and interdependence,
  60–61
indexicals, 169–70
intelligibility, 62, 89, 139, 141, 148,
  225. *See also ming*; *specific topics*
internalism vs. externalism, 219–20
ironic coherence, 87–88, 139, 185,
  195–97. *See also specific topics*
 defined, 86, 87, 195–96
 vs. non-ironic coherence, 10–11, 49,
  84–88
 transition to, 131–37
ironic Daoism, 133, 140–42, 153. *See
  also Laozi*
ironic meaning, 85
ironic tradition, 93, 139. *See also specific
  topics*
 central irony of, 157
is-ought problem, 53
Ivanhoe, Philip J., 95, 96, 156, 269n2

James, William, 44–45, 274n20
Jingxi Zhanran 荊溪湛然, 1
Jixia 稷下 Daoism, 132

Kant, Immanuel, 25, 38, 43, 46, 91,
  109, 273
Kline, T. C., 296n3

knowing, role of, 187–88
knowledge, 51
  forms of, 149–50, 188–91

language. *See also* grammar
  in Chinese thought, status and role of, 19–21
Laozi 老子, 156, 158–60, 293n72
Laozi 老子, 139–42
  ironic coherence in, 139–46
  omnipresence and, 146–62
Laozi tradition and desiring w/holes, 139–42
Lévy-Bruhl, Lucien, 26–28, 32–33, 57
  on correlative thinking, 47
  "logic of participation," 57
  on logical/rational thought, 26–27, 31, 33, 47, 57, 77
  on primitive participatory collectives, 26, 31
Li 理, 22, 83, 244
  centrality and, 223, 254
  coherence and, 9–17
  Dao and, 277n20
  human nature and, 78
  meanings, 22, 123
  Mencius and, 122, 123
  nature of, 9
  Neo-Confucianism and, 11–12, 47, 62, 78, 84, 222, 269n2, 278n34
  omnipresence and, 15
  qi and, 78
  ritual and, 202–3
  toward, 265–68
  value and, 12, 15, 69–70
  Xunzi and, 131, 201–3
Li, Chenyang, 22, 64–65, 69, 278n35
  on grammar, 113
location, simple. *See* simple location
logical/rational thought
  characteristics, 31
  Lévy-Bruhl on, 26–27, 31, 33, 47, 57, 77
  vs. prelogical thought, 26–28

magnetic center paradigm, 287n22

Makeham, John, 250
Manyul Im, 73
mass-noun hypothesis, 33, 50–52, 72
Matter, 37
matter and form, 160–61
Mencius (孟子Mengzi), 68, 71, 280n20
  (pragmatic) nominalism and, 115–17, 122, 124–26, 212, 220
  classes and types in, 114–26
  coherence and omniavailability of value in, 89–94
  Confucianism and, 219, 224, 240
  Daoism and, 115, 127–28, 135–36, 224
  on the Decree, 127
  Gaozi 告子 and, 115–17
  on the Good/Goodness, 90, 115–18, 120, 130, 241
  harmony and, 123
  on Heaven, 95, 98, 100
  on human nature (*xing*), 68, 100, 115–17, 119, 120, 122, 124–26, 130, 210, 216
  moral theory, 126
  omnipresence in, 127–31, 136
  qi 氣 and, 128–30, 134–36
  on *tian* 天, 100
  on virtue, 121
  Xunzi 荀子 and, 200, 201, 204, 210, 211, 215, 216, 219, 220
methodological pluralism, 92
metonymy and metaphor, 53–54, 85
mind, nature of, 50–51
ming 名 ("name"), 146, 147, 149, 150, 162, 174
Mohism, 53, 68, 72, 101, 298n12
  Confucianism and, 92, 171, 183, 195, 251
Monkey Keeper, story of the, 176
monogenetic sacrificial systems, 58
"Mother," 144
Mozi 墨子, 192, 194

namelessness, 145, 286n20
names, 147–48, 284n9
naming, Dong's theory of, 250–51

Nanguoziqi, 165, 166
Neo-Confucianism, 221, 269n2
  Li and, 11–12, 47, 62, 78, 84, 222,
    269n2, 278n34
Nivison, David S., 92
nominalism, 54
  definition and nature of, 7, 43
  Mencius and, 115–17, 122, 124–26,
    212, 220
  performative, 114, 211–12
  pragmatic, 115–17
  vs. realism, 7, 43, 44, 80, 89,
    115–17, 126, 128, 220, 266
    beyond the dichotomy of, 7, 10,
      11, 43–46, 55–56, 59, 62–63,
      76, 94, 98, 107, 116–17, 122,
      130, 205–6, 208–10
  "soft," 204
  Xunzi 荀子 and, 204–6, 208–12
Non-being and Oneness, connections
    between, 288n29
non-ironic coherence, 87
  aspects involved in, 139, 221
  defined, 86–87
  themes, 89
nourishing life, 184

obvious, the, 171, 174, 188
  illumination of, 172, 184
Occidental idea of universals, 33
omniavailability, 130
  of value in Confucius and Mencius,
    89–94
omnipresence, 128, 136
  and coherence in Xunzi, 215–20
  Confucius and, 92–95, 127–28, 130,
    131
  and ironic coherence in Laozi,
    146–62
Omnipresent, two opposite derivations
    of the, 38–47
One, 157
one-many problem, 6, 8, 45, 49, 52,
    55, 59
ontology, 22
opposites (and oppositions), 174–76,
    230–31, 251, 301n17

paradoxical simultaneity of, 145

parallelisms of position and function,
    246–47
participation, 32, 59
  law of, 27
  logic of, 57
participatory collectives/collections,
    primitive, 31
pendulum model, 77–83, 86, 99, 100
Perfect Unseen Coherence, 226
Perkins, Franklin, 100
perspectival knowledge, 163
philosophical positions, critiques of, 17
Plato, 4, 5, 37, 73–75, 160
  harmony, 278n35
  paradox, 178, 192
  realism and, 56
Platonism, 4, 5, 73
pleasure, 66, 90, 111
poly-essentialism, 14
polygenetic sacrificial systems, 58
potentiality, pure, 38
pragmatic nominalism, 115–17
pragmatic vs. semantic referent, 73
pragmatism, 44–45
pre-ironic Daoism, 132, 133, 137, 140
presence. See omnipresence
primitive mentality vs. rational
    thought, 26
process orientation vs. substance
    orientation, 21–22
progeny, 66, 84. See also continuance
proto-Daoism, 87, 140, 221
  qi-omnipresence and the empty
    center in pre-ironic, 131–37
Puett, Michael, 58, 59
Putnam, Hilary, 274

qi 氣, 96, 128–31, 134–36, 283n39
  Dao and, 135–36
  Li and, 78
  Mencius and, 128–30, 134–36
  Yin-Yang and, 231, 251, 252
qi-omnipresence and the empty center
    in pre-ironic proto-Daoism,
    131–37

Qian (yang/heaven), 234, 237, 238, 246–49
Qian Mu 錢穆, 81, 82, 292n70
   on Chinese thinking, 276n20
   pendulum, 77–84, 224, 226, 244–45

rational thought. *See* logical/rational thought
rational vs. aesthetic order, 275n15
real, abstract universals
   doctrine of, 35
realism, 24, 43, 266
   defined, 43
Record of Ritual (Liji 禮記). *See Doctrine of the Mean; Great Learning*
Rectification of Names (正名), doctrine of, 111–14
relativism, 61, 178, 178, 190–95
ren 仁, 105–8, 113
ritual
   vs. law, 103–11
   negotiated identity as a function of, 111–14
ritual practice, arguments for a proposed change of, 106–7
Russell, Bertrand, 271n15

sacrifice, systems of, 58–59
same and different. *See also* sameness
   distinction in mainstream Western philosophy, 23–37
   in form and matter, 37–38
   rethinking, 2–8
same-different paradox, 31
sameness
   difference and, 196. *See also* same and different
   negotiability of, 5
   Xunzi and regulation of, 199–214
   toward a theistic non-ironic theory of, 251
   of type, 68–69
self-divination, 58, 59
semantic vs. pragmatic referent, 73
set theory, 72
sex, 236
sexual desire, 149, 158

sheng 生, 114. *See also* human nature; *xing* 性
Shi Bo, 65–66
Shun, Kwong-loi, 114, 121, 125, 134, 281n23
simple location, 34, 36, 39, 40, 44
   doctrine of, 34
simpliciter, 67, 74, 223, 246, 268
Slingerland, Edward, 219–20
solipsism. *See under* wild card
Spinoza, Baruch, 40–41, 44
stillness, 132–35, 149, 216–17, 221, 288n27. *See also* sustainability
stomach desires, 148–51, 154, 157–60
Strawson, P. F., 51
subject-predicate form, dogma of, 35
sustainability, 149–52, 238, 287n23

Tao Te Ching. *See Daodejing*
Tang Junyi, 49–50, 120–22, 142, 161–62
tian 天, 95, 96, 99, 100, 279n9
time, cyclical, 257–61
totemism, systems of, 58
transcendence, 60, 61
transcendental universals/categories, doctrine of, 34
transformation, 163
truth, 22–23
types. *See under* Mencius

unconditioned determination, paradox of, 44
unhewn, the, 142, 161, 196
   five meanings of, 146–62
unintelligibility, 140, 166
unity, 62–63, 66, 157, 201, 207–9, 216–18
universals, 38. *See also* essences; Omnipresent
   vs. "common notions," 40–42
   doctrine of, 38, 43, 49
   "magical" nature of, 41–42
   particular vs. universal, 93
   problem of, 33
   relations between, 38
Universals, 25, 37, 38

valuation, objects of, 148–50
value, 89, 118, 139, 183, 293n72,
    301n17. *See also specific topics*
    Yin-Yang and, 239
Van Norden, Bryan, 90, 92, 192–94,
    206, 296n3
virtue, paradox of, 92
virtue ethics, 90–91
virtuosity and harmony, 275n19

walking two, 193, 194, 292n70
"Walking Two Roads," 176, 189
Wang, Robin, 302n19, 302n22
Wang Bi, 285n13
Way of Earth, 226–27
Way of Heaven, 93, 147, 192–95,
    226–27, 253
when a white horse is not a horse. *See*
    White Horse Dialogue
White Horse Dialogue, 71–77, 170,
    278n29
Whitehead, Alfred North, 33, 34, 36,
    46–47
whole/part epistemology, 215–16
whole/part ontology, 50, 55–56, 69
w/holes, desiring, 139–42
wild card, 182, 196, 197, 267–68.
    See also Zhuangzi: and thing as
    perspective
    against objective truth and subjective
        solipsism, 188–95
    using the, 183–88
Wittgenstein, Ludwig, 70
Wong, David B., 296n3
wu 無, 93–94, 141, 286n20, 290n34
wu-wei, paradox of, 219
wuwei (non-doing), 134, 285n18

xing 性, 84, 103, 114–17. *See also*
    human nature; *sheng* 生
Xunzi 荀子, 266, 279n14, 296n3,
    298nn13–14
    ethics, 210–11
    Mencius 孟子 and, 200, 201, 204,
        210, 211, 215, 216, 219, 220
    naturalistic atheism, 195

omnipresence and coherence in,
    215–20
and regulation of sameness and
    difference, 199–214
on relations of man and nature,
    206–8
theory of human nature, 210–11
Xunzi 荀子, 220–21

Yan Ying, 65
Yang Xiong 揚雄, 88
    Taixuanjing, 255–63
yi 易, 125
    meanings, 21, 125
Yin and Yang, 140, 301n17. *See also*
    specific topics
    meanings, 229, 230
    Zhuangzi 莊子 and, 215, 230, 249–50
Yin-Yang 陰陽
    qi and, 231, 251, 252
Yin-Yang compromise, 229–50
Yin-Yang divination system, an
    alternate, 255–63
Yin-Yang polarity, emphases
    constructing the development of
    various versions of, 230–31
Yin-Yang theism in Dong Zhongshu,
    250–55
You of Zhou, 65–66

Zai Wo 宰我, 106–10
Zhang Zai 張載, 93
Zhouyi 周易 (*Book of Changes*), 21,
    238–40, 243–44, 255–57
    commentaries to, 21, 232, 235,
        241–42, 255
Zhu Xi 朱熹, 254, 301n17
Zhuang Zhou 莊周, 162–63, 267–68,
    289–90nn31–32
Zhuangzi 莊子, 76, 85, 290n34,
    292n65, 295nn83–85. *See also* wild
    card
    on absolutism, 194
    Aristotle and, 291n47
    on Axis of Courses, 175–76

on changing the world, 186
Course, 185, 192
on Dao, 183–84
Daoism, irony, and, 283n2
doubt and, 169
on emptiness, 178
on "genuine knowledge," 188–91, 295n85
on Heaven, 183–84
heavenly potter's wheel, 292n70
Huizi and, 163, 290n32
on independence and freedom, 164
intuitionism, 174
ironic coherence and, 195–96
on knowledge and identity, 187–89
Li and, 22
as monist, theist, and fatalist, 191, 192
on oneness, 195, 197
on the Perfect Man, 21
perspective of, 172
perspectivism and, 1, 6, 211, 212

"Pivot of Dao(s)," 223–24
"regarding all things as one," 179–80
relativism and, 191–95
technique of "illumination of the obvious," 172
themes at the heart of his project, 163
and thing as perspective, 162–82
on value and anti-value, 293n72
view of experience, 178–79
on walking two, 193, 194, 292n70
on White Horse Dialogue, 76
Ziporyn's, 192–93
Zhuangzi 莊子, 88, 215, 286n20, 287n22
core of the philosophy of, 165
ming 名 and, 147, 149, 162
notions of coherence in, 23
on virtuosity, 275n19
Yin and Yang 陰陽 and, 215, 230, 249–50
Zigong 子貢, 92–94, 101

Printed in Great Britain
by Amazon

48500464R00189